LAW, RELIGIOUS FREEDOMS AND EDUCATION IN EUROPE

Cultural Diversity and Law

Series Editor:
Prakash Shah, School of Law, Queen Mary, University of London, UK

Around the world, most states are faced with difficult issues arising out of cultural diversity in their territories. Within the legal field, such issues span across matters of private law through to public and constitutional law. At international level too there is now considerable jurisprudence regarding ethnic, religious and cultural diversity. In addition, there are several layers of legal control – from communal and religious regulation to state and international regulation. This multiplicity of norm setting has been variously termed legal pluralism, inter-legality or inter-normativity and provides a fascinating lens for academic analysis that links up to cultural diversity in new and interesting ways. The umbrella of cultural diversity encompasses various population groups throughout the world ranging from national, ethnic, religious or indigenous groupings. This series particularly welcomes work that is of comparative interest, concerning various state jurisdictions as well as different population groups.

Also in the series

Law, Religious Freedoms and Education in Europe

Edited by

MYRIAM HUNTER-HENIN
University College London, UK

ASHGATE

Published by
Ashgate Publishing Limited
Wey Court East
Union Road
Farnham
Surrey, GU9 7PT
England

Ashgate Publishing Company
Suite 420
101 Cherry Street
Burlington
VT 05401-4405
USA

www.ashgate.com

British Library Cataloguing in Publication Data
Law, religious freedoms and education in Europe. – (Cultural diversity and law)
   1. Religious minorities–Education–Europe. 2. Religious education–Law and legislation–
Europe. 3. Freedom of religion–Europe.
   I. Series II. Hunter-Henin, Myriam.
   344.4'0796-dc22

Library of Congress Cataloging-in-Publication Data
Hunter-Hinin, Myriam.
Law, religious freedoms and education in Europe / by Myriam Hunter-Henin.
   p. cm. – (Cultural diversity and law)
   Includes bibliographical references and index.
   ISBN 978-1-4094-2730-8 (hardback : alk. paper) – ISBN 978-1-4094-2731-5 (ebook)
   1. Religion in the public schools–Law and legislation–Europe. 2. Religious minorities–
Legal status, laws, etc.–Europe. 3. Freedom of religion–Europe. I. Title.
   KJC6275.H86 2011
   342.408'52–dc23

2011040152

ISBN 9781409427308 (hbk)
ISBN 9781409427315 (ebk)

Printed and bound in Great Britain by the
MPG Books Group, UK.

To my older daughter, Melanie.
May she forgive me for spending her 6th birthday at the conference from
which this book was born.

To my husband, for his patience and support over the numerous weekends
dedicated to this book and to the conference that preceded it.

Contents

List of Figures and Tables

Figures

Tables

Notes on Contributors

Eric Barendt (University College London), Emeritus Professor of Media Law at UCL, was the first person to hold a chair in media law in the United Kingdom: he was Goodman Professor of Media Law from 1990 until 2010. He had previously been a Fellow of St Catherine's College, Oxford. His books include *Freedom of Speech* (2007), 2nd edition, Oxford University Press; *Introduction to Constitutional Law* (1998), Oxford University Press and *Academic Freedom and the Law* (2010), Hart. He has also written extensively on libel and privacy law, and media regulation, and is one of the editors of the *Journal of Media Law*, published by Hart. He has been a Visiting Professor at Santa Clara University, California, at LaSapienza University, Rome, at Paris II, and the Universities of Melbourne and Auckland.

Anna Buchanan (Cardiff Law School) graduated from Cardiff Law School in 2009 having undertaken an LLB and the Bar Vocational Course. She was called to the Bar by Middle Temple in July 2009. She currently works for the Older People's Commissioner for Wales and is also a Research Associate with the Centre for Law and Religion at Cardiff University. Anna's undergraduate dissertation examined the law on collective worship in schools in Wales. It is this research that underpins her contribution to this book. Anna delivers an annual lecture on the Law of Religion and Education to students on Cardiff University's LLM course in Canon Law.

Blandine Chélini-Pont (Université d'Aix-en-Provence) is a Senior Lecturer in contemporary history. She holds a PhD in History from The Institut d'Etudes Politiques de Paris and a PhD in Law at the University Paul Cézanne, Aix-en-Provence, France. She teaches Law and Religion, French Political History, European Political Culture and Religious Geopolitics at the Faculty of Law and Political Science of Aix-en-Provence. She is the editor of the French journal on Law and Religion (*Annuaire Droit et Religions*) published by Presses de l'Université d'Aix-Marseille and is an associate member of the *Groupe de Sociologie des Religions et de la Laïcité*, Ecole Pratique des Hautes Etudes de Paris. Her areas of research are on Political Catholic. Her latest book, *Rome and Washington from the Independence of the United States to the Cold War*, is to be published by Desclée de Brower publishers.

Yuko Chiba is an independent researcher and a former Research Fellow at the School of Law, Queen's University Belfast. She holds a PhD in Social Sciences from University of Ulster. Her research interests include the democratic process and human rights in Northern Ireland and the inclusion/exclusion of incomers in divided societies.

Martine Cohen (CNRS Paris) realized studies about the French Catholic Charismatic Renewal, as well as about the issue of 'cults'. Since the end of the 1980s, she has engaged into a sociological study of French Jews, proposing comparative analysis between Catholic and Jewish renewals, as well as between Jews' and Muslims' integration process in France, along the changing forms of French secularism. Her current focus is now on the reshaping of 'franco-judaism', through the study of the institutional and ideological changes of the organized Jewish community. Her publications include: 'Jews and Muslims in France: changing responses to cultural and religious diversity' (2009) in *Legal Practice and Cultural Diversity*, edited by R. Grillo, Ashgate; 'Les déclinaisons historiques du franco-judaïsme et ses critiques contemporaines', *Archives de Sciences sociales des religions*, n.144, October/December 2008, 141–61.

Frank Cranmer (Cardiff Law School) is a Fellow of St Chad's College, Durham, and an Honorary Research Fellow at the Centre for Law and Religion, Cardiff, where he teaches on the LLM in Canon Law. Recent publications include Human rights and the Christian tradition: a Quaker perspective (2010) in *New Directions in Law and Religion*, Peeters and, with Javier García Oliva, The cultural heritage of faith-communities in the United Kingdom (2010) 5 *Derecho y Religión*. As well as writing on religion and human rights, he contributed to several of the Scots law entries to the recent third edition of *Jowitt's Dictionary of English Law*.

Peter Cumper (University of Leicester) is a Senior Lecturer in the School of Law in the University of Leicester, where he teaches Constitutional and Administrative Law, Human Rights Law, and Law and Religion. He has published in a number of books and journals in the UK and overseas on issues related to human rights, law and religion.

Heinrich de Wall (Friedrich-Alexander-Universität, Erlangen) is Professor of Ecclesiastical Law, Constitutional and Administrative Law at the University of Erlangen-Nürnberg and the Director of the 'Hans-Liermann-Institut für Kirchenrecht'. His fields of interest are in State/Church law, the law of the German Protestant churches, history of church law, German constitutional law, political thought in early modern Germany. Publications include: with A. von Campenhausen, *Staatskirchenrecht* (2006), 4th edition; with Stefan Muckel, *Kirchenrecht* (2010), 2nd edition; with Andreas Gestrich, 'Germany' (2010) in *The Dynamics of Religious Reform in Church, State and Society in Northern Europe, c. 1780–c. 1920. Vol. 1: Political and Legal Reform*, edited by Keith Robbins.

Javier García Oliva (Manchester University) studied Law at the University of Cádiz, where he obtained his first degree, LLM and PhD (cum laude and European distinction). After finishing his first degree, he became a lecturer at the University of Cádiz (1996–2000) and a Research Fellow at the Centre for Law and Religion, Cardiff University (2001–2004). Javier was appointed as a lecturer at the University of Wales Bangor in 2004, where he stayed until January 2011, when he took up a lectureship at the University of Manchester. He is also a Teaching Fellow at University College London (UCL) and the University of Oxford. Furthermore, he is a Research Associate at the Centre for Law and Religion (Cardiff University), the convenor of the SLS Public Law section and the Book Review Editor of *Law and Justice*.

Mark Hill QC (Cardiff Law School/3 Pump Court Chambers) is a practising barrister specializing in cases concerning religious liberty and is Honorary Professor of Law and Religion at Cardiff University. He sits as a judge in the civil courts as a Recorder on the Midland Circuit and in the ecclesiastical courts as Chancellor of the Diocese of Chichester and the Diocese of Gibraltar in Europe. His publications include *Religion and Law in the United Kingdom* (2011), *Ecclesiastical Law* (2007) now in its third edition, *Religious Liberty and Human Rights* (2002) and *English Canon Law* (1998) as well as numerous articles in periodicals and chapters in edited books. He is editor of the *Ecclesiastical Law Journal* and a member of the International Consortium for Law and Religion Studies, the European Consortium for Church and State Research, the Church of England's Legal Advisory Commission and the Inter-Faith Legal Advisors Network at Cardiff Law School's Centre for Law and Religion.

Myriam Hunter-Henin (University College London) is a Senior Lecturer in Law and co-Director of the Institute of Global Law. Before her appointment at University College London, she studied and taught at Paris I Panthéon-Sorbonne University. Her areas of research are on Comparative Law in the areas of Religion and Education; Religion and Family Law; and Human Rights. Recent research is concerned with the regulation of religious symbols in France and its interaction with *laïcité* and the European Convention on Human Rights.

Arif A. Jamal (National University of Singapore) is an Assistant Professor of Law at the National University of Singapore (NUS). Educated in Canada, the United States and the United Kingdom, Arif was called to the Bar of British Columbia (Canada) and obtained his doctorate from the Faculty of Laws, University College London. His recent publications include: 'Moving out of Kazanistan: liberal theory and Muslim contexts' (2010) in *Muslim Societies and the Challenge of Secularization* edited by G. Marranci, Dordrecht: Springer; and, with Arjona Sebastia, C., Menkel-Meadow, C., Ramraj, V. V., and Satiro, F. (forthcoming), 'Senses of Sen: a review essay of Amartya Sen's "The Idea of Justice"', *International Journal of Law in Context*.

Tobias Lock is a lecturer at the School of Law of the University of Surrey where he teaches EU law and public law. Before joining Surrey, he was the DAAD/Clifford Chance Lecturer at the Faculty of Laws, University College London from 2007 until 2011. His work is mainly in the area of EU law and especially on the relationship of the EU with other legal orders. His latest publications are concerned with the EU's accession to the ECHR. Furthermore, he conducts research in EU fundamental rights law and comparative constitutional law.

Alison Mawhinney (Bangor University) is a lecturer in the School of Law at Bangor University. Her main research interests are freedom of religion in schools, religious discrimination in employment and the human rights obligations of non-state service providers. She was Principal Investigator on a recent AHRC/ESRC funded research project entitled 'Opting out of religious education: the views of young people from minority belief backgrounds'.

Christopher McCrudden (Lincoln College, Oxford) is Professor of Human Rights Law in the University of Oxford; a fellow and tutor in law at Lincoln College, Oxford; a practising barrister-at-law (Gray's Inn), and a William W. Cook Global Law Professor at 8 Michigan Law. Specializing in human rights, he concentrates on issues of equality and discrimination as well as the relationship between international economic law and human rights. At the Michigan Law School, Professor McCrudden teaches in the areas of international, European, and comparative human rights. He serves on the European Commission's Expert Network on the Application of the Gender Equality Directives and is a scientific director of the European Commission's network of experts on non-discrimination.

Ulrike Niens (Queen's University, Belfast) is a lecturer in the School of Education, Queen's University Belfast. Her research and teaching focuses on peace education and inclusion, identity and citizenship. Having secured and managed a number of externally funded research projects, the findings based on quantitative as well as qualitative research methods have been published internationally and informed educational policy in Northern Ireland. Ulrike is chair of the School of Education's Ethics Committee and editorial board member of *Compare* and *Peace & Conflict: The Journal of Peace Psychology*.

Farid Panjwani (The Aga Khan University, London) is an Assistant Professor at Aga Khan University's Institute for the Study of Muslim Civilisations in London. With background in the Philosophy of Education, International Development and Islamic Studies, Farid is particularly interested in the interface between religious and citizenship education, and the philosophical questions posed by the need for social cohesion in contemporary multicultural societies. His recent publications include: 'A destructive vacuum: the marginalisation of local knowledge and reassertion of local identities' (2009) in *Multiple Modernities in Muslim Societies*, edited by Sadria, Aga Khan Award for Architecture/IB Tauris; 'Religion, citizenship and hope: civic virtues and education about Muslim traditions' (2008) in *Sage Handbook of Education for Citizenship and Democracy*, edited by Arthur/ Davis/Hahn, Sage Publications.

Norman Richardson (Stranmillis University College, Belfast) has worked as a teacher in primary and post-primary schools in London and Belfast and now lectures in teacher education programmes at Stranmillis University College, Belfast. His main areas of teaching and research are in religious and cultural diversity, inclusive Religious Education and intercultural education. He is also actively involved in a range of community relations and inter-religious programmes in Northern Ireland and elsewhere.

Russell Sandberg (Cardiff Law School) is a lecturer at Cardiff Law School where he researches at the Centre for Law and Religion. In 2005, he graduated from Cardiff Law School with First Class Honours and in 2010 he successfully defended his doctoral thesis at Cardiff examining the relationship between religion, law and society. Russell is the author of *Law and Religion*, published by Cambridge University Press in 2011 and is co-author (with Mark Hill QC and Professor Norman Doe) of the United Kingdom monograph on Religion Law. This forms part of the Kluwer Law International Encyclopaedia of Laws Series and has also been published as a paperback book entitled *Religion and Law in the United Kingdom*. He is also co-editor (with Professor Norman Doe) of the edited collection *Law and Religion: New Horizons* (2010), Peeters. He is a Specialist Contributing Editor for the 2010 edition of *Jowitt's Dictionary of English Law* working on the Ecclesiastical Law team. With colleagues at the Centre for Law and Religion at Cardiff, he coordinates the Interfaith Legal Advisers Network (established in 2007) and chairs the Law and Religion Scholars Network (established in 2008).

Anna Van den Kerchove (IESR Paris) holds an MA in History, Paris XII-Créteil and Paris IV-Sorbonne, an MA and PhD in Religious Studies, EPHE/Sorbonne, Paris. She studied ancient languages at the Institut Catholique de Paris and EPHE/ Sorbonne, Paris and is now a teacher and researcher at the Ecole Pratique des Hautes Etudes (EPHE) in Paris. She has participated in various projects, such as the *Redco* Project. Publications include: *Histoire du Christianisme, Documentation photographique* (2009) La Documentation française, n. 8069; With D. Borne, *Jésus, Récits primordiaux* (2010), La Documentation française; 'Teaching about religious issues within the framework of the French "Laïcité"' (forthcoming) in a volume edited by P. Loobuycjk and L. Franken (Antwerpen University).

Lucy Vickers (Oxford Brooks University) is Professor of Law at Oxford Brookes University. Her main research area is the protection of human rights within the workplace and aspects of equality law. She has written extensively on issues relating to harassment at work, religious discrimination and age discrimination.

She is the author of *Freedom of Speech and Employment* (2002) Oxford University Press, *Religious Freedom, Religious Discrimination and the Workplace* (2008) Hart Publishing, and a report for the European Commission on Religion and Belief Discrimination in Employment – The EU Law (2007).

Lorenzo Zucca (King's College London) is Reader in Jurisprudence at King's College London. He holds the degrees of Maîtrise (Paris 2 Assas), DEA (Paris 1 Sorbonne), Mjur (Oxford) and PhD (EUI, Florence). Lorenzo's special interests are in jurisprudence, constitutional theory, EU constitutional law, and human rights. He is the author of *Constitutional Dilemmas – Conflicts of Fundamental Legal Rights in Europe and the USA* (2007), Oxford University Press and of articles on European human rights law and theory. He is currently working on the place of religion in the European public sphere. He also publishes in the fields of legal theory and is particularly interested in theories of human rights. Lorenzo has been speaker at many European and International Universities, including the Hebrew University of Jerusalem and Mofid University of Qom-Iran where he lectured on Law and Religion.

Foreword

Robert Jackson

This important book recognizes that issues of religion and education in Europe need to be addressed in an interdisciplinary way. Not only do research methods from the social sciences and humanities need to be applied, but insights from a range of disciplines are also necessary for a broad understanding of the issues, especially those resulting from the pluralization of societies in consequence of migration, globalization and issues concerned with human rights. The inclusion of law as an academic field is vital, and the conference on which this book is based was a landmark in bringing together legal specialists with others from education, the social sciences and the humanities.

Much of the book deals with themes which recur in different societies in Western Europe. Each nation has its unique history of religion and State, and these have resulted in some very different attitudes and policies towards the study of religion in schools. They range from the policy of *laïcité,* as in France (Massignon 2011, Willaime 2007), where traditionally religion has been confined to the private sphere, to suspicion of any treatment of religion in schools in some post-Soviet countries, such as Estonia (Schihalejev 2010), to aiming to teach about religious diversity impartially in public education, as in Norway (Skeie 2007) or England and Wales (Jackson and O'Grady 2007, Dinham and Jackson forthcoming), to the public funding of schools teaching the beliefs and values of different specific religions and philosophies, as in the Netherlands (ter Avest et al. 2007), to the favouring of a particular religion or religious denomination in public education, as in Spain (Dietz 2007, Álvarez Veinguer et al. 2011).

In addition to teaching religions or teaching *about* religions, there are recurrent issues relating to religious dress and symbols, worship in schools, separate religious schooling, and the rights of children, parents and teachers in various contexts. This book explores all of these through themes such as identity (whether personal, group or national identity), and the role of the State through policies intended to lead to integration or perhaps to assimilation. Often the borderline between public and private space is difficult to locate and there are ongoing debates as each Sate looks to its own history as well as to the various global or supranational forces operating on it. This is why it is important to look at developments at the European level, as well as national policies and debates. Some national issues have been taken to the European Court of Human Rights, as in the cases of Norway and Turkey (Lied 2009, Relaño 2010). However, it is in institutions such as the Council of Europe and the Organization for Security and Cooperation in Europe that we find attempts at policy discussion relevant to European States in general. Such discussions are relatively recent and need to be seen in interplay with accounts of national situations.

Within the documentation of key European institutions concerned with human rights and education, education about religions and beliefs (as distinct from intercultural education and antiracist education) rarely got a mention in the decades leading up to the millennium. Despite significant differences within individual states, the predominant view in European institutions was that religion was a private matter and that religious education was an issue for parents, religious communities and private schools. The emergence of discussions about religion and education was gradual, but the events of 11 September 2001 in the United States of America and their ongoing global consequences served as a catalyst for the entry of discussions of religion and education within the public sphere (Jackson 2010).

Thus, in 2002, the Council of Europe began its first project on religion and education. Much work had been done earlier on education for democratic citizenship and intercultural education, with the latter seen as a subset of the former. I was at a meeting at the Council of Europe late in 2002 when the issue of how to formulate a rationale for education about religions in publicly funded schools was discussed. Great care was taken to avoid the idea that support was being given for the propagation of a particular religious view or of religious views in general. The argument for learning about religions in schools which finally emerged was a cultural one, although there was no intention whatsoever to suggest that religion could simply be *reduced* to culture. The argument was that, since people practise religion in society, all should be able to agree that, at the least, religion is a part of human culture. Thus, some knowledge and understanding of the religious diversity of Europe should be part of the intercultural education of all European young people.

Specialists in religions and education and in intercultural education from different European States were brought together to participate in the Council of Europe's first project on 'The New Challenge of Intercultural Education: Religious Diversity and Dialogue in Europe'. There were various positive outcomes from the project, including the publication of a reference book for use as a resource in schools across Europe (Keast 2007), but the most important output was a Recommendation from the Committee of Ministers – the Foreign Ministers of the 47 member states of the Council of Europe – on teaching about religions and non-religious convictions in European public schools (Council of Europe 2008). This Recommendation is of great importance and deserves to be studied and discussed by educators, politicians, policy makers, parents and young people across Europe. It is possible here to do no more than indicate the general 'flavour' of the document. For example, its underlying principles include the view that intercultural dialogue, including its dimension of religious and non-religious convictions, is a precondition for the development of tolerance and the recognition of different identities on the basis of human rights. Its objectives include developing a tolerant attitude and respect for the right to hold a particular belief; nurturing a sensitivity to the diversity of religions and non-religious convictions as an element contributing to the richness of Europe; ensuring that teaching about the diversity of religions and non-religious convictions is consistent with the aims of education for democratic citizenship, human rights and respect for equal dignity of all individuals; and promoting dialogue between people from different cultural, religious and non-religious backgrounds. Its educational preconditions include sensitivity to the equal dignity of every individual; the capacity to put oneself in the place of others in order to establish an environment where mutual trust and understanding are fostered; inclusive and cooperative learning; and provision of safe learning space to encourage expression without fear of being judged or held to ridicule. Many other issues are addressed directly on the Recommendation, including the Foreign Ministers' views on the development of resources for teaching and learning and on teacher training.

During the period of this project there was discussion within the Council of Europe about the establishment of European centres to promote education about religions and beliefs and education for democratic citizenship. Following a feasibility study, the decision was made in principle to develop a single European Centre dealing with a broadly understood education for democratic citizenship, incorporating human rights education and intercultural education and including education about religions and beliefs. The Norwegian authorities came forward to offer financial and organizational support and, in May 2008, the European Wergeland Centre was established in Oslo (named after the nineteenth-century Norwegian poet Henrik Wergeland) with a brief to disseminate the results of European projects, to create networks of scholars and teachers and to provide web-based resources in the fields covered by the Centre (www.theewc.org). Among its many activities, the European Wergeland Centre is collaborating currently with the Council of Europe in promoting the dissemination of the Ministerial Recommendation on teaching about religions and beliefs.

Independently from the Council of Europe, another major European institution concerned with human rights also considered the place of the study of religions and beliefs in public education. This is the Organization for Security and Cooperation in Europe (OSCE). The OSCE was founded in the 1970s, and includes as participant States most European countries, plus the USA and Canada. The security brief of the OSCE includes the human dimension as well as the military/political and economic dimensions; hence it has an Office for Democratic Institutions and Human Rights (ODIHR). As with the Council of Europe, the ODIHR conducted a project to identify principles on which participant States could develop policy and practice for teaching about religions and non-religious beliefs in schools across its huge geographical region. The result was the publication of a standard setting document, the *Toledo Guiding Principles on Teaching about Religions and Beliefs in Public Schools*, named after the city in which the drafting team first worked on the text, and in recognition of Toledo's historical role in communication between those of different religions (OSCE 2007). An important feature of this document is that the drafting team included leading international legal specialists in religion, human rights and education, including Silvio Ferrari, Malcolm Evans, Cole

Durham and Jeremy Gunn among others, as well as educators and other social scientists. Again, this important document should be studied and used as a tool by educators, policy makers and politicians across Europe and North America and beyond.

However, the development of policy requires much more than the discussion of generic recommendations. Policy makers need detailed knowledge of what is actually happening 'on the ground', so to speak. In this respect, it is important to understand particular societies – their history, social composition, public attitudes, current educational practices and the views of students and teachers. One large scale inter-European research project involving eight countries, the REDCo (Religion, Education, Dialogue, Conflict) Project, has provided large amounts of relevant data at the national level to complement and inform European policy recommendations (Jackson 2011). The empirical findings of the REDCo project are complemented by the wealth of material made available for the first time in the wide-ranging contributions to the present volume.

References

Álvarez Veinguer, A., Rosón Lorente, F.J. and Dietz, G. 2011. Under the shadow of Al Andalus? Spanish teenagers' attitudes and experiences with religious diversity at school. *British Journal of Religious Education* 33(2), 143–58.

Dietz, G. 2007. Invisibilizing or ethnicizing religious diversity? The transition of religious education towards pluralism in contemporary Spain, in *Religion and Education in Europe: Developments, Contexts and Debates,* edited by R. Jackson, S. Miedema, W. Weisse and J.-P. Willaime. Münster: Waxmann, 103–31.

Dinham, A. and Jackson, R. forthcoming 2012. Religion, welfare and education, in *Religion and Change in Modern Britain,* edited by L. Woodhead and R. Catto. London: Routledge.

Council of Europe. 2008. Recommendation CM/Rec (2008) 12 of the Committee of Ministers to member States on the dimension of religions and non-religious convictions within intercultural education. Available at: https://wcd.coe.int// ViewDoc.jsp?Ref=CM/Rec(2008)12&Language=lanEnglish&Ver=original& BackColorInternet=DBDCF2&BackColorIntranet=FDC864&BackColorLog ged=FDC864 [Accessed: 10 April 2011].

Jackson, R. 2010. Religious diversity and education for democratic citizenship: the contribution of the Council of Europe, in *International Handbook of Inter-religious Education*, Volume 4: *Religion, Citizenship and Human Rights,* edited by K. Engebretson, M. de Souza, G. Durka and L. Gearon. Dordrecht, the Netherlands: Springer Academic Publishers, 1121–51.

Jackson, R. 2011. Religion, education, dialogue and conflict: editorial introduction. *British Journal of Religious Education* 33(2), 105–9.

Jackson, R. and O'Grady, K. 2007. Religions and education in England: social plurality, civil religion and religious education pedagogy, in *Religion and Education in Europe: Developments, Contexts and Debates*, edited by R. Jackson, S. Miedema, W. Weisse and J.-P. Willaime. Münster: Waxmann, 181–202.

Keast, J. (ed.) 2007. *Religious Diversity and Intercultural Education: A Reference Book for Schools* (Strasbourg: Council of Europe Publishing).

Lied, S. 2009. The Norwegian *Christianity, Religion and Philosophy* Subject *KRL* in Strasbourg. *British Journal of Religious Education* 31(3), 263–75.

Massignon, B. 2011. Laïcité in practice: the representations of French teenagers. *British Journal of Religious Education* 33(2), 159–72.

OSCE 2007. *The Toledo Guiding Principles on Teaching about Religions and Beliefs in Public Schools.* Warsaw: Organization for Security and Cooperation in Europe, Office for Democratic Institutions and Human Rights. Full text available at: http://www.osce.org/odihr/29154 [Accessed: 10 April 2011].

Relaño, E. 2010. Educational pluralism and freedom of religion: recent decisions of the European Court of Human Rights. *British Journal of Religious Education* 32(1), 19–29.

Schihalejev, O. 2010. *From Indifference to Dialogue? Estonian Young People, the School and Religious Diversity.* Münster: Waxmann.

Skeie, G. 2007. Religion and education in Norway, in *Religion and Education in Europe: Developments, Contexts and Debates,* edited by R. Jackson, S. Miedema, W. Weisse and J.-P. Willaime. Münster: Waxmann, 221–41.

Ter Avest, I., Bakker, C., Bertram-Troost, G. and Miedema, S. 2007. Religion and education in the Dutch pillarized and post-pillarized educational system: historical background and current debates in *Religion and Education in Europe: Developments, Contexts and Debates*, edited by R. Jackson, S. Miedema, W. Weisse and J.-P. Willaime. Münster: Waxmann, 203–19.

Willaime, J.-P. 2007. Teaching religious issues in French public schools: from abstentionist *laïcité* to a return of religion to public education, *Religion and Education in Europe: Developments, Contexts and Debates,* edited by R. Jackson, S. Miedema, W. Weisse and J.-P. Willaime. Münster: Waxmann, 87–101.

Preface

This collection on Law, Religious Freedoms and Education in Europe is based on a conference[1] organized under the auspices of the Institute of Global Law (University College London) and Maison française d'Oxford which was held in Oxford, at Maison française d'Oxford, on 8 and 9 October 2010.

My warmest thanks go to all the colleagues and enthusiasts for Law and Religion or/and Human Rights and Comparative Law who supported the event: Professor Luc Borot (Director of the Maison française d'Oxford), Dr Frédéric Audren (Maison française d'Oxford); Dr Ioannis Lianos and Dr Florian Wagner-von-Papp (co-directors with myself of the Institute of Global Law, UCL); Dr George Letsas and Dr Saladin Meckled-García (Directors of the Institute for Human Rights, UCL); Phil Baker and Lisa Penfold (administrator and events manager at UCL); Professor Norman Doe (Director of the Centre for Law and Religion at Cardiff Law School), Dr Russell Sandberg (Centre for Law and Religion at Cardiff Law School), Dr Javier García Oliva (Manchester University), Dr Tobias Lock (UCL), Dr Prakash Shah (Queen Mary, University of London) and The Institute of Advanced Legal Studies.

I would also like to express my gratitude to the generous sponsors who offered financial contributions towards the conference on which this book is based:

- The Pentland group
- Grand challenges at University College London
- The Laws Faculty at University College London
- The Institute for Human Rights (UCL)
- The Institute of Global Law (UCL)
- CHERPA, 'Croyance, Histoire, Espace, Régulation Politique et Administrative', Sciences Po Aix
- IESR, 'Institut européen en science des religions'
- LEJP, 'Laboratoire d'études juridiques et politiques', Cergy-Pontoise University
- ENS Paris, L'Ecole Normale Supérieure
- The Cultural Department of the French Embassy in the UK

Moreover, gratitude is of course owed to all the contributors to this book whose analyses share a new light on religious freedoms in the sphere of education: Prof.

---

1 For the full programme of the conference, see http://www.ucl.ac.uk/laws/global_law/content/docs/law_religion_oct2010_v2-1.pdf. For audio recordings of papers, see http://www.mfo.ac.uk/en/audio/by/conference_lecture/law_religion_education.

Eric Barendt, Dr Anna Buchanan, Dr Blandine Chélini-Pont, Dr Yuko Chiba, Prof. Martine Cohen, Frank Cranmer, Peter Cumper, Prof. Heinrich de Wall, Dr Javier García Oliva, Prof. Mark Hill QC, Dr Arif Jamal, Dr Tobias Lock, Dr Alison Mawhinney, Prof. Chris McCrudden, Dr Ulrike Niens, Dr Farid Panjwani, Norman Richardson, Dr Russell Sandberg, Dr Anna Van den Kerchove, Prof. Lucy Vickers and Dr Lorenzo Zucca.

Finally, acknowledgement and recognition are due to Arman Sarvarian, PhD student at UCL, for his immense and precious help in editing this collection, and for the kind support provided by Ashgate Publishers.

Myriam Hunter-Henin
London

Introduction

Religious Freedoms in European Schools: Contrasts and Convergence

Myriam Hunter-Henin[1]

This edited collection brings together chapters by sociologists, political scientists, historians and legal specialists who consider how contemporary cultural and religious diversity challenges and redefines national constitutional and legal frameworks and concepts and how these frameworks and concepts – spontaneously or under social pressure and/or prompting from the European Court of Human Rights – respond to this diversity in the highly sensitive and topical sphere of education.

The Scope of the Book

Law, Religious Freedoms and Education in Europe

The approach adopted in the book is multidisciplinary and comparative because legal solutions are impossible to understand independently of the sociological, political and historical contexts in which and for which they are adopted. Moreover, the broader European context cannot be ignored. Human rights develop under the watch of judges from the European Court of Human Rights and positions taken in other countries may impact sociologically on the support afforded to given national positions. The contributions deal mainly with Western Europe: specifically England and Wales, Northern Ireland, France, Germany and Spain. If multicultural societies in Western Europe have all been faced with the challenges of accommodating minority religious communities,[2] the responses chosen to meet those challenges have varied greatly, with the most striking differences arising in the context of education.

However, a common trend has been the emergence of a human rights discourse in which law and religion issues are now being phrased in terms of 'religious

---

1   I would like to thank Frank Cranmer (Cardiff Law School), Dr Russell Sandberg (Cardiff Law School) and Prof. Martine Cohen (CNRS Paris) for their comments on earlier drafts of this chapter. Any errors remain mine.
2   Kymlicka 1995.

freedoms'.[3] Whatever their legitimate interest in upholding their particular traditions – systemic legal coherence, constitutional integrity and values – States must acknowledge the individual dimension of religion as a freedom belonging to each of us.[4] In England and Wales, particular protections used to be afforded on grounds of religion prior to the Human Rights era but these owed more to 'the tradition of religious tolerance and accommodation than to any sophisticated notion of religious liberty as a widespread positive right' (Hill Chapter 15, Sandberg Chapter 16).

Despite starkly diverging traditions and approaches, European countries unite around article 9 of the European Convention on Human Rights. Article 9 paragraph 1 proclaims religious freedom as a right belonging to each of us: 'Everyone has the right to freedom of thought, conscience and religion; this right includes freedom to change his religion or belief, and freedom, either alone or in community with others and in public or private, to manifest his religion or belief, in worship, teaching, practice and observance.' Once litigants have proved that there has been an interference with the manifestation of their religion or belief under article 9(1), the onus is then on the State to demonstrate that the interference was justified under article 9(2). To that end, paragraph 2 promotes a case by case approach designed to assess whether or not the interference, proven to be prescribed by law and pursuing a legitimate aim, does on the facts of the case respond to a pressing social need and is proportionate to the aim pursued. McCrudden (2011) rightly states that the *Human Rights Act 1998* has produced 'a shift in British constitutional thinking, in which pragmatic empiricism has been supplemented, if not replaced, by a constitutional idealism that focuses much more on principles'. And yet, the emphasis that is placed on the justification stage under article 9(2) will lead inevitably and gradually to a balancing process which requires a careful weighing up of all the circumstances of a particular case and the exclusion of decisions based on principle.[5] All European States are therefore in that sense encouraged to move towards a more individualistic and more factually based approach. The same conclusion applies under the framework of the European Union, more specifically under the *EU directive 2000/78/EC* prohibiting discrimination at work on the ground, inter alia, of religion. More generally, it has been said that 'the overall picture in the European Union is one of *balance* between religious and secular influences which is struck in differing ways in the various Member States' (McCrea 2010).[6]

The principle of equality, emerging as a paramount principle in law and religion matters, has come to protect individual self-identity through judicial

---

3   Bradney 2000.

4   Cf. underlying the importance of freedom of religion, ECtHR 20 September 1994 *Otto Preminger Institut v. Austria, JCP* 1995.I.3823; *RTDH* 1994, 441.

5   For a similar methodological evolution in the context of privacy, Fedtke, Hunter-Henin and O'Cinneide 2005.

6   Emphasis added.

activism rather than economically disadvantaged groups through legislative redress (McCrudden Chapter 6). In turn, this individual focus, combined with the multiplicity of prohibited grounds of discrimination, has generated conflicts between the different grounds of non-discrimination as well as between freedom of religion under article 9 of the European Convention and non-discrimination claims, to be resolved by litigation. McCrudden (Chapter 6) concludes that 'clashes of principle appear more likely to result in rules having to be introduced to attempt to resolve them, leading to greater inflexibility when the individual case is considered'. But these conflicts may also be read as an encouragement for a case by case analysis, in order to ascertain in each case the exact gravity of and justification for the alleged interferences. Overall, the general methodological trend seems, therefore, to be in favour of an individually and factually focused reasoning.

But changes in methodology are slow. English judges, for example, do not always carry out a proper assessment of the proportionality test required by European case law. Instead, they sometimes make a priori judgments about the extent to which schools should be allowed to discriminate rather than carrying out a careful examination of the merits of each case (Vickers Chapter 4, Sandberg Chapter 16); and one can occasionally read crude dismissive statements as to the existence of infringements under article 9(1) of the European Convention, again irrespective of the merits of the case (Hill Chapter 15, Sandberg Chapter 16). Similarly, the case law of German courts on issues of anti-discrimination law under the EU directive is still lacking in sophistication and nuance (Lock Chapter 17). Paragraph 23 of the *Directive 2000/78/EC*, under which discrimination is only allowed in 'very limited circumstances' would require more attention to the facts of each individual case than is currently displayed (Lock Chapter 17). From a comparative perspective, the observation is therefore one of slow and methodological convergence, by contrast to the harmonization endeavours at work in other legal fields.[7] The goal is not, therefore, to create a new and different model for Europe[8] nor to ascertain what model would be the best one for Europe,[9] but to make sure that each national model evolves in a way that is respectful of religious freedoms. This modest scope in comparative terms avoids numerous pitfalls. Instead of approximating national laws or bringing them closer together, promoting a 'unique' model for Europe may actually create new divergences and reinforce nationalistic reactions (Sefton-Green 2010). How could we identify the best model for Europe? It is assumed that the best national model would be one that most serves multiculturalism (Modood 2010). But if imposed as a paradigm for the whole of Europe, the most multiculturalism-friendly national model may (ironically) affect multiculturalism adversely since it may cause potential damage

---

7   Sefton-Green 2010.

8   Beck and Giddens 2006.

9   Cf. presenting 'moderate secularism' as a model for multicultural European societies, Modood 2010.

in terms of a 'welfare loss caused by legal rules that are less or not at all tailored to national and cultural preferences' (Van Dam 2009, Sefton-Green 2010). Moreover, the quest for the 'better' national model for the relationship between law and religion may often be characterized by cultural insensitivity. As often seen in other contexts with 'better law' projects,[10] a particular standpoint (influenced by a single, often idealized, system or solution) tends to work as a filter for analysis of all national models. Unsurprisingly, the national system or rule used as a prism then turns out to be the winner because, inevitably, it will be the best one to fit the chosen mould of analysis. Possibly aware of these pitfalls, the European Court of Human Rights has shown at least a degree of deference to national traditions in matters of religion at school.

Law, Religious Freedoms and Education in Europe

Religious freedoms vary in scope and meaning according to the national context in which believers or non-believers wish to exercise their freedom of (or freedom *from*) religion, because of the margin of appreciation recognized by the European Court of Human Rights to member States in deciding on the best way to accommodate religious freedoms.[11] Tensions between a systemic approach, sensitive to States' heritages and legal frameworks, and an individual approach, more attuned to individual rights and beliefs, are now at the heart of law and religion issues in Europe. Within this tension between state and individual reasoning an added complication (or enrichment) stems from claims of collective rights,[12] whereby groups seek respect for their own religious ethos even, at times, against more general frameworks or individual aspirations and beliefs. Furthermore, the emphasis placed by the European Court of Human Rights on individual rights cannot hide the fact that the human rights discourse is in itself a framework and that the fusion of human rights and religion may not be unanimously accepted. Might the role of religion not be somewhat restricted if it were thought to exist only within the framework laid down by human rights instruments? Depending on one's point of view, might one not fear or welcome a dilution of religion which would no longer be protected for itself but as a human right amongst others?[13]

Alternatively, the human rights discourse may *itself* be seen as a form of religion or theology. Thus, as Edge (2001) puts it, 'rather than international law being seen as a qualitatively different mode of thought which can be used to evaluate religious systems, it may be more accurate to see the interaction between international law and religious systems as a unique form of interfaith dialogue.' Ruston (2004: 270) goes so far as to suggest that the concept of human rights can be traced, at least in part, to an *imago Dei* theology that goes back at least

---

10   See for a criticism of the method in family law, Bradley 2004.

11   On the margin of appreciation, see Sweeney 2005.

12   On the notion of collective rights, Rivers 2001.

13   Evans 2000.

as far as Augustine of Hippo and which, he suggests, '... owes little to secular Enlightenment sources and everything to an enduring religious tradition shared by both Catholics and Protestants, even though not consistently practised by them'.

Within the human rights framework itself, the consecration of religion as a human right was questioned by some as an unnecessary step: for instance, would freedom of religion not already fall under the ambit of other human rights such as freedom of expression or privacy?[14] Despite these controversies and the general decline in religious practice – as opposed to religious beliefs (Davie 2002: 5) – it seems that the emergence of religious freedoms in a human rights framework has contributed to the growing importance of religious issues in the legal sphere across Europe. The question is no longer whether or not we should have religious freedoms but, rather, how we are to accommodate them. That said, however, in meeting these new challenges as to the 'how', previous controversies about the 'why' – the purpose and role of religion within legal frameworks – inevitably resurface. In addition to possible tensions generated by the relationships between 'religious' and 'legal' frameworks and by the different possible levels of perspective – individual, national, infranational or supranational – the concept of religious freedoms *itself* is often at the source of misunderstandings and potential conflicts.

The freedom recognized for schoolchildren under the right to religious freedoms may therefore give rise to different interpretations. In France, for example,[15] religious freedom may seem to blur the distinction which is drawn in a school context between freedom of conscience and freedom of thought:

> Freedom of conscience along with its constituents freedom of religion and freedom of belief guarantees diversity of belief in society and the freedom to express those beliefs. Freedom of thought ensures the right to independently reexamine beliefs received from family, social groups and society as a whole. This way a person can freely adhere to these beliefs, adapt them or turn away from them to something else. Naturally, this is a conceptual distinction and clearly daily life produces constant disharmony between these two freedoms. But the perspective is not the same and the French view school as the perfect institution to teach future citizens to exploit their faculties of reason and to help them exercise freedom of thought.[16]

Behind those conceptual subtleties lie fundamental questions about the meaning of individual freedom of thought and conscience. In the name of individual freedom and in compliance with the distinction drawn above, the French have banned the ostentatious display of all religious symbols in state schools:[17] a move than most

---

14   Nickel 2005.

15   For an illuminating analysis on the French position, see McGoldrick 2006: chapter 2.

16   Baubérot 2003: 461.

17   Loi no. 2004–228 of 15 March 2004 encadrant, en application du principe de laïcité, le port de signes ou de tenues manifestant une appartenance religieuse dans les

other Western countries would construe as an attempt at state indoctrination and the very opposite to freedom of thought and conscience.

If the meaning of the autonomy granted under the right to religious freedom is thus unclear, so is the holder of that right: are we acknowledging children's religious freedoms or parental beliefs? Under article 9 of the ECHR children are entitled to freedom of religion; but parents are also entitled to have their children educated according to their own beliefs under article 2 of Protocol 1.[18] In practice, children's rights tend to be merged into those of their parents.[19] This is slightly at odds with other areas where the entitlement of children as right bearers has been more willingly recognized.[20] Would it be realistic completely to separate the child's and the parents' perspectives? To attempt to ascertain whether a child's claim that his or her religious freedom had been infringed was truly motivated by the child's individual beliefs or by family opinion or pressure would be riddled with difficulties. Could a judge realistically embark on a systematic questioning of the reasons underlying a given religious commitment? Would the coincidence between family tradition and religious adherence strengthen the religious commitment or would it weaken it on the grounds that – allegedly – it had been embraced not by the child as an individual but as part of the family? The French position could be seen as protecting children's autonomy against possible parental and social pressure whereas the English approach could be seen as favouring family choices.[21]

More uncertain still are the meanings of 'religious' and 'religion' under the right to religious freedoms and right to freedom of religion. Are we referring to the way that individuals perceive their beliefs or to the way that religious communities define themselves and their members? Indirectly, albeit based on

---

écoles, colleges, lycées publics, *JO* 17 March 2004, 5190 (Act regulating, by virtue of the principle of '*laïcité*', the wearing of religious symbols or clothing in state primary and secondary schools).

18   Article 2 of Protocol 1 of the ECHR reads as follows: 'No person shall be denied the right to education. In the exercise of any functions which it assumes in relation to education and teaching, the State shall respect the right of parents to ensure such education and teaching in conformity with their own religious and philosophical convictions.'

19   ECtHR *Valsamis v. Greece* (1996) 24 EHRR 294, Kilkelly 1999.

20   See in England and Wales, the *Gillick* case, *Gillick v. Western Norfolk and Wisbech AHA* [1986] AC 112 and the *Children Act 1989* and, in the context of the United Nations, the *United Nations Convention on the Rights of the Child*. Those landmark texts and decision mark a shift in the thinking about children. The idea that children have the capacity and more fundamentally the right to make decisions for themselves began to emerge. See for a reflection of the theoretical underpinnings of children's rights and a case in favour of children's rights, MDA Freeman: 1983 and 1997: chapters 1, 2 and 4.

21   *R (on the application of Begum) v. Head Teacher and Governors of Denbigh High School* [2007] AC 100 where Baroness Hale was the only member of the House of Lords to appreciate that the 14-year-old girl concerned might have a different opinion from her parents on dress. See Freeman 2010: 7.

racial discrimination, the decision of the UK Supreme Court in the *JFS* case[22] may be read as a victory for the individual perspective of religion over its collective dimension. In that case, a Jewish faith school had refused to admit a candidate on the ground that he was not halachically Jewish. Whatever the degree of the applicant's self-identification as Jewish and his involvement in the Jewish community, he was not regarded as Jewish because his mother's conversion to Judaism was not recognized as valid by the Office of the Chief Rabbi and, as a result, he did not meet the school's admission criteria. Although the UK Supreme Court did not directly arbitrate the conflict between these two conceptions of Jewishness but, strictly speaking, only ruled on the scope of the *Race Relation Act 1976*, the outcome gives precedence to the individual dimension. The race discrimination angle lent support to a more generous approach of Jewishness. As Cranmer (2010: 82) puts it 'if a child of Jewish parents (even if its mother, in the eyes of some Jews, has been improperly converted) practices Judaism as he or she understands it and self-identifies as Jewish, it is difficult to see how a claim by the child to be ethnically-Jewish can be lightly set aside – whatever the view the religious authorities may take about his or her Jewishness'. By rejecting the school's policy as constituting discrimination based on ethnicity, the Court indirectly gives weight to how individuals define their religious affiliation.[23] This is all the more striking given that, for the Orthodox Jewish faith, individual conscious affiliation is not a defining feature of Jewishness (McCrudden 2011).

The recognition of 'religious' freedoms also raises questions for the protection of non-religious believers. Does the recognition of 'religious' freedoms imply that one must always give a voice to religion? Can we ever have a true recognition of religion in French schools if all 'ostentatious' religious signs have to be left outside school premises and faith has to pass the impossible test of rationality? Or is this complete blank space the very condition of religious recognition in a *laïc* State? How much attention should be given to minority religious opinions? Can we ever have recognition of minority religion in the United Kingdom if mainstream views are implicitly given precedence? Or is priority to mainstream views a necessary condition for harmonious religious coexistence in a multicultural society? Can we respect individual religious freedom fully without losing sight of the meaning of

---

22   *R (on the application of E) v. The Governing Body of JFS and the Admissions Appeal Panel of JFS and others* [2009] UKSC 15.

23   This subjective approach was also adopted in the case of *Williamson, R v. Secretary of State for Education and Employment and Ors ex parte Williamson and Ors* [2005] UKHL 15, paras 22 and 23 where Lord Nicholls of Birkenhead declared: '[I]t is not for the court to embark on an inquiry into the asserted belief and judge its "validity" by some objective standard such as the source material upon which the claimant founds his belief or the orthodox teaching of the religion in question or the extent to which the claimant's belief conforms to or differs from the views of others professing the same religion. Freedom of religion protects the subjective belief of an individual.'

'religious' and giving way to all sorts of personal whims?[24] Can we adequately guarantee freedom *from* religion in States where the majority is overwhelmingly religious? If the adjective 'religious' in religious freedoms is to include non-religious beliefs as explicitly prescribed by the European Court of Human Rights and not to be limited to beliefs held by the majority, how are we to define what beliefs are to be protected, what balance is to be reached between conflicting beliefs and, to go back to our starting point, what equilibrium is to be struck between individual belief (and identity) and national values (and identity)? These tensions and fundamental questions arise in other contexts such as the workplace (Vickers 2008) but are particularly acute in the sphere of education.

Law, Religious Freedoms and Education in Europe

For a variety of reasons, the problems linked to the accommodation of religious freedoms in Western Europe are more sensitive in the sphere of education than in other fields such as the workplace. Whereas the workplace engages adults, the activity of education is mainly addressed to children who are possibly more vulnerable to proselytism than are workers.[25] Schooling is vital – and compulsory – for children. It is the place 'where they learn about the world, about the place they will occupy in it, about powers and inequality'.[26] If it is true that the workplace contributes to the common good as a factor for harmonious social relations and economic prosperity, the influence of education on individuals' minds and a nation's mentality are even more profound. State schools are both the bedrock of a nation's values and the means by which it helps to form good citizens. In secular States such as France, schools are entrusted with the important mission of teaching the values of republicanism, individualism, equality and democracy.[27] But this national dimension of state school education is not unique to *laïc* States. Non-*laïc* States such as the United Kingdom and Germany also regard schools as vital places for the building of a cohesive society[28] and for the transmission of the nation's cultural heritage – including its religious traditions.[29] Generally speaking, 'education is the first building block to promote a genuinely plural and tolerant society' (Zucca Chapter 1). Education, moreover, clearly belongs to the public sphere which includes the state education system. State schools represent

---

24   See however ECtHR *X, Y and Z v. UK* (1982) 31 D&R 50, stating that only beliefs with some cogency, seriousness, cohesion and importance could fall within the ambit of article 9 of the European Convention.

25   ECtHR *Dahlab v. Switzerland*, Application no. 42393/93; *Asmi v. Kirklees Metropolitan Council* [2007] ICR 1154.

26   Freeman 2010: 6.

27   Corbett 1996.

28   The *Education and Inspections Act 2006* imposes a duty on governors of state schools in England to promote community cohesion in their conduct of their school (s.38).

29   Haüßler 2001: 465.

emblematically the chosen national model of Church/State relationships – and that model is often the result of historical conflicts in which schools were the battleground. Consequently, any challenge to a given legal solution aimed at accommodating religious freedoms in school is often perceived as a direct threat to a nation's identity.

This collection will explore the challenges posed by religious freedoms in the sphere of education in Western Europe. The role of this introduction is first and foremost to present the main questions that have arisen before setting out the approaches adopted by the contributors. The question as to whether or not religious plurality is being accommodated within schools – or indeed whether or not it should be so accommodated – is widely debated in Western Europe and a number of perspectives and tensions may be identified: between national and religious identities; between separatist and cooperationist approaches between State and religion; between the public and private spheres; between integration, assimilation, segregation and equality.

The Themes of the Book

National and Religious Identities

Recognition of religious freedoms as a human right is justified because of the importance of religious beliefs for an individual's self-perception and self-construction. Religious beliefs 'define a person's very being – his sense of who he is, why he exists, and how he should relate to the world around him. A person's religious beliefs cannot meaningfully be separated from the person himself: they are who he is.'[30] National identities, proclaimed and protected through national constitutions or constitutional arrangements and conventions, are valued as a cement for cohesive societies.[31] Both national and individual religious identities generally mingle and the historical, political and legal background of a given country will certainly influence the way in which it individual citizens express and perceive their religious identity. But there will not always be harmony between the manifestations of national and religious individual identities, leaving conflicts to be arbitrated under a supranational human rights framework. Religious identities may also be national, with the State establishing one particular church as a national church. More complex still, the State may recognize a variety of national churches, as is the case in the United Kingdom with the Church of England, the Church of Wales and the Church of Scotland (see Sandberg and Buchanan Chapter 5)

---

30   Conkle 1988: 1164–5.

31   See for example the debates on Britishness in the House of Lords, HL Deb, 19 June 2008, c. 1140–c. 1172 and the Library notes for debates [Online] available at htpp://www.parliament.uk/documents/lords-library/lln2008–015.pdf. [Accessed: 14 March 2011].

or a variety of federal entities.[32] There are further subtleties in the relationships between State and Church in those countries that have official churches. National churches need not always be 'established by law' and can have a high degree of autonomy, as is the case in Great Britain.[33] Moreover, religious identities within a single State can themselves become an element in different national allegiances – as in Northern Ireland where '"Catholics" (…) describe the community that tends to Irish nationalism, and a greater identity with Ireland, whereas "Protestants" tend to Unionism, and a greater identity with Great Britain' (McCrudden Chapter 6). Finally, beyond individual and state religious identities, groups and institutions may also seek to have their own religious identities and ethos recognized and protected. All of those different levels of identities are to be found in the school context.

Group religious identities: religious schools
One way of promoting religious identity in the education sector has been to encourage the emergence of schools which seek to enforce a religious ethos.

In the United Kingdom, 'faith schools' are a common feature of the state school system. But not all of them actually promote a strong religious ethos nor are they afforded the level of autonomy that one might suspect: only 'voluntary aided schools with a religious character' are granted a relatively high degree of autonomy, whereas foundation or voluntary controlled schools with a religious character mostly have to abide by the rules applicable to schools without a religious character (Sandberg and Buchanan Chapter 5). And the divide between these categories does not necessarily reflect a higher or lesser degree of religiosity in the schools in question, with the result that the recognition of a religious character of a given school tells us little about the legal framework applicable to that school or the strength of its religious ethos. Similarly, the general observation that French religious schools (which are necessarily private) lack a strong religious ethos is undeniably true of Catholic schools which represent 98 per cent of the private schools in France (Chélini-Pont Chapter 7) but can hide contrary minority trends. Thus, even if French private religious schools under state contract are to be very inclusive, one may detect a revival of religious identity in Jewish schools: 'the Jewish sector differs from the general private one by its strong religious character' albeit with a few Jewish schools opposing to this trend of religious radicalization a 'cultural-secular' option (Cohen Chapter 2).

---

32   In Germany, the organization of schools thus falls under the competence of German states (*Länder):* Basic Law Art 70 (Lock Chapter 17). In Switzerland, the regulation of the relationship between the Church and the State is the responsibility of the Cantons: Federal Constitution Art 72.

33   Under *the Church of England Assembly (Powers) Act 1919*; the *Welsh Church Act 1914* and *the Church of Scotland Act 1921*. Strictly speaking, the latter did not confer independence on the Church of Scotland but only recognized its inherent existing independence. See Cross and Livingstone 1997. I am grateful to Frank Cranmer for pointing this out to me in an earlier draft.

Beyond the complexities of the religious ethos of schools and individual beliefs, States may themselves, as mentioned above, claim a religious identity, either explicitly through an established or official Church or, more implicitly, through the endorsement of religious practices and symbols which have become part of a nation's culture and history.

State religious identities and individual freedom from religion
How can a State claim its own religious identity and yet remain neutral and respectful towards all religious beliefs? The question was indirectly raised in the *Lautsi* case where Italy, albeit a secular State claiming no religious identity, allowed its Catholic heritage to be displayed in the form of crucifix in the classroom. The ECtHR first held in a chamber judgment that the presence of a crucifix in state classrooms was incompatible with pupils' freedom not to be subjected to religion,[34] before ruling on appeal, in Grand Chamber,[35] that the relevant Italian 'authorities (had) acted within the limits of the margin of appreciation left to the respondent State' (para. 76). The Grand Chamber did not deny the religious connotation of the crucifix nor the preponderant visibility it gave to Christianity (para. 71) but given the essentially passive nature of the symbol (para. 72) and the overall openness of Italian state schools towards all religions (para. 74), it considered that the decision to display crucifix was within the margin of appreciation granted to Member States. The same question was raised in Germany before the Federal Constitutional Court in 1995.[36] Having established that the cross was a religious symbol, the German Constitutional Court held that its presence in state schools amounted to a direct interference by the State with pupils' freedom from religion or from Christian religion. The main rationale for the German Constitutional Court's decision was the inescapability of the cross: school pupils were thus forced to study under the cross (Lock Chapter 17).

Laïc States and individual freedom of religion
In States such as France where national religious identity is hardly acknowledged, the thorny recurring issue will be whether or not the importance of religion for individuals (and groups) can nevertheless be sufficiently recognized and preserved. In France, citizens are defined in their common humanity and equality before the law (Zucca Chapter 1). Any differences in terms of gender, race, position, status or religion should be irrelevant before the law. Similarly, any membership of minority groups and any claims for minority rights will be discarded as threatening the equality accorded to *individuals*. There is a fear that minority rights would serve groups rather than individual members and, at a conceptual level, French

---

34 ECtHR *Lautsi v. Italy* 3 November 2009, Application no. 30814/06.
35 ECtHR Grand Chamber *Lautsi v. Italy* 18 March 2011, Application no. 30814/06.
36 BverfGE 93,1.

identity will therefore ignore its underlying religious identities.[37] There is debate as to whether *laïcité*, at least in some of its most militant versions, operates as a hindrance to the integration of immigrants,[38] especially those of Muslim origins. One may at least wonder whether the abstract construction which derives from the concept of *laïcité* in France does not conveniently hide the difficulties that the population of Muslim origin often faces in fact. At school, might not the ban on all ostentatious religious symbols run the risk of erecting national secular and individual religious identities as conflicting entities, confronting individuals with impossible choices? Most probably it will; but empirical research would be needed to confirm that this is indeed the outcome of the law and to rebut the evidence that many pupils in French state schools actually welcome the opportunity given to them by the ban to escape other impossible choices between preferences expressed by their families, friends and society as a whole.[39] Beyond those controversies, the desire which lies at the very heart of the concepts of *laïcité* and formal equality to have a common destiny and to erase the inequalities which religion and social memberships may trigger should certainly not be scorned. Valuing diversity (which is the option favoured in the UK) is no certain guarantee of a peaceful and cohesive coexistence because it is always possible that socio-cultural and economic gaps between groups will make mutual increasingly impossible (Zucca Chapter 1). Moreover, one should be careful not to caricature national positions and exaggerate differences between them. The concept of *laïcité* for example is but one way of accommodating religious plurality and should not be seen as the negation of religion.[40]

Whatever the 'model', the consequences that it carries in the sector of education are unclear. Does the goal of a common destiny prescribe a national uniform syllabus, devoid of any religious content? Conversely, what does the recognition of 'diversity' mean at school? Can any type of symbol be allowed and any derogation from the national syllabus authorized, so long as they are inspired by religious motivations?

Separatist or Cooperationist Models

Laïcité and rationality
Macklem (2000) argues that it is the fact that religious views are based on faith rather than reason that gives rise to the need to protect them. This argument would be particularly problematic in France in a school context, where rationality is unquestionably given priority. *Laïcité*, historically linked to the revolutionary

---

37   This is at the antipode of the notion of consciational democracy, a political system where entitlements and responsibilities are given to (religious) communities rather than to individuals, as in Northern Ireland (McCrudden Chapter 6).

38   Freedman 2004.

39   Sage 2005.

40   I am grateful to Prof. Martine Cohen for underlining this point.

ideas of '*l'Esprit des Lumières*' does not only summarize the ways in which France has chosen to deal with Church/State relationships, it also expresses a positive belief[41] with its own teaching and its own places of worship: town halls, official state buildings and state schools).[42] This positive dimension of *laïcité* distinguishes it from notions of secularism and mere neutrality which only seek to maintain a neutral position and minimize state interference into religious beliefs. The presentation of *laïcité* as an opinion may, however, be misleading because it may suggest that *laïcité* could have its own subject in the shape, for example, of a civic education class alongside religious education classes. But *laïcité* as an ideal goes much further. It implies the possibility of escaping all mention of religion as a social grounding, of avoiding the necessity to position oneself as a believer or non-believer and of thinking outside all reference to religion.[43] Following that logic, religion should not be taught in *laïc* state schools *at all*. Freedom of religion is taken into account in France insofar as pupils are granted one afternoon a week off school in order to attend religious instruction outside school premises should they wish to do so (Van den Kerchove Chapter 12). Moreover, French state secondary schools may allow the presence of chaplaincy on school premises if parents request it[44] (Chélini-Pont Chapter 7).

This is, however, but one (rigid) form of *laïcité*.[45] A more open version of the concept, whilst still advocating some separation between State and religion, could accommodate individual manifestations of religious beliefs at schools, either through clothing or chosen teaching of Religious Education. The accommodation of religious symbols worn by pupils and the organization of religious education classes does not necessarily entail State/Church cooperation. In that sense, neither necessarily conflict with the requirements of *laïcité* per se, as indeed illustrated by Italy, where the *laïque* nature of the Republic[46] is no obstacle to the presence of religious symbols and classes in Italian state schools or by earlier case law of the French *Conseil d'Etat*.[47] Even under the most radical forms of *laïcité* there is at least a tenable argument for teaching about religion where not to do so would deprive pupils of the tools and general cultural background that are needed for a sound understanding of social events, history and art. From that intellectual perspective, a revival of religion can be detected in French *laïc* schools (Van den

---

41 Ronan 1991.Against this conception of *laïcité* as an opinion or belief in itself, Caye and Terré 2005: 34.

42 Cf. suggesting to establish a bank holiday dedicated to 'Laïcité' on 9 December, date of the 1905 Act on the separation of Church and State, Philippe Vitel MP from the party UMP (Var), Question to the Prime Minister no. 68744, *JO* 19 January 2010, 443.

43 Kintzler 2005: 54.

44 Art R 141–2 and R 141–4 of the Code of Education.

45 For the variations in the concept of *laïcité*, see Bouchard-Taylor 2008: chapter 7, 131–153; Baubérot and Milot 2011.

46 Based on Art. 7 of the Italian Constitution, amongst other constitutional provisions.

47 CE 27 November 1989 Avis, *RFDA* 1990, 1, where religious symbols worn by students were not per se seen as conflicting with the requirements of an 'open *laïcité*'.

Kerchove Chapter 12; Debray 2002). To enter the perimeter of French *laïc* state schools, religion thus needs to wear the cloak of rationality; and rather than to be studied as a separate subject, as 'religion' it is to be examined within other core subjects as a '(religious) issue' influencing history or art. This particular way of teaching about religion or, more accurately, about religious issues, is perceived as a guarantee of the objective presentation of religious matters. Indeed, teachers of French state schools, most of whom are civil servants, are not allowed to display their own beliefs; and if they were to discuss faith directly it would be seen as exposing them to too high a risk of subjectivity. The incorporation of religious issues into core subjects such as history or history of arts is, however, no reliable protection against subjectivity and biases. The content of history textbooks, for example, reveals a great imbalance in favour of Christianity. Other religions are largely ignored or only mentioned from the perspective of Christianity (Van den Kerchove Chapter 12). But even so, these trends represent a new perspective on religious issues in French state schools. In fact, one may detect a resurrection of religion in French schools.[48]

Interestingly, discussion of religion under the cloak of rationality echoes claims made in US schools – but the goal of presenting religion in that way is the opposite one of that sought in France. Unlike in France, the objective in the US is not to foster a greater awareness of religion as a social issue – a dimension that hardly anyone would contest in the US – but to present religious beliefs, and in particular beliefs about the creation of the world, as scientific theories (Barendt Chapter 13). Beyond the question of *how* one should discuss religion in the classroom, these claims of rationality question *what* religion actually is. The US Supreme Court offers interesting lessons for Europe. One of the key factors put forward by the Supreme Court is the educational purpose (or lack of purpose) of the proposed measure (Barendt Chapter 13). For example, according to the US constitutional case law, the proposed introduction of the Book of Genesis in a biology class would not fulfil such a purpose because its aim is not to broaden pupils' minds and deepen their knowledge (an objective which could be claimed for the introduction of the Book of Genesis in religious education classes) but to promote religious views of the world by presenting them in competition with or in lieu of other accounts of the beginning of the Earth and humankind. Conversely, purely for educational purposes the teaching in history classes about religion in France could arguably be enhanced and improved without necessarily putting into jeopardy the French model of *laïcité*. By contrast to France, in most European States, religion will be the object of a separate subject at school.

---

48   See evidence of this renewal in the research and publications undertaken and gathered by the IESR (Institut Européen en Science des Religions), [Online] available at: http://www.iesr.ephe.sorbonne.fr/ [Accessed: 30 March 2011].

Neutrality through opt-outs

Religious education/instruction is in most European States a traditional part of the national school syllabus and debates surrounding religion do not focus on whether religion or not should be present in the syllabus or where it should feature but on how religious education/instruction classes should be taught in order to accommodate all beliefs. Respect for freedom *of* religion and freedom *from* religion is generally guaranteed by the optional nature of the course.[49] However, this general model has not been enforced without controversy and is regularly challenged as being insufficiently neutral and inclusive for our multicultural societies. The most acute debates have concerned the right of non-believers not to be subjected to religious instruction.[50]

In the UK, the pervasiveness of religion is reflected in the provisions relating to religious worship. All schools in England and Wales, whether of a religious character or not, must hold a daily act of worship.[51] Moreover, the presence of religion raises the question of which religion should be present. England and Wales prescribe a broadly Christian character both for the act of daily worship[52] and for the content of religious education classes.[53] Respect for minority beliefs is to be guaranteed mainly by the right to opt out. However, the efficacy of the opt-out system on the ground has been questioned, not least because little is done actually to inform pupils of its existence (Mawhinney et al. Chapter 11). Moreover, does not the premise of freedom of choice on which the opt-out system is based underplay the risk of peer pressure on pupils and their parents to conform to the norm (Cumper Chapter 10)? Finally, how much of a choice do parents have if little is offered in the way of a worthwhile alternative to those who choose to opt out (Cumper Chapter 10)? Should civic education be offered as an alternative? But would such a non-religious course be compatible with the duty of neutrality of the State towards religion? Could the introduction of such a course be suspected of promoting a kind of 'state religion'? Many in Spain have argued that such a course, if compulsory, would affect children's and parents' right to freedom of religion even if a course on religious education were to be offered in parallel. Alternatively, could students who chose to follow religious instruction/education classes not legitimately complain that in doing so they were deprived of the possibility also to follow the course on civic education, as if one could not be both a citizen and a believer (García Oliva Chapter 9)? Would the way forward therefore be to change the content of religious education classes so as to make it more inclusive and therefore acceptable to all?

---

49   See for example in England and Wales, *School Standards and Framework Act 1998*, s.71.

50   See ECtHR *Grzelak v. Poland*, Application no. 7710/02, 15 June 2010 (Cumper Chapter 10).

51   *School Standards and Framework Act 1998*, s.70.

52   Schedule 20 to *School Standards and Framework Act 1998*.

53   *School Standards and Framework Act 1998* and *Education Act 1996*, s.375(3).

Neutrality through inclusiveness in religious education
It is difficult to design a religious education syllabus which would be inclusive enough to justify the mandatory nature of the course.[54] The shift from religious instruction to religious education classes in many countries is already a step in the direction of inclusiveness (Cumper Chapter 10). In England and Wales, for example, legislation stresses that 'religious education is the study *of* religion rather than the study *in* religion' (Sandberg and Buchanan Chapter 5). But is there not a risk that in opening up the scope of religious education one may fail to convey the 'heritage of the nation'[55] or dilute the religious component of a course[56] which many still see as an integral part of religious education classes?

> It may be preferable for a teacher of history of religions to be atheist, or at least agnostic, rather than a believer. He or she will be more objective. However, a teacher appointed by the church in order to transmit its teachings and its mysteries of faith should logically be a believer and become an example or a model for his pupils with his own life. If this is not required, I understand nothing ...[57]

Must the religious or secular tradition of a given State be abandoned for the sake of inclusiveness? What, in other words, are the relationships that the public and private spheres should enjoy in this context?

Public and Private Spheres

Teachers v. students
The traditional French approach tends to assign religious practices to the private sphere[58] and, in an educational context, to private schools. But most of those private (and possibly religious) institutions are in fact closely monitored and supported by the State, in compliance with the framework set out in the *Loi Debré* 1959. French private Catholic schools are highly integrated into public education: 'the choice is

---

54   EctHR 29 June 2007 *Folgerø and others v. Norway*, Application no. 15472/02, condemning Norway for introducing a mandatory course on Christian Knowledge and Religious and Ethical Education whose content was judged to be insufficiently critical, objective and pluralistic (Zucca Chapter 1).

55   Which is the justification for the broadly Christian character of religious worship and religious education in England and Wales.

56   A denominational religious education course will however be taught in England and Wales in voluntary aided schools, known as faith schools, in accordance with the tenets of the religion or religious denomination specified in relation to the school (*School Standards and Framework Act 1998*, Schedule 19 para. 4) but parents can ask for their children to opt out and receive instead the non-denominational course provided in other schools (Sandberg and Buchanan Chapter 5).

57   Bejarano 2001, quoted by García Oliva: Chapter 9.

58   Laborde 2005: 318, more generally, Trigg 2007.

one of massive presence rather than a reduced denominational presence' (Chélini-Pont Chapter 7). As a result, both students and teachers attending or working in Catholic schools will also be part of the public system and as such will be allowed to refuse to take part in events displaying the school's religious ethos. In practice, therefore, the distinctive religious character of Catholic schools will constantly be challenged[59] despite the classification of those schools as being on the private side of the divide. The result is that the divide between the public and private *spheres* does not coincide perfectly with the divide between public and private *schools*.

Private schools can be heavily involved in the public sphere and be restricted by public duties, as the French example shows. Conversely, in States attached to the concept of neutral cooperation rather than of *laïcité* such as Germany, the public duty to remain religiously neutral will only concern teachers who owe the State a duty of loyalty[60] and its extension to *pupils* will be more problematic (Lock Chapter 17). Nor will the duty of loyalty owed by teachers equate to the duty of neutrality of the State itself towards religion. If the two duties were assimilated, teachers would lose their own fundamental rights to religious freedom: a dimension whose importance was underlined by the German Constitutional Court in the *Ludin* case[61] (Lock Chapter 17). At the other end of the spectrum, teachers in Northern Ireland will be trained either in Catholic or in Protestant teacher training colleges and will then teach either in Catholic or Protestant schools (McCrudden Chapter 6); the concept of a public sphere that transcends religious allegiances is simply non-existent in the non-secular and bipolarized Northern Irish system. In England and Wales more complex categories will apply, with the public/private law divide being completely blurred by finer distinctions between different types of schools: foundation schools, academies, voluntary aided schools, controlled schools and, more recently, free schools. Many of these will have a religious character despite being largely funded by the State (Vickers Chapter 4).

A relative and problematic divide

Overall, the division between the public and the private spheres never appears to be absolute[62] even in secular States such as France where a strict separation between the State and religion is proclaimed. The very principle of a divide between public (non-religious) and private (possibly religious) spheres may, generally speaking, appear too crude[63] and does not sit well with many systems of religious belief. The law may forbid the wearing of the Islamic veil in public spaces, precisely where an observant Muslim woman will feel that wearing it is

---

59 Cf. Chélini-Pont: Chapter 7, pointing to the SUNDEP (teachers' unions) fighting against the involvement of teachers in any assemblies and events relating to the distinctive religious character of Catholic schools.

60 Article 33(5) of the Basic Law.

61 Bundesverwaltungsgericht, 2 C 21.01 (4 July 2002).

62 Oliver 1999.

63 Habermas 1991.

a religious requirement, and allow it in the private sphere, where the religious need to protect women's modesty[64] does not arise. From the point of view of religious institutions, the crucial challenge will be to reconcile State requirements flowing from the participation of religious institutions in public services with the preservation of their own religious ethos. Cooperation with or absorption into the state system does not entail giving up the religious ethos which characterizes a particular school: private schools under state contracts in France, for example, will have their 'specific character' recognized under the *Loi Debré*, while any foundation or voluntary school in England and Wales may be designated by the Secretary of State as having a religious character where he is satisfied that the school was established by a religious body or for religious purposes[65] (Sandberg and Buchanan Chapter 5). But this participation in the public sector may carry with it special duties such as, in England and Wales,[66] the duty to promote community cohesion[67] and, more recently,[68] the duty to promote equality (Vickers Chapter 4).

In most jurisdictions,[69] state involvement will preclude religious schools from implementing their religious ethos in a discriminatory way: tolerance towards other believers and non-believers will have to be secured even where this might undermine the core beliefs of the religion to which the school adheres. So is individual religious freedom being enforced at the cost of groups' and schools' religious ethos or is the dilution of religiosity in religious schools a consequence of the secularization of society as a whole (Cohen Chapter 2) rather than an effect of a human rights or discrimination law discourse? The exact equilibrium to be reached between the regard to be granted to a school's ethos and the respect to be given to individual freedom of religion may vary within the state school system itself, depending on the type of school concerned. In England and Wales, voluntary controlled and foundation schools and voluntary aided schools with a religious character are allowed to discriminate in the appointment and management of their staff and the latter schools to a greater extent than the former. Yet the distinction between voluntary controlled and voluntary aided schools relates to questions of funding and governance and may not be necessarily be significant in terms of the religious ethos of the school (Vickers Chapter 4, Sandberg Chapter 16). So should the distinction really carry any weight when deciding the extent to which schools may be allowed to discriminate against their staff on grounds of religion?

More generally, the tension between a group religious ethos and individual religious freedoms feeds into wider debates on integration. How can we reconcile

---

64   Surah XXIV, verse 31.

65   *School Standards and Framework Act 1998*, s.69(3).

66   More generally, see *Associated Society of Locomotive Engineers and Firemen (ASLEF) v. United Kingdom* (2007) 45 EHRR 793.

67   *Education and Inspections Act 2006*, s.38.

68   Under section 149 of *the Equality Act 2010* (in force since April 2011).

69   There is no legal prohibition of religious discrimination in schools admissions in Northern Ireland and state schools in Northern Ireland are almost exclusively Protestant.

integration into the nation as a whole with integration within given (religious) communities?

Integration, Assimilation, Segregation and Equality

In Western European countries, 'Integration is foremost a value per se, insofar as it rests on the fundamentally democratic notion that, in spite of divergence of their beliefs and their experience and their allegiances, people who have respect for what is right and in particular for human rights can live in harmony.'[70] All Western European countries in search of harmonious social cohesion therefore have to ensure that the recognition of difference (in the name of the diversity of religious beliefs) does not erect an impossible hurdle in the way of more global thinking where believers (of all creeds) and non-believers alike can be seen as united. The concept of religious freedom offers the key to reconciling diversity within unity and unity within diversity. Even if each and every one of us is the bearer of an individual right to freedom of religion and even if the contours of that right essentially rely on the bearer's own evaluation of his or her beliefs[71] – thus leading to a myriad of potential interpretations of what areas religious freedoms may cover – unity is nevertheless provided by the overall human rights framework.

However helpful it may be, the concept of religious freedoms tells us little about how to accommodate the religious freedoms of groups versus the religious freedoms of individuals (and vice versa). How inclusive do religious schools therefore need to be in order to respect individual rights to freedom of religion? National responses vary.

Integration and autonomy of religious schools

The autonomy granted to religious groups is more limited in *laïc* States than it is in neutral States or States with an established or official religion. In France, religious schools under state contracts will not be allowed to invoke their specific religious character in order to derogate from the general syllabus nor may they impose discriminatory entry requirements on pupils or make religious teaching and practices at school mandatory (Cohen Chapter 2). Far from being 'islands of exclusivity',[72] the majority of (Catholic) private religious schools in France welcome pupils from varied religious backgrounds who often switch back and forth between the state and the private school systems. This integration of private schools into the state educational system, however, only applies to schools that have opted for a partnership with the State (under a 'state contract'). Even then,

---

70 Schnapper 1994.

71 The State should not ascertain whether particular religious beliefs or the means to express such beliefs are legitimate, ECtHR *Hasan and Chaush v. Bulgaria*, Application no. 30985/9634 (2002) EHRR 55.

72 Expression used by Esau 1993.

the proximity between the state and private sector may vary in practice given the lack of effective control by state authorities of the implementation of the terms of this state contract. For example, despite being under state contract, French Jewish schools close to the Orthodox or Ultra-Orthodox communities have refused admission to non-Jewish children, including children born to non-Jewish mothers who have not undergone a conversion regarded as valid under Orthodox religious law (Cohen Chapter 2). When the *JFS* (*Jewish Free School*) in England tried to do the same, the practice was held to be illegal.[73] The UK Supreme Court considered that the requirement that candidates be Jewish by reason of descent from a Jewish mother – because it excluded children of non-Jewish mothers who had not been validly converted[74] – amounted in effect to a discrimination on grounds of *race* and was therefore illegal. The *JFS* case illustrates that a practice which may not be clearly discriminatory on the ground of religion may well come under attack as constituting race discrimination. For different reasons, French courts would no doubt also hold such selective admission criteria to be illegal (as violating the duty of schools under state contract to open admission) were there to be a challenge in court. But in the absence of litigation, the practice prospers. The irony is thus that French private schools under state contract which are legally bound to a wide admission policy may in fact in some instances be more selective than English schools with a religious character which are lawfully allowed to restrict entry based on religion or belief provided that, principally, the school is oversubscribed.[75] However, in the vast majority of cases, the religious ethos of the 'faith school' will be far more present in English schools than in French private religious schools.[76]

More generally, faith schools in Britain have been at times accused of exacerbating social divides (on the issue see Jackson 2003). But these debates have to be put into a broader context:

> The crucial issue is the *quality* of education provided by the State. If you only have a right to do something mediocre, then you may just as well waive it in order to have a better education provided by the private sector. Regrettably, the poor quality of state provided education entrenches class differences based upon economic means (Zucca Chapter 1).

---

73   See note 22 *supra*.

74   This ethnic test could be overcome by non-Jewish mothers converting to Judaism in a manner recognized by the Orthodox branch but this possibility only confirmed the ethnic discrimination in the eyes of the majority of the Supreme Court. Such a conversion was indeed seen as a significant burden which was only applicable to those who were not born with the requisite ethnic origins.

75   *Schools Admission Code* for 2007, paras 2.41–3. See Sandberg and Buchanan: Chapter 5.

76   See Chélini-Pont Chapter 7.

From that perspective, British faith schools, the vast majority of which belong to the state sector, may on the contrary be seen as alleviating class differences by providing high-quality education regardless of economic means.

Integration, parents' autonomy and protection of children
Another frequent argument put forward in support of faith schools is parental autonomy. The creation of religious schools may to some extent be seen as a consecration of parental choices in education. For Catholics in Northern Ireland, the creation of separate Catholic schools represented a haven of self-determination (McCrudden Chapter 6). Within the context of multi-faith schools, rights to opt out of classes with a religious content are further manifestations of a certain deference to parental views in education. In most jurisdictions, freedom of choice is – at least formally[77] – granted to parents. The same is, however, not usually true in respect of the main protagonists: young pupils.[78] Invariably, their freedom of religion seems to be merged into the educational choices made for them by their parents. But what if a particular child wished to manifest his religious belief in a way that his parents disapproved of or vice versa, if parents wanted to impose their religious convictions against their children's wishes? If children's human rights are to be taken seriously and children's right to religious freedoms given any substance, parental educational rights should not, logically, be allowed systematically to trump their children's views and legal frameworks should give scope for the expression of such views. In England and Wales, pupils – whatever their age – cannot as of right withdraw themselves from religious education classes (Cumper Chapter 10); curiously, the right of withdrawal granted to sixth-formers is limited to the obligation to attend acts of daily worship.[79] In the *Williamson* case,[80] the parents' religious belief that corporal punishment was to be used on their children whilst at school was not seen as fundamental enough to justify trumping the statutory ban[81] against corporal punishment imposed on all school teachers. Although one may suspect that the children concerned might not have been very fond of the form of punishment claimed by their parents, the issue was not examined as one of conflict between parental choices and children's views.[82] Only Baroness Hale of Richmond described the case as being as much about the rights of the

---

77   For the limits and constraints surrounding this choice, see page 21 *supra*.

78   The UN Convention on the Rights of the Child proclaims that children have a right to education (Art 28), freedom of expression (Art 13), thought, conscience and religion (Art 14). The Convention has been largely ratified but has not usually been incorporated into national laws nor has been made fully binding on national courts. The Children's Rights Bill was moved to the House of Lords in an attempt to make the Convention part of English Law but was abandoned.

79   *Schools Standards and Framework Act 1998*, s.71A.

80   *R v. Secretary of State for Education and Employment and Ors ex parte Williamson and Ors* [2005] UKHL 15.

81   *Education Act 1996*, s.548.

82   On this, see Dwyer 1998, Narisetti 2009, Lees and Howarth 2009.

child as the rights of parents: 'this is, and always has been, a case about children, their rights and the rights of their parents and teachers. Yet there has been no one here ... to speak on behalf of the children. The battle has been fought on ground selected by the adults'.[83] However, the interests of children in general to be protected against violence came into play under article 9(2) of the European Convention in order to assess whether the infringements made against the parents' freedom of religion were justified. Nevertheless, the recognition of children's rights as being part of the equation was no reason for dismissing their parents' rights to religious freedoms. So long as parents genuinely and strongly believe that corporal punishment is a tenet of their faith, judges will be reluctant to question the religious nature of their belief and deny them protection under article 9 paragraph 1 of the European Convention on Human Rights (Cranmer Chapter 14). However, as reflected in this case, the broader scope of what may constitute a religious belief for the purposes of article 9 paragraph 1 does not necessarily mean that religious beliefs will be afforded greater protection in practice. Indeed, recognition of a particular belief as warranting protection leaves open the question as to whether or not its particular manifestation can legitimately be restricted under article 9 paragraph 2. The outcome will therefore normally depend on the particular facts of each case, unless additional filters are introduced under paragraph 1. Under the 'specific situation rule', even if the practices in question are found to constitute a manifestation of religious belief, claims will fail under article 9 paragraph 1 where claimants have voluntarily accepted the restrictions on their exercise and other means are available for them to practise their beliefs without undue any hardship or inconvenience. Mark Hill (Chapter 15) analyses and criticizes the rather crude application of this rule by English judges:[84] 'it is somewhat regrettable that the courts have sought artificially to limit the universal application of such rights (to religious freedoms) rather than systematically developing an exposition of the qualifications to those rights.'

The Structure of and Contributions to the Book

This overall methodological tension between conceptual debates and *in concreto* analysis is reflected in the structure adopted for this book – which leads us from a study of key concepts (Part I) to an analysis of case studies (Parts III and IV) via an examination of national models (Part II).

In the first part of this collection, the tensions and interactions between the key concepts of integration, *laïcité*, identity and discrimination are approached from a theoretical (Zucca), sociological (Cohen for France and Jewish schools and Jamal and Panjwani for England and Muslim Schools) and legal (Vickers) perspective.

---

83   *Williamson* 2 FLR 374, 395.

84   For example see *R (on the application of Begum) v. Headteacher and Governors of Denbigh High* School [2006] UKHL 15, [2006] 2 WLR 719.

Lorenzo Zucca studies the concepts of integration and accommodation in a school context and finally rejects both in order to propose his own model of the 'classroom as a tolerance lab'. Under that model, inclusiveness and solidarity would reign, both in respect of the content of the syllabus – with the introduction of a compulsory course in civic and religious education in the broadest possible sense – and in respect of the school system itself – with an emphasis being placed on funding good quality, inclusive state schools rather than faith or private schools.

Martine Cohen analyses the shift towards an increased religiosity in Jewish private schools in France as an attempt to stress Jewish identity in an increasingly secular society. However, she suggests that there need not be a binary opposition between a strong national secular identity and a strong (Jewish) religious minority. Pluralist religious schools, she concludes, could also emerge and may also be welcome, provided they are not limited to the better off and better educated families.

Arif Jamal and Farid Panjwani focus on Muslim religious identities in a school context. They show that for different reasons, in both Muslim and Western countries the teaching of Muslim tenets has become an object of study alongside other subjects of the syllabus such as science and history: 'the enchanted history and beliefs of religion became scrutinized and interpreted by the standards of disenchanted historical and empirical methods'. This objectification of religion in the classroom matches a similar tendency in the courtroom where judges – though often reluctantly – sometimes seek to define a religious tradition against so called objective criteria. Jamal and Panjwani argue that such an approach is flawed for two reasons. First, it violates the subjectivity of the experience of the believer, contrary to the subjective basis that should legally underpin the individual right to religious freedom. Secondly, it fails to reflect the diversity of meanings and traditions that exist amongst Muslims.

Lucy Vickers' analysis of the relevant legal framework relating to religious discrimination in English schools reveals the conceptual and practical difficulties that the implementation of potentially contradictory texts and directions are likely to raise. Vickers' focus is on teachers in faith schools. Vickers argues that the discrimination that is presently allowed in voluntary aided schools to affect all staff beyond those involved in the teaching of religious education and regardless of the actual degree of religious ethos observed by the particular school may not be compatible with the *Employment Equality Directive 2000/78* under which exceptions must be proven to be legitimate and proportionate. She also wonders whether the recent extension, under the *Equality Act 2010*, of the public sector equality duty to religion and belief will improve matters. Given the uncertainties of what religious beliefs may be covered under the new duty and the ambiguities of what equality would entail in practice, the best way forward, she argues, would be for schools to view their new duty to promote equality as part of the well-established duty to promote social cohesion.

These key concepts of integration, *laïcité*, identity and discrimination cannot be read and understood fully outside of the social, historical, political and constitutional contexts of national systems which are the focus of the second part of this book.

National models reveal a broad range of options between the complex and overall broadly Christian model in England and Wales (Sandberg and Buchanan), the highly segregationist and bipolar – Catholic and Protestant – structure in Northern Ireland (McCrudden), the separationist and *laïc* French system (Chélini-Pont) and the neutral secularity of Germany (de Wall) and Spain (García Oliva). All reveal that the interplay of religion and education is deeply embedded in historical and political national contexts.

Russell Sandberg and Anna Buchanan present and analyse (theoretically and empirically) the English and Welsh model. They reveal discrepancies between schools labelled as being without a religious character but yet subject to the obligation to organize a daily act of worship and schools officially recognized as having a religious character and yet lacking sufficient autonomy to uphold their religious ethos. Beyond these contradictions, fundamental questions are raised as to the role, reality and meanings of daily worship in school practice, as to the place of minority religions vis-à-vis Christianity, and as to the place of Welsh law on religion vis-à-vis United Kingdom statutes. The increasing powers of the Welsh Assembly could, they suggest, be an opportunity to develop a law on religion in schools more in tune with twenty-first century society.

Christopher McCrudden's analysis of religion and education patterns in Northern Ireland reveals the bicommunalism that underpins the Northern Irish model, described as a 'highly segregated, denominational and non-secular education system' – itself the product of a consciational approach to democracy involving the sharing of power between segments of society joined together by a common citizenship but divided by ethnicity, language, religion or other factors. Despite an unmet need for places in mixed-religion schools, the scope for change is, he suggests, still limited: the impact of legislation on discrimination remains restricted in scope and the political context highly relevant.

Blandine Chélini-Pont's analysis of the French system reveals that the dichotomy between a *laïc* state school system devoid of all religious manifestations and a private and religious school system is not a fair characterization of the French model. Indeed, the dichotomy undermines the high degree of involvement of Catholic private schools in French public education. She suggests that this high numerical presence of Catholic schools in a secularized public education system has led to a secularization of the Catholic school system itself, both as regards its teachers and its pupils. The challenge that French Catholic schools now face, she concludes, is to maintain their openness and non-denominational nature without losing all of their distinctive religious character.

Heinrich de Wall analyses the meaning and consequences for the school context of the German notion of state religious neutrality. Unlike the French concept of *laïcité*, religious neutrality does not require the absence of religion in the public sphere but merely demands that the State abstain from showing a preference or dislike for a particular religion or for religion in general. De Wall examines the consequences of the concept in respect of religious instruction classes in German state schools. Provision of religious instruction in state schools complies with the concept of neutrality so long as it does not confer any advantageous or disadvantageous status on any particular religious group. Mindful of the need to respect state neutrality whilst at the same time respecting the rights of religious groups to self-determination, the German system has opted for a denominational form of religious instruction in which religious communities are highly involved. De Wall argues that this system is not only respectful of religious groups (which are thereby associated as crucial actors in the public sphere) but – thanks to a right to opt out granted to parents and, from the age of 14, to pupils themselves – is also respectful of parents' and pupils' rights to religious freedom. However, he concludes that the real challenge for the German model will come from the current demands of Muslim pupils and parents for Islamic religious instruction classes in state schools. It is only if those demands are accommodated and current institutional hurdles overcome (notably the lack of an umbrella Muslim organization able to speak out for German Muslims and decide on the issues surrounding religious instruction classes) that the German denominational model of religious instruction will have a future in a religiously pluralist German society.

Javier García Oliva's analysis of the Spanish model reveals that the cooperationist approach of Spain towards Church/State relationships hides a high involvement by church authorities in religion at school: religious education is denominational and teachers of religious instruction classes are proposed by the relevant church authorities. These features, García Oliva concedes, may be at times difficult to reconcile with the demands of equality: to what extent, for example, should Catholic Church authorities be allowed to dismiss or penalize teachers of Catholic religion whose conduct has been deemed not to be compatible with the tenets of the Catholic faith? Conversely, to what extent should the requirements of equality interfere with the right of churches to have their own identity and autonomy respected? So far as pupils are concerned, how can one ensure equality between pupils who study religious instruction and those who opt out and yet also ensure that religious instruction is treated like any of the other subjects in the school syllabus (as required under the agreement between Spain and the Holy See)? However delicate this conciliation may be, García Oliva concludes, the denominational nature of the course on religious instruction need not disappear and the involvement of church authorities be abolished. Denominational teaching of religion can be inclusive and involvement of church authorities, within limits, welcome and justified. On the whole, however, because of the controversial nature of denominational religious teaching and the problems related to finding a suitable alternative subject, the author expresses a preference for a compulsory subject of non-denominational religious education.

Unsurprisingly, the oppositions revealed in Part I and Part II in the understandings of key concepts and national traditions amongst countries of Western Europe are reflected in the judicial or legislative solutions given in different jurisdictions to particular issues regarding religion at school. However, common features are also to be noted, not least because of the convergent effect of the decisions of the European Court of Human Rights. Two particular areas of vivid dispute are considered: teaching content (Part III) and religious symbols (Part IV).

Religion at school in most jurisdictions is a subject as such. Unsurprisingly, many of the debates in our multi-faith European societies focus on the way in which the subject, whether described as 'religious education' or 'religious instruction', should be taught (Cumper, for an analysis of European case law and Mawhinneyet al. for an empirical study). But religion can also influence the syllabus of public schools in separatist systems (Van den Kerchove for France and Barendt for the US) or have repercussions beyond teaching content on other issues such as discipline (Cranmer).

Peter Cumper's chapter offers a study of the challenges presented by the provision of religious education in multi-faith and secular European societies. If, as he argues, the provision of religious education itself has a lot to offer, notably as a way of 'helping to build bridges between people of different faiths in religiously diverse societies', the question of how it should be provided remains controversial. In a European context where, Cumper argues, States are reminded by the European Court of Human Rights to be mindful of pupils from minority faiths, the very feasibility of the opt-out model may be questioned as inevitably subjecting those pupils to the risk of stigmatization. He concludes that the crucial question in the coming years may be more about the content (and as a consequence about proper funding) of religious educational classes. In crude terms, the options for the future lie between a mainly confessional and Christian syllabus or a more comparative curriculum inspired by a broad range of religions and beliefs.

Alison Mawhinney, Ulrike Niens, Norman Richardson and Yuko Chiba analyse the implications of the right to opt out from religious education classes for minority-belief pupils in Northern Ireland. They reveal that opt-out provisions are not the best way to address religious diversity in schools. Even when properly implemented – which would require better information for families and good quality alternatives for opted-out pupils – opt-out provisions do not fully meet minority-belief families' expectations. Opted-out pupils, especially those of a younger age, may feel a sense of marginalization and exclusion. Moreover, and more fundamentally, opt-out mechanisms fail positively to recognize and value the beliefs of minority families. Rather than to allow pupils to 'exclude themselves' from religious classes of 'essentially Christian' content, a better option, Mawhinney et al. argue, would be to redesign the Northern Irish religious education syllabus in a more inclusive way.

Anna Van den Kerchove's analysis reveals that religion is no longer a taboo topic in French *laïc* schools. Now recognized as an integral part of society, religious issues appear in most recent history textbooks used in French secondary schools. Teachers, though still forbidden to display their own beliefs, may thus engage in discussion on religious matters. But this trend in favour of a revival of religion mainly benefits Christianity. More is now being said about religion (or rather about religious issues) in French state schools, she concludes; but more should also be said and could be better said about non-Christian beliefs.

Eric Barendt's chapter on teaching evolution, creationism and intelligent design in US schools raises questions which are of particular relevance for European debates. The key justification that emerges from US constitutional case law in respect of the presence of religion in state schools is the educational purpose it can fulfil. Religious views which are presented in order to 'inform students and promote their understanding of minorities' would thus comply with such a purpose and be held to be constitutional whereas measures which seek to promote religious views of the world would not. The analysis of the US experience, he concludes, has a lot to tell us about the interplay of religion, education and the law.

Frank Cranmer's analysis of the *Williamson* case, its prelude and its aftermath, provides clues as to how English courts approach religious questions at school. In *Williamson*, the claimants argued that corporal punishment was an essential element of their Evangelical Christian faith and that they should as a consequence be allowed to delegate to teachers the right physically to discipline their children. The importance of the decision, Cranmer tells us, goes far beyond this simple question. The value of the decision lies in the tension it reveals between the extreme reluctance of courts to judge the validity of a particular belief on the one hand and, on the other, the need to assess whether or not a particular manifestation of that belief is sufficiently fundamental as to merit protection. *Williamson*, he concludes, is thus a perfect illustration of and justification for the case-by-case approach of common law judges.

Beyond how religion is to be taught at school, the most high-profile cases have dealt with how (if at all) religion is to be seen at school, hence a final part on religious symbols.

The *Human Rights Act 1998* and the new law prohibiting discrimination on grounds of religion or belief have been described as the two pillars of twenty-first century religion law in Britain.[85] The first two chapters confirm the statement in relation to religious symbols worn in English and Welsh schools by pupils (Hill, in respect of the influence of the human rights era) and by staff (Sandberg, with a focus on anti-discrimination law). The third and final chapter addresses legal issues raised by religious symbols in German state schools (Lock). Interestingly, a human rights discourse in Germany on these matters has developed through a national rather than a European impetus.

Mark Hill's analysis reveals how English courts have adapted to the methodological shift triggered by article 9 of the European Convention on Human Rights which turned religious freedom into a positive individual right. English courts, he observes, tend to adopt a broad approach to what may amount to religious beliefs under article 9 paragraph 1 of the Convention and yet often conclude that those beliefs have not been interfered with. As illustrated in the case of *Begum* (and others that followed), the House of Lords held that the school's

---

85 Sandberg 2011: 115.

refusal to allow Miss Begum to wear the *jilbab* did not interfere with her right to religious freedom under article 9(1). Their reasoning was based on the notion of the 'specific situation', where a person voluntary submits to a particular system of rules. That reasoning, Hill suggests, is flawed. A school pupil does not voluntarily accept a school uniform policy and there is no contractual relationship between school and pupil. A far more satisfactory approach, he concludes, would be to abandon the 'specific situation' rule and develop reliable criteria for legitimate qualifications to religious freedoms under article 9(2).

Russell Sandberg's chapter on religious symbols worn by staff in British schools studies the respective usefulness of article 9 of the ECHR and anti-discrimination law. Given the broad (and he suggests unfortunate) construction by English courts of the 'specific situation' rule, claims under article 9 are unlikely to succeed. Teachers and other staff, he observes, will typically have agreed to restrictions of their religious freedom under their contract of employment and will be barred from subsequently claiming that this restriction interferes with their article 9 right. Consequently, Sandberg concludes that school employees would be better advised to rely upon discrimination law, under which more scope is given by English judges to the consideration of the merits of individual cases. However, employees who wish to wear symbols which manifest a belief only held by a few individuals may find that their claims fall outside the scope of anti-discrimination protection. Sandberg is highly critical of this exclusion of those minority beliefs. A far better approach, he suggests, would be to abandon distinctions according to beliefs and decide all of those claims on the grounds of justification. That would allow courts to reach more nuanced decisions, reflecting the context in which the claimant operated.

Tobias Lock's contribution focuses on a few high profile and very instructive German constitutional cases relating to religious symbols in German state schools. Lock's analysis reveals the criteria for distinguishing between the treatment of static religious symbols such as a cross affixed to the wall of a classroom and manifestations of religion at school through prayers or religious education. Whereas the former are of a compelling nature because pupils cannot escape from them and are thus forced to 'study under the cross', the latter can accommodate diverging views through opt-out rights. There are also convincing reasons, Lock argues, for distinguishing between static religious symbols such as crosses in the classroom and portable religious symbols such as Muslim veils worn by teachers or pupils. Whereas the former is a direct result of the action of the State, bound by a duty of neutrality, the latter involves another crucial dimension: the religious freedom of the teacher or pupil concerned. Finally, religious symbols worn by teachers may be seen in a different light from religious symbols worn by pupils: because of the duty of loyalty owed by teachers to the State, a ban on religious symbols worn by teachers will be held constitutional, always provided it has a clear and precise legislative basis. The duty of neutrality of the State in matters of religion is not, Lock concludes, akin to the concept of *laïcité* and yet, in respect of teachers at least, the situation in many German *Länder* may be very similar. However, Lock suggests that in Germany similar bans would be more problematic in respect of pupils. Moreover, anti-discrimination law may in time provide successful grounds for challenge by teachers banned from wearing religious symbols.

Conclusion

The chapters in this collection were assembled with a view to assisting the reader in reflecting critically on the extent and meanings that are given to religious freedoms at school across Europe. All the contributions reveal that the concept of religious freedom is of growing importance in European schools. One may legitimately fear that 'heavy or exclusive focus on the facilitation of religious freedom (may) tend to underplay the complexity of broader issues raised by the relationship between religion and the law. In particular, such an approach can fail to acknowledge sufficiently that more religious freedom for some can come at the cost of less freedom for others.'[86] However, the present chapters suggest that the growing importance of the concept of religious freedoms in Europe is tied to a growing balancing process between conflicting rights and viewpoints. The concept of religious freedom is thus a counterforce to potentially monolithic assimilationist state models of integration, a factor towards increased diversity within individual and collective religious identities and an impetus for a methodological shift in judicial reasoning. The accommodation of collective religious freedom – and in particular the right of 'faith schools' in England and Wales – to promote their religious ethos must be balanced in each case against the freedom of religion (or freedom from religion) of staff. Moreover, the State's duty to religious neutrality or schools' commitment to community cohesion should only justify infringements to individual religious freedom of pupils and staff that are legitimate and proportionate. Finally, the religious freedoms of parents (and their ensuing right to educate their children according to their own religious beliefs) can come into conflict with the religious freedoms of children themselves, as illustrated by the *Williamson* case.[87] Of course, this balancing process between state duties and individual freedoms, between conflicting collective and individual freedoms or between clashing individual religious beliefs always take place in a given national model of State/Church relationship. Indeed, the concept of religious freedoms has not so far undermined the historical and subtle compromises that the respective European States have achieved with the Church or the Churches in the sphere of education: from the *laïc* French model to the religious and segregated approach in Northern Ireland, via the denominational but neutral option adopted in Germany and Spain and the complex system in England and Wales which combines a non-denominational but broadly Christian model of non-religious state schools with

---

86   McCrea 2010: 1.
87   Note 23 *supra*.

state 'faith schools', no model is per se seen as contrary to the demands of religious freedoms, as the recent Grand Chamber decision in the *Lautsi* case[88] shows.

Viewed together, these contributions highlight how the relationships between individual religious freedoms and collective and state identities or between religious freedom and other human rights are the object of an ongoing social experiment and underline the difficulties and risks involved in seeking to identify *the* best solution or best model for Europe.

References

Adhar, R.J. 2000. Parental religious upbringing in a children's right era, in *Christian Perspectives on Law and Relationism*, edited by P. Beaumont and K. Wotherspoon. Carlisle: Paternoster Press.

Adhar, R.J. 2000. Children's religious freedom, devout parents and the state, in *Law and religion in Contemporary Society. Communities, Individualism and the State*, edited by P.W. Edge and G. Harvey. Aldershot: Ashgate,93–105.

Bagni, B.N. 1979. Discrimination in the name of the Lord: a critical evaluation of discrimination by religious organizations. *Columbia Law Review* 79, 1514.

Baubérot, J. 2003. Secularism and French religious liberty: a sociological and historical view. *Brigham Young University Law Review* 2, 451–64.

Baubérot, J. and Milot, M. 2011. *Laïcités sans Frontières*, Paris: Editions du Seuil.

Beck, U. and Giddens, A. 2006. L'Europe telle qu'elle est: un point de vue cosmopolitique. *Raisons Politiques* 5, 7–15.

Bouchard, G. and Taylor, C., 2008. *Fonder l'Avenir. Le Temps de la Conciliation*. [Online]. Available at http://www.scribd.com/doc/3053017/rapport-de-la-commission-BouchardTaylor-version-integrale [Accessed: 30 March 2011].

Bradley, D. 2004. A family law for Europe? Sovereignty, political economy and legitimation. *Global Jurist Frontiers* 4(1), Article 3.

Bradney, A. 2000. Religion and law in Great Britain at the end of the second Christian millennium, in *Law and Religion in Contemporary Society. Communities, Individualism and the State*, edited by P.W. Edge and G. Harvey. Winchester: Ashgate Publishing, 17–30.

Caye, P. and Terré, D. 2005. Le neutre à l'épreuve de la puissance. Les conditions métaphysiques de la laïcité, in *La Laïcité, Archives de Philosophie du droit*, Dalloz 48, 27–41.

Chauvin, N. 2003. Le Port du voile islamique par une enseignante. *Revue française de droit administratif*, 536–45.

Collins, H. 2003. Discrimination, equality and social inclusion. *Modern Law Review* 66, 16–43.

Conkle, D.O. 1988. Toward a general theory of the establishment clause. *Northwestern University Law Review* 82, 1113.

---

88   Note 35 *supra*.

Corbett, A. 1996. Secular, free and compulsory republican values in French education, in *Education in France*, edited by A. Corbett and B. Moon. London: Routledge, 5–21.

Cranmer, F. 2010. Who is Jew? Jewish faith schools and the Race Relations Act 1976. *Law & Justice* 164, 75–83.

Cross F.L. and Livingstone, E.A. 1997. Scotland, Christianity in *The Oxford Dictionary of the Christian Church*, edited by F.L. Cross and E.A. Livingstone. Oxford: Oxford University Press, 1471–3.

Davie, G. 2002. *Europe: The Exceptional Case*, London: Darton, Longman and Todd Ltd.

Debray, R. 2002. *L'Enseignement du fait religieux dans l'école laïque*. Paris: Odile Jacob.

Dwyer, C. forthcoming. Faith in the system: state-funded faith schools and contested geographies of identity integration and citizenship. Paper presented at the annual conference of the Association of American Geographers, Washington DC, April 2010.

Dwyer, J.G. 1998. *Religious Schools v. Children's Rights*. Ithaca NY: Cornell University Press.

Edge, P.W. 2000. Religious rights and choice under the ECHR. *Web Journal of Current Legal Issues*, 3.

Edge, P.W. 2001. *Legal Responses to Religious Differences*. The Hague/London/New York: Kluwer.

Esau, A. 1993. Islands of exclusivity. Religious organizations and employment discrimination. *University British Columbia Law Review* 33, 719.

Evans, C. 2004. Religious freedom in European human rights law, in *Religion and International Law*, edited by M. Janis and C. Evans. The Hague: Martinus Nijhoff, 339.

Evans, M.D. 2000. Chapter 9 in *Law and Religion in Contemporary Society. Communities, Individualism and the State*, edited by P.W. Edge and G. Harvey. Winchester: Ashgate Publishing, 177–97.

Freedman, J. 2004. Secularism as a barrier to integration? The French dilemma. *International Migration* 42(3), 5–27.

Freeman, M.D.A. 1983. *The Rights and Wrongs of Children*. London: Frances Pinter.

Freeman, M.D.A. 1997. *The Moral Status of Children: Essays on the rights of the Child*. The Hague, London, Boston: Martinus Nijhoff.

Freeman, M.D.A. 2010. The human rights of children. *Current Legal Problems*, Oxford University Press, 1–44.

García Oliva, J. 2010. Church, State and establishment in the United Kingdom in the 21st century: anachronism or idiosyncrasy. *Public Law* 3, 482–504.

Ghanea, N. et al. (eds) 2007. *Does God Believe in Human Rights? Essays on Religion and Human Rights*. Leiden: MartinusNijhoff Publishers.

Habermas, J. 1991. *The Structural Transformation of the Public Sphere: An Inquiry into a Category of Bourgeois Society*. Cambridge, MA: MIT Press.

Haüßler, U. 2001. Muslim dress codes in German state schools. *European Journal of Migration Law* 3, 457–74.

Hill, M. and Sandberg, R. 2007. Is nothing sacred? Clashing symbols in a secular world. *Public Law*, 488–506.

Horwath, J. and Lees, J. 2009. Religious parents just want the best for their kids: young people's perspectives on the influence of religious beliefs on parenting. *Children & Society* 23(3), 162–75.

Hunter-Henin, M.,O'Cinneide, C. and Fedtke, J. 2005. Privacy, in *Encyclopedia of Comparative Law*, edited by J.M. Smits. London: Edward Elgar Publishing, 554–65.

Jackson, R. 2003. Should the State fund faith based schools? A review of the arguments.*British Journal of Religious Education* 25 (2), 89–102.

Jackson, R. 2006. Promoting religious tolerance and non-discrimination in schools: A European perspective. *Journal of Religious Education* 54 (3), 30–8.

Jackson, R., Miedema, S., Weisse, W. and Willaime, J.-P. (eds) 2007. *Religion and Education in Europe: Developments, Contexts and Debates*. (Münster: Waxmann).

Kilkelly, U. 1999. *The Child and the European Convention on Human Rights*. Aldershot: Ashgate Publishers.

Kintzler, C. 2005. Laïcité et philosophie, in *La Laïcité, Archives de Philosophie du droit*, Dalloz 48, 43–56.

Kymlicka, W. 1995. *Multicultural Citizenship*. Oxford: Oxford University Press.

Laborde, C. 2005. Secular philosophy and Muslim headscarves in schools. *Political Philosophy* 13(3), 305–29.

Langlaude, S. 2006. Indoctrination, secularism, religious liberty and the ECHR *International and Comparative Law Quarterly* 55(4), 929–44.

Langlaude, S. 2007. *The Right of the Child to Religious Freedom in International Law*. Leiden/Boston: Martinus Nijhoff Publishers.

Macklem, T. 2000. Faith as a secular value. *McGill Law Journal* 45, 1–63.

McCrea, R. 2010. *Religion and the Public Order of the European Union*. Oxford: Oxford University Press.

McCrudden, C. 2011. Multiculturalism, freedom of religion, equality, and the British constitution: the *JFS* case considered. *International Journal of Constitutional Law*, 1–37.

McGoldrick, D. 2006. *Human Rights and Religion. The Islamic Headscarf Debate in Europe*. Oxford and Portland, Oregon: Hart Publishing.

Modood, T. 2007. *Multiculturalism: A Civic Idea*. London: Polity Press.

Modood, T. 2010. Moderate secularism, religion as identity and respect for religion. *The Political Quarterly* 2010, 4–14.

Modood, T, Triandaffyllidou, A., Zapata Barrero, R. (eds) 2005. *Multiculturalism, Muslims and Citizenship: A European Approach*. London: Taylor and Francis.

Narisetti, I. 2009. *Forced into Faith: How Religion Abuses Children's Rights*. New York: Amherst.

Nickel, J. 2005. Who needs freedom of religion? *University Colorado Law Review* 76(4), 941.

Oliver, D. 1999. *Common Values in Public and Private Law*. London: Butterworths.

Oliver, P., Scott, D. and Tadros, V. (eds) 2000. *Faith in Law, Essays in Legal Theories*. Oxford Portland Oregon: Hart Publishing.

Rivers, J. 2001. Religious liberty as a collective right, in *Law and Religion, Current Legal Issues*, edited by R. O'Dair and A. Lewis. Oxford: Oxford University Press.

Ronan, J. 1991. La Laïcité comme religion civile. *Esprit* 175, 108–15.

Ruston, R. 2004. *Human Rights and the Image of God*. London: SCM Press.

Sage A, 2005. Headscarf ban judged a success as hostility fades. *The Times*, 5 September.

Sandberg, R. 2011. *Law and Religion*. Cambridge: Cambridge University Press.

Schnapper, D. 1994. Muslim communities, ethnic minorities and citizens, in *Muslims in Europe*, edited by B. Lewis and D. Schnapper. London and New York: Pinter Publishers, 148–60.

Sefton-Green, R. 2010. Multiculturalism, Europhilia and harmonization: harmony or disharmony? *Utrecht Law Review*, 50–67.

Sweeney, J.A. 2005. Margins of appreciation: cultural relativity and the ECHR. *International Comparative Law Quarterly* 54, 459–74.

Thomas, S. 2004. The global resurgence of religion: international law and international society, in *Religion and International Law*, edited by M.W. Janis and C. Evans. Leiden: Martinus Nijhoff,321–38.

Trigg, R. 2007. *Religion in Public Life: Must Faith Be Privatized?* Oxford: Oxford University Press.

Van Dam, C. 2009. Who is afraid of diversity? Cultural diversity, European co-operation and European tort law. *King's Law Journal* 20, 281–308.

Vickers, L. 2008. *Religious Freedom, Religious Discrimination and the Workplace*. Oxford and Portland Oregon: Hart Publishing.

PART I
Key Concepts:
Laïcité, Integration, Identity
and Discrimination

Chapter 1

The Classroom as a Tolerance Lab

Lorenzo Zucca

I grew up in Italy and attended a state school where a crucifix was hung on the wall of the classroom. I am in the unique position of being a potential victim and a potential perpetrator of that situation. I am a potential victim since I am a secularist and I always opted out from the weekly class of religious education taught by a person appointed by the Roman Catholic Church. Yet, at the same time I am a potential perpetrator because I was raised as a Catholic and belong to the majority of people who do not find the crucifix (or, for that matter, any of the other Christian symbols in Italian public places) particularly intrusive simply because it was such a part of our daily life. The explanation lies in Italy's cultural and social homogeneity, which held true until the end of the 1980s. Under these conditions, integration was not a central preoccupation. Why would one promote integration in a place that is already very cohesive? Integration becomes necessary when there is a social, cultural or ethnic gap that makes it increasingly difficult to live together peacefully. If that is the case, then one may speak of a progressive disintegration of the social fabric. Any State that experiences disintegration has to respond with a politics that promotes integration.

Integration is, however, not always regarded as the best remedy to a lack of social and cultural cohesion. This is because States believe socio-cultural homogeneity to be desirable; many States are committed to an ordered political realm that leaves ample room for the development of socio-cultural pluralism. In this case, instead of integration one speaks of accommodation.

The realm of education, I shall argue, is the main laboratory wherein the State can test its policies concerning the harmonious organization of a society and the recognition of the place of religion within it. States committed to integration promote one school for everyone, in which pupils are turned into full citizens of a society. States committed to accommodation, instead, allow a certain leeway for religious communities to organize and deliver education through faith schools or other private schools funded by the State. Since I believe both approaches to have strengths and weaknesses, the model I present seeks to steer a middle course between the two. In particular, I shall suggest that, in order for the State to improve on social cohesion, it has to create the preconditions for mutual understanding and solidarity between members of different socio-cultural groups. In other words, the classroom should be a laboratory for engaging in the practice of tolerance.

My analysis will be theoretical and comparative. In section 1, I begin with a brief inquiry into the notion of integration and contrast it with the notion of accommodation. My position – which I term 'the classroom as a tolerance lab' – steers a middle way between integration and accommodation. In section 2, I focus on three major European States: Italy, France and the UK. Italy is an obvious choice because it is involved in the high profile *Lautsi* case[1] before the European Court of Human Rights ('ECtHR') which prompted this discussion.[2] France, at the beginning of the Third Republic, put religious education at the core of its political project through the laws of Jules Ferry entrenching a right to free education.[3] The UK is also an interesting case as it sponsors multiculturalism through state-funded faith schools. The three States are under pressure as they struggle to square religious claims with liberal and republican principles. In each of them, there have been very high profile cases: the saga of the *foulard islamique* has captivated France during the past 20 years and the Supreme Court of the UK opened its first judicial year with a case on discrimination in faith schools (McCrudden 2011). I end with a discussion of the *Lautsi* case as a possible illustration of how the State should promote education as a tolerance lab.

Integration

The most general notion of integration portrays society as a whole and individuals, or groups, as its parts. A harmonious whole includes every individual and every group. If someone is left out, then integration is necessary to bridge that gap. Understood in this broad sense, I can hardly think of anyone opposed to integration. In theory, the purpose of a common society is to integrate everyone regardless of class, sex or religion. In practice, however, there are tensions that make integration quite a difficult business – and not always desirable. In relation to the whole, there are centripetal and centrifugal forces. The most important centripetal force is equality: since no one enjoys being negatively discriminated against, minority religious groups as a consequence will demand recognition of the same privileges provided to religious groups of the majority. The strongest centrifugal force is freedom: everyone wants their thoughts and beliefs recognized and protected and religious groups in particular ask for the respect of their own beliefs. One can readily see that liberty and equality, as understood above, pull in opposite directions.

---

1   EtCHR *Lautsi v. Italy* 3 November 2009, Application no 30814/06.

2   The Grand Chamber has now handed down its own decision: ECtHR Grand Chamber *Lautsi v. Italy* 18 March 2011, Application no 30814/06.

3   Loi du 16 juin 1881 établissant la gratuité absolue de l'enseignement primaire dans les écoles publiques. Loi dite 'Jules Ferry' et 'Bert Paul', [Online] available at: http://mjp. univ-perp.fr/france/1881enseignement.htm. [Accessed: 2 April 2011]. Lois du 28 mars 1882 sur l'enseignement primaire obligatoire, [Online] available at: http://www.r-lecole. freesurf.fr/doc-hist/loiferry.html [Accessed: 2 April 2011].

Integration, in the most general sense, is an aim or goal of the State and it is close to what some call the goal of social cohesion. In all European States, people are encouraged to develop bonds that keep them together, bonds that go beyond the mere respect of the same law and form a common set of principles guiding life in common. 'Integration as an aim' should be distinguished from 'integration as a process'. The latter is what a State deploys as a means to attain the goal of integration. For example, France deploys a strategy of integration by setting conditions of belonging to the republican nation in order to promote the goal of integration – that is, in order to turn individuals into republican citizens. Integration as a process is not universally embraced; many States prefer to promote the goal of integration (or, more precisely, social cohesion) through the process of accommodation (Choudri 2008).

Integration as a process is centripetal: it attracts everyone to one socio-cultural centre as in France. Accommodation as a process is centrifugal: it allows for divergence in order to avoid disintegration.

Table 1.1   Integration and accommodation processes

	Ideal	Corruption	Evil
Integration	Centripetal	Assimilation (France)	Uniformity
Accommodation	Centrifugal	Atomized separation	Segregation

Both strategies of integration and accommodation have risks and problems. Integration, for example, can easily slip from a virtuous process towards assimilation at best and uniformity at worst. The problem with assimilation is that it is not responsive to the needs of the cultural minorities. Either they take it or they leave it. Uniformity is even worse because it not only requires parts to adapt to the whole but it also requires the whole to minimize its internal diversity as much as possible. An example of blind uniformity is that imposed by Soviet Russia in which cultural and religious differences were repressed by an overarching, egalitarian ethos.

Accommodation presents parallel risks and problems. Accommodation without a plan can easily result in aimless diversification, which may amount to atomized societies. Everyone and every group is accepted provided that it does not impinge upon the life of others. We live like boats passing one another in the night, we are not interested in others and others should refrain from becoming interested in our lives. Diversification is not intrinsically bad but is a perilous slippery slope that sometimes leads to segregation whereby a society is ruled by the motto 'separate but equal'. The USA pre-*Brown v. Board of Education* exemplifies such a risk.[4]

---

4   *Brown v. Board* of Education of Topeka, 347 U.S. 483 (1954).

This should not allow one to forget that the aim of both is to promote integration. I am not sure whether one strategy is better than the other overall. Essentially, I think that it is a contingent matter dependent on history and other local variables. However, I hope it is clear that both processes are potentially problematic and have to be closely monitored – in particular, in relation to the treatment of religious minorities.

Republican States such as France have always used integration as a keyword. Multicultural States such as the UK prefer to talk about accommodation. The difference between the two chiefly lies in their conceptions of the whole. In France, the whole is static and the parts must be fitted into that whole. In the UK, the whole is dynamic and the parts contribute to a reframing of the whole. Thus, 'republicanism' and 'multiculturalism' stand at opposite ends of the spectrum. French republicans, who favour a formal conception of equality, speak of the need of integration of discriminated people into the common society. British multiculturalists, who favour freedom as non-interference, speak instead of accommodation of minorities as parts of a larger whole.

Buried behind those theories lie some assumptions as to what a society should look like. France, for example, believes that there should not be any intermediary between individuals and the State. Groups and communities cannot be regarded as speaking for a set of people and are not considered to be legitimate representative of a worldview that differs from that of the State. Thus, religious communities cannot present themselves as having a collective voice in the public sphere. Equality in the French republican sense amounts to a very formal ideal according to which the State is blind vis-à-vis any sexual, religious or ethnical difference. This ideal of equality present some obvious problems and stand in opposition to the ideal of liberty as non-interference defended by multicultural States such as Britain who believes in the desirability of giving to groups and communities a voice and recognize them as representing a valuable diversity. Even if laudable, the mere recognition of diversity does not guarantee a peaceful and cohesive coexistence because it is always possible that socio-cultural and economic gaps between groups make mutual understanding increasingly impossible.

Both republican and multicultural strategies seem to be ill-equipped to face the challenges of religious pluralism. In particular, their insistence on abstract understandings of liberty and equality is deeply problematic as they aim at imposing controversial understandings of what a society should be like – only to blame individuals and groups when they do not conform to this or that model of an ideal society. Moreover, those ideal understandings seem very little concerned with the value of solidarity between individuals and groups of different socio-cultural origins. Solidarity as a value greatly differs from liberty and equality as it can only be understood, nurtured and promoted on the ground rather than from the abstract eagle eye perspective of the State looking down on its citizens.

The State has an obligation to secure the preconditions for solidarity to hold between individuals and groups. In order for this to be possible, individuals and groups need to disregard prejudices and stereotypes regarding their neighbours whose origins and roots are poorly known. Living side by side harmoniously requires a certain amount of mutual trust that can only come if one's neighbour is not regarded as an agent of disturbance but an individual, like any other, with his/ her own religious, political, cultural background.

The only possible way to promote a certain measure of trust and mutual knowledge is by giving a chance to individuals and groups to experience parts of life in common. Education provides the necessary space where people can attain mutual understanding and dispel prejudices and stereotypes about each other. The classroom can perform the vital role of bridging socio-cultural gaps by exposing people to different cultures within a common environment. Sadly, this experience is doomed to fail if some people are excluded from the outset from classes as is the case, for example, with Muslim pupils wearing the scarf. Also, the experiment is not going to happen if the State encourages groups and communities to organize themselves autonomously, as with faith schools in Britain.

The classroom should be a real tolerance lab where everyone engages in an experiment from the start. At stake is the very possibility of coexistence and cohabitation, so every State should take this experiment very seriously and promote the practice of tolerance on the ground instead of imposing an idealized and moralizing vision of an ideal society starting from an abstract understanding of the values of liberty or equality. In the next section, I will explore the extent to which European States have an obligation to promote a tolerant environment through education from the viewpoint of the right of education protected by Article 2 of Protocol 1 of the European Convention on Human Rights 1950 ('ECHR').

State, Religion and Education

In the past 20 years since the first *foulard* case in 1989,[5] courts in all European States have been flooded with cases about the place of religion in primary and secondary education. The cases can be divided in three broad categories. First, they concern religious symbols in the classroom. Secondly, they concern religious syllabuses in public schools. Thirdly, they concern the way in which States organize the systems of state, private and religious schools. Much has been said about the first, less about the last two. Here, I want to say something about all of them through the discussion of the general right to education entrenched in Article 2 of Protocol 1 of the ECHR and the way in which it influences the mission of the State as promoter of tolerance.

---

5   Avis du Conseil d'Etat Section de l'intérieur 27 novembre 1989, no. 346893, Avis 'Port du foulard islamique'. [Online] available at: http://www.rajf.org/spip.php?article1065 [Accessed: 2 April 2011].

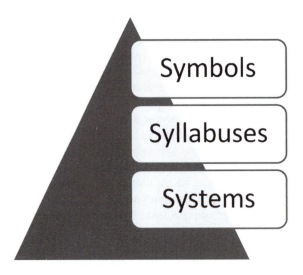

Figure 1.1   Three categories of concern

This section offers some considerations on the nature of the right to education, the role of the State in its implementation, and the place of religion in schools. The point I am trying to buttress is that education is the first building block to promote a genuinely plural and tolerant society. There are several issues blurring the general picture, the first of which is the distracting power of religious symbols. In *Lautsi*, the issue of the crucifix is the most visible tip of the iceberg but the most important problem is the nature of the right to education and the corresponding obligation of the State to organize a system of education that is inclusive and that allows for different individuals and groups to come together in a tolerant environment. The question is the following: what is the role of the State in regulating education in order to promote tolerance? Article 2 of Protocol 1 ('right to education') of the ECHR reads as follows: 'No person shall be denied the right to education. In the exercise of any functions which it assumes in relation to education and to teaching, the State shall respect the right of parents to ensure such education and teaching in conformity with their own religious and philosophical convictions.' The interpretation of this article immediately raises three problems. First, the article does not clarify who the right-holders are. It is ambiguous, for example, whether from the viewpoint of the children education is a right or an obligation. Secondly, it is necessary to understand the scope of the obligation of the State in providing education. Thirdly, it raises the issue of conformity between the education offered by the State and the religious and philosophical convictions of parents.

The second chamber of the ECtHR in *Lautsi* outlined some clarifications in a formulaic way.[6] First, the main fundamental right is that of education and is held by children. In this context, parents have an ancillary right to the respect of their religious and philosophical convictions. Secondly, the obligation of the State is to guarantee that education provided to students be objective, critical and impartial. The Court draws a distinction between 'education' and 'indoctrination' and strictly prohibits the latter. Finally, the State has a duty of neutrality and impartiality; for the Court, neutrality particularly guarantees the right to believe or not to believe of all parents and children. The ECtHR adds that Article 2 of Protocol 1 should be read in conjunction with Articles 8, 9 and 10. In other words, it does not seem to be a self-standing right but a subsidiary duty like the prohibition of discrimination under Article 14. The central idea seems to be that of neutrality as a necessary precondition for pluralism. The Grand Chamber breaks free from the idea of neutrality as a central duty of the state and claims instead that Italy has a wide margin of appreciation concerning the symbols in the classroom since the presence of a religious symbol does not amount to indoctrination. To reach this conclusion, the Grand chamber uses the controversial notion of a 'passive symbol.' It is hard to make sense of this idea since passive symbols cannot be opposed to active symbols, a symbol being always passive. What the Court seems to hint at is that the teaching of religion is more intrusive and can amount to indoctrination. Moreover, the person who teaches the class should be free from religious symbols.[7]

None of those principles are free from controversy. Moreover, there remain some unanswered questions as to the so called 'right to education'. In most European States, education is regarded as a duty on children. The age requirements vary but may go up to the age of majority. Yet, at the same time, education must also be a right of children. If the State did not make any provision for education, children through their parents would have a claim against the State. But what are exactly the rights of parents *vis-à-vis* the State? Is it about the State offering a choice between state and private schools? Or is it about the State offering a state system of schools?

The scope of the obligation of the State raises even more important problems. The crucial issue is the *quality* of education provided by the State. If you only have a right to something mediocre, then you may just as well waive it in order to have a better education provided by the private sector. Regrettably, the poor quality of state provided education entrenches class differences based upon economic means.

I believe the UK *JFS* case[8] could be read from the alternative viewpoint of the State obligation to provide quality education. UK state schools offer a very basic

---

6   ECtHR *Lautsi v. Italy* 3 November 2009, Application no. 30814/06, para. 47

7   The court prohibits the wearing of an Islamic scarf on the part of the teacher. See ECtHR, *Dahlab v. Switzerland* 15 Febuary 2001, Application no. 42393/98.

8   *R (on the application of E) (Respondent) v. Governing Body of JFS and the Admissions Appeal Panel of JFS (Appellants) and others* [2009] UKSC 15.

service when it comes to education. It is not a mystery that private schools provide a better start in life and entrench class difference based on economic means. The rich will be rich and well educated; the poor will be poor and poorly educated. One way of bypassing the class divide in educational matters is to attend faith schools that are often very well ranked in national tables and offer a very high standard of education.

The Jewish Free School ('*JFS*'), for example, is often classed amongst the very best schools in the country. Despite being funded by the State, faith schools practise discrimination at the entrance point based upon religious criteria. If one belongs to the religion of the school, then in principle one is eligible for a place. The applicant (M) had been raised by his father and his mother, an Italian Catholic converted to Judaism in Israel. The problem in the case was that the criterion employed by the school followed an Orthodox understanding of Judaism that excluded M because his mother had not converted according to acceptable standards. The criterion was criticized on the basis that it introduced racial discrimination under the cloak of religion.

This case regarded from the viewpoint of the right to education raises the issue of whether the State should fund faith schools that will inevitably exclude some on religious, if not apparently racial, grounds. Is there a right to education in a religious institution? Article 2 of Protocol 1 does not seem to give a conclusive answer as it states that: 'the State shall respect the right of parents to ensure such education and teaching in conformity with their own religious and philosophical convictions.' Does this mean that the State should simply permit the existence of faith and other private schools? Or does it mean that the State should fund those schools? The ECtHR in *Lautsi* held that the provision does not discriminate between public and private schools. This probably means that the State is free to choose on how best to structure and fund education provided that it does not prohibit faith and other private schools. This seems to be reasonable, but it does not tell us the exact scope of the State's obligation to guarantee education.

France has put education at the heart of its republican project since the nineteenth century. Prime Minister Jules Ferry established the principle of free state schools with the law of 1881.[9] In 1882, he made them both compulsory and *laïques* – that is, ostensibly free from any religious element.[10] The central idea was to promote social advancement and integration of all through public education. If education is to be understood as an instrument for individual development and improvement of social status, then the right to education only makes sense if it imposes a strong duty on the State to guarantee the highest possible standard of education to everyone. This is not incompatible with having faith schools or other private schools. However, the State should give priority to the funding of State schools in order to maintain them as competitive as possible. Any other standard would simply defeat the purpose of public schools as the great social levellers.

---

9   Loi du 16 juin 1881, note 3 *supra*.

10   Lois du 28 mars 1882, note 3 *supra*.

As part of their obligation to secure a right to education, States need to send a clear message to State schools and private schools in order for them to strive to create a pluralistic environment wherein tolerance can flourish. The French saga of the veil shows that France betrayed its original republican intent. To put Muslim students in a situation of having to choose between wearing the *hijab* or leaving school achieves the opposite result to the one originally intended by Jules Ferry: it pushes them to give up their right to education in a public school in order to find a more tolerant environment in which they can feel at ease with their identity. Most of the Muslim pupils who wear a scarf seek refuge in Catholic schools that are more tolerant than state schools towards religious symbols and people.

Tolerance in the religious context is a difficult value to practice because it requires striking a balance between opposite reactions of acceptance and opposition towards diversity. Such a value is, by definition, very unstable as the context can often tip the balance in one way (mostly in the direction of opposition) or the other. In order to be consciously tolerant, it is necessary to know the object towards which we direct our acceptance or opposition. This requires much nurturing that can best be achieved through education. The State should introduce in state schools a mandatory class in civic education for the purpose of creating the preconditions for toleration. Such a course should include the knowledge of civic and political institutions as well as religious institutions understood in the broadest possible sense.

Given this premise, it is open to discussion whether the ECtHR rightly sanctioned Norway for introducing a compulsory course on 'Christian Knowledge and Religious and Ethical Education' in 1997. The Grand Chamber in *Folgerø* considered that the curriculum was insufficiently critical, objective and pluralistic to justify its mandatory character.[11] The intent of the course was, among other things, to promote dialogue between faiths. However, the Court believed that it was not *objective* enough and as such it had to be made optional. It is difficult, however, to delineate the precise standards of objectivity required by the ECHR. It is safer to assume that, on these issues, local knowledge would help to shape the best possible curriculum. It does not seem to be the prerogative of a supranational court in any event.

The importance of education on religious and civic matters has to do with the cognitive dimension of tolerance. When we extend our knowledge of the external world and we come to the conclusion that there is nothing dangerous with a group or a practice, then we give up opposition even if we are not prepared to embrace that practice. Moreover, knowledge through a balanced education helps to form much more stable and reasonable judgements. Even when one disagrees with someone, this does not constitute a ground for opposition. On the contrary, it may well prompt cultural enrichment. Of course, after deliberation and disagreement one may rightly consider another person's opinion to be wrong. Yet, even that

---

11 ECtHR *Folgerø v. Norway* (2008) 46 EHRR 47.

cannot constitute a good reason for opposition in that 'wrong' opinions do not curtail freedom of thought or action.

Back to Symbols: *Lautsi* and the Crucifix in the Classroom

In *Lautsi v Italy*,[12] the Chamber of the Second Section of the ECtHR found that the presence of the crucifix in Italian state schools violated the right to education in conjunction with the right to freedom of conscience, thought and religion (Article 9, ECHR). This case provoked a strong and passionate reaction from the Catholic Church as well as the majority of politicians and a substantial number of private citizens in Italy. As it is often the case, the heat of those debates was inversely proportional to the light shed by them. The government filed a request to hear the case before the Grand Chamber, which was accepted on 2 March 2010. On 18 March 2011, the Grand Chamber reversed the decision of the second section and concluded that the presence of the crucifix was not incompatible with the right of parents to have their children educated in line with their own philosophical convictions.[13]

As mentioned above, the issue of religious symbols is only the most visible tip of a much bigger iceberg. European States are experiencing signs of tension when regulating religion in public schools. One of the explanations for this is the crystallization of a conception of secularism that rules out religion from any intervention in the public sphere. This position is often inconsistent with the compromises the State has reached with dominant religions in each country. The changing cultural, social and political landscape in Europe casts light on the arbitrary compromises that the secular State has reached with local religions. From this finding emerges a competing understanding of secularism as a default framework within which religious and non-religious people can both contribute to the shaping of public policies (Zucca 2008).

Education is the first laboratory and exercise room for the difficult practice of tolerance. The State as we saw has to invest on state schools in order to promote greater mutual knowledge, which is the best instrument to allow for tolerance to flourish. Moreover, opposition is bred by socio-economic gaps that education is meant to bridge in the first place. A State that does not successfully promote social advancement through education is already failing in the mission of avoiding social and cultural conflicts.

Religious and civic education is a necessary element of any state school curriculum. How can we possibly study the history, philosophy, literature and art of our countries without understanding the role religion played and how it shaped along with other intellectual sources our moral and political landscape? Armed with these points, we can go back to the initial issues: is the presence of the

---

12   *Lautsi v. Italy*, note 1 *supra*.

13   ECtHR, *Lautsi v. Italy* 18 March 2011, Application no. 30814/06.

crucifix interfering with the right to education of children? Is it interfering with the philosophical and religious convictions of their parents? And more importantly, is the presence of the crucifix preventing the creation of a more tolerant environment? Firstly, as I suggested, the criterion to judge state schools is the overall quality of their curriculum. There is no doubt that Italian schools offer a high standard education for everyone and for free. It is still possible to choose a private school if parents so desire. In the post-war experience of Italian state schools, the presence of the crucifix never interfered with the critical, objective and pluralistic nature of public education. The main limit of that system lies in the presence of a course of religious education which is run by a teacher appointed by the Vatican. That course, however, is not mandatory and it is easily possible to opt out. In line with my previous points, it would be desirable that the State replace that course with a compulsory course on pluralistic religious education.

The idea that the State must be 'neutral' in the sense of completely expunging religion from public schools is based on a contested notion of exclusive secularism that is in sharp opposition to more inclusive conceptions. The ECtHR in *Lautsi* seems to have embraced an understanding of exclusive secularism that is more likely than not to lead to major confrontations between States and religions. The Grand Chamber had a great chance to formulate a more inclusive understanding of secularism that allows for a place of religions in the classroom and in the public sphere – a secularism that truly promotes tolerance and pluralism in the best tradition of the Court itself. However, the Grand Chamber decided to frame the problem in the narrowest possible terms: the issue is only about the compatibility of the crucifix with the right of education and freedom of religion. It controversially holds that the decision has nothing to do with the compatibility of the crucifix with the principle of secularism (para. 57).

I believe that the Grand Chamber's decision lacks subtleness and articulation. In the remaining pages I want to discuss my preferred solution taking as a cue the pleadings presented by Professor Weiler before the Court in its general hearings. I address here both the general principles raised by the *Lautsi* case[14] and Professor Weiler's brief (Weiler 2010). In the interests of space, I will only mention the most essential arguments.

In its decision, the Second Chamber dealt with the nature and scope of the right to education as encapsulated in Article 2 of Protocol 1. Therein lies an important tension between the *obligation* of the State to provide equal access to education for all and the *obligation* of the State to guarantee pluralism and diversity through the respect of parents' convictions. To achieve the latter aim, it has to promote an environment where everyone can identify with the school – including its syllabus and its symbols. The central question, as I understand it, is the following: how can the State treat people with different religious and philosophical convictions in a way that guarantees equal concern and respect? This tension is encapsulated in the Chamber's judgment:

---

14 *Lautsi*, note 1 *supra*, para. 47.

> Respect for parents' convictions must be possible in the context of education
> capable of ensuring an open school environment which encourages inclusion
> rather than exclusion, regardless of the pupils' social background, religious
> beliefs or ethnic origins. Schools should not be the arena for missionary
> activities or preaching; they should be a meeting place for different religions
> and philosophical convictions, in which pupils can acquire knowledge about
> their respective thoughts and traditions. [paragraph 47c]

When faced with such a fundamental conflict, judges should exercise a good degree
of empathy – that is, the natural human capacity of putting oneself in someone
else's shoes trying to avoid the trap of dividing the camp in two sharply separate
camps of the secular or the religious. This is often difficult in legal settings where
the binary logic tends to polarize the discussion. I firmly believe that in order to
deal with conflicts one needs to go beyond that binary logic in order to find a better
compromise.

Professor Weiler's analysis is thought-provoking and engaging but falls in the
legalistic trap of dividing the world into two halves for the purpose of showing that
the choice of a side is never neutral. His discussion follows three main lines that
mirror the three legal principles he singles out from the case. The first principle
is the affirmation of the right to freedom of religion and freedom from religion,
which though hardly an object of contention, is often difficult in its application.
The second principle concerns the need for a classroom that inculcates tolerance
and pluralism and is bereft of religious coercion. Here, I would like to briefly say
that prima facie everyone may agree with that idea but the practical implications
are far from clear. As explored above, the ECtHR conceives of schools as meeting
places for different religions and philosophical convictions. In order to create
this environment, the State has to deal with three main policy issues that are
all interlinked. First, the State has to set up a system in which equal access to
education is promoted; this requires a judgement as to whether, for example, faith
schools should be funded by the State. Secondly, the State should make sure that
the school's syllabus promotes the knowledge of diversity so that it cannot simply
impose a religious course of a given confession without giving the possibility of
opting out. Ideally, the course would promote pluralism by presenting different
faiths as well as the secular position on ethical issues. Thirdly, and I want to stress
here that this is only the tip of a much bigger iceberg concerning the place of
religion in education, the State should decide which symbols to display and refrain
from embracing symbols that may hamper equal membership and diversity.

It is the third principle that chiefly concerns Professor Weiler. This is the
principle of neutrality as articulated by the court: 'The State's duty of neutrality
and impartiality is incompatible with any kind of power on its part to assess the
legitimacy of religious convictions or the ways of expressing those convictions.'[15]He
criticizes the rationale of neutrality proposed by the Court by using one conceptual

---

15   *Lautsi*, note 1 *supra*, para. 47

argument and two sets of dichotomies. The conceptual argument has to do with the understanding of 'freedom of religion'; Professor Weiler suggests that the individual freedom of and from religion is complemented by the freedom of the State to define its own national identity by selecting, among other things, its religious symbols. The two sets of dichotomies concern the definition of a *laïc* / non-*laïc* State and the factual situation of having a symbol or not having one. Here, I will attempt to argue against what I regard as a conceptual mistake and as false dichotomies. More generally, I will criticize the binary logic that splits society into secular and religious camps and which, albeit typical of legal reasoning, is very detrimental when one attempts to solve a social and legal conflict.

The first conceptual mistake concerns the distinction between individual freedom of religion and the freedom of the State 'when it comes to the place of religion or religious heritage in the collective identity of the nation and the symbology of the State (Weiler 2010). Freedom in constitutional terms is defined in relation to the established constitutional authority of the State. The State has the power to change legal relations in ordinary law but finds its limit in the existence of individual freedom which signpost immunity from regulation on the part of the individual as well as a disability to regulate on the part of the State. So to say that the State 'has freedom' is inaccurate. The State has the power to determine the place of religion or religious heritage in its own collective identity by choosing the symbols it prefers but this power can be limited by the exercise of freedom on the part of an individual or a group who can reasonably show to have been discriminated against.

Professor Weiler argues that in Europe the State is not obliged to follow a given model of Church/State relationship. This is correct but even in this context it is inaccurate to claim that the State has a freedom to decide its own model as this would suggest that the ECtHR has the ultimate authority to decide these issues and the State only has residual authority. However, the truth is that the ECtHR can only point to a violation of Convention rights whilst the authority to determine the collective identity of the State remains in the hands of the State itself. The Grand Chamber takes up this suggestion and avoids imposing a single model of State/ Church relationship. Today, that is not an issue anymore. What is at stake is the way in which the secular state deals with diversity in a society that is growingly pluralist and less and less homogeneous. Unfortunately, the Grand Chamber shirks from taking a position as to the obligation of the state to show genuine respect for those people that are not comfortable with Christian religious symbols exposed in a public place. That said, the main responsibility still lies with the national state.

What kind of choice can the State make? Here, Professor Weiler uses the first false dichotomy between *laïc* and non-*laïc* States. French *laïcité* represents one paradigmatic form of secularism whereas England is described as a typical non-*laïc* State. There are two problems with this dichotomy. The former is that *laïcité* is far from being a representative form of secularism; if anything, it is a radical (and often ideological) exception in Europe. It is radical because it has imposed, since 1905, a very strict separation between Church and State which was created after a bitter conflict between the French State and the Catholic Church. More problematically, it is ideological as it claims to provide the foundation of a set of values common to all the citizens of France. But of course the suggestion that once stripped of religious beliefs we would all converge towards a common national identity defined in purely political terms is just an illusion. *Laïcité*, in this ideological sense, is not compatible with freedom of belief.

The second problem with the dichotomy is that the polar opposite of a *laïc* State is defined in purely negative terms: non-*laïc* States. This is hardly accurate and as a consequence not very helpful. England, the example used by Weiler, is a very complex case. It certainly cannot be defined as *laïque* but it has many secular elements along with elements of establishment. In brief, as Julian Rivers (2010) points out, the English system encapsulates a tension between establishment and secularism. Instead of positing such a dichotomy, it would be more stimulating to propose a typology of the variety of secularism in Europe.

I want to raise, in passing, another problem for Weiler's argument. The Italian Constitutional Court singles out *laïcité* as one of the constitutional principles embedded in the foundational text (although not explicitly mentioned). Concerning the crucifix in the classroom, it refused to rule on this issue because it lacks jurisdiction for reviewing an administrative decree. But the constitutional judge decided as a matter of internal regulation to remove the crucifix from the courtroom, thereby taking a side in the debate. It would seem that, from a constitutional viewpoint, were we to draw the appropriate consequences of the principle of *laïcité* as recognized by the constitutional court, crucifixes would have no place in school classrooms. However, Italy is for the moment an in-between case that shows a tension between its secular (or more precisely *laïque*) character and the acceptance of certain elements of religion in public institutions. I personally believe that the Italian State holds inconsistent positions as to the place of religion in public institutions. But I also believe that it is for the State to decide what form of secularism suits itself and to draw from it all the necessary conclusions. Conversely, it is not the mission of an international court to suggest which form of secularism is the most appropriate. An international court can, however, pinpoint to an existing contradiction between principle and practice.

The final and most important false dichotomy is that between a wall with a symbol and one without. Professor Weiler's parable of Marco and Leonardo, two children who are equally perplexed by the presence and the absence of the crucifix, aims to illustrate that neither of these two choices is neutral. It may be true that a naked wall is not a neutral solution in particular in this case where emptiness would be the conclusion of an act of rejection. It does not follow, however, that the presence and the absence of crucifix are equivalent. Moreover, those two options do not exhaust the realm of the possible. I do believe that a solution can be found in an alternative arrangement.

Besides the two polar opposites, there are at least two more positions. The first option is well known and consists of having several symbols rather than one. Having several symbols would be more consistent with so called pluralist ethics since one symbol is reasonably to be interpreted as capturing a monistic position. Moreover, the solution in favour of a plurality of symbols was the position initially adopted by the Italian State which used to require having on the wall a picture of the valiant king along with a crucifix. It can then be argued that Italian walls should not be emptied but filled with other symbols that may capture the increasing diversity in the classroom. Alternatively, one could of course have a picture of the President or the Prime Minister but it is doubtful that this would be acceptable to all!

There is another completely different position to consider which requires the active engagement of all interested parties. Given that one, two or more symbols or none at all are alternative positions, it would be desirable to spark a debate about which option pleases most the local community of parents, teachers and pupils in the school. One problem remains: where to start? Should the debate take place from scratch or should it take account of the status quo? This decision is better left to the State as the constitutional authority charged with the selection of national symbols. This may mean that we would have to start with the default position of the crucifix, even though as I said this is inconsistent with a self-avowed commitment to *laïcité*. However, the point here is not to bow or to resist to the State authority but to take this tension as an opportunity for local deliberation and mutual learning. On this point, the Grand Chamber ends up leaving too wide a margin of appreciation for the national state. The ECHR should have put more pressure on Italy to engage in a serious national debate as to the desirability of the crucifix in the classroom. As things stand, Italy will simply ignore this issue until the next major litigation.

I am not arguing that the symbol should be removed as a matter of principle. One can well imagine a scenario in which the rule for everyone would be unchanged: the Italian State elects the crucifix as a symbol to be hung in classrooms. However, it should be possible to apply for an exemption to this rule. The exception could work according to a deliberative model. The debate could have two stages: first, parents (and/or pupils depending on their age) would have to present reasons for and against the crucifix in the classroom. If they agreed to keep the crucifix, then the deliberation would end there. If they agreed to have an exemption to the general rule, then they would have to decide what best arrangement to put in place instead: another symbol, several symbols or a white wall. In this way, the power of the State to determine its own national symbols would be preserved and not overruled by the ECtHR. The second is that freedom of and from religion would equally be enhanced although not in a way that is openly polarized and exclusive but in a way that is inclusive, pluralistic and tolerant. Individual freedom is a powerful weapon that may be abused by some individuals who are not able to accept that compromises are at the core of democratic societies. Thus, the Grand Chamber had the opportunity to put forward an understanding of the right to education that is sensitive to the idea that classrooms should be the laboratory of tolerance in so far as they are the best places whereby one can live pluralism and develop mutual understanding. The presence of the crucifix in Italian classrooms is not always incompatible with the respect of parents' convictions. However, and this is what is missing in the Grand Chamber's decision, the State has to show a real concern and respect for those parents that disagree with that rule by giving the possibility of an exemption mechanism. If the State can devise a system whereby the crucifix can be regarded as a starting point for a local debate on what symbols bind us together then it will perhaps be acceptable. The overarching goal is not to impose unilaterally a secular or a religious view of what the symbols in the classroom should look like. The aim should be to provide an environment within which the exchange between religious and non-religious people is possible, creative and productive. The classroom as a tolerance lab does not require as a matter of principle to remove the crucifix once and for ever. Instead, it demands that the decision on what symbols should be displayed in a classroom be dependent on mutual understanding and respect. Unfortunately the Grand Chamber treats the notion of respect very ambiguously. It first states that respect requires more than mere 'acknowledgement' or 'taking into account.' Respect imposes a positive obligation on the state. This is a good starting point, however the Grand Chamber goes on to say that respect varies from one State to another and depends on European consensus. Lacking consensus on the requirements of respect, the Court has to accord a wide margin of appreciation to the national State.

The Grand Chamber fails to show respect for the notion of respect. Unfortunately, it gives the state a blank cheque which does not require any extra step to be taken. This is not ideal as there remains a big tension between those people who regard the crucifix as desirable and those who see it as an unacceptable presence.

Conclusion

Symbols should not occupy us for too long. The State has a general obligation to organize a system of education which values religious communities without giving them the chance to isolate themselves from other religious and non-religious people. In other words, the system of education that a State device should protect pluralism while promoting a vision of education as an experiment – a laboratory – in the practice of tolerance. In the UK, it is highly doubtful that faith schools can create a place where diversity meets in order to foster mutual understanding and tolerance. It is all the more suspect when a school excludes pupils on debatable religious grounds, as it was the case in the *JFS* school.[16] The State should not subsidize educational environments where socio-cultural, not to speak of ethnic, homogeneity is the norm and diversity only the exception. In France, republican schools that are engaged in the mission of forming republican citizens cannot pretend that everyone who enters the educational environment accepts blindly republican values. If those values are strong, education will be able to pass them

---

16   *R(E) v. Governing Body of JFS* [2009] UKSC 15.

on and require individuals to reflect upon them and embrace them because they are desirable – not because they are imposed.

European States that are seeking to enhance social cohesion cannot rely on strategies of integration or accommodation that reinforce and entrench assumptions about ideal societies. I have sought to demonstrate in this chapter that States are better advised to take into account the fact of pluralism on the ground and to organize it in such a way that mutual understanding between various groups of a society is possible. Of course, tensions between individuals and groups will not be totally dispelled; this would in fact be very worrying as it would be the sign of uniformity. On the contrary, those tensions could play an important role in pushing people to reflect on their own commitments and on the necessity for diversity. This could be the lesson of the crucifix if taken as a starting point for engaging with others in order to understand oneself better.

I started by saying that I was both a potential victim and a potential perpetrator of the presence of the crucifix in Italian classrooms. I would like to suggest that that is not because I am inherently irrational or lack the ability to take a clear stance. It is because I can see a tension between my secularist position and my sense of belonging to a culture that is imbued with religious elements and symbols. To feel that tension means to be able to see that there are important reasons that militate in favour of either position and I do not want to simply prioritize one above another. Instead, I believe that that tension is a starting point for a further reflection on the secular State and the presence of religions within it. It is in the classroom that such a reflection should start and can only take place if we conceive of the classroom as a tolerance lab.

References

Choudri, S. (ed.) 2008. *Constitutional Design for Divided Societies – Integration or Accommodation.* Oxford: OUP.

McCrudden, C. 2011. Multiculturalism, freedom of religion, equality, and the British constitution: the JFS case considered. *International Journal of Constitutional Law*, 1–37.

Rivers, J. 2010. *The Law of Organized Religions – Between Establishment and Secularism.* Oxford: OUP.

Weiler, J.H.H. 2010. Editorial – State and nation; church, mosque, and synagogue – the trailer. *International Journal of Constitutional Law* 8(2), 157–66.

Zucca, L. 2008. The crisis of the secular state. A reply to Prof. Sajo. *International Journal of Constitutional Law* 7(3), 494–514.

Chapter 2
Jewish Day Schools in France: Mapping their Jewish Identity Proposals

Martine Cohen

The Jewish schooling sector must first be analysed with reference to the general religious-private educational system in France. General data will then be given about the importance and the recent evolution of Jewish schools before addressing the topic of their diverse Jewish identity proposals. Specific Jewish criteria (such as religious practices or the content and extent of Jewish teachings) will help to clarify their differences and to highlight a religious-secular polarization within the organized community. However, the challenge of ideological pluralism is not the only one. Indeed, as for French society at large, the Jewish schools' landscape also shows socio-economic and cultural differentiations within the Jewish community.

The Religious-Private Educational Sector in France

Education was historically a major field for the State/Church conflict. Indeed, the building of a public educational system (notably with the Ferry laws in the 1880s (Baubérot 1997) was intended to eliminate the Catholic Church's monopoly on schooling and religious teaching congregations were regularly expelled from France. However, in the same way the Ferry laws had established a free day during the week to allow religious courses to be given, further positive legal steps, among which the 1905 Separation Law between State and Church, were clearly taken throughout the twentieth century, in a spirit of compromise by always facilitating religious practice. Among these steps was the *1959 Loi Debré* which provided private schools (mostly religious Catholic ones) with the possibility of receiving state financial support under certain conditions.

Basic Principles of the 1959 *Loi Debré*

The *Loi Debré* is based on mutual commitments by the State and those schools which freely decide to contract with the State.[1] State commitment essentially

---

1   Two types of 'contract' exist. Since the vast majority of private schools have chosen today the 'associational contract', we will limit our analysis to this type of contract. Under

involves a substantial financial support which covers mainly teachers' salaries (only for teachers of the general curriculum) as well as general running costs of the school. This support does not oblige the school to give up its religious ethos since the State fully respects its 'specific character' (the same principle applies for other kinds of private schools). In exchange, the school has to comply with three main requirements: it must strictly follow the general curriculum, including possible controversial subjects such as biology, philosophy and history. It also has to accept all pupils, regardless of their religious belonging or faith; finally, this non-discrimination principle goes along with another principle, namely, that of freedom of conscience (which includes freedom of religion): religious teachings and practices must be optional for *all* pupils of the school. This clearly implies the possibility for non-Catholic children to attend a Catholic school where they may be offered a course in their own religion.[2]

The private general educational sector gathers today 17 per cent of the total number of French pupils – more than 2 million pupils, of whom 95 per cent attend Catholic schools (Toulemonde 2009).[3] State support for the private sector remains today more or less on the same level, irrespective of shifts in balance between the private and public sectors.[4] Indeed, more and more parents are worried about the quality of public schools either in respect of their general organization or their pedagogical environment. The result is that only 7 per cent of pupils are exclusively schooled in the private sector, whereas 40 per cent of them switch back and forth between public and private schools. This shows a relative normalization of the private sector, in which less than 10 per cent of parents declare a religious motivation for their choice. This general trend, which also implies a global secularization of the Catholic schooling system is analysed by some as a progressive movement towards a more pluralist 'public' service.[5] It

---

this contract, the degree of commitment of parties is greater. For historical and judicial details, see Poucet 2009, Toulemonde 2009.

2 The fact that many Catholic schools have difficulty maintaining their 'specific character' is not due to a lack of freedom of religion but rather to the general trend of secularization of French society: Catholic practitioners are fewer and fewer; in addition, private schools, of which Catholic ones remain the vast majority, are often chosen not for their religious orientation but for the quality of their teaching and pedagogical environment.

3 Catholic schools do not constitute a uniform sector: the degree of their religious ethos varies and some are more prestigious and sought after by rich or well-educated families (either Catholic or not) whereas some are situated in poor areas and often attended by children born from immigrant families.

4 Under an informal agreement, reflecting previous figures, the State is to take in charge salaries of 20 per cent of newly appointed private sector teachers out of the total of teaching positions created per year. Other expenses, concerning school buildings or running costs, will vary, depending on the particular relationships between the local Catholic Church and public authorities.

5 We may thus speak of a de facto convergence between the French and the English schooling systems (see Sinclair 2010). However, two features still differ from the English

must, however, be counterbalanced by the fact that new inequalities are appearing along socio-economic criteria, *both in the public and the private sectors*, between 'protected' and prestigious sought after schools and others of a lower quality (Toulemonde 2009, Poucet 2009, Oberti 2007).

The Jewish Educational System: General Data[6]

The Jewish school sector represents a very small part of the general private-religious sector: 30,000 Jewish pupils out of 2 million. If we add to this number about the same number of Jewish children attending Catholic schools,[7] the result is that about 60 per cent of Jewish school-age pupils attend private schools. This is far above the average national percentage of 17 per cent. Furthermore, this is a true 'revolution' compared with the historical adhesion of Jews to the public educational system in particular and the Republic in general. Obviously, Jews are much more anxious than the average population about the quality of the public system – notwithstanding other motives such as a new fear of anti-Semitism. In the same way, the Jewish sector differs from the general private one by its strong religious character, which does not encourage non-Jewish parents to enrol their children – even in schools under contract with the State where they theoretically have the choice to opt out from religious instruction.

Let us now present general data about the evolution of Jewish schools and their organizational aspects before giving a more precise view of this sector.

The Growth of Jewish Schools since 1945

Two Jewish day-schools existed in 1945, counting approximately 400 pupils (Fonds Social Juif Unifié 2003).[8] The figures are much higher today, the increase having occurred essentially during the 1980s and the 1990s: in 2009, 102 schools enrolled 30,000 pupils. These schools vary in size, their structures being of modest or large capacity (14 pupils for the smallest; over 1,500 for the biggest ones). Jewish schools have become increasingly state funded: today, 72 per cent of their

---

situation: first, French religious schools remain strongly perceived as 'private' ones, even when they contract with the State and have subsequently to convert their religious orientation to an optional choice. This opt-out proposal is the second difference with the English system.

6   The only source of numerical data on Jewish schools is the *Fonds Social Juif Unifié* (FSJU), a Jewish central institution dedicated to social work and cultural activities. For a general history of Jewish schools, see Elmaleh 2006; for a sociological analysis, see Cohen 2011.

7   According to the FSJU.

8   *Fonds Social Juif Unifié* (2003). Two new schools were created in 1948 (in Strasbourg and Paris) so the proper estimate may be around 600 pupils at that date.

pupils are taught in state supported classes. Most of the schools which do not choose to contract with the State are small primary schools and belong essentially to the more religious sector.

The organizational framework of Jewish schools includes several school networks (each with its own specificity) and an umbrella organization in charge of their loose coordination.

Networks and Independent Schools

Jewish schools do not present a unified or uniform landscape. Several networks are in competition. There are also 'independent' schools which in fact form an informal network.

In considering the formal networks, we have to first single out the oldest ones that have existed since the nineteenth century. They are linked to the Consistory (the principal Orthodox institution) and to the *Alliance israélite universelle* ('AIU'). These two historical networks were dedicated to the 'regeneration' of Jews which, in the nineteenth century, meant opening up to secular teachings – mainly French language and Mathematics. The Consistory developed its schools in France, whereas the AIU developed its network outside France, in countries belonging to the French Colonial Empire as well as in areas under French influence (notably the Ottoman Empire). Another network sharing the same orientation is that of the *Organization, Reconstruction, Travail* ('ORT') founded in 1880 in Russia to train young Jews in manual and agricultural works and whose first school in France was built in 1934. These networks would later evolve following the general changes of the Jewish population and its needs.

The newest networks, mainly the Chabad (or Lubavitcher Hassidim) and the Ozar Hatorah schools, were founded after the war, notably in the seventies and eighties. They are largely dedicated to 'proselytizing' among the Jews in order to encourage their 'conversion' or return to a more rigorous Judaism.

An Umbrella Body

The *Fonds Social Juif Unifié* ('FSJU') was founded in 1949 with the support of American Jewry and modelled after the American United Jewish Appeal in order to centralize fundraising as well as to coordinate all social and educational initiatives among the Jewish organized population. It has grown in importance and appears today to be a quasi-official partner of the State in these areas in spite of the recent emergence of significant competitors having their own relationship with public authorities in the social and educational spheres.

The Department for Jewish Education of the FSJU functions as an umbrella body for all networks and independent schools. It has progressively attained this position throughout the 1980s, notably through its alliance with the Catholic Church in 1984 in its battle against the governmental project to create a 'unified public service', which was seen by Catholic parents at that time as a way to reduce their schooling choice. In particular, the Department for Jewish Education is in charge of the annual negotiation concerning the opening of new state funded classes (with state paid teachers). Hence, it has an important role as 'coordinator' between the different networks and the schools which all have to reach on an annual basis a common decision as to which schools are to benefit from state financial support.[9] However, this coordinator status is counterbalanced by its lack of financial power whereas private donators and family foundations may support schools which are not yet state funded. The FSJU Department also created in 1993 the 'Neher Institute' for various programmes of teacher and director training.

Jewish Schools and their Jewish Identity Proposals

A Typology of Jewish Schools' Proposals

Options offered by Jewish schools do not correspond exactly to parents' preferences: pupils form a group which is more diverse and even heterogeneous in its degree of religious practice and life style than the existing orientations of schools. Only in more religious schools is a high degree of orthodox uniformity guaranteed.

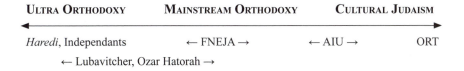

ULTRA ORTHODOXY	MAINSTREAM ORTHODOXY	CULTURAL JUDAISM
Haredi, Independants	← FNEJA →	← AIU → ORT
← Lubavitcher, Ozar Hatorah →		

Figure 2.1   Jewish identities

The different networks and independent schools may be organized along a continuum line, from the pole of 'Ultra Orthodoxy' at one end to that of a 'Cultural Judaism' at the other end, via the 'Mainstream Orthodoxy' option. Let us briefly describe these poles and positions, established principally by reference to the degree of religious practice, before describing in more details the criteria which allow us to distinguish between them as well as to explain the in-between positions.

    Towards the Cultural Judaism pole, one can find the two historical networks of ORT and AIU. As already mentioned, the *Alliance israélite universelle* opened

---

its schools in the nineteenth century for Jews outside France in countries which were often part of the French colonial empire. With the end of the Empire (and of the French influence), the AIU changed its orientation from 'frenchification' of traditional Jews to an emphasis on Jewish religious education in its newly created schools in France since Jews are today well integrated and may be seen by some as too assimilated.[10] The ORT network shared with the AIU the same aim of 'regeneration' by training Jews in 'practical' and 'useful' professions; today it has renewed its purpose, training pupils for new technical professions (optics, computer engineering, ...).

Towards the Ultra Orthodox pole, one may distinguish several streams. The *Haredi* sector (an indigenous term whose meaning is 'people fearful of God') corresponds to the historical stream that refused any compromise with modernity and rejected trends of emancipation which sought, on the basis of equal rights, to allow individual Jews to choose their destiny.[11] Independent schools are also close to the *Haredi* sector but they may be more open to non-strictly Orthodox Jews. Unlike the *Haredi*, the Lubavitcher (Chabad) and Ozar Hatorah networks share a missionary aim. This basically implies that they accept non-strictly Orthodox Jews in their schools in order to 'convert' them to a more rigorous practice.

Mainstream Orthodoxy (network 'FNEJA') is historically identified with the Consistory institution.[12] This stream is ideologically characterized by its basic acceptance of the main religious obligations subject to only a few reforms which are viewed as minor and not altering the general architecture of the Orthodox system. Sociologically, the Mainstream Orthodoxy is in fact open to all *individual* Jews regardless of their degree of practice. Schools in this sector were created by the Consistory or by founders close to it. In the 1980s, the largest ones (which have become autonomous schools) proposed to constitute a loose federation linked to the FSJU – a secular institution in itself but close to the religious norms of the Mainstream Orthodoxy – in order to acquire more weight relatively to the new Ultra Orthodox networks which were multiplying (Lubavitcher, Ozar Hatorah).

---

10   According to Enos-Attali (2010), the move away from the public educational framework began, albeit with some hesitation, in the 1970s following the arrival of North African Jews in France. It was confirmed at the end of the 1980s, but with remaining emphasis on sensitivity towards French values and the quality of general education. According to a major actor of this change (personal interview, January 2011), in 1985–1986, after having closed almost all its schools in North Africa (only four remain today in Morocco), the AIU was ready to give up. But new projects were brought by the then President and his followers. Among them, were the creation by AIU of new schools in France and a policy of 'affiliated' schools in and outside France (in Israel, Europe and North America, mainly Quebec).

11   As we know, equal rights was a theoretical principle and even in France, which was the first country to grant this equality, discriminations or persecutions did not cease in one day.

12   We may also speak of this stream as simply 'Orthodoxy'.

The different poles are of unequal importance. Where Cultural Judaism represents less than 10 per cent of the pupils, the Ultra Orthodox pole and its close networks (Lubavitcher and Ozar Hatorah) enrol about 58 per cent of them and the remaining 32 per cent correspond to the FNEJA and AIU networks (Cohen 2011).[13] Taking into account the fact that part of the Orthodox schools incline towards the Ultra Orthodox pole, as the graph shows, there is a visible imbalance in favour of the radical religious option while the secular pole appears in a minor position.

Two Main Criteria for Differentiation

Two main criteria help determine the global differentiation between the poles as well as the in-between positions: the *degree of religious practice* required at school and sometimes also from the family and the *content of the Jewish curriculum and its importance* in relation to the general curriculum.

The degree of religious practice required from pupils can be exemplified by some radical practices such as a strict dress code for the girls, single-sex classes and 'no TV at home' policy. These practices, which mainly concern gender norms and the openness towards global society, help to distinguish Ultra Orthodoxy and Orthodoxy and to clarify the middle position of the Lubavitcher and Ozar Hatorah networks as well as the attraction of some Orthodox schools towards the Utra Orthodox pole.

In Ultra Orthodox school community life, as well as in their personal lives, girls are required to follow a strict dress code: long skirts, long sleeves and covered legs. Additionally, boys and girls are taught in separated classes. In the same vein, Ultra-Orthodox directors will explicitly require families not to have any television sets at home. By contrast, Mainstream Orthodox schools may allow girls to wear trousers at school (practices differ from one school to another), and do not ask them to follow a strict dress obligation in their personal life. They will not evoke the question of TV at home. Their attraction towards the Ultra Orthodox pole can be seen by their inclination to propose more and more religious courses (upon, they claim, pupils' requests), by their preference for single-sex classes during these religious courses and by the obligation which some of them maintain for girls to wear skirts.

Between these two poles, Lubavitcher and Ozar Hatorah schools are more flexible towards these radical requirements in order to attract non-Ultra Orthodox Jews: they do not ask families not to have TVs at home and they do not always separate boys and girls in classes. But they do require a strict dress code for the girls, as in the Ultra Orthodox schools.

---

13   The estimate has been established on the basis of FSJU statistics. The *Alliance israélite universelle* network is the smallest one (about 5 per cent of the total), gathering also schools which are loosely affiliated.

On the Cultural Judaism pole, none of these radical practices are required; the stress is put more on a cognitive than a normative approach to Judaism. Pupils are free to organize and to attend religious services inside the school; the only religious requirement is the respect of Jewish dietary law (*Kashrut*) within the school community.

In this cognitive approach, differences appear as to the content of the Jewish curriculum and its importance in relation to the general curriculum which is our second criterion. Where Cultural Judaism schools give priority to the study of Jewish History and main Jewish folkloric festivals, both Orthodox and Ultra Orthodox schools give priority to the study of religious texts. However, Ultra Orthodoxy diverges from Orthodoxy in the content of this traditional study: in Ultra Orthodox schools, boys must study a large range of Bible commentaries (the abstract part of the Talmud) while girls are taught only 'practical commandments' which will help them to properly fulfil their future duties as wives and mothers. Girls are also more oriented towards a short curriculum in order to encourage them to marry at an early age and to become teachers for young children in their own schools. In that sense, Ultra Orthodox schools tend to constitute a self-perpetuating system.[14]

The middle position of the *Alliance israélite universelle* schools between Orthodoxy and Cultural Judaism must be interpreted as a lesser attraction towards the Ultra Orthodox norms along with a particular sensitivity to parental insistence that schools open pupils towards 'general culture' in accordance with the historical ideology of this Institution to cultivate a sense of belonging to France.

Three Fundamental Key Factors for Differentiation

A general differentiation appears between a cognitive secular approach to Judaism for the Cultural pole, which still includes some religious practices and references to the main collective festivals, and the strictly normative religious approach of the Ultra Orthodox schools which exclude any secular comprehension of their lifestyle choice. At the heart of this differentiation, gender norms and the openness towards global society represent central issues, embodied by three fundamental key factors: (1) women as *a key section of the population*, (2) individual freedom as *a key value*, and (3) History as *a key discipline*.

Women are considered by the Orthodox law (the *Halacha*) as the 'natural transmitters' of Jewish identity.[15] Their role as 'guardians' of Jewish identity is strongly emphasized among the Ultra Orthodox groups. Thus, girls from these groups are strictly controlled and oriented towards short-term studies. Historicity as a social process conducted by human beings as well as individual freedom, is

---

14   I am grateful to Nathalie Harbonne for the information she provided me on Jewish Ultra Orthodox sectors.

15   This does not prevent the possibility of conversion to Judaism or the educational role of men.

seen by Ultra Orthodox as the main factor of change for Jewish identity; hence, it is associated with a loss of Jewish identity. This is the reason why history (of the Jews) as a modern critical discipline is rejected whereas 'Jewish history' is taught through the religious texts and viewed as essentially conducted by God. This explains as well their rejection of any celebration of the Israeli Independence Day (seen as a human-conducted event). Lubavitcher and Ozar Hatorah schools broadly share these options but show an ambivalent position on the issue of celebrating Israeli Independence Day.

As for the Mainstream Orthodox schools, they generally admit modern values of individual freedom and historicity as a human process. However, their attraction towards the Ultra Orthodox position is reflected in their teaching of 'Jewish history' more as a legend narrative than as a scientific history – at least for ancient times, when considering the period of foundation of the 'Jewish people'. For modern times, some of these schools would be reluctant to include teachings on Jewish modern philosophers or writers but – unlike Ultra Orthodox ones – they celebrate with great fervour Israeli Independence Day. On the issue of female freedom, they appear more open than the Ultra Orthodox but they still maintain a traditional conception of women as spouses and mothers.

The more we go towards the Cultural Judaism pole, the more individual freedom is accepted and even encouraged, in particular for women. In the same way, the history of the Jewish people plainly becomes a product of human beings – hence, the positive attitude towards the creation of the modern State of Israel – and history is well received as a scientific discipline.

In this general perspective, the continuum line also points to the degree of openness towards change in Jewish Law (the *Halacha*) as well as, on specific matters of admission criteria at school, the acceptance (or not) of children born from non-Jewish mothers. These children are not considered as Jews by Orthodox and Ultra Orthodox sectors; consequently, they are not admitted in their schools unless the mother has been converted by an Orthodox rabbinical court. By contrast, towards the Cultural Judaism pole, all the ORT schools and two AIU-affiliated schools (one of which is characterized by a more Cultural Judaism approach than the other) explicitly admit non-Jewish children. Other AIU schools run a case by case policy on this matter but all of them inquire into parental motivation for a Jewish education.

These various admission policies regarding the status of children raise the issue of pluralism within Jewish schools. First, admission of non-Jewish children – which is an obligation for schools under an 'associational contract' with the State – is implicitly refused by the vast majority of them out of their right to preserve their 'specific character'.[16] Likewise, pluralism may also be sought

---

16   It seems that requests from non-Jewish parents for their children to attend Jewish schools are very few, if any, given the more or less strict religious way of life required. This *de facto* selection, which differs from the openness of Catholic schools, would be held illegal, were parents to sue one of these schools. But in the absence of litigation and of any

after in respect of the variety of conceptions of Jewishness, including the legal/ religious definition of 'who is a Jew'. On this point, while it is understandable that Cultural Judaism schools do not require any rabbinical certificate of Jewishness, it is more remarkable that a recently created primary school (founded by Reform and Conservative synagogues and now affiliated with the AIU network) maintains a strongly religious orientation and yet admits children born from non-Jewish mothers as well as children born from mothers converted by a Reform or Conservative synagogue (who would not be considered as Jewish by the Orthodox and Ultra Orthodox).[17] According to one Ultra Orthodox school director, this unusual option raises more confusion among the Ultra Orthodox and Orthodox sectors which strongly hold to an unchanged *Halacha*, than the non-normative practices of the Cultural Judaism schools.[18] However, this case corresponds quite well to the growing reality of Jews who marry non-Jews who then convert to Judaism (either with an Orthodox, Conservative or Reform rabbinical court) and thus remain religiously involved.

Conclusions: Competing Schools' Networks – Facing the Two Challenges of Pluralism

Jewish Schools' Networks within a New Denominational Framework

A shift has occurred within the Jewish community over the past 40 years. Until the end of the 1960s, the vast majority was integrated within the Consistory system on the basis of a 'soft consensus' around the mainline Orthodoxy. This consensus was characterized by an openness to all Jews regardless of their effective degree of practice and belief. Ultra Orthodox circles were few and marginal (not really visible) whilst the tiny Reform current was in fact close to the Consistory sharing with it the same strong adhesion to the Republic and to its Humanistic culture. Intellectual personalities often circulated between Consistorial circles and the Reform synagogue. Since then, religious pluralization has led to a quasi-*denominational framework* though the Consistory remains the official state partner. The religious radicalization of some groups, even within the Consistory system,

---

state control on this point, the practice continues unhindered. In any case, as already said, Ultra Orthodox schools generally choose not to contract with the State and are thus not bound by an obligation of open admission anyway.

17 Named as '*Ecole Juive Moderne*', the school explicitly stresses on its 'open Judaism' and its pluralism. The case can be compared to the new Jewish school which opened its doors in London in September 2010 and is explicitly religiously pluralist. Named 'JCoSS' ('Jewish Community Secondary School'), it stresses on 'inclusion' and is self-characterized as 'unique on the "map" of faith schools in the UK'. [Online], Available at: http://www.jcoss.org/ [Accessed: 26 January 2011].

18 Personal interview (March 2010).

sparked others to create 'secular Judaism' associations to counter this trend. Hence we may speak of a shift *from (individual) diversity to (organized) pluralism.*

This shift is visible as well within the educational sector. Jewish schools remained few in number during the time Jews manifested their overt confidence in the public system. At that time, attending a Jewish school did not reflect any mistrust of the Republic or Enlightenment ideals but only a stronger attachment to Jewish identity or to traditional religious practices than shown by the average French Jew. Since the end of World War II, new religious movements (some coming from North America, the USA or Canada) began developing their schools' networks – each with its own conception of Jewish identity and the Jewish way of life. Competition between networks has intensified since the 1980s, which has led to a religious escalation and polarization, as well as an enlargement of Ultra Orthodox circles through the multiplication of their schools. This trend was accompanied by a growing mistrust toward the public system – a mistrust actually shared by parts of the French population – which generated a diversification of parents' expectations towards Jewish schools.

Jewish parents' expectations obviously include a stress on 'Jewish identity'. However, the content of this concept of 'Jewish identity' may cover several meanings and does not necessarily indicate a preference for a radical religious stance. Thus, we may speak of a partial discrepancy between parents' expectations and the options that Jewish schools offer. If religious escalation towards a more and more rigorous practice obviously represents one major trend, the development of new religiously pluralist schools alongside other schools emphasizing Cultural Judaism seems to point out to new demands.

Jewish Schools' Networks vis-à-vis Socio-Economic and Cultural Differentiations

About one-third of Jewish school-age pupils attend a private *non-Jewish* school. Parents' motivation in this case is clearly a wariness of the public system either because of its supposed decreasing quality or because of a growing climate of violence or because of a new fear of specifically anti-Jewish attacks. These various motivations are shared as well to some degree by those who choose a private Jewish school. However, in the same way that Jewish schools do not offer the same kind of Jewish content, they do not all propose the same general curriculum either.

Moreover, just as a ranking has appeared between 'good' and allegedly deficient public schools, a similar hierarchy between sought after and supposedly defective schools has also appeared among Jewish schools (and among private schools in general as well). Some of the former cultivate their good reputation by excluding feeble pupils before the final examination of the secondary school, thus obtaining high rates of success.[19] Others are known for the quality of their pedagogy and

---

19   In September 2009, a 'second chance' secondary Jewish school was created in order to gather some of these excluded pupils. These pupils may also turn to private non-religious schools where they may constitute a large majority.

teachers' team. 'School-hunting' is then ruled either by the cost of school enrolment or by the level of parental involvement in their children education. Hence, the socio-economic level of families and/or their cultural background do play a role and create subtle differentiations between schools.

A first demarcation exists between schools which favour short-term studies and are thus more interested in an instrumental approach of knowledge. This first split of the Jewish schooling framework seems to be more or less consistent with a socio-economic differentiation, based on the schooling costs or with a high priority given to the Jewish religious curriculum. A second differentiation among schools which offer long-term studies also exists between, on the one hand, those which give priority to scientific or economic fields and, on the other hand, those which are keen on the overall quality of the curriculum, including the humanities. Here one can notice a historical shift of Jewish schools, since only *one of them* offers today at secondary level an 'arts' (literature) option. Indeed, this shift corresponds to a more general trend within the French population where humanities are more and more neglected studies. Is the trend also true for the whole of the Jewish population or only for those who choose a Jewish school? My hypothesis, which has yet to be confirmed, would be that this trend exists in both sectors but may be weaker within the general Jewish population.[20]

If the development of Jewish schooling is linked to the general growth of the private sector, Jewish schools illustrate as well the socio-economic and cultural splits within the Jewish community. They also seem to accentuate the Jewish community's alienation from humanities or general culture. A tendency towards ethnic separateness thus combines with a search for socio-economic or cultural demarcation (a social '*entre-soi*').

References

Baubérot, J. 1997. *La Morale laïque contre l'ordre moral sous la Troisième République*. Paris: Seuil (2nd edition, Archives Karéline, 2009).

Cohen, M. 2011. De l'école juive ... aux écoles juives. Première approche sociologique. In *L'Etat et l'enseignement privé*, edited by B. Poucet. Rennes: Presses Universitaires de Rennes, 237–61.

Elmaleh, R. 2006. *Histoire de l'éducation juive moderne en France. L'école Lucien de Hirsch*. Paris: Biblieurope.

Enos-Attali, S. 2010. Vers une nouvelle Alliance?, in *Histoire de l'Alliance israélite universelle, de 1860 à nos jours*, edited by A. Kaspi. Paris: Armand Colin, 405–49.

---

20   It would be of interest to compare the range of subjects chosen by Jewish children attending Jewish schools with those chosen by Jewish children attending other private schools.

Fonds Social Juif Unifié. 2003. *L'école juive en France, 1945–2003. Etat des lieux*, Paris.

Fonds Social Juif Unifié. 2008. *Document interne*, 1.

Kahn-Harris, K. and Gidley, B. 2010. *Turbulent Times. The British Jewish Community Today*. London/New York: Continuum International Publishing Group.

Oberti, M. 2007. *L'Ecole dans la ville. Ségrégation – mixité – carte scolaire*. Paris: Les Presses de Sciences-Po.

Poucet, B. 2009. *La Liberté sous contrat. Une histoire de l'enseignement privé*. Paris: Fabert.

Sinclair, C. 2010. Le Système scolaire anglais: entre judéo-christianisme, laïcité et multiculturalisme, in *Pluralisme religieux et citoyenneté*, edited by M. Milot, P. Portier and J.P. Willaime. Rennes: Presses Universitaires de Rennes, 195–208.

Toulemonde, B. 2009. L'enseignement privé, in *Le Système éducatif en France*, edited by B. Toulemonde. Paris: La Documentation française, 253–64.

Chapter 3

Having Faith in Our Schools:
Struggling with Definitions of Religion

Arif A. Jamal and Farid Panjwani

As Jurgen Habermas (2006) has noted: 'A devout person pursues [his or] her daily rounds by *drawing* on belief. Put differently, true belief is not only a doctrine ... but a source of energy ... and thus nurtures his or her entire life'. What Habermas' comment illustrates is that, in their everyday lives, religious faith is simply part of the make-up and outlook of believers – of 'who they are' – experienced usually without seeking to define belief. Although the need for definition may arise from time to time in individual study, conversation with friends and colleagues or reflective moments, at most times faith is an everyday affair like breathing. As the believer engages with the symbols of his tradition in the context of his community, myriad and nuanced understandings of his tradition emerges. So long as faith is engaged in this manner, it may also be socially seamless without any conflict between the individual and society.

When, on the other hand, believers encounter situations which demand or impose formal definitions on the lived experience a great deal of 'friction' can ensue. This friction results from diverse and subjective religious convictions being narrowed and constrained by definitions of the belief that may well seem entirely alien, and indeed alienating, to the person of the tradition. This friction is not only an irritant to the individual, the community or to society at large but may also compromise the manifestation/expression of his faith and, ultimately, his freedom of religion. In this chapter, we look at two situations within the area of education in which objective definitions of religious traditions are either sought or required. First, we examine a series of cases – beginning with the Jewish Free School ('*JFS*') case in the UK – in which courts have struggled with religious definitions. These examinations will illustrate that when courts are asked to consider religious definitions (concerning admissions policies, school attire or in other circumstances) there emerges a fundamental, and perhaps irreconcilable, tension between freedom of religion or religious expression, on the one hand, and the need for adjudication about religion or religious expression on the other. We note the tension that comes from trying to define religious beliefs for the purposes of adjudication, as well as the undesirable social implications that arise when courts become the arbiters of religious definitions. We explain these concerns in legal as well as in broader sociological terms, drawing upon the analysis of religion studies scholarship.

Second, we consider the issue of religious definitions in the context of the religious education of Muslims. We examine a particular result of the interaction between religion and education in the context of the modern State in countries of Muslim majority and of Muslims in the West. It will be noted that through a variety of ways, these interactions have led to the objectification of religious traditions in all of these environments. In both situations – the legal and the educational – therefore, we show that the process of defining a religious tradition against objective criteria violates both the subjectivity of the experience which should underpin the right of freedom of religion (and its cognate freedom of religious expression) and also fails to understand that religious traditions cannot be essentialized without being misrepresented.

Religious Definition and Case Law

The JFS Case

There are some cases that courts do not wish to decide and others in which they are not well placed to do so. In *Wisconsin v. Yoder*,[1] the United States Supreme Court declared, on the one hand, that 'religious freedom – the freedom to believe and to practice strange and, it may be, foreign creeds – has classically been of the highest values of our society' (*Braunfield v. Braun*, 366 US 599, 612 (1961) *per* Brennan J, concurring and dissenting). On the other hand, the Court stated that '[t]oday, education is perhaps the most important function of state and local governments' (*Brown v. Board of Education*, 347 US 483, 493 (1954)). Inevitably, these values and interests sometimes conflict. When they do, as the Court noted, they can '… involve the kind of close and perhaps repeated scrutiny of religious practices … which the Court has heretofore been anxious to avoid'.[2]

When the UK Supreme Court encountered the *JFS* case,[3] it faced a similar situation. Lord Phillips remarked: 'While the court has appreciated the high standard of the advocacy addressed to it, it has not welcomed being required to resolve this dispute'.[4] The Court acknowledged that it was a case that it did not wish to decide but may not, however, have fully recognized why this was also as much a case that it was ill-equipped to decide. To get to an understanding of why this is the situation we can begin by elaborating the challenge that the *JFS* case raised and then proceeding to consider, briefly, aspects of other cases which reinforce this challenge. By the time that the *JFS* case made it to the Supreme Court, the issue that had originally prompted the case – namely the denial of admission of a child,

---

1   406 US 205 (1972).

2   Per White J, concurring.

3   *R (on the application of E) (Respondent) v. Governing Body of JFS and others (Appellants)* [2009] UKSC 15; [2010] 2 WLR.

4   Ibidem, para. 8.

M, to the *JFS* school because he was not recognized as Jewish by the standards of the Office of the Chief Rabbi ('OCR') – had been substantively settled between the parties and the remaining question that confronted the court was whether the school policy constituted racial discrimination under section 1 of the *Race Relations Act 1976* (the 'RRA'). Ultimately, the Court decided, in a split decision, that the policy did violate the RRA. We do not discuss here their assessment of the policy in light of the RRA. Rather, we look at how they encountered and assessed the criteria of 'Jewishness' which were raised.

Lord Phillips began his judgment with the seventh chapter of Deuteronomy and stated that '[i]t is a fundamental tenet of the Jewish religion, derived from the third and fourth verses [of Deuteronomy], that the child of a Jewish mother is automatically and inalienably Jewish' and that this is the 'matrilineal test'.[5] The certainty and seeming clarity of this test, however, breaks down in the case of M whose mother had converted to Judaism in a manner that was not in accordance with the requirements of Orthodox Jews, and thus acceptable to the OCR, even though the conversion *was* recognized by Masorti, Reform and Progressive Jews.[6] To reiterate, the question considered by the Court in *JFS* was not about the different orientations of Judaism but rather whether the criteria used, based on the OCR definition of who is a Jew, violated the RRA. However, in discussing the differing interpretations and traditions within Judaism, the Court ventured into the territory of religious definitions. In his judgment, Lord Mance noted that M was recognized as a Jew by Reform and Masorti synagogues but he also remarked parenthetically that the Court was told that before the late eighteenth century these sorts of distinctions in Judaism did not even exist.[7] These factors are a significant context for the *JFS* case as Lord Hope, who wrote the lead minority judgment, pointed out:

> It is accepted by all sides in this case that it is entirely a matter for the Chief Rabbi to adjudicate the principles of Orthodox Judaism. But the sphere within which those principles are being applied is that of an educational establishment whose activities are regulated by the law that the civil courts must administer. Underlying the case is a fundamental difference of opinion among members of the Jewish community about the propriety of the criteria that the [OCR] applies to determine whether a person is or is not Jewish.[8]

And it is here that the challenge arises: it did not arise directly in *JFS* because the court did not have to discuss the appropriateness of the OCR's Jewishness criteria; only to assess the admissions policy against the Act. However, in other cases courts have gone further.

---

5   Ibidem, para. 2.
6   Ibidem, para. 6.
7   Ibidem, para. 74.
8   Ibidem, para. 160.

The Shabina Begum Case

In the well-known *Shabina Begum*[9] case, at the Court of Appeal, Brooke LJ observed: 'Very strong religious beliefs [were] close to the centre of this dispute'.[10] In this case, the courts (Administrative, Court of Appeal and then House of Lords) had to assess whether the school's uniform policy which permitted some forms of dress common to Muslim students but not others violated Miss Begum's rights under Article 9 of the European Convention on Human Rights 1950 ('ECHR'). The courts split on the substantive issue: the Administrative Court did not find any violation of Miss Begum's Article 9 rights but the Court of Appeal did. The House of Lords reversed the Appeal Court's decision and reinstated the overall conclusion of the Administrative Court though, in their different speeches, the law lords expressed varying degrees of sympathy with the opinions expressed in the Court of Appeal. What is most interesting for our purposes, however, is the analyses by the courts of the nature of the religious beliefs that Miss Begum was asserting.

In formulating their judgments, the courts reviewed opinions about the types of dress that were appropriate for Muslim girls and women. Unsurprisingly, there was a range of diametrically opposed and mutually excluding opinions but the courts emphasized that the critical issue was not what others thought was appropriate or required as part of their religious beliefs or expression but rather what Miss Begum herself felt. For example, the Court of Appeal considered the judgment of the European Court of Human Rights ('ECtHR') in *Chaus v Bulgaria*,[11] where the European Court recalled that, 'but for very exceptional cases, the right to freedom of religion as guaranteed under the Convention [the ECHR] excludes any discretion on the part of the State to determine whether religious beliefs or the means used to express such beliefs are legitimate'.[12] This was cited approvingly by Scott Baker LJ, who went on to say:

> The fact that this [Shabina Begum's] view is held by a minority, or even a small minority, is in my judgment nothing to the point in considering the issue of whether Article 9(1) is engaged. There is in my view force in the criticism that it is not for school authorities to pick and choose between religious beliefs or shades of religious beliefs.[13]

---

9   *R (on the application of Begum) v. Headteacher and Governors of Denbigh High School*, [2005] EWCA Civ 199, [2005] 1 WLR 3372.

10   At para. 8.

11   ECtHR 26 October 2000, Application no. 30985/96. (This SHOULD reference the Court – ECtHR)

12   Ibidem, para.78.

13   Ibidem, para. 93.

This sentiment was echoed when the case was appealed to the House of Lords, with Lord Bingham saying:

> It is common ground in these proceedings that at all material times the respondent sincerely held the religious belief which she professed to hold. It was no less a religious belief because her belief may have changed, as it probably did, or because it was a belief shared by a minority of people. Thus it is accepted, obviously rightly, that article 9(1) is engaged or applicable.[14]

Of course, all of this makes the point that religious beliefs depend on the conscience and interpretations of the parties, and in this sense are subject-dependent. Indeed, this has been acknowledged by courts themselves in other cases. As Lord Nicholls said in *R (on the application of Williamson) v. Secretary of State for Education and Employment*:[15]

> It is not for the court to embark on an inquiry into the asserted belief or judge its 'validity' by some *objective standard* such as the source material upon which the claimant founds his belief or the orthodox teaching of the religion in question or the extent to which the claimant's belief conforms to or differs from the views of others professing the same religion. Freedom of religion protects the *subjective belief* of an individual.

Recognizing this, courts must also recognize that they are ill-equipped to have to settle issues about religious definitions. Was the school's dress policy sufficiently accommodating of Muslim senses of clothing propriety? Was the definition of Jewishness in accordance with Jewish tradition? Courts cannot answer these questions well for two reasons. The first is that they cannot assess these matters against any objective standard. Although the courts try to avoid making these assessments they cannot but acknowledge that such issues form the context and, to some extent, the substance of the cases. Courts are thus put in the rather impossible situation of having to assess the subjective right of freedom of religion (and, in the case of the ECHR and analogous statutes, freedom of religious expression) in an objective way. It is difficult, if not impossible, to see how they can square this circle, recognizing as they also do that they are not supposed to make 'religious' judgements. One judicial approach that commends itself, however, was the position taken by the Supreme Court of Canada in *Syndicat Northcrest v. Anselem*[16] in which the majority held that a religious practice should be tolerated when the individual sincerely believed it to be connected to their religion – even if it was not required by the relevant religious authority, *The Beximco Case*.

---

14   [2006] UKHL 15, para. 21. See also Lord Hoffman's speech at para 50.
15   [2005] UKHL 15; [2005] 2 A.C. 246, para. 22 [emphasis added].
16   [2004] 2 S.C.R. 551.

The second, and related, reason why courts are ill equipped to deal with religious definitions is more sociological – though it too has arisen in case law. In the case of *Beximco Pharmeceuticals Ltd v. Shamil Bank of Bahrain E.C.*, the English Court of Appeal had to interpret a contract that was '[s]ubject to the principles of the Glorious Shari'a'.[17] After hearing expert evidence, the Court concluded:

> Finally, so far as the 'principles of ... Sharia' are concerned, it was the evidence of both experts that there are indeed areas of considerable controversy and difficulty arising not only from the need to translate into propositions of modern law texts which centuries ago were set out as religious and moral codes, but because of the existence of a variety of schools of thought with which the court may have to concern itself in any given case before reaching a conclusion upon the principle or rule in dispute ...[18]

In other words, the Court acknowledged that even in a context outside of an individual right and that is subjectively understood, like the situation of a commercial contract in *Beximco*, it is ill equipped to sift through the variety of opinions, schools and interpretations that exist in any religious tradition. This understanding is reinforced by scholarship coming from religious studies, as the scholar and expert on Islam Carl Ernst (2003) asserts:

> Although it is common to hear people say, for example, 'Christianity says that ...' or 'according to Islam ...' the only thing that can be observed is that individual people who call themselves Christians or Muslims have particular positions and practices that they observe and defend. No one, however, has ever seen Christianity or Islam do anything. They are abstractions, not actors comparable to human beings (in the same spirit see also Panjwani 2004).

Ernst's observation makes the sociological point that any search for an objective identity of a religious tradition is a misguided exercise from the outset. Moreover, if we do have to focus on what the human beings within religious traditions do or say we are led, as the Court of Appeal was in *Beximco*, to one inevitable conclusion: they do not all do the same thing or say the same thing even if and when they do so from the same tradition. In short, there is *intra*-tradition variation and interpretational diversity at any one place and any one time but even more so over time and over place. We are led, therefore, to a subject-orientated understanding of what religious traditions mean.

---

17   [2004] EWCA Civ 19 at para. 1.
18   At para. 55.

Further Implications

Efforts, whether voluntary or not, to define religious traditions in objective terms run the risk of generating two other socially problematic results. First, and related to the above, they suggest static conceptions of religions (Brettschneider 2010). We have just made the point that religious traditions cannot be viewed as static, even if a snapshot is taken of one tradition at one time. For example, on 30 November 2004 *The Guardian* newspaper reported the results of a survey of British Muslims conducted by ICM.[19] At the same time, it relayed the outcomes of roundtable discussions – 8 tables, 8 subjects, 103 young Muslims – that were arranged as part of news story. These roundtables evidenced the great range of views from young British Muslims. For example, the article reports the following discussion from Table 5 on 'How the faithful live in a secular society' (No Author 2004):

> When Asif Dawood, a member of Hizb ut-Tahrir, declared that Islam and democracy were incompatible, there was an uproar at the table, with Mr Yousafazi [a member of Young Citizens in the West Midlands] rejecting the idea outright and insisting that the principles of democracy came out of Islam.There was an assumption, added Sohaib Saeed Bhutta from the Muslim Association of Britain, that there was such a thing as British Islam, when there were differences 'within even Glaswegian Islam'.

This diversity of opinion illustrates the difficulty of articulating any credible, objective definition of a religious tradition. In addition to this problem, however, efforts at objective definitions raise the greater difficulty of doing harm to the ability of adherents of religious traditions to maintain their inherent diversity, especially in public discourses. This is especially so for minority traditions and those which do not have church-like corporate bodies that might express 'official' positions. Thus, while it may be possible to seek objective definitions (though almost certainly not definitions shared by all) of, say, Catholic doctrine by reference to the teachings of the Catholic Church and to talk about objective definitions of Anglican or Methodist doctrine due to the church structures within these communities, this does not work well in other traditions. There is, for example, no equivalent body to the Catholic Church for all Muslims or for all Sunni or Shia Muslims even though within certain sub-communities there are types of hierarchical authorities. However, even such authorities are not always fully comprehensive or unchallengeable. As the *JFS* case demonstrated, there is also no one Jewish body even though here too there are certain hierarchies within the subgroupings. We can recall that while the parties in *JFS* accepted that definition of a Jew as determined by the OCR was the standard to be used for the case, it was acknowledged in the Court's own words that this was only one understanding of Judaism. If one considers other religious traditions, for example Hinduism and

---

19 [Online] available at http://www.icmresearch.co.uk/ [Accessed: 1 April 2011].

Buddhism, which have more plural and diffuse varieties of religious authority, or Sikhism which again has more diffuse and often more locally centred authorities, then determinations of what religious traditions might mean objectively becomes not only restrictive invidious but as Susanna Mancini (2010) has noted:

> ... [J]ust as in the *JFS* decision, non Christian minorities are offered the choice between preserving their diversity by keeping it strictly within the private sphere, or accessing the public sphere under the condition of assimilating to a significant degree into the majority religious culture ... This trend, which is spreading across Europe, has a strong destructive potential, because by applying a concept of equality that implies homogenization of behaviours and values, it ends up restricting the room for diversity that is necessary for a genuinely pluralistic society.

Due to the importance of the right to freedom of religion on the one hand and the State's interest in education on the other, issues of religion and education (especially in an environment like the UK, which allows for faith based schools) can and do end up in the courts. When they do, courts are put in an unenviable situation. Their first hope is to avoid having directly to adjudicate about religious definitions and they are sometimes able to do this. Even when they do, however, they acknowledge that the issues of religious definitions are part of the context of their decisions. When courts cannot avoid dealing with religious definitions, however, they must encounter the fact that they are very ill-equipped to make such determinations for two reasons: (1) legally, because rights to freedom of religion are subjectively defined and based, ultimately, on individual perception and conviction, without there being any sort of objective metric that the courts could use to assess religious definition; and (2) sociologically, because there is no way to interrogate a religious tradition as to its terms, meanings or definitions since religious traditions can only speak through individual adherents who do not express a single view concerning their religious traditions. What is being suggested, therefore, is that courts must always recognize that participation and understanding of a religious tradition is *subjective* and that any rights that might flow from adherence to a religious tradition should be interpreted with this subjective context in mind. There will, of course, be times when courts will have to make assessments about the terms or tenets of religion to address practices that impinge upon the right of others or which may be offensive to public policy. When such judgements do have to be made, however, the criteria for restricting religious expressions would better be set against relevant societal concerns, rather than as being outside of some objective definition of what the religious tradition requires. In addition to the above, however, religion and education also meet in schools where the lived context of religion gets transformed into curricular form as a school subject. Here, one encounters the problem of defining religious traditions.

Educational Curricula and the Objectification of Religious Traditions

Religion and education have a long history together. Religion needs education to pass its teachings to the next generation. And, until modern times, much of the education was around religion and provided by religious institutions. In England, for example, the State started to set up schools only from 1870 onwards, after the famous *Forster's Act* (Cruickshank 1963).

In the history of Muslims, from a very early time, institutions emerged that helped pass on religious texts and doctrines to the new generations. The *maktab*, *madrasa* and *hawza* are among the main examples of such institutions.[20] From the nineteenth century onward these long-standing but already largely declining educational institutions faced new epistemological and organizational challenges. One of the embodiments of these challenges was the modern education system that came to be transplanted across the Muslim societies in the nineteenth and twentieth centuries. While many governments became interested in modern education for its military and economic potential for the State, a few people, among them Sayyid Ahmad Khan (1817–1898), a South Asian reformer, saw the philosophical challenge underpinning the new education (Troll 1978):

> My friends! You know well that in our time a new wisdom and philosophy have spread. Their tenets are entirely different from those of the former wisdom and philosophy [of the Greeks]. They are as much in disagreement with the tenets of ordinary present day Islam as the tenets of Greek wisdom and philosophy were with the tenets of customary Islam during their times … Today doctrines are established by natural experiments and they are demonstrated before our eyes. These are not problems of the kind that could be solved by analogical arguments or which can be contested by assertions and principles that the learned classes of former times have established. Take for instance the question of piercing of the roof of heaven (*kharq*) and the closing of [the doors of] heaven (*iltiyam*), which is a very big issue in the sciences of our tradition and which has lived on in our learning and teaching. … But of what use is this doctrine now and what utility is there in studying and teaching it, since it has been established that the way in which former philosophers and ulema decided upon the existence of heaven is wrong? What is needed now is to reflect upon what 'heaven' means, and for this it is necessary to work out new principles and tenets instead of calling to memory the worn out and obsolete doctrines.

---

20   Though often used today in the sense of school, in historical terms, a *madrasa* is an educational institution offering instruction in Islamic subjects including, but not limited to, the Qur'an, the sayings (Hadith) of Prophet Muhammad, jurisprudence, theology and law. Historically, *madrasas* were distinguished as institutions of higher studies and existed in contrast to more rudimentary ones called *kuttab* (sing. *maktab*) that taught mainly the Qur'an, and in some cases, reading and writing.

This philosophical challenge remains unanswered; in fact hardly even engaged with. Rather, the main response from Muslim societies has been to create a juxtaposition of the new and the old, of the traditional and the modern schools/universities. Turkey under Kemal Ataturk was the main exception where the kuttab-madrasa system was abolished (Agai 2007).[21]

In the South Asian context, for example, this educational duality was reflected in Aligarh's Muhammadan Anglo-Oriental College founded by Sayyid Ahmed Khan and the Deoband's *Dar-ul 'Uloom* established by Mohammad Qasim Nanotwi (Kukucan 1994, Metcalf 1978). These two institutions became early symbols for a dual system of education in the Indian Muslim context, divided along what came to be known as the secular and religious lines. Similar dual systems evolved in most Muslim societies during the late nineteenth and early twentieth centuries (Charfi 2005, Hefner 2007, Tibawi 1972). In the immediate post-colonial era, as Muslim countries embarked on modernization, although the dual system remained entrenched material success and political power came to be associated increasingly with the modern system which consequently became predominant (Cook 1999, Tibawi 1972). The traditional religious system, however, retained its moral relevance and continued to flourish. Institutions such as al-Azhar in Egypt, Zaytunia in Tunisia and Deoband in India retained their religious authority with various negotiated arrangements with the State. Thousands of *kuttab* and *madrasas* across the Muslim world continued to provide religious education (Hefner and Zaman 2007). The dual system has been a cause for lament amongst many Muslims. A major conference on education in Muslim societies held in Makkah in 1977, for example, found it to be one of the major causes of the 'crisis of education' (Husain and Ashraf 1979):

> There are at present two systems of education. The first, traditional, which has confined itself to classical knowledge, has not shown any keen interest in new branches of knowledge that have emerged in the West or in new methods of acquiring knowledge important in the Western system of education ... The second system of education imported into Muslim countries, fully subscribed to and supported by all governmental authorities, is one borrowed from the West. At the head of this system is the modern University, which is totally secular and hence non religious in its approach to knowledge. Unfortunately, these people educated by this new system of education, known as modern education, are generally unaware of their own tradition and classical heritage.

The two systems may differ on many grounds but they also share a deep commonality. Both reflect a major cause and an outcome of the way religion

---

21   Even in Turkey the dual system operated until Ataturk's time and was in fact never completely abolished – a few madrasas were allowed to continue under strict government control and new form of religious training institutions were established soon thereafter (Agai 2007).

and education has interacted in modern Muslim context: the *objectification of the religious tradition*. This is perhaps easier to see with regard to the place of religious education in modern school system where it is one subject amongst others. Dennis Lawton (1975) famously wrote that a curriculum is a selection from culture. While this is so, a curriculum is also the transformation of experiences into abstract and measurable fragments of learning. Like a procrustean bed, a school curriculum demands that the religious life of a community must take the shape of propositions which can then be passed on as a subject-matter. Moreover, it must fit the prescribed hours of teaching, it must be examinable, it must have some order and sequence and it must be teachable by classroom instruction methods. Further, being juxtaposed with other subjects such as history and science, the 'enchanted' history and beliefs of religion get scrutinized and interpreted by the standards of 'disenchanted' historical and empirical methods. Thus, making Islam a school subject is to make it an object, alongside the objects of study in science and history and other subjects, which must be 'explained' and 'understood' (Eickelman 1992).

Further, the transformation of religion into a modern school subject takes place within the broader framework of the modern State. In Muslim contexts this was often, particularly in the immediate post-colonial period, the State which proclaimed secular orientation and thus viewed religion from a particular angle. The education systems in which Islam became a subject of study were deeply shaped by the policies and ideologies of the respective States. As Starrett (1998) puts it, with reference to Egypt: 'the expansion and transfer of religious socialization from private to newly created public sector institutions over the last century has led to a comprehensive revision of the way Egyptians treat Islam as a religious tradition'. The State was 'putting Islam to work' to help it achieve its goals of a variety of kinds. The observation holds for many other parts of the Muslim world as well.

The objectification of religion is also observable in the case of *madrasas*, which also went through a transformation and were increasingly administered along modern, bureaucratic lines. The Deoband Madrasa in South Asia was arguably the first attempt within the *madrasa* setting to impart religious teachings along the organizational lines of modern educational practice. The founders sought to emulate the British bureaucratic style for educational institutions: a sequential curriculum with a fixed course of studies, an examination system, student records and annual reports. None of these features are to be found in traditional *madrasas*. Over time such 'reforms' were carried out in many countries and today most *madrasas* work along these lines, such that whereas their curriculum may be traditional, their management is thoroughly modern (Dinar 2004). Thus, the history of the reforms of *madrasas* in different parts of the Muslim world is essentially a history of their bureaucratic re-organization in line with the demands of modern state and society. As Hefner and Zaman (2007) note: 'Whatever its root in Islamic tradition, then, the *madrasa* is now thoroughly embedded in the modern world.'

A further point needs to be made. The *madrasa* of Deoband was established under a colonial regime at a time when Islam was no longer the state religion in South Asia with the ruler responsible for the preservation of the *Shari'a*. Accordingly, Deoband and other *madrasas* were seeking to preserve Islamic tradition as they understood it in the absence of state support. They were seeking – and still continue to seek – to create a body of religious leaders able to serve the daily legal and spiritual needs of their fellow Muslims apart from government ties. Effectively, this is a process of the privatization of religion. Another way to see this is that in the face of the declining Muslim political presence, *madrasas* and mosques became concrete evidence of Muslim cultural presence.

Thus, despite their apparent differences, the two institutional arrangements for religious education – the modern school and the reformed *madrasa* – contributed to what Asad (1993) has called 'the construction of religion as a new historical object' The traditions of Muslims were to pass on from one generation to another as much, if not more, through structured educational experience as through the processes of upbringing in families, mosques and neighbourhood; they were to be taught as well as caught.[22]

When Muslims moved to the West in large numbers in 1950s and 1960s, they brought with them this new relationship between religion and education. However, the taught aspect was to gain an even greater importance in the West for the reasons below. Though shaped by modern forces, the cultures whence Muslims had come retained their Islamic character in public symbols, in communal *adab* (broadly, social ethics and etiquette), in salutations, architecture and many other forms. The modern school system within Muslim contexts also operated in this larger framework. Religion was not far from discussions in science, literature or social studies classrooms. It was also present in the school assemblies and reflected in dress code, dietary customs and so on. Even a non-Muslim in such a place would absorb the culture of 'Islam', without necessarily accepting its theological commitments. This larger cultural context was absent in the West. Instead of Islamic symbols there was, for the most part, a mixture of secular and Christian symbols in society generally which was mirrored in the school system. Thus those among Muslims who were concerned to pass on their religious tradition had to engage in more conscious and systematic efforts.

One avenue to make for such efforts was in family life. However, here there were limits imposed by the economic conditions of many migrants. They worked long hours and spending time at home and with children was often a struggle. In such cases, the economic necessity limited the role of the family as a vehicle for transmission of the religious heritage. In these circumstances, some Muslims came to see schools as the place where Islamic religious traditions could be passed on to the new generation. How this crystallized into the idea that Muslims ought to have their own schools if they wanted to preserve their religious tradition – or at least how the process is remembered – is captured in this quote from a interview

---

22   There are also private modern schools in most Muslim countries. However, the curriculum of religious education in such schools is often either determined by the State or is in line with the state curriculum.

conducted in Leicester in 2008 with Dr Mukadam, Chairman of the Association of Muslim Schools:

> Among the Muslim communities in Britain there are those who consider themselves as practising Muslims, who value their faith and regard the transference of faith and values as their religious duty, first and foremost. They regard this as a duty that comes from authorities – the Qur'an and Sunna – which ask us to safeguard our children from the fire of hell. And the most important element to safeguard in children is *iman* [faith] and *akhlaq* [morals]. Now how do you preserve that Iman, transfer those values that you have inherited from your parents – they asked these questions. They asked them in 1970s when families joined the already existing mostly male community. Can we do it through state schools? Can we do it privately? Some of the 'ulema' and the educationist said let's look around what normal comprehensives were doing. These people realised that Christians have their own faith schools, and the Jews have their own schools. Why are they having them? What were the reasons? There must be reasons. This led to the exploration of the aims and objectives. It dawned upon Muslims that the reason Jews and Christians have their own schools separate from normal comprehensive is primarily that they want to preserve and transfer their faith and values. So you see there is no difference between these aims and the aims of Muslims. Muslims felt that there is a big danger here if our children would go to their schools which are secular and where there is no religious environment. Our children must be saved from such an environment. Then first schools began to emerge.

The reference here is to schools which are commonly called Muslim or Islamic school or, more officially, schools with Islamic religious character.[23] Today, there are more than 140 such schools, 11 of which are publicly funded.[24] The main underlying educational objective of Muslim schools, as gleaned from the schools' websites and promotional literature, is to produce good Muslims and to make Islam a central force in the belief, thoughts and practices of the new generation.[25]

---

23   Some people make a distinction between an 'Islamic' and a 'Muslim' school. They claim that a Muslim school is a matter of demography and governance. Any school with majority Muslim children or run by Muslims can be called a Muslim school. An Islamic school, according to them, is a school which is run along the lines of Islamic education and principles of religion. The distinction does not concern us here.

24   DfES. [Online], available at: http://www.education.gov.uk/schools/leadership/typesofschools/b0066996/faith-schools [Accessed: 20 February 2011].

25   It is important to note that the demand for Muslim schools is by no means universal among Muslims. A vast majority of Muslim children in the UK, as many as 95 per cent by some estimates, go to state or Christian denominational schools. Some of this majority may move to Muslim schools if there were a greater supply of them but it is unlikely that this will shift the balance too much. There are many sections of Muslim community which actively oppose the establishment of Islamic schools.

A Muslim school operates in a geographical and sociological space in which Muslims from a variety of backgrounds, doctrinal orientations and theological persuasions reside. One may consider the case of Britain, which arguably has one of the most diverse Muslim populations in the world that reflects not just national cultural diversity but also doctrinal and theological diversity. The catchment area of a Muslim school is likely to have Muslims of many persuasions, indeed it almost always does. Understandings of what the fundamentals of Islam are and hence what it means to be a 'good Muslim' will inevitably vary amongst these Muslims. Thus, when an educational institution in Britain aims to produce good Muslims and make Islam a central force in the lives of its pupils, it cannot avoid answering the questions – even if it does not consciously ask them – about whose understanding of Islam will be taught and what definition of good Muslim will be adopted? Curriculum, after all, demands selection.[26]

A school can take the position that it will provide space for a plurality of ways in which Islam is understood, thereby accommodating various doctrinal persuasions from which its students come. But several factors militate against this possibility. The first is the absence of a theology accommodating intra-religious diversity. Though the doctrinal diversity within Muslims is nothing new, it has been the hardest matter for Muslims to come to terms with. Historically, beyond linguistic formula such as the *Shahada* (creedal declaration of basic tenets), reverence for the Prophet Muhammad and the Quranic text (albeit with different interpretations of the text and of the Prophet's legacy) and belief in the ideas such as the hereafter, there is almost nothing that can be considered as uncontested and uniform amongst Muslims. Much has been written about this diversity and so elaboration is not needed here. Suffice to say that whether we take metaphysical notions such as *nabuwah* (prophecy), *qiyama* (the day of resurrection) or socio-economic ideas such as *riba* (usury) or the very status of the Quran, there are many Muslim interpretations but no Islamic consensus. And yet, these interpretations have often existed side by side, more or less non-violently, though sometimes in tension with each other. Most *madrasas* across the Muslim world, for instance, teach Islam from particular orientations. In most cases, as noted above, even States have specific theological orientations which in turn shape their legal and educational approaches.

Related to this is the practical pedagogical limitation. It is very difficult to find teachers, or educational materials, capable of creating an educational experience which reflects the internal diversity among Muslims. The close proximity in which various doctrinal and theological orientations find themselves is an educationally novel development.

---

26 Obviously, the question of whose understanding of Islam the educational system will pass on is raised in majority Muslim counties as well. However, in most cases there the issue acquires a legal character because the States often have an official religious orientation which settles the issue for the educational system. Iran has the *Twelver Shi'i* orientation while Saudi Arabia has a *Hanbali* orientation, for example.

Given the above, it is perhaps not surprising that in almost all cases, Muslim schools have come to define Islam and Muslims along traditional sectarian lines. Officially, schools are open to children of all theological persuasions within Islam, but in practice most schools operate along Shi'a or Sunni lines, predominantly the latter; and within that schools may follow *Deobandi, Jama'at-e-Islami* or other orientations.[27] Muslim schools undoubtedly have rich diversity of pupils but it is reflected in ethnic, national and linguistic diversity, and not theological or doctrinal diversity. Whether it is in terms of student population, teacher profile, representation of history, doctrines or concepts, there are hardly any Muslim schools in Britain that reflect intra-religious Muslim diversity.

Interviews conducted by one of the authors (Panjwani) with school officials, found that when asked about the religious composition of pupils, a frequent answer given was that there used to be both Shi'a and Sunni students but at present there were only the former or the latter (depending on the school). It is possible that initially schools may have received pupils from various doctrinal persuasions, but given the schools' focus on one particular orientation, pupils from other orientations may therefore have left. The same can be noted in the portrayal of events, concepts and interpretations in Muslim history which too are mostly based on a singular rather than multiple perspectives. An example is the presentation of emergence of post Prophetic authority in Muslim history. The question of who ought to have inherited the leadership of the nascent community of Muslims after the Prophet's passing is a fateful question in Muslim history and the answers to this question undergird the key divisions in Islam between the Shi'a and Sunni traditions. None of the schools surveyed in the author-conducted interviews mentioned above teach their students the importance of this question and the various points of views that have emerged around it. Each school teaches only the way its own particular theological orientation interprets the issue of the succession to the Prophet.[28]

---

27 *Deobandi, Jam'at-e-Islami* and Barelvis are among the various orientations that emerged in the South Asian context as Muslims came to define themselves in the process of engaging with the changing circumstances of the last two hundred years or so. The Deobandis take their name from the seminary established in 1867. It has a reformist goal and stresses inner spiritual life through adherence to scripturalist practices as against the folk traditions, such as the practices around saints' shrines. The Barelvis consider folk practices and local expressions of Islam – sometimes called popular Islam – very important. Founded in the late nineteenth century this movement is rooted in South Asian sufi traditions. Jama'at-e-Islami was founded in 1940s by Mawdudi. It seeks socio-political change in Muslim societies along the lines of its interpretation of Islamic teachings covering all aspects of modern life. For details of these and other movements, see Jones 1989.

28 Although the focus of this paper has been schools with Islamic religious character, the monolithic representation of Muslim religious tradition is equally an issue in the so called secular schools. For secular schools, the religious education syllabus (called Agreed Syllabus), which includes Islamic religious education, is developed at the local education authority level in consultation with a Standing Advisory Council for Religious

These brief observations about the interaction between education and religion in a formal school settings show that whether in the modern educational systems of Muslim majority countries or the reformed institutionalized system of *madrasas* or in the Muslims schools in the West, the objectification of religious tradition is part and parcel of the patterning of a religious tradition into a deliverable school subject and an examinable learning experience. The process reflects a selection, a reformulation and a negotiation. It is a selection from 1,400 years of Muslim religious history with immense doctrinal, ritual, literary and artistic variety. It is a reformulation of an experience into teachable and examinable propositions. It is a negotiation between the State and believers and among believers of various persuasions. Finally, at present there is a growing demand for an Islamic perspective on a variety of aspects from economics and science to bioethics and fashion. To what extent, is this trend a result of the objectified understanding of religion, distributed by various educational systems, within which the new generations of Muslims have grown up? Once a religious tradition has been reified, it is a small step to attach this reified object to other objects such as science or economics. It does not seem unreasonable to posit that when children learn religion in the same way as they learn science and economics many of them eventually come to expect scientific and economic guidance from religion. Education, in this case, seems to have created a new form of understanding of religion.

The elites – at the level of State, *madrasa* and among the Muslims in the West – may have aimed to systematize and control the understandings of religion. The outcome of these efforts seems to be an understanding that sees the religion of their parents as perversion, conflating and confusing culture with religion. Instead, many in the new generation seek a religion that works like a system, provides propositions to follow and can claim to solve problems of modernity. As Starrett (1998) observed, the objectification of religion through education has created a need 'for religious information, the tendency to look toward religion for certain things, the creation of certain compartments in a conceptual order that can only be filled by something, regardless of its specific content, labelled "Islamic"'.

Conclusion

We have looked at two types of definitional processes. First, we considered selected legal cases where the issue of religious definitions has been salient. Second, we have examined the process of establishing curricula for educating about Islam in state and traditional schools in countries of Muslim majority as well as in Muslim

---

Education (SACRE). Under the 1988 legislation, each local education authority is required to establish a SACRE which is a mechanism to take into account the religious views of the local population. A survey of the resulting Agreed Syllabuses and the textbooks that followed shows that the process of the objectification of religious tradition is equally at play here (Ipgrave 1998, Panjwani 2005).

schools in the West. In both situations, we see that, for different reasons, there develops a strong, institutional need to define religious tradition in objective terms notwithstanding the recognition in both contexts that any religious tradition in general, and certainly Islam, inevitably has a great deal of interpretational variation and diversity. One is accordingly left with a highly problematic incongruence between institutional pressure for singularity and objectification on the one hand and the existence of subjectivity and plurality on the other.

We note the serious consequences this incongruity has not only for the representation of religious traditions, and for those within the traditions who may be isolated from the diversity of their own religious heritages but also for our legal determinations and our educational policies. As we have suggested, it would be wrong for courts to premise legal rights to freedom of religion or religious expression on objective understanding of religious traditions. Similarly, it would be wrong to develop educational curricula – or establish any school – about any religious tradition in general based upon a constrained narrative of the intra-tradition diversity. Thus, we call for an embrace of the subjectivity of religious experience, belief and understanding. This does not make the task of courts or schools any easier; quite the contrary. It may, however, make their work more true to what they seek to understand and to teach. As an alternative, a subjectively defined approach such as that suggested by Lord Nicholls and employed by the Supreme Court of Canada in the *Syndicat Northcrest* case, applied within the constitutional limits of a liberal State, commends itself. Similarly, in the educational context, it seems imperative that schools provide pupils with an introduction to a wider range of interpretations and theological positions within any religious tradition in order to reflect more authentically the historical and contemporary circumstances of religious traditions.

References

Agai, B. 2007. Islam and education in secular Turkey: state policies and the emergence of the Fethullah Gulen group, in *Schooling Islam: The Culture and Politics of Modern Muslim Education*, edited by R.W. Hefner et al. Princeton: Princeton University Press, 149–71.

Asad, T. 1993. *Genealogies of Religion: Discipline and Reasons of Power in Christianity and Islam*. Baltimore and London: Johns Hopkins University Press.

Brettschneider, C. 2010. A transformative theory of religious freedom: promoting the reasons for rights. *Political Theory* 38(2), 187–213.

Charfi, M. 2005. *Islam and Liberty: The Historical Misunderstanding* (trans. P. Camiller). London: Zed Books.

Cook, B. 1999. Islamic versus Western conceptions of education: reflections on Egypt. *International Review of Education / Internationale Zeitschrift für Erziehungswissenschaft / Revue internationale de l'éducation* 45(3–4), 339–58.

Cruickshank, M. 1963. *Church and State in English Education*. London: McMillan & Co.

Dinar, A. 2004. *Social Role and implications of Madrasa Education: A Study of Deeni Madaris in Karachi, 1947–2004*. Unpublished PhD Thesis, Faculty of Social Sciences and Humanities, Hamdard University, Karachi.

Eickelman, D. 1992. Mass higher education and the religious imagination in contemporary Arab societies. *American Ethnologist* 19(4), 643–55.

Ernst, C.W. 2003. *Following Muhammad: Rethinking Islam in the Contemporary World*. Chapel Hill: UNC Chapel Hill Press.

The Guardian. 2004. Young, Muslim and British, 30 November, 17–20.

Habermas, J. 2006. Religion in the public sphere. *European Journal of Philosophy* 14(1), 1–25.

Hefner R.W. and Zaman Q. 2007. *Schooling Islam: the Culture and Politics of Modern Muslim Education*. Princeton, N.J.: Princeton University Press.

Husain, S.S. and Ashraf, S.A. 1979. *Crisis in Muslim Education*. Jeddah: Hodder and Stoughton.

Ipgrave, J. 1998. Issues in the delivery of religious education to Muslim pupils: perspectives from the classroom. *British Journal of Religious Education* 21(3), 146–57.

Jones, K.W. 1989 *Socio-religious Reform Movements in British India*. Cambridge: Cambridge University Press.

Kucukcan, T. 1994. An Analytical Comparison of the Aligarh and the Deobandi Schools. *The Islamic Quarterly* 38(1), 48–58.

Mancini, S. 2010. To be or not to be Jewish: The UK Supreme Court answers the question. *University of Bologna School of Law/SAIS Johns Hopkins University Working Paper Series* [Online], 1–17. Available at http://papers.ssrn.com/sol3/papers.cfm?abstract_id=1693127 [Accessed: 10 January 2011].

Metcalf, B. 1978. The Madrasa at Deoband: A model for religious education in modern India. *Modern Asian Studies* 12(1), 111–34.

Panjwani, F. 2004. The 'Islamic' in Islamic education. *Current Issues in Contemporary Education* 7(1).

Panjwani, F. 2005. Agreed syllabus and un-agreed values: religious education and missed opportunities for fostering social cohesion. *British Journal of Educational Studies* 53(3), 375–93.

Starrett, G. 1998. Putting Islam to Work: Education, Politics and Religious Transformation in Egypt. Berkeley/London: University of California Press.

Tibawi, A.L. 1972. Islamic Education: Its Traditions and Modernization into the Arab National Systems. London: Luzac.

Troll, C.W. 1978. *Sayyid Ahmad Khan: A Reinterpretation of Muslim Theology*. New Delhi: Vikas.

Chapter 4

Religious Discrimination and Schools: The Employment of Teachers and the Public Sector Duty

Lucy Vickers

The Employment of Teachers in Faith Schools

The English state school system is made up of a range of different types of school such as foundation schools, academies, voluntary aided and controlled schools, with free schools now becoming part of the mix. Unlike many countries, in England many of these schools have a religious ethos despite being largely funded by the State.[1] Over 30 per cent of the 22,000 maintained schools in England have a religious character.[2] To an extent, the existence of such a large number of 'faith schools' reflects the fact that many of them were founded as church schools prior to the development of the public provision of education. However, the continued existence of faith schools is not merely a product of their history as the number of faith schools is currently expanding and the Church of England is still very actively involved in their governance. The overwhelming majority of faith schools are Christian and so it is this group of schools that will be the focus of this chapter (Vickers 2009).

The pros and cons of faith based state schools in the state school sector are often debated, with most of the focus being on the way in which faith schools affect admissions and parental choice of school. However, another issue has begun to be raised more recently that is the subject of this part of the chapter, namely, the effect of rules governing faith schools on the employment of teachers and their career progression. In essence, the large proportion of faith schools, particularly at the primary level, means that the number of opportunities for teachers to work outside the faith school system is reduced.

---

1 Faith schools receive grants (of up to 90 per cent of the total cost) towards capital costs of the buildings and 100 per cent of running costs (including teachers' salaries) from the State: [Online]. Available at: www.atl.org.uk/atl_en/education/postition_statements/faith_schools.asp [Accessed: 17 January 2008].

2 Over 7,000 schools: [Online]. Available at: http://findoutmore.dfes.gov.uk/2006/02/religious_educa.html [Accessed: 3 January 2008].

The Role of Faith Schools

Prior to the introduction of universal education, much public education was provided by the Church, leading to the establishment of thousands of church-run schools. Although state provision of education gradually developed, this was always shared with the Church resulting in the inclusion of Church schools into the state system, as voluntary schools, by the time of the *Education Act 1944* (Harte 2002). This enabled church schools to benefit from the greater funding available from the State, but also spared the State from having to fund the capital costs involved in setting up new schools; church schools were permitted to opt to become either 'voluntary controlled' or 'voluntary aided' with land and buildings owned by the Church in both cases, but different arrangements regarding control of admissions and the appointment and employment of staff.[3]

Although the number of faith schools has decreased overall since 1944, there remain a very large number of mainly a Christian nature and within that, predominately Church of England. Moreover, both Government and faith groups are actively pursuing the increased involvement of faith groups with the provision of state education. The promotion of a faith schools' agenda was part of education policy during the Labour government[4] and continues as part of the Coalition policy of promoting free schools: of the first 16 new free schools announced, seven had a religious character.[5]

Although a large proportion of schools have a religious character, it has to be acknowledged that the role of faith within these schools can vary. Some are only nominally religious in nature, with a day-to-day ethos indistinguishable from any other school. They are multicultural, welcome children of all religions and none and aim to instil moral and civic values in their pupils but with no more than nominal adherence to the faith which governs their constitution. Under the *Education Act 1944* all state schools (faith based or not) are required to have a daily act of collective worship and to teach religious education, though in practice this is often not religious in character and many faith schools are equally nominal in terms of their creation of an explicitly religious identity. Yet, though not all faith schools are particularly religious in nature there are faith schools that are more clearly religious with religious acts of worship every day and more explicit reference to religion in the creation of the school ethos.

---

3 September 2008 saw the launch of *Accord*, a coalition of organisations working to end the special treatment of religion in schools in terms of admissions, syllabus and the employment terms of teachers: [Online]. Available at: http://www.accordcoalition.org.uk/ [Accessed: 2 December 2010].

4 Of 47 academies opened between 2000 and 2007, 16 had a faith designation. See *Faith in the System* (2007), *Building on Success in Schools* (2001).

5 [Online]. Available at: http://www.education.gov.uk/schools/leadership/typesof-schools/freeschools/a0066077/free-school-proposals-approved-to-business-case-and-plan-stage [Accessed: 23 December 2010].

Moreover, it seems that the Christian churches involved in the provision of education have become more explicit in their aim to use education as opportunity to reach to a wide range of individuals with the Christian message, as seen in the Church of England's policy document *The Way Ahead* (2001). This document states that 30 years ago 'the emphasis was on the Church's mission of service to the community, through education'[6] whereas the new policy notes that schools can provide churches with an opportunity to reach out to parents through the children attending its schools. Concerning the employment of staff, *The Way Ahead* is equally clear in that it actively aims to encourage Christians to enter the teaching profession and suggests that ways need to be found to offer 'enhanced opportunities for Christians seeking Qualified Teacher Status' by offering additional qualifications for new entrants to work in church schools as well as developing training for head teachers. This commitment to 'enhancing opportunities' for Christians to teach or become head teachers in church schools suggests that the Church of England has become more active in encouraging the employment of Christians at all levels in its schools.

Of course, it has always been the case that involvement in state education provides a massive opportunity for outreach for faith groups and it is unsurprising that they are keen to exploit the opportunities available. However, viewed from the perspective of members of the teaching profession, such a strategy may be more problematic as it may significantly curtail the freedom of teachers who do not share the faith of the majority of faith schools to develop their careers across the full range of state funded schools. This is particularly the case outside large urban areas, where the choice of where to work may be more limited and there may be a small range of options available. It is in this context that the special rules that regulate the employment of teachers in faith schools will now be considered.

The School Standards and Framework Act 1998 ('SSFA')

The SSFA protects teachers in non-faith schools from religious discrimination[7] but allows faith schools to impose requirements regarding religion and belief on teaching staff and allows voluntary aided schools to impose religious requirements and require certain standards of conduct from teaching staff and non-teaching staff.[8] Teachers and some support staff in faith schools are governed by the SSFA and religious discrimination is allowed in some circumstances. The SSFA generally protects teaching staff in non-faith schools from discrimination on grounds of religion but it provides exceptions for schools with a religious character which are allowed to discriminate in favour of staff who share the religious ethos of the school. The provisions of the SSFA are complex because the rules vary depending on the type of school involved: voluntary aided, voluntary controlled, community

---

6   Ibidem para. 3.15.
7   SSFA, s.59.
8   *Education and Inspections Act 2006*, s.37(2).

schools or foundation schools.[9] The differences were outlined above, but will be briefly reiterated. All types of school are run by school governors but there is divergence in who funds the school and who employs the staff.[10] In voluntary controlled church schools, the land and buildings are owned by the church but the local authority funds the school and employs the staff. By contrast, in voluntary aided church schools the land and buildings are owned by the church and the school is funded by the local authority but the governing body employs the staff.[11] In community schools, the local authority owns the buildings, provides funds, and employs staff. In foundation schools, funding is provided by the local authority, but buildings are owned by the governing body, and the governing body employs the staff.

The distinctions between different types of schools therefore relate to questions of funding and governance and the legal question of who employs staff. They are not based on the level of religious input or the extent to which a Christian ethos is promoted within the school.[12] For example, a school may be voluntary aided but its ethos may be very multicultural and the school may embrace and celebrate many faiths. As long as it complies with the legal obligations concerning the Christian content of assemblies, this will be perfectly lawful and consistent with its voluntary aided status. Similarly, a voluntary controlled school may, in practice, have a very Christian ethos; for example, having prayers said at the start and end of each day, regular attendance at church for Christian festivals and the presence of significant numbers of religious symbols displayed around the school. Again, as long as the correct religious education syllabus is followed in terms of covering other faiths this is perfectly lawful and consistent with the voluntary controlled status.

Yet the distinctions between voluntary controlled and voluntary aided status, while not necessarily of significance in terms of the ethos of the school, are of great significance regarding the extent to which staff are free to exercise their freedom of religion because the status of the school effects the extent to which schools can discriminate in favour of religious members of staff and against those who do not share the religion of the school.

The main distinction within the SSFA is between schools with a religious character and those without. Concerning schools which do not have a religious

---

9   Other schools which receive state funding are academies set up under the *Learning and Skills Act 2000*. These are partly funded by the business sector. In addition, there are city technology colleges, funded directly by the Government, rather than via a local education authority, and the new free schools.

10   There are also differences in terms of who controls admissions but this issue is not within the scope of this chapter.

11   Some funding may come from the voluntary organisation, usually a church.

12   However, as a general rule, faith schools are usually voluntary aided or voluntary controlled. Foundation schools (many of which were formerly grant maintained schools) may or may not be faith based, and community schools are rarely faith-based.

character, the Act provides that teachers cannot be refused employment, dismissed or deprived of promotion or other advantage by reason of their religious beliefs, failure to attend religious worship or refusal to give religious education.[13] In the case of non-faith schools, then, the Act provides similar protection to that provided under the *Equality Act 2010*, which protects all workers against direct and indirect discrimination subject to the 'genuine occupational qualifications' exception. In most cases, the genuine occupational requirement would not apply to teachers in non-faith schools and so the general Equality Act provisions protect against most forms of discrimination. For example, refusal to employ a teacher in a non-faith school because of her religious beliefs would be direct discrimination. Refusal to allow a teacher to have time off for religious observance or to wear religious dress to work would potentially be indirect discrimination but could be justified where necessary. An example of the application of these rules can be seen in *Asmi v. Kirklees Metropolitan Council*[14] where a Muslim teaching assistant was dismissed for refusing to remove a face veil when in class. Whilst the dismissal could be indirectly discriminatory (the requirement of the school that Asmi have her face visible in class was particularly disadvantageous for a female Muslim), the requirement to remove the veil was proportionate given the need to uphold the interests of the children in having the best possible education, thus justifying the potential discrimination.

Regarding schools with a religious character, the legal position is very different in that schools are allowed much greater freedom to impose religious requirements on staff. The SSFA distinguishes between different types of faith school, providing greater freedom to 'voluntary aided' schools than to others. The different provisions will be considered in turn.

Voluntary controlled and foundation schools

In religious voluntary controlled or foundation schools, religion can be taken into account in appointing the head teacher and regard may be had to his or her 'ability and fitness to preserve and develop the religious character of the school'.[15] In addition the school can 'reserve' up to a fifth of its teaching staff who can be 'selected for their fitness and competence' to give religious education in accordance with the tenets of the faith of the school.[16] The regulations also permit failure to comply with the tenets of the religion to be grounds for dismissal for the head teacher and reserved staff. The SSFA protects other (non-reserved) teachers

---

13   SSFA, s.59. The provision applies to working as a teacher and being employed for the purposes of the school otherwise than as a teacher.

14   [2007] ICR 1154.

15   SSFA, s.60 as amended by *the Education and Inspections Act 2006*, s.37.

16   SSFA, s.58. After amendment by section 37 of the *Education and Inspections Act 2006*, if the head teacher is appointed to teach religious education, the head teacher counts as a reserved teacher. This means that the additional religious requirements can be imposed on the head teacher.

and support staff in voluntary controlled schools from discrimination on grounds of religious opinion, failure to attend religious worship or refusal to give religious education at the school.

Effectively, then, the SSFA allows for religious discrimination in the appointment of the head teacher and reserved staff and for the imposition of requirements on them to live in accordance with the tenets of the religion. This suggests that under the Act teachers can be dismissed because of a failure to comply with religious tenets on lifestyles. Thus a 'reserved' teacher or a head teacher in a voluntary controlled school could potentially be dismissed for living in a relationship outside marriage or for marrying a divorced person, even though this may bear no relation to his or her ability to teach. This provision stands in strong contrast to the requirements that apply to other employment sectors under the *Equality Act 2010* that religious requirements be genuinely 'occupational' in that they must relate to the conduct of the job. Moreover, under the *Equality Act 2010* occupational requirements must be proportionate. The SSFA has no proportionality requirement. This means that the question of whether the requirement is really necessary, or could be achieved through less discriminatory means, is not addressed.

Voluntary aided schools

The freedom of voluntary aided schools to discriminate on grounds of religion is even greater, as religious requirements can be imposed on all teaching staff – not just the head and 'reserved teachers'. Preference can be given in connection with the appointment, remuneration or promotion of staff on the basis of religious belief and attendance at worship. Moreover, in decisions to dismiss, regard can be had to conduct which is incompatible with the precepts of the religion, or with the upholding of its tenets.[17] This means that staff could be dismissed for failing to comply with requirements relating to religious lifestyles as well as dismissal for failure to share the faith of the school in question. However, in contrast to the situation in voluntary controlled schools, in voluntary aided schools this freedom to discriminate is not limited to just the one fifth reserved teachers and head teachers.

The possibility of applying faith and lifestyle requirements to all teachers and some support staff in such schools, whether or not they are engaged in teaching religion, seems to go well beyond what might be lawful under the *Equality Act 2010* were it to apply to such schools. Moreover, the SSFA does not have a requirement that any religious requirements imposed on staff should be proportionate. Thus, there is no requirement to consider the proportionality of any religious requirement having regard to the ethos of the school, nor having regard to whether any less discriminatory means to achieve the school's aim could be found. This is troubling given that voluntary aided status reflects the legal constitution of the school, rather than its practical commitment to a religious ethos, and the fact that voluntary aided church schools may be no more religious in nature than other schools.

---

17   SSFA, s.60.

The effect of the SSFA on teaching staff who do not meet requirements to share the religious ethos of the school could be significant. Although many church schools do not use their powers under the SSFA to recruit exclusively or predominantly Christian staff, the option is there for them to do so and there is some evidence that some schools do require religious adherence from staff.[18] Moreover, it is quite open to schools to take account of the 'enhanced opportunities' in terms of training which the Anglican Church suggests should be developed in *The Way Ahead* in decisions which are made regarding advancement or promotion of staff in faith schools. Thus, Christian teachers may come to enjoy significant advantages in career terms over staff of other faiths or those with no religion. Moreover, there is no compensating or equivalent advantage for those of other religions in other schools: the numbers of schools run by other faith groups are very small and non-faith schools cannot discriminate at all on grounds of religion or non-religion.

Is the Freedom of Religion of Teachers Adequately Protected?

Certainly, the position of teachers with regard to their religious freedom at work is reduced below that of other workers. The general protection against discrimination on grounds of religion and belief contained in the *Equality Act 2010* only allows for discrimination where it is the result of an occupational requirement and it is proportionate to impose the requirement in the circumstances. In assessing proportionality, the religious ethos of voluntary aided schools would be taken into account as the employer in these cases is the Church. Nonetheless, it is notable that the SSFA offers significantly reduced protection by not including a proportionality test.

The lower level of protection against religious discrimination available for staff under the SSFA raises the question of whether the provisions of the SSFA are compatible with the requirements of the *Employment Equality Directive 2000/78*. Article 4(1) of the Directive provides a general exception to discrimination where there is a genuine occupational requirement for it, where it serves a legitimate aim and the discrimination is proportionate to that aim. Article 4(2) of the Directive allows for broader exceptions for religious organizations to maintain a religious ethos and require loyalty from staff to that ethos. Whilst exceptions to the non-discrimination principle can be acceptable within the Directive, therefore, the limits on the non-discrimination principle provided in the SSFA are so broad that they may well not comply with the requirement in Article 4 that exceptions be legitimate and justified.

In the case of voluntary controlled schools, where the employer of staff is the local authority, the decision in *Glasgow City Council v. McNab*[19] shows that these are not religious ethos organizations. Thus, any exceptions must not only meet the higher standard of Article 4(1) where exceptions must be proportionate

---

18   See *McNab*'s case at note 19 *infra* and '[m]y lack of faith stopped me being accepted', *The Guardian*, 4 December 2007.

19   [2007] IRLR 476.

but also any religious requirements of the job must be genuine and determining requirements and no reference is made to assessing this in the light of the religious ethos of the organization. In *McNab* (a Scottish case, so the SSFA did not apply) it was held that that it was not essential for a pastoral care teacher in a Catholic school to be Catholic as the responsibilities of the job involved giving advice on a large number of issues, only a few of which required knowledge of Catholic doctrine and those could be assigned to a different teacher. This illustrates that, under the *Equality Act 2010* whose provisions regarding religious discrimination are based on the Directive, it would not be easy to argue that teachers in faith schools must share the faith of the school. This suggests that the provisions of the SSFA, as they apply to voluntary controlled schools, are not compatible with Article 4(1) of the Directive.

In the case of voluntary aided schools, the broader Article 4(2) exception would apply because the employer of staff is the school governing body – a religious ethos organization. Nonetheless, the extension of the provisions of the SSFA to such a broad range of staff beyond those involved in teaching religious subjects and the fact that the rules apply on the basis of the status of the school as a voluntary aided school, without regard to the level of religious observance within the school, means that the rules in the SSFA are probably too broad to come within the exceptions provided by the Directive, which provides that exceptions must be justified and that regard should be had to the organization's ethos in making this judgement.

The failure of the SSFA to include a proviso that any religious discrimination in schools must be proportionate may make the protection of the SSFA incompatible with that provided for in the Directive. Of course, in some cases discrimination may be proportionate but the SSFA prejudges this issue by providing that such religious discrimination against teachers *is* lawful rather than following the approach of the Directive which requires this judgement to be made subject to proportionality of the particular case.

If the provisions of the SSFA allowing discrimination against teachers on grounds of religion and belief were to be made subject to a requirement of proportionality, this would allow for an assessment to be made as to how an appropriate balance should be maintained between upholding the rights of faith schools to maintain their religious ethos and of teachers to pursue their careers free from religious discrimination. A criterion of proportionality would enable each case to be considered rather than pre-judging that discrimination against the teacher is always acceptable. This could entail considering whether there are other options available to a teacher to teach or look for promotion elsewhere. For example, where there is only one religious school among several others in a particular location, such as a city, the practical effect of discrimination by an employer may differ from where either a faith school is the only maintained school in a locality or where a large proportion of schools in an area are faith schools. It is suggested that, for these purposes, a third of schools would count as a large proportion because it is sufficient to have a significant effect on the job opportunities of teachers. The consideration of proportionality might also involve an assessment of a school's actual ethos, based on current practice, rather than basing the employment rights of teachers on the constitutional and governance arrangements of the school.[20]

The Role of the State and Social Cohesion

Clearly, it is always going to be difficult to balance the rights of faith organizations to retain a religious ethos with the rights of staff to be free from religious discrimination. In most contexts, this difficulty is addressed by requiring proportionality in the imposition of any faith requirement by enabling employment tribunals to assess contextual factors such as the nature of the job, the extent to which religious belief is a defining element, the size of the undertaking, the impact of the requirement on the job opportunities for other workers, the extent to which other employment opportunities are available to potential applicants.

An additional fact which may be relevant to the question of proportionality, and which is also relevant to the question of whether the wide exceptions to the non-discrimination principle are acceptable, is that regardless of whether the employer is the local authority or the school governors each of these schools receives the vast majority of its funding from the State. This fact of itself provides additional reasons against allowing much wider exceptions to the non-discrimination principle in state schools than in other employment sectors.

First, as has been mentioned above, in some sectors the State is effectively a monopoly employer. In relation to schooling, the state sector educates 93 per cent of the school population in England[21] and so most teachers spend their careers within that sector. Of course, staff remain free to choose other forms of employment but nonetheless the religious freedom of staff will be significantly restricted if they are excluded from large parts of the sector on grounds related to religion.

Secondly, greater religious neutrality in the state sector enables the State to encourage equal participation in the work force from a range of religious groups (Rawls 1999). Equal employment rights in the state sector enables the State to send a symbolic message to the rest of society that all citizens are equal and valued. This enables the State to encourage social cohesion by improving access to employment and improving integration between social groups who make up society.

Thirdly, the protection for religious discrimination takes on a special significance in the public sector as employment practices carry with them the implied endorsement of the State. Moreover, the State may be said to owe a duty to encourage social cohesion by employing individuals who reflect the range of communities which make up our society. Indeed, the *Education and Inspections Act 2006* imposes a duty on governors of state schools in England to promote

20   This is likely to be related to the settlement made in 1944, often based on the extent of a particular parish's financial resources at the time.

21   6.4 per cent of children were in independent schools in 2007. See Hansard, 3 July 2007: Column 981W.

community cohesion in their conduct of the school.[22] The freedom of state schools to discriminate against staff on grounds of religion sits somewhat uncomfortably alongside their duty to promote community cohesion. This will be further considered below in relation to the public sector equality duties.

The Religion and Belief Public Sector Equality Duty

Although the *Equality Act 2010* is largely a consolidating statute, it also introduces some new measures including the creation of new public sector equality duties to cover religion and belief, age, sexual orientation, maternity and pregnancy. These new duties will be added to duties which already exist with regard to race, gender and disability and can be seen as an attempt to harmonize or 'level up' the protection available to the newer equality grounds. It may also be useful to see the duties in the school context as complementing the duty to promote community cohesion imposed on schools by section 38 of the *Education and Standards Act 2006*.

The extension of the equality duties can clearly be welcomed as part of a drive to eliminate discrimination and promote equality in schools. However, it may be that the religion and belief duty could give rise to some difficulties and could also cut across the duty to promote community cohesion unless implemented very carefully.

Overview of the New Religion and Belief Equality Duty

Most of the provisions of the *Equality Act 2010* came into force in October 2010 but the newly extended public sector equality duty only came into effect in April 2011. The duty is contained in section 149 of the Act and is imposed on public authorities, including governing bodies of maintained schools.[23] It provides:

S.149 (1) A public authority must, in the exercise of its functions, have due regard to the need to:

> (a) eliminate discrimination, harassment, victimization and any other conduct that is prohibited by or under this Act;
> (b) advance equality of opportunity between persons who share a [religion or belief] and persons who do not share it;
> (c) foster good relations between persons who share a [religion and belief] and persons who do not share it …

Exactly what is required to comply with the new duty is not yet clear; however, some guidance can be found from the experience with the earlier public sector

---

22   *Education and Inspections Act 2006*, s.38.
23   *Equality Act 2010*, Schedule 19.

duties on grounds of race, gender and disability. Cases have rarely been litigated[24] but the success of these duties is better seen in the range of initiatives undertaken in schools in response to these duties. Most schools and governing bodies have introduced equality policies and undertake significant range of activities designed to promote gender race and disability equality in schools.

The extent to which schools tackle discrimination and promote equality is also one of the areas evaluated by OFSTED. Inspectors are required to evaluate how effectively the school actively promotes equal opportunity and tackles discrimination. Areas reviewed by OFSTED include the performance and experience of different groups of children (for example by gender and race), the extent to which the school develops understanding about differences and values diverse experiences, and the emphasis the school gives to processes to promote equality and eliminate discrimination and ensure that stereotypical views are challenged.[25] The focus on the promotion of equality as part of the OFSTED framework means that schools have been established as a key area in which the promotion of equality can be achieved. As discussed above, the duty on governing bodies to promote community cohesion is also well established and forms part of an overall pattern in which schools have become a key forum in which discrimination is tackled and good relations between communities are fostered.

It might seem, then, that the addition of new grounds of equality to the list already protected may not add much to the equality agenda in schools. Indeed, in order to meet the community cohesion agenda and as part of a general ethos of promoting equality many schools already have equal opportunities and diversity policies addressing a wider range of equality grounds beyond gender, race and disability to also include age, religion, belief and sexual orientation. To an extent, the new equality duties introduced from April 2011 may not lead to a great change in practice as the new grounds are already being protected in most schools as part of a well-established community cohesion agenda.

However, it is worth thinking a little more closely about the introduction of the new duty as it may be that the addition of religion and belief in particular to the list of public sector duties could cause some difficulties to schools.

The Potential Impact of the Religion and Belief Duty

Definitional issues

A number of concerns can be raised about the extension of the public sector duty to religion (Lester and Uccellari 2008, Vickers 2011). For example, a preliminary

---

24 Although see *R (on the application of Janet Harris) v. Haringey London Borough Council and others* [2010] EWCA Civ 703 and *R (on the application of (1) Kaur (2) Shah (Claimants) v. Ealing London Borough Council (Defendant) & Equality & Human Rights Commission (Intervenor)* [2008] EWHC 2062 (Admin).

25 See the Evaluation Schedule for Schools published by OFSTED. [Online]. Available at: http://www.ofsted.gov.uk/ [Accessed: 3 December 2010].

concern is that the term 'religion and belief' is not defined clearly in the legislation.[26] This leaves an element of uncertainty in the protection and may well leave schools unclear about the scope of the new duty.

Of course, it is relatively easy to ensure that practices of mainstream religions in any geographical area are accommodated in its schools and many schools already ensure that a variety of religious festivals are marked in school, religious forms of dress are accommodated and religious dietary requirements can be met. However, difficulties can arise where individuals or groups have their own interpretations of religious requirements. In such cases, it may be difficult for schools to be clear how far they should accommodate any religious requests. For example, in *R. (on the application of Begum (Shabina)) v. Denbigh High School Governors*[27] a school refused to allow a Muslim pupil to wear a *jilbab* to school. The school already had a uniform permitting the wearing of religious dress, including a headscarf, but one pupil wished to wear the more religiously conservative dress. Whilst, on the facts of the case, the House of Lords ruled that the school had not breached the individual pupil's religious freedom, it is noteworthy that it recognized that individual religious beliefs (namely, the pupil's belief that she should wear the *jilbab*) should be protected (where doing so does not interfere with the rights of others) and there is no need to show a minimum number of adherents before such protection can be granted.

Thus, in promoting equality and fostering good relations schools should be careful not to assume that accommodating majority versions of religious faiths will be sufficient; it may be necessary also to offer to accommodate minority or even single person religions or beliefs as well. Unlike the other public sector duties, then, the scope of the religion and belief duty is much less certain as a primary definitional issue is left ambiguous and schools may well be uncertain about how far this duty extends.

Moreover, in some cases, the duties to eliminate discrimination and to foster good relations between groups may not lead to the same outcome when trying to determine their scope. In the *Begum* case, for example, the school had agreed its uniform in consultation with the local Muslim community and so it could be said that adopting the agreed uniform would foster good relations with that particular community; one of the reasons for maintaining its rule was the wish to protecting other Muslim students from family or societal pressure to wear more conservative styles of dress and so it could be seen to foster good relations on grounds of gender as well as religion as between different religious groups. Yet, at the same time, it did not help to eliminate religious discrimination against the one pupil who wished to wear an alternative uniform.

---

26   Religion means 'any religion' and belief means 'any religious or philosophical belief': *Equality Act 2010*, s.10.

27   *R (on the application of Begum) v. Headteacher and Governors of Denbigh High School* [2006] UKHL 15.

An additional related issue regarding definition is that many religions and beliefs are highly contested even within their own communities. If a school is trying to develop ways in which good relations may be fostered between groups, it may struggle to identify clearly what the religious group believes. Most religious groups contain a variety of voices so that, if religious equality is to be promoted, it is important to ensure that one voice does not predominate. In these cases, determining who represents the religion, and thus whose equality needs to be advanced, or whose good relations need fostering, can be very difficult. It may involve selecting the 'authentic' voice of the religion or belief – a decision that teachers and governors are not in a strong position to make.[28]

It may be that, for ease of reference, schools decide to celebrate or showcase fairly simple representations of particular religious groups but in the process they may fail to represent the complexity of the beliefs in question. Using Christianity as an example, children may learn that Christians celebrate that Jesus was the son of God, born at Christmas and that he was born in a stable, and so on. However, many Christians do not share this belief in a literal sense, and it can be hard to express in a school context the range and depth of Christian concepts of incarnation. Thus, it may well be that attempts to promote religious equality leads to representations of religion that satisfy no one. Simple representations of each faith may leave those who share the religion feeling that they have been misrepresented but those who do not share the religion may not be happy for school children to be involved in the deeper theological discussions that would be required for them to attain a fuller, more meaningful understanding of the religious beliefs.

Additional concern about the lack of definition may be raised by the case of *Nicholson v. Grainger PLC*[29] in which the EAT held that beliefs about climate change could amount to a protected belief. If this definition is carried across from the employment context to the context of the public sector duty in schools, it could mean that attempts to promote a 'green' agenda would come within the public sector duty. This would mean that schools would need to take steps to foster good relations between those who share the belief and those who do not. This could possibly provide a publicly funded boost to those who do not support a 'green' agenda and could cause difficulties for schools who regularly promote environmental awareness. Of course, this was not the aim of the legislation and it was made clear in the *Nicholson* judgement that the decision related only to the employment context but the judgment itself relied on several precedents from the European Court of Human Rights ('ECHR') from contexts other than employment, and it is possible that it could be used as precedent in contexts such as education giving rise to such unintended consequences.

---

28 Note 27 *supra*.
29 [2010] I.C.R. 360.

Protecting those without a religion or belief

Even apart from the definitional problem for the scope of the duty, more fundamental concerns arise concerning the religion and belief duty. This is because the 'religion and belief' ground includes within it those with a religion and belief and those without. This means that it may be difficult for a school to demonstrate that it is treating equally members of both groups. The problem arises because the two groups' interests are likely to be in conflict because the promotion of understanding between religious groups by schools is unlikely to be compatible with providing equality for those of no faith and who do not want to see religion featuring in schools at all.

For example, if a school celebrates Christmas it may be thought suitable and a relatively straightforward step in the interests of fostering good relations on grounds of religion and belief to also to allow for some observance of Hanukah, Eid and Diwali as well and indeed such a multicultural and inclusive approach to assemblies and religious festivals is very common in schools. However, with the imposition of a legal duty to foster good relations between those with a faith or belief and those without matters become less clear as it is uncertain how the interests of those without a religion or belief should be brought within such an approach. Would a 'celebration' of atheism be needed? And would a separate celebration be appropriate for agnosticism? Moreover, if, for example, each religion were to be given a special assembly, would equality for the non-religious be promoted by having one non-religious assembly or would four such assemblies better reflect equality with the four different religious assemblies? Some might feel that good relations with those with no religion would be best served by allowing no religious celebrations in school at all, rather than by giving quantitative equal treatment. There are clearly no simple answers to these questions, but what they illustrate is that some deeper underlying questions remain about how to meet the equality duty, when applied to religion and belief, which will be left to individual schools to determine. Identifying good practice in this area may be more difficult than in relation to the more established grounds of race, gender and disability.

Of course, the equality duty is not merely about school assemblies and Christmas plays and, sensitively implemented, the duty should be able to achieve its objectives of enhancing equality. However, there remains a risk that the promotion of equality and the taking of steps to foster good relations between groups on the basis of religion may lead to greater focus on religion in schools and thus to enhanced sensitivity to religious difference. There is a danger that attempts to foster good relations between religion groups will fail and may even increase tension between groups by drawing attention to religious differences.

In summary, there are clearly a number of problems that can be identified with the religion and belief equality duty that may make it difficult to implement in schools with confidence. Although the issues identified are particular to the religion and belief duty, they also reflect a fundamental tension within equality law. In order to find guidance on how the duty may be best implemented, it will be instructive to consider briefly the current debates regarding the various meanings of equality.

Definitions of Equality

There has been extensive academic debate about the meanings and purposes of equality (Barnard and Hepple 2000, Fredman 2002 a and b, Hepple 2008, Vickers 2011). The first and most obvious meaning is formal or symmetrical equality, in which like cases are treated alike. The difficulties with this approach are well recognized in that it can be difficult to tell when likes are indeed alike (Westen 1982) and the approach can lead to levelling down of treatment so that everyone is treated 'equally badly' (Barnard and Hepple 2000, Fredman 2002a). The formal approach to equality would not lead to a very active duty on schools to promote equality because it only requires equal treatment rather than positive steps to be taken to promote equality or good relations between groups. The idea of the public sector duty entails a richer view of equality as it involves fostering good relations between groups and the active promotion of equality.

At least three more substantive models of equality can be identified in the literature: the first, a model of equality that focuses on the link between equality and individual dignity and identity; the second, a model which focuses on disadvantage and redistribution (Barnard and Hepple 2000); the third, a model based on equality as a means of addressing social exclusion and promoting participation (Fraser 2000, Fredman 2002b, Collins 2003). These broader concepts of equality will be explored further here as they may help develop a way of viewing the equality duty which will help to determine how to apply it in relation to religion and belief in a way which avoids the difficulties identified above.

The first concept of equality views it as a reflection of human dignity (Kant 1963): all people share an essential dignity as human beings and are equal in their humanity and moral worth. A concept of equality based on dignity acknowledges that full equality will only be achieved when individuals enjoy social and cultural equality. Schools can play a significant part in achieving this as they are an obvious meeting point for all parts of a community. They may well be able to promote equality and foster good relations between groups by ensuring that different religious identities are reflected and recognized in school. However, basing the public duty on this understanding of equality also gives rise to some reservations, particularly with respect to religion and belief. Not only can it be difficult to determine which religious views are protected but also there can be concern that action to promote equality on religious grounds is viewed as providing some official endorsement of religion, which may be criticized by those who believe that religion should be kept out of the public sphere. In this context, it is worth noting that the religion and belief duty will apply to faith and non-faith schools.

The problem of state endorsement of religion is avoided if a second concept of equality is used, which instead is concerned with overcoming disadvantage. This approach sees the wrong of religion and belief discrimination as causing disadvantage rather than in its lack of recognition of different identities. In this equality model, religion and belief is included as a ground of equality because it acts as a proxy for disadvantage rather than because the characteristic is intrinsically valued. For example, if monitoring of academic progress showed uneven performance across a school on the basis of pupils' religion it would be appropriate for a school to try to address the causes of underperformance in particular religious groups. Such targeted intervention would not infer that the religion per se is valued by the school and the school would not have to ensure the same treatment for every religious group. Instead, a focus on religion within the school could uncover a link between religious groups and a particular form of disadvantage, thus enabling that disadvantage to be targeted.

However, if adopting this approach, care needs to be taken to ensure that religion is indeed reliable as a proxy for disadvantage. Moreover, multiple identities mean that there may be very great differences in disadvantage between, for example, Sikh boys and Sikh girls, black Christians and white Christians or working-class Muslims and middle-class Muslims. This makes it hard to identify where disadvantage lies and how it is caused.

A third concept of equality is based upon the idea of inclusion, which embraces both dignity and disadvantage with equality seen as a means of promoting respect for the equal dignity of all and affirming community identities and facilitating full participation in society (Fredman 2002b). In effect, the argument is that minority groups need to be encouraged to participate in civic life so that their voice within the community can become stronger, leading to an end to their marginalization and disadvantage and at the same time enhancing their dignity (Collins 2003). In this model, promoting dignity and ending disadvantage are seen not as ends in themselves but as ways to achieve a more equal society in terms of economic distribution and social harmony.

A focus on social inclusion provides a basis for more positive action in order to achieve equality and so provides perhaps the best theoretical underpinning for the public sector duty. It avoids many of the problems identified above with the introduction of the religion and belief duty into schools. It avoids seeming to 'value' religion and belief, arguably an inappropriate aim (especially in non-faith schools). It also avoids the problem of definition and questions such as whether beliefs in climate change are included because the focus is on promoting good social harmony rather than quantitative equal treatment for each belief group. Such an approach is instead compatible with the proactive approach of the public sector duties which seek to put thinking about equality at the heart of public authority (and therefore school) decision-making.

What is striking about such an approach in the school context is that it has so many resonances with the existing duty to promote community cohesion. This duty was introduced in 2006 and schools have made significant efforts to ensure that they can meet it. Examples of good practice in this regard are very similar to what one might expect to see as examples of good practice for the public sector duty in schools. For example, Government 'Guidance on the duty to promote community cohesion'[30] states that by community cohesion, we mean working towards a society in which there is a 'sense of belonging by all communities; a society in which the diversity of people's backgrounds and circumstances is appreciated and valued; a society in which similar life opportunities are available to all; and a society in which strong and positive relationships exist and continue to be developed in the workplace, in schools and in the wider community'.[31]

The difficulties identified above with the expansion of the public sector duties to the religion and belief would be largely overcome if schools were to view the duty to promote equality and foster good relations as part of the duty to promote community cohesion. The aims and values of the equality duty and the duty to promote community cohesion are, after all, shared. By regarding them as largely co-extensive, schools can then continue to build on the good practice they already developed on this issue.

Conclusion

A number of concerns have been identified with regard to the employment provisions of the SSFA and the suggestion has been made that the Act may not be in accordance with the *Employment Equality Directive 2000/78*. It was also suggested that the freedom of faith schools to discriminate against staff on grounds of religion and belief (as well as in admissions) may not sit well with their duty to promote community cohesion, though this is not to deny that many faith schools perform very well in terms of measures of their work in this regard.[32]

At the same time, the extension in the *Equality Act 2010* of the religion and belief duty has the potential to create practical difficulties for schools as they seek to ensure that they correctly balance the interests of different groups (religious and non-religious) and avoid seeming to endorse religious views through the implementation of policies designed to celebrate the different communities which they represent. It is suggested that a continued focus on the well-established duty to promote community cohesion may be a way for schools to overcome many of these difficulties. Such an approach would also accord with a theoretical underpinning for the duty in which equality is based on inclusion and full participation in society for all.

---

30   [Online]. Available at: http://www.teachernet.gov.uk/wholeschool/Communityco-hesion/ [Accessed: 3 December 2010].

31   Ibidem, p.3.

32   27 November 2009. 'Faith schools "strong on community cohesion"'. [Online]. Available at: http://news.bbc.co.uk/1/hi/education/8381090.stm [Accessed: 14 December 2010].

References

Barnard, C. and Hepple, B. 2000. Substantive equality. *Cambridge Law Journal* 59, 562.

Church of England. 2001. *The Way Ahead*. London: Church House Publishing.

Collins, H. 2003. Discrimination, equality and social inclusion. *Modern Law Review* 66, 16.

Fraser, N. 2000. Rethinking recognition. *New Left Review* 3, 107.

Fredman, S. 2002a. *Discrimination Law*, Oxford: OUP.

Fredman, S. 2002b. *The Future of Equality in Britain*. EOC, Working Paper Series no. 5, London: Equal Opportunities Commission.

Harte, J.C.D. 2002. The development of the law of employment and education, in *Religious Liberty and Human Rights*. Cardiff: University of Wales Press.

Hepple, B. 2008. The aims of equality law, in *Current Legal Problems* edited by O'Cinneide and Holder. Oxford: OUP.

Kant, E 1963. *The Moral Law: Kant's Groundwork of the Metaphysics of Morals* (trans H.J. Paton) London: Hutchinson.

Lester A. and Uccellari P. 2008. Extending the equality duty to religion, conscience and belief: proceed with caution. *European Human Rights Law Review*, 567.

Rawls, J. 1999. *A Theory of Justice*. Oxford: OUP.

Vickers, L. 2011. Promoting equality or fostering resentment. *Legal Studies*, 135.

Vickers, L. 2009. Religion and belief discrimination and the employment of teachers in faith schools. *Religion and Human Rights* 4, 1–20.

Westen, P. 1892. The empty idea of equality. *Harvard Law Review* 95, 537.

PART II
National Models

Chapter 5

Religion, Regionalism and Education in the United Kingdom: Tales from Wales

Russell Sandberg and Anna Buchanan

The period surrounding the First World War witnessed a number of important developments concerning the regulation of religion in the United Kingdom. The *Church of England Assembly (Powers) Act 1919* recognized the self-autonomy of the Established Church by creating its own legislative assembly. The *Church of Scotland Act 1921* recognized the Church of Scotland's independence in 'matters spiritual'. And the *Welsh Church Act 1914* disestablished the Church of England in Wales. The period saw a number of key legal developments which continue to be important today and which stressed the autonomy of the Christian churches.[1]

Indeed, an argument could be made that the *Welsh Church Act* remains one of the most important pieces of modern religion law.[2] In elucidating how the Welsh Church was no longer to be 'established by law', the Act arguably provides the fullest explanation of what establishment means in the English context. Given that there is no one statute establishing the Church of England,[3] the *Welsh Church Act 1914* (somewhat ironically) is the closest there is to an 'establishment' Act. Moreover, the Act also provides the clearest statutory elucidation of the legal status of religious groups in England and Wales other than the Established Church. The Act re-established the Church in Wales as a voluntary society whose members were bound by the existing ecclesiastical law of the Church of England 'in the same manner as if they had mutually agreed to be so bound'.[4] This reflects the legal status of all members of religious groups other than the Church of England. All religious groups in England and Wales are treated as voluntary associations where two or more people voluntarily agree to be bound together for common purposes and to undertake mutual duties and obligations.[5] However, there is no general statute concerned with the recognition of religious groups in England and

---

1   For example, notably in 1917 Catholic Canon Law became codified for the first time.

2   That is: 'law created by the State or international bodies which affect religious individuals or groups'. For a fuller elucidation of the concept, see Sandberg 2011.

3   For a comparison with the *Church of Scotland Act 1921*, see Sandberg 2011: chapter 4.

4   Subject to modification or alteration, according to the constitution and regulations of the new institutional Church in Wales. See section 3 of the Act.

5   See *Forbes v. Eden* (1867) LR 1 Sc & Div 568 and Sandberg 2011: chapter 4.

Wales and so for a statutory explanation of this doctrine of 'consensual compact' one is left once again looking at the Welsh Church Act (Doe 2002: chapter 1).

Despite the importance of the *Welsh Church Act*, little attention has been paid to the question of whether the interaction between law and religion in Wales now differs from the English model.[6] Unlike Scotland, which is often considered separately since it has its own legal system; Wales is often dealt with in the same breath as England. This is unsurprising given that much of religion law is common to both England and Wales. Indeed, despite disestablishment, many of the incidents of establishment remain in Wales (Watkin 1990, Doe 2002: chapter 1). These 'vestiges of establishment' continue in terms of the legal right to be married in the parish church,[7] burial rights[8] and the provision of chaplains in prisons.[9] Moroever, many of the new laws enacted to regulate religion apply as much in Wales as they do in England.[10]

However, there are signs that a distinctive Welsh religion law is emerging. The advent of the Welsh Assembly and further powers of devolution have led to greater regulation of religious matters by Cardiff Bay. This is particularly so in relation to education law. The Welsh Assembly has considerable (and growing) powers in relation to religious worship and education in schools and the recognition of schools with a religious character (which are commonly but erroneously known as 'faith schools'). Interestingly, there has long been a crucial difference between the English law on these matters and the position in Wales. Whereas in England representatives of the Established Church are entitled to sit on the local regulatory bodies which monitor religious education and worship in schools (the Standing Advisory Councils for Religious Education or 'SACREs'),[11] this particular aspect of establishment does not apply as a 'vestige' in Wales. Whilst the disestablished

------

6 For a notable exception, see Oliva and Lambert 2010.

7 *Welsh Church (Temporalities) Act 1919*, s.6; *Marriage Act 1949*, s.78(2). Indeed, the *Marriage (Wales) Act 2010* extends the categories of persons entitled to be married in the parish church beyond 'parishioner' to include others having certain 'qualifying connections'. This brings the Church in Wales in line with the Church of England, following the *Church of England Marriage Measure 2008*.

8 *Welsh Church (Burial Grounds) Act 1945*.

9 Welsh prison chaplains must be clerics of the Church in Wales: *Prison Act 1952*, s.53(4).

10 As shown by the famous litigation concerning Shambo the sacred bullock: *R (on the Application of Swami Suryananda) v. Welsh Ministers* [2007] EWHC (Admin) 1736.

11 These were first set up under the *Education Act 1944*. They are required to be made up of four committees. Committee A is made up of Christian denominations and such other religions and religious denominations as, in the opinion of the Local Authority, will appropriately reflect the principal religious traditions in the area. In England only, there is a Committee B which comprises representatives of the Church of England. Committee C is made up of teacher associations whilst Local Authority representatives sit on Committee D. See Department for Children, Schools and Families Non-Statutory Guidance 2010: Religious Education in English Schools.

Church in Wales continues to enjoy many vestiges of establishment in relation to marriage, burial and prison law it enjoys no special position in education law.

This chapter examines the Welsh picture concerning religion and education in greater depth, exploring how a distinctively Welsh religion law on education could develop. It is divided into three parts. The first provides an outline of the current law on religious education and worship and the establishment of schools with a religious character in England and Wales. The second draws upon empirical work by Buchanan (2008) to examine the extent to which the law is understood and followed in practice in Welsh schools, focusing upon the legal provisions concerning religious worship. The third then examines the growing competencies of the Welsh Assembly in this area and asks whether it is now time for the Assembly to act in order to provide a legal framework which is fit for purpose in the twenty-first century.

The Legal Framework

Religious education and daily worship remain compulsory in all schools that are maintained by the State. However, this general rule is subject to three major qualifications. First, whilst the law provides the general framework concerning religious education and worship the detail is left to the local level. Religious Education is not part of the National Curriculum; its content is instead determined locally by the SACREs. These SACREs also have a monitoring role and have been given the power to suspend the requirement for Christian collective worship in a particular school. The second is that education law grants parents a right to withdraw their children from the religious education and worship provided by the school and, in relation to worship, this right is now in the hands of sixth-formers. The third qualification is that the rules on religious education and worship differ substantially in schools which have been designated as having a religious character. The legal requirements differ greatly depending on the status of the school with a religious character (voluntary, foundation, and so on). The following section unpacks the law on these matters in greater depth, examining the current law on religious education and worship and the establishment of schools with a religious character as it applies in England and Wales.[12]

---

12 For a further examination, see Sandberg 2011: chapter 8.

Turning first to Religious Education ('RE'),[13] the *School Standards and Framework Act 1998* ('SSFA')[14] places a legal obligation upon the Local Education Authority ('LEA') the governing body of schools and head teachers to ensure that RE is taught in accordance with the locally agreed syllabus.[15] This syllabus must 'reflect the fact that the religious traditions in Great Britain are in the main Christian whilst taking account of the teaching and practices of the other principal religious represented in Great Britain'.[16] However, despite this Christian starting point, it is also stressed that RE is the study *of* religion rather than a study *in* religion. It is forbidden for RE to be given to pupils 'by means of any catechism or formulary which is distinctive of a particular religious denomination (but this is not to be taken as prohibiting provision in such a syllabus for the study of such catechisms or formularies)'.[17] The precise balance is determined at a local level by the SACRE.[18] It is compulsory for every LEA to establish a SACRE, which consists of 'representative groups' and other 'persons co-opted as members of the council by members of the council'. The 'representative groups' must include 'a group of persons to represent such Christian denominations and other religions and denominations of such religions as, in the opinion of the authority, will appropriately reflect the principal religious traditions in the area' and, as noted above, in England, there must be 'a group of persons to represent the Church of England'.[19]

There is also a right for parents to request that their child 'be wholly or partly excused' from receiving RE.[20] Section 9 of the *Education Act 1996* states that in exercising their powers LEAs should 'have regard to the general principle that pupils are to be educated in accordance with the wishes of their parents, so far as that is compatible with the provision of efficient instruction and training and the avoidance of unreasonable public expenditure'. This ensures that domestic law is compatible with the standards of the European Convention on Human Rights ('ECHR'). Under Article 2 of the First Protocol of the ECHR, the State must

---

13   In addition to Religious Education, the academic subject of Religious Studies is often taught as an optional subject at GCSE and 'A' level. The syllabus followed by such courses are determined by exam boards, though schools are often afforded a degree of choice, meaning that whilst some Religious Studies courses may focus on Christian theology others may focus upon other world religions or religious questions concerning philosophy or ethics.

14   This is the latest in a long line of statutes: see also the *Education Reform Act 1988*, the *Education Act 1944* and the *Elementary Education Act 1870*.

15   SSFA, s.69. The syllabus may be different for different schools, classes or pupils.

16   *Education Act 1996*, s.375(3).

17   Schedule 19 to the SSFA.

18   The syllabus is adopted after receiving the advice of a periodic conference convened for that purpose. The Conference is a smaller group, usually drawn from the SACRE, and must reflect the representative groups of the SACRE: *Education Act 1996*, Sch.31.

19   *Education Act 1996*, s.390.

20   SSFA, s.71.

respect the right of parents to ensure for their children education conforming to the parent's own religious and philosophical convictions. The UK has entered a reservation in relation to this accepting it only in so far as it is compatible with the provision of efficient instruction and training and the avoidance of unreasonable public expenditure. The law also recognizes the religious freedom of teachers):[21] no teacher can be required to give religious education nor is he to 'receive any less remuneration or be deprived of, or disqualified for, any promotion or other advantage ... by reason of the fact that he does or does not give religious education'.[22]

Turning next to religious worship, the SSFA provides that it is compulsory for schools to hold a daily act of collective worship.[23] This will normally be held on school premises[24] but it does not have to be held at the beginning of the day; and separate acts of worship may be held for pupils in different ages or school groups.[25] Schedule 20 of the SSFA states that 'the required collective worship shall be wholly or mainly of a broadly Christian character'. However, it clarifies that collective worship is of a broadly Christian character 'if it reflects the broad traditions of Christian belief without being distinctive of any particular Christian denomination'. Moreover, not every required act of collective worship needs to be of broadly Christian character, 'provided that, taking any school term as a whole, most such acts which take place in the school do comply'.[26]

Again, the precise balance is determined at a local level. One of the functions of the SACRE is to advise the LEA on 'such matters connected with ... religious worship in community schools or in foundation schools'.[27] The SACRE has the power to disapply the requirement in prescribed schools, for particular classes or for particular descriptions of pupils.[28] The law also provides for the religious freedom of parents, teachers and, in this context, sixth-formers. Parents have a right to withdraw their children, and sixth-formers have a right to withdraw themselves from daily worship.[29] Moreover, no person is to be disqualified from being a teacher at a school or being employed or engaged for any other purpose at the school by reason of his or her religious opinions or for attending or omitting to attend religious worship.[30] Also, no teacher 'shall receive any less remuneration or be deprived of, or disqualified for, any promotion or other advantage ... by

---

21 See further Sandberg: this book Chapter 16.

22 SSFA, s.59(3).

23 Ibidem,s.70.

24 However, if the governing body is of the opinion that it is desirable for worship on a special occasion to take place elsewhere than on the school premises, it may make arrangements after consultation with the head teacher.

25 SSFA, Schedule 20.

26 See also *R v. Secretary of State for Education ex parte R and D* [1994] ELR 495.

27 *Education Act 1996*, s.391.

28 Ibidem, s.394(1), (5), (6).

29 SSFA, ss.71, 71A.

30 Ibidem, s.59(2).

reason of his religious opinions or of his attending or omitting to attend religious worship'.[31]

The rules outlined so far apply in relation to all maintained schools which have not been designated as having a religious character. In schools which have been so designated, the rules differ substantially and moreover there is some variation between the different types of school. The *School Standards and Framework Act 1998* organizes maintained schools into five statutory categories.

(a) community schools
(b) foundation schools
(c) voluntary schools, comprising
  (i) voluntary aided schools
  (ii) voluntary controlled schools
(d) community special schools
(e) foundation special schools

Any foundation or voluntary school may be designated by the Secretary of State as having a religious character where he is satisfied that the school was established by a religious body or for religious purposes.[32] The designation must state the religion or religious denomination of the school.[33] However, a distinction must then be drawn between, on the one hand, foundation or voluntary controlled schools which have a religious character, and on the other hand, voluntary aided schools which have a religious character. In short, voluntary aided schools enjoy more freedom (Petchey 2008): state law recognizes their autonomy to function according to their religious character and they more closely resemble representations of 'faith schools' found in the media.

This is particularly true in relation to the law on Religious Education. In a foundation or voluntary controlled school with a religious character, the rules are similar to those which apply to schools without a religious character. Religious education must be in accordance with an agreed syllabus but the difference is that the agreed syllabus is one adopted for the school or for a class of pupils.[34] As with schools without a religious character, the agreed syllabus must be non-denominational.[35] However, where parents request that their children receive religious education in accordance with the religion or religious denomination specified in relation to the school then the governors are under an obligation to

---

31   Ibidem, s.59(4).

32   Ibidem, s.69(3).

33   Ibidem, s.69(4). Where more than one religion or religious denomination is so specified, this is to be construed as including a reference to any of those religions or religious denominations (s.142). The procedure is governed by the *Religious Character of Schools (Designation Procedure) Regulations 1998*.

34   SSFA, Schedule 19, para. 3.

35   Ibidem, para. 2(5).

'make arrangements for securing that such religious education is given to those pupils in the school during not more than two periods in each week' unless special circumstances render it unreasonable for them to do so.[36] This means that whilst the general law affecting schools without a religious character provides a parental right to opt out, the law in relation to foundation or voluntary controlled schools with religious character provides a parental right to opt in. However, it is unclear how this rule operates in practice.

In voluntary aided schools with a religious character, the rules are closer to stereotypical expectations of a faith school. Religious education must be in accordance with the trust deed or with the tenets of the religion or religious denomination specified in relation to the school.[37] There is a parental right to opt out of this denominational education.[38] This takes the form of a request that their child receive the kind of non-denominational RE that would be found in other schools.[39]

Different rules also apply in relation to teachers (Sandberg this book: Chapter 16, Vickers 2009). Once again, voluntary aided schools with a religious character enjoy more freedom. In foundation or voluntary controlled schools which have a religious character, the matter is governed by the same rules that apply in schools that do not have a religious character unless the member of staff is a 'reserved' teacher. Provided that there are more than two teachers, 'reserved' teachers can be appointed who can be treated differently on the basis of their religion or belief in connection with remuneration or promotion.[40] In voluntary aided schools which have a religious character, the rules which apply to reserved teachers in other schools with a religious character may be applied to all teachers.[41] This, coupled with the different rules as to religious education, underscores how voluntary aided schools which have been designated as having a religious character are in a very different legal position than foundation or voluntary controlled schools which have a religious character. However, there are some advantages that are enjoyed by all schools which are designated as having a religious character. This is the case in relation to religious worship. No distinction is made between foundation, voluntary aided and voluntary controlled schools with a religious character. In all schools with a religious character, the daily act of collective worship must be in accordance with the trust deed or with the tenets of the religion or religious

---

36   Ibidem, para. 3(3).

37   Ibidem, para. 4.

38   This is not to say that other faiths are not studied. In 2006 faith leaders entered into a non-statutory agreement with the Department of Education for religious schools to teach about other religions, primarily to demonstrate the need to understand other faiths and to combat ignorance and prejudice. See Department for Children, Schools and Families 2007: *Faith in the System.*

39   SSFA, Schedule 19 para. 4(3)–(4).

40   SSFA, s.58. See Sandberg: this book Chapter 16.

41   Ibidem, s.60(5).

denomination specified in relation to the school.[42] The governing body are under an obligation to ensure that any denominational education given to pupils and the content of the school's collective worship are inspected.[43]

However, the chief advantage afforded to all schools which have been designated as having a religious character relates to admissions. A school designated as having a religious character can lawfully restrict entry based on religion or belief if three requirements are met. First, the school must be over subscribed.[44] Second, the school's actions must fall within the exception afforded to schools so designated under the *Equality Act 2010*.[45] This exception covers admissions[46] to the school and the way in which they provide education.[47] However, the exception does not extend to excluding pupils from school or by subjecting pupils to any other detriment.[48] Schools that have a religious character are not exempt from the general law on these matters – which means that although they could refuse to admit a child on grounds of religion or belief they could not subsequently exclude that child or disadvantage him if he or his parents subsequently changed or lost their faith (Addison 2006: 94). The third requirement is that the school's actions must be on grounds of religion or belief.[49] The exception, found in paragraph 5(a) of Schedule 11 to the *Equality 2010 Act*, only applies in relation to religion or belief discrimination. Schools with a religious character cannot discriminate on any other ground, such as on grounds of race or ethnicity. This has proved problematic since a watertight distinction cannot often be drawn between race and religion (Barber 2010, Cranmer 2010).[50]

---

42   Ibidem, Schedule 20, para. 5.

43   *Education Act 2005*, ss.48–50.

44   *Schools Admission Code* for 2007, paras 2.41–3. Section 84 of the *School Standards and Framework Act 1998* provides that admission authorities must act in accordance with this Code. See Rivers 2010: 255.

45   The exception is now found in Paragraph 5(a) of Schedule 11 to the *Equality Act 2010*. This replicates provisions previously found in the *Equality Act 2006*, s.50(1)(a). Paragraph 6 provides that there cannot be any discrimination on grounds of religion or belief 'in relation to anything done in connection with acts of worship or other religious observance organized by or on behalf of a school (whether or not forming part of the curriculum)'. Note also the exceptions provided for LEAs and other public authorities: see *Equality Act 2010*, Schedule 3 paragraph 11. The previous law was found in the *Equality Act 2006*, ss.51–2.

46   *Equality Act 2010*, s.85(1).This covers the refusal to admit a person as a pupil as well as the arrangements and terms concerning admissions.

47   Ibidem, s.85(2)(a)–(d). This includes the way it does not provide education and the ways it affords and does not afford the pupil access to a benefit, facility or service.

48   Ibidem, s.82(2)(e)–(f).

49   However, attendance or abstaining from attending a Sunday school or a place of worship cannot be required as a condition of attending a maintained school: *Education Act 1996*, s.398.

50   See *R (on the application of E) v. JFS Governing Body* [2009] UKSC 15, in which a school's admission requirement stipulating a restricted definition of Jewishness in accordance with the teaching of the Office of the Chief Rabbi was held to be discriminatory

In sum, the current legal framework assumes that Christianity is the norm but permits SACREs to make allowances for local variations and gives parents and sixth-formers the right to withdraw. The law also allows for a variety of different schools with a religious character where, again, the general legal provisions can be altered. However, in a religiously diverse and often sceptical society, many argue that an approach that gives Christianity preferred status is outmoded. Many humanist organizations lobby for the reform of religious education and the abolition of collective worship. New non-statutory guidance on religious education in English schools was published in 2010.[51] This guidance broadens the meaning of 'principal religions' to include the Baha'i faith, Buddhism, Jainism, Zoroastrianism and Humanism, as well as the traditionally accepted principal religions such as Hinduism, Judaism, Islam, and Sikhism. The new guidance, however, does not make updated provision for collective worship.

The next section will draw upon empirical work carried out by Buchanan which asked Welsh head teachers about their understanding of the current law on collective worship, how it is operating in their schools and whether they believe it still has a place in Wales today.

The Law in Practice

The legal framework outlined above raises many questions that need to be addressed empirically. For instance, empirical investigation may shed light on whether the legal distinctions between different types of school which have a religious character are observed in practice. However, perhaps the ripest area for empirical investigation is that of religious worship. There is a popular perception that the general law mandating a daily act of worship is simply not observed. Cox and Cairns (1989: 42), for example, make the wry observation that collective worship in schools today, if carried out to the letter of the law, demands almost as much commitment from children as from adult members of monastic orders. Furthermore, it is strongly suspected that the law is unsatisfactory. As long ago as 1994, the General Secretary of the Secondary Heads Association stated that 'a law which cannot be obeyed or enforced is a bad law, and it should be amended. This is undoubtedly the case with regard to collective worship in schools' (Cumper 1998). Such concerns have not gone away. In 2010, when the Coalition Government made the novel request for members of the public to nominate 'bad laws' to be repealed, many respondents nominated the laws on collective worship.[52]

---

since in effect it was a test of ethnicity which is unlawful under the *Race Relations Act 1976*, regardless of its religious content.

51   Department for Children, Schools and Families Non Statutory Guidance 2010: *Religious Education in English Schools*.

52   See the now archived 'Your Freedom' website [Online], available at: http://webarchive.nationalarchives.gov.uk/20100824180635/http://yourfreedom.hmg.gov.uk/

The view that such law should be repealed is held by many, including a number of those headteachers who are charged with the duty of implementing the law. The compromise found in the current law was actually reached over 20 years ago in 1988 during the passage of the Education Reform Bill. Prior to that Bill in 1985, a government committee known as the Swann Committee produced a document entitled 'Education for All: Report of the Inquiry into the Education of Children from Ethnic Minority Groups'.[53] With reference to religion and education, the Committee argued that in a pluralistic, multicultural society, 'a major task in preparing *all* pupils for life ... must ... be to enhance their understanding of a variety of religious beliefs and practices'[54] To this end, the Committee urged that religious education become phenomenological[55] in its approach rather than confessional[56] and concluded that acts of collective worship should no longer be compulsory[57] since they would no longer be appropriate in a non-confessional context. The Committee held that the right to withdraw a child from religious education would necessarily become null and void since all religious education would be 'informative' rather than requiring personal participation.[58]

These proposals did not find their way into the Education Reform Bill. Indeed, the amendments proposed by the House of Lords to that Bill were likely a reaction *against* the Swann Committee's proposals. When the Bill came to the House of Lords in April 1988, it was met with much critical comment and insistence by a number of Peers that the legislation specify a predominantly Christian nature to religious education and collective worship.[59] The Bishop of London was entrusted with work on amendments to ensure that the Bill did not represent a move towards secularism or a move away from traditional Christian values. The Bishop's amendments were successfully tabled to the Bill and continue to underpin the legal framework discussed above. In the House of Lords debate, the Bishop stated that these amendments were based upon five main principles:

> We have sought to provide a framework for worship which,
> first, maintains the tradition of worship as part of the process of education, giving proper place to the Christian religion;
> secondly, maintains the contribution of the collective act of worship to the establishment of values within the school community;

[Accessed 23 January 2011].

53   Cmnd 9453 (1985).

54   Ibidem, 466 (emphasis in the original).

55   That is 'presenting religion in a way that faithfully captures its nature while simultaneously showing its relevance to the experience of pupils at different levels of intellectual, social and emotional maturity': Barnes 2007: 163. See generally Cox 2006.

56   Cmnd 9453 (1985) 474.

57   Ibidem, 497.

58   Ibidem, 498.

59   Hansard, House of Lords, 18 April 1988, Col. 1232.

yet, thirdly, does not impose inappropriate forms of worship on certain groups
of pupils;

fourthly, does not break the school up into communities based on the various
faiths of the parents, especially in that it makes some groups feel that they are
not really part of the community being educated in the school;

and, lastly, is realizable and workable in practical terms of school accommodation
and organization.[60]

In the twenty-first century, some would say that it may be timely to revisit and
reassess these principles. Moreover, there are those who would claim that the
law today does not fulfil these principles. Contrary to the Bishop of London's
statement, many would argue that the law *does* 'impose inappropriate forms of
worship on certain groups of pupils', *does* 'break the school up into communities
based on the various faiths of the parents' and is *not* 'realizable and workable in
practical terms of school accommodation and organization'. Buchanan's empirical
work sought to examine the extent to which the law is followed in practice, and the
strengths and weaknesses of the status quo, by surveying head teachers as to their
current practices and their views upon the law.[61]

Buchanan sent a questionnaire[62] to 10 per cent of schools in Wales (209
schools). Schools were selected on a random basis using the National Grid for
Learning's website[63] list of schools and selecting every tenth school in each of
the LEA lists, which meant that 10 per cent of schools in each LEA received a
questionnaire. Questionnaires were sent to 172 primary schools and 37 secondary
schools. Of these questionnaires, 112 were returned[64] (a little over 50 per cent)
meaning that the research findings are based on a sample of 5 per cent of schools
in Wales. Of the schools which responded, 71 were primary schools without a
religious character while 21 schools were primary schools with a religious
character. There were 20 responses from secondary schools. Only two of these
schools had a religious character.

The first question asked was: 'At the last school inspection, did your school
meet the statutory requirement for collective worship?' and head teachers were
asked to indicate 'yes', 'no', or 'report did not mention it'. All schools which have
been designated as having a religious character reported that they had passed the
inspection. The record is similarly high in relation to primary schools which do not

---

60   Hansard, House of Lords, 7 July 1988, Col.434.

61   The following draws upon empirical work conducted by Buchanan for the purpose
of her unpublished LLB Dissertation at Cardiff University: Buchanan 2008.

62   Buchanan carried out two surveys: one addressed to head teachers at schools
and one addressed to SACRE clerks. The following focuses only on the first survey. For
discussion of the second survey see Buchanan and Sandberg (forthcoming).

63   Available   at: http://www.ngfl-cymru.org.uk/6-0-0-0_schools_in_wales.htm
[Accessed 23 January 2011].

64   Four questionnaires were returned by the Post Office because the schools had closed.

have a religious character. All but one of these schools reported that it had passed its inspection of collective worship.[65] The head teacher of the school which did not pass indicated that they were unlikely to pass the next inspection given that collective worship took place just three times a week. The head teacher seemed opposed to collective worship and commented: 'I feel strongly that schools other than faith schools should not have any obligation to provide worship.'

The picture for secondary schools without a religious character was more mixed. Nine schools reported that they had fully passed the collective worship element of their inspection whilst eight schools reported that they had not. One school which failed was confident that it would pass the next inspection since pupils now participated in a daily act of worship. Of those that failed, four head teachers believed that collective worship had no place in secondary schools today. Many head teachers said that collective worship should still have a place in schools today because 'some children wouldn't have any experience of collective worship unless provided by school' and 'it is the only contact with formal worship that 90 per cent of school children have. It is important to give them opportunities to explore and learn about spiritual matters'. The remaining four agreed with the principle of collective worship but made comments such as '[it should be] left as a matter of professional judgement in terms of where it sits within the PSCHE[66] framework' and 'the practical issues, that is, lack of appropriate space, need to be considered'. Both of these comments hint at a misunderstanding of the legal provisions; a myth that the law on collective worship requires an entire school to meet in one place at one time. One school which did pass stated that it would not pass the next inspection, although no reason for this impending failure was given, the head teacher commenting, however, that he did 'not believe that schools were places of worship'.

The answers to this question suggest that in many schools that failed their inspection, the head teachers seem to be unconvinced of the merits of collective worship. Indeed, there seem to be some head teachers who have no intention whatsoever of putting the law fully into practice. The questionnaire suggests that a number of secondary schools without a religious character did not pass the statutory requirements for collective worship at their last inspection. Official statistics support this conclusion. In Wales, collective worship is monitored by Estyn, the office of Her Majesty's Inspectorate for Education and Training in Wales.[67] Figures on their website[68] indicate that between 2001 and 2005, 81 out of 149 schools inspected in Wales failed to meet the legal requirements for collective worship. Estyn inspection reports on non-faith secondary schools in Cardiff identified by

---

65   One school said that the report did not mention it.

66   Personal, Social, Citizen and Health Education.

67   Estyn is independent of, but funded by, the National Assembly for Wales under section 104 of the *Government of Wales Act 1998*.

68   Available online at: http://www.estyn.gov.uk/inspection_reports [Accessed: 23 January 2011].

Buchanan at the time in which she carried out the questionnaire showed that 6 out of 14 schools did not satisfy statutory requirements for a daily act of collective worship. Five schools did pass the inspection of collective worship, two reports failed to mention collective worship at all and one report stated that, although the school had passed, the *quality* of collective worship lacked consistency.

The second question sought to examine whether the legal requirements pertaining to religious worship were understood. It asked: 'What does the law say about collective worship in Welsh schools?' The answers to this question were sketchy at best, perhaps illustrating the methodological limits of the questionnaire. Fifteen schools did not answer the question which perhaps might indicate a reluctance to write about the law. However, the answers that were given were telling. One head teacher from a primary school with a religious character answered, 'I do not know' whilst a head teacher from a secondary school without a religious character admitted that they had 'no idea'. Other responses showed that the law was misunderstood. One head teacher of a primary school with a religious character wrote that the law required collective worship 'as far as is practicable' whilst other head teachers wrote that the law required 'at least one act of collective worship a week', '20 minutes per day', and worship 'at the start of each day'. One head teacher wrote that the law required 'collective worship for [the] whole school daily'. It was not clear whether they appreciated that the whole school did not need to be gathered together for the statutory requirements to be met. Another head teacher wrote that the law was 'the same as in England, as per the 1944 Act', which is, in some respects, quite right.

Some answers suggested that the legal requirements were understood. Every school, bar 11, made reference to the 'daily basis' requirement. However, just 11 of 71 primary schools without a religious character and 2 of the 18 secondary without a religious character specified the need for worship to be of Christian character. It was of note that schools with a religious character were as non-specific about the law as schools without.[69] This is of interest since, as noted above, the law pertaining to schools which have a religious character differs. A total of nine schools out of the total number of responses mentioned that collective worship can take place as a single act or separate acts. One hundred head teachers did not mention the right of parents to withdraw their child from collective worship. Overall, these answers suggest that some of the legal requirements are generally understood but a number of misunderstandings exist. In particular, there seems to be little appreciation of the differences between worship in schools with a religious character and those without.

The third question asked was: 'How often would an individual pupil in your school participate in an act of collective worship?'[70] The responses to this question

---

69   However, one head teacher at a primary school with a religious character observed that it was 'desirable that all teaching staff attend daily'.

70   The responses to this question need to be treated with some caution given that this question appeared after the question on inspections and the question which provoked many

indicated that in a majority of primary schools a pupil would experience daily collective worship whilst in the majority of secondary schools they would not. Interestingly, three primary schools without a religious character and one primary school with a religious character were the only schools to go further than the law requires – saying that a pupil would experience collective worship more than once a day. Fifty-three primary schools without a religious character said that the worship was daily, two said that it was twice a week, three said that it was three times a week, one said it was four days a week while one said that it was once a term and one just said that it was held 'regularly'. In relation to primary schools with a religious character, 17 of 21 such schools said that it was held daily, one said that it was held at least once a day, one said that it was held 'most days' whilst one said that it was held just once a week. All the secondary schools with a religious character said that collective worship was held daily. In secondary schools without a religious character, just 7 out of the 18 schools that responded said that it was held daily. Two said that it was held two days a week whilst another two said that it was held once a week. Other responses indicated that collective worship was held 'once or twice a week', 'two or three times a year' and 'rarely'. The responses to question three suggest that the general trend is that schools with a religious character and primary schools (with or without a religious character) seem to comply with the law. It is of note that those primary schools which do not have a daily act of worship do tend to have a number of acts of worship a week, rather than nothing at all; the same is not generally true of those secondary schools which do not have a daily act of worship. Moreover, if the answers to questions one and three are collated they appear to provide evidence that the inspection of collective worship in schools is inconsistent. The answers to question three suggests that in a number of the schools that did pass the inspection of their collective worship, an individual pupil does not take part in a daily act of collective worship. Of the primary schools which passed, one meets once a week, another meets twice a week, three meet three times a week, one meets four days a week and another just once a term. Amongst the 11 secondary schools reported as passing inspection, one reported that they had worship 'at least twice a week' whilst another candidly stated that 'during the year before inspection it was daily'.

Questions four and five asked who was responsible for organizing collective worship in the school and whether or not they had had any training to help them with the task. It is not clear from the law whether head teachers or governing bodies may delegate the task of organizing collective worship to another member or members of staff but it would seem reasonable to expect this to be permissible – not least to protect the religious freedom of head teachers who are opposed to collective worship.[71] In the vast majority of primary schools the findings show that

---

respondents to note that the law required a daily act of worship. Many head teachers would have been aware that the 'correct' answer to this question was 'daily'.

71   Of course, delegating the organization of religious worship does not mean that the head teachers and Governors are no longer responsible for ensuring that the legal

head teachers organize collective worship themselves. This was the case in 50 of the 71 primary schools without a religious character and in 14 of the 21 primary schools with a religious character. In eight of primary schools without a religious character the matter is organized by the Senior Management Team while in four the task was delegated to the assistant head teacher. In 18 of these schools the organization is delegated to the RE coordinator.[72] Other responses to this question in primary schools without a religious character said that it was organized by 'staff on a rota basis' or by a 'designated member of staff'. One response said that it was organized by a vicar.[73] In primary schools with a religious character where the collective worship is not organized by the head teacher, it tends to be organized by an RE Coordinator. This was the case in seven schools. In other primary schools with a religious character the organization was delegated to 'a designated teacher' or a 'collective worship coordinator'. One response said that 'all teachers' were responsible whilst one again referred to the 'local vicar'.

In contrast, it appears that secondary head teachers do not take on the responsibility of organizing collective worship. Just 2 of the 20 secondary head teachers organized collective worship in secondary schools and, interestingly, both of these were in schools without a religious character. The RE coordinator was responsible for the organization of worship in the two secondary schools with a religious character, though one respondent also named the chaplain. In secondary schools without a religious character, the organization of religious worship seems to be a matter for the Senior Management Team. This was the case in 10 of the 18 schools. In the other schools, the organization was similarly delegated to a team of senior teachers. In one school it was delegated by the 'pastoral team', in another by the 'Heads of Year' and in the third by 'Key Stage Coordinators'. No mention was made of local clerics by head teachers of secondary schools without a religious character. Overall, the general picture seems to be that religious worship is organized by head teachers in primary schools and by teams of senior teachers in secondary schools. However, the lack of coherence provided in the responses of secondary school head teachers may point to a lack of leadership in this area of school life.

The question about whether the organizer of collective worship had had any training received varied responses; the majority of respondents answered 'none'. This was especially true in the schools that did not have a religious character.[74] Only 4 of the 21 primary schools with a religious character answered 'none'

---

requirements concerning collective religious worship are met.

72   This suggests a blurring between Religious Education and Religious Worship which is not found in the law.

73   The denomination was not given. It would be interesting to see if this was the parish priest of the Church in Wales by default (notwithstanding the provisions of the *Welsh Church Act 1914*).

74   This was the case in 42 of the 71 primary schools without a religious character and 14 of the 18 secondary schools without a religious character.

whilst all the secondary schools with a religious character responded that the RE coordinators responsible for collective worship had had theological training. In primary schools without a religious character, the training seemed to be provided by the head teacher and senior management team and by a variety of courses. Some of these courses were said to be run by the LEA, others by the SACRE. Reference was also made to training days which in some cases were organized by churches.[75] In one case the respondent noted that the training had occurred through 'courses years ago'. One response referred to the organizers' background: 'Sunday school teacher/church experience', 'Religious Studies degree' and '30 years of teaching experience'. Similar trends can be found in the secondary schools without a religious character. In the four schools where training was said to have occurred, respondents referred to teaching meetings, teacher training, LEA training and in one case the organizer's role as 'RE teacher for 25 years'. In the primary schools with a religious character, in addition to references to staff training through the LEA, reference was also made to training through the Archdiocese and in one case the organizer was said to be on a 'working party for Anglican worship in schools'. Question six asked if head teachers were aware that the Welsh Assembly may offer grants to persons employed at schools in order to equip them to conduct, or assist in conducting, collective worship.[76] Every school bar one was unaware of this provision. The question also asked if head teachers would be interested in such funding. Unsurprisingly, just 10 schools said that they would *not* be interested in the funding.[77] The majority of those 10 have head teachers who had made it plain elsewhere in the questionnaire that they had little interest in collective worship. The seventh question asked, in the case of anyone coming into the school to help with collective worship, which religious tradition(s) they represented.[78] A range of answers were given to this question. Some of the primary schools without a religious character reported that they had been visited by a range of Christian ministers of religion (including clerics from the Church in Wales, the Catholic Church, the Methodist Church and Pentecostal Church) as well as lay preachers and non-ordained practising Christians. Representatives of the Salvation Army were also named. The extent to which religions other than Christianity were invited was not clear. Some schools also referred to 'a Muslim representative' whilst some said 'all the major faiths'. Respondents also said that youth workers and people from

---

75   No details were given as to which churches. Reference was also made to courses held though the Education and School Improvement Service (ESIS).

76   The *Education (Education Standards Grants) (Wales) Regulations 2001*, Schedule 1, paragraph (h)(i) provides that 'training for persons employed at schools which is aimed at equipping (or better equipping) them to conduct, or to assist in conducting, acts of religious worship at such schools in accordance with section 70 of the 1998 Act'.

77   All 10 of these schools did not have a religious character.

78   The questionnaire did not ask whether anyone came into the school to help with collective worship meaning that it is not possible to determine how many of the schools do not have external help in this way.

the voluntary sector and charities had been invited. Respondents from secondary schools without a religious character made similar but less specific responses such as 'ministers', 'representatives of various religions', 'Christians' and 'secular and Christian charitable organizations'. A similar range of visitors had been invited into schools with a religious character. Although such schools referred to the minister of religion with whom their school was linked, a number also referred to representatives of other faiths. This is surprising since it is often implied by those who oppose 'faith schools' that such schools are places of indoctrination where other religious views are not welcome.

Question eight focused on the right to withdraw children from collective worship. It asked how many children in the school were withdrawn by their parents from collective worship. The responses suggest that the numbers withdrawn are very low. In the vast majority of schools, no children have been withdrawn: this is the case in relation to 51 of the 71 primary schools without a religious character, 19 of the 21 primary schools with a religious character, 10 of the 18 secondary schools without a religious character and all of the secondary schools with a religious character. Even in secondary schools without a religious character, respondents were quick to point out that the numbers withdrawn were 'very few' in relative terms. No more than five students had been withdrawn in any of the primary schools. Fourteen primary schools without a religious character and one primary school with a religious character said that between one and five of the pupils had been withdrawn. Five responses from primary schools without a religious character volunteered the information that the pupils withdrawn were Jehovah's Witnesses.[79] In secondary schools without a religious character, six schools reported that fewer than 5 pupils had been withdrawn, one said that between 11 and 15 pupils had been withdrawn whilst one estimated the figure at around 15 to 20. These figures were fairly small in comparison to the size of these schools. This may suggest that the use of the parental right to withdraw is limited. However, further research is needed to verify this. In particular, it would be useful to examine which religious or non-religious groups request opt outs and how this functions in different types of school with a religious character since the law applying to different types of these schools differs significantly.

Further questions asked about the administration of collective worship. The answers to these questions revealed that a majority of the schools had a written, publicly available, policy on collective worship. This was the case in 58 of the 71 primary schools without a religious character, all of the primary schools with a religious character and half of the secondary schools which did not have a religious character. Only one of the two secondary schools with a religious character had

---

79   Jehovah's Witnesses commonly withdraw their children from religious education and collective worship because it is felt that this is the province of the parent alone. They do not want their children to be involved in any festivals relating to other world faiths and do not celebrate Christmas or Easter because they believe that they are rooted in Paganism and are not biblical.

a written policy which existed 'only as part of the school prospectus'. Of those schools which had a written policy only two of the schools said that they had encountered complaints about it or had experienced problems in administering it.[80] The questionnaire responses also indicated that schools were generally not in regular contact with their respective SACREs. In primary schools without a religious character, 12 said that they were never in contact, 13 said that they were rarely in contact, four said that they were only in contact where necessary and 10 did not answer the question. However, 23 primary schools said that they are in touch with their SACRE once a year or more. Three primary school without a religious character said that members of their staff were members of the SACRE. The same was broadly true of primary schools with a religious character: three were never in contract, four were rarely in contact, two were in regular contact, one was in annual contact and two had members of staff on the SACRE. One school commented that it used the SACRE's website resources whilst another said that they had had one visit in five years. The figures for secondary schools without a religious character were also similar: three were never in contact, five were rarely in contact, four were in regular contact, four were in annual contact and in three schools members of their staff were members of the SACRE. The picture for secondary schools with a religious character seemed to be more mixed. One said that they were never in contact whilst the other said that they liaised on a 'half-termly' basis. However, it is not possible to extrapolate wider conclusions from this very small sample. Overall, the general trend seems to be that most schools have some form of written policy on collective worship which has not proved problematic; this lack of difficulty may explain in part why schools and SACREs do not appear to be in regular contact. It is also worth noting that the requirement for collective worship had not been set aside by the SACRE in any of the schools surveyed.[81] It would have been interesting to compare a school that had experienced this. However, the random sampling of schools had not made this possible.

The final question was an open question asking the head teachers whether they believed that collective worship still had a place in Welsh schools today. The answers to this question indicated that it was mostly the head teachers of secondary schools without a religious character who doubted the place of collective worship. Eight of the secondary schools without a religious character were in favour whilst 10 were against. This might be in part caused by the timetabling and practical difficulties that the daily act of worship causes for many large secondary schools. By contrast, only five of the primary schools without a religious character said that collective worship no longer had a place.[82] Unsurprisingly, schools with a

---

80   One was a primary school with a religious character; the other was a primary school which did not have a religious character.

81   A response to a recent Freedom of Information request by Buchanan to all local authorities in Wales indicated that there has only been one dis-application in Wales. This was in relation to a secondary school with a large Hindu and Sikh intake.

82   Three respondents expressed no opinion.

religious character overwhelmingly stated that there was a place for collective worship. The lone dissenting voice was the head teacher of one primary school with a religious character who wrote that they thought the school should be able to represent on an equal basis all faiths in its collective worship but that 'at present as the law stands we are unable to do so'.

The responses across the board to this question proved fascinating, particularly those from schools without a religious character.[83] In primary schools without a religious character, a number of the respondents who said that there was a place for collective worship maintained that it was crucial in that it, as one respondent put it, 'sets aside quality time for pupils to reflect upon religious, moral and cultural issues'. A number of these respondents said it fulfilled rather different functions: some saw it as being an important part of PSHE; one said that it was a 'good source to maintain strong discipline' whilst another said that it 'allows staff time to discuss their expectations of their pupils'. There was a difference of opinion as to whether collective worship should be Christian. Some responses were firmly in favour of Christian worship. Several responses identified Christianity as being part of British society and said that worship in school was needed since many children did not attend Church.[84] A small number of head teachers in primary schools without a religious character made reference to their own religious beliefs to justify their support for collective worship: one wrote 'as a practising Christian I feel the Christian traditions and values need to be embedded in children thus resulting in respect and love for one another'.[85] Other respondents, although supportive of collective worship, doubted any need for it to be specifically Christian. As one respondent put it, collective worship 'should be less prescriptive in content and participation'. Interestingly, the responses from primary schools without a religious character who did not believe that worship had a place today seemed to rely upon objections to religion in general rather than objections to focusing on Christianity in particular. Two respondents said that religious worship should be a matter for parents whilst another expressed the view that 'we live in an increasingly secular society and religion/collective worship does little to bring societies together'. Two of these responses said that they believed in the value of school assemblies but that this should be done without any worship.[86] Two of

---

83   In contrast, schools with a religious character unsurprisingly referred to the ethos of the school as providing the rationale for collective worship. Many made reference to 'Christian values' but some spoke more broadly about spirituality, moral issues and the transmission of behavioural expectations.

84   Reponses included: 'Christianity is the core of British society. Many children do not go to church or experience any Christian teaching' and 'Christian values are very important and form the basis of our mission / vision policies'.

85   Another response stated: 'I have come to know Jesus as Lord and Saviour and realize that following his teaching works and provides us with all we need to live fulfilling lives.'

86   One of these respondents also said that their doubts as to religious worship did not affect their belief in the value of teaching children about religion.

the five negative responses raised questions concerning whether the legal right to withdraw from collective worship – bestowed upon parents, sixth-formers and teachers – work in practice. As one respondent put it, 'Teachers are often unable to opt out (despite their rights) and parents are given the choice of either going along with it or making their children feel ostracised and different.'[87]

Interestingly, all of the positive responses by head teachers of secondary schools without a religious character focused on the ethical importance of collective worship – saying that it helped to support the ethos of the school, was part of PSHE and promoted moral behaviour. Views as to the content of collective worship were rarely expressed. One respondent in favour of collective worship said that it should not occur 'in a religious context'. However, by contrast, one respondent simply wrote 'faith matters'. The nearest any respondent came to making the kind of arguments found in some of the responses by primary head teachers was the comment by one respondent that: 'The religious heritage of our schools is fundamental to our ability to call ourselves civilized.' The responses from head teachers of secondary schools without a religious character who opposed religious worship were much stronger in their condemnation of religious worship than their primary school counterparts. Whilst, again, many stressed that they saw the value of non-religious assemblies, many expressed the view that schools are not places of worship. One respondent said that the current legal framework as it currently stands is 'nonsense' as it is 'not observed in practice by the vast majority of schools … any observance is linked to inspection'. Another said that, 'As in France, there should be a division between the state education system and religion' whilst a third said: 'It has absolutely no place in modern Wales. The law should be repealed to allow schools to focus on delivering quality, secular, inclusive experiences which develop the ethos of the school and the standards society expects.'

The extremes of opinion are easily demonstrated. Many of those in favour of collective worship based their arguments on claims that Wales is still a Christian country, whilst many of those against based their claim on the argument that Wales is a secular country. It is also of note that whilst some primary school head teachers saw collective worship as replacing the worship that many children do not experience within their families, some of the secondary school head teachers argued that because many 'families do not participate in collective worship' then it is should certainly have no place at school. It is also significant that the comments by head teachers to this final question do not reveal any major misunderstandings of the law.[88]

87	The other respondent commented that 'I do not believe in God myself and therefore feel hypocritical encouraging pupils to worship', suggesting that they felt unable to exercise their right to opt out.

88	Only one response seemed to misunderstand the law pertaining to the daily act of worship saying that 'Logistical planning to accommodate 1,400 students in one place is impossible for an assembly'.

In sum, however, the responses to the questionnaire suggest that collective worship is a truly divisive issue in Welsh schools. This is especially true of secondary schools without a religious character. Reponses to the questionnaire (and figures from the Estyn website) suggest that a significant number of these secondary schools were considered not to meet the legal requirements regarding the collective worship during their last inspection; and a number of head teachers at schools which failed continue to be unconvinced of the merits of collective worship and appear to be unlikely to do anything to pass the next inspection. The legal requirements do not seem to be generally well understood by the head teachers questioned. Many know of the daily requirement but do not seem to appreciate the nuances found in the law allowing different acts of worship for different classes. Indeed, the fact that the worship has to be daily seems to be seen as the definitional feature of the law (much more so than, for example, the requirement that it be 'of broadly Christian character'). Many of the objections to collective worship are more specifically objections to *daily* collective worship.

Indeed, this may help to explain the different responses from primary and secondary school head teachers. Whilst in primary schools, pupils tend to experience daily acts of worship; this does not seem to be the case in most of the secondary schools surveyed. And there is a noticeable difference between some of the head teachers' own comments on the frequency of collective worship and the judgement by inspectors as to whether these schools have met the legal requirements. The other major difference between primary and secondary schools is that whilst primary school head teachers are usually responsible for collective worship, secondary head teachers seem to delegate this. The tendency for Religious Education coordinators to deal with this is concerning given the different purposes of Religious Education and collective worship found in the law. It is also of concern that those who organize collective worship seem to have little training and little contact with SACREs. The responses to Buchanan's questionnaire also highlight the extent to which the right to opt out by parents, sixth-formers and teachers is effective in practice. Given these findings it is unsurprising that head teachers seem torn as to whether collective worship should still have a place in Welsh schools. Whilst there seems to be consensus about the value of school assemblies in terms of spiritual and moral reflection and forming a clear identity for schools, there is notably less support for the inclusion of religion. Interestingly, the requirement that collective worship be 'of broadly Christian character' does not appear to be singled out for criticism by many head teachers. Any criticism is levelled at religious content in general and not at Christianity in particular. Further empirical work is needed to reveal the extent to which collective worship is 'broadly Christian' in schools without a religious character.

Conclusions: A Welsh Solution

The elucidation of the legal framework concerning religion in schools revealed a number of contradictions and absurdities. The letter of the law requires schools without a religious character to be very religious indeed whilst certain types of school with a religious character are by no means afforded by the law the level of autonomy that one might suspect, given the popular stereotypes that exist concerning 'faith schools'. It also appears that the current compromises found in the law are anachronistic. They are the result of a battle fought over 20 years ago. The relationship between religion and the State has moved on: as shown by the large amount of legislation concerning religion enacted in recent years and the significant number of religion law disputes that have come before courts (Sandberg 2011, Sandberg this book: Chapter 16), it is not surprising that many respondents to Buchannan's questionnaire and the Coalition Government's request for nominations of 'bad laws' have argued for changes to the law. Although some of these calls come from those who are ideologically opposed to the existence of religion in the public space, a number of critics have called for reform on the basis that the current law is not working. A new twenty-first century approach seems necessary.[89]

For those who seek change in Wales, their focus needs to be on lobbying Cardiff Bay not Westminster. The Welsh Assembly now enjoys significant powers concerning education. And these powers are growing meaning that the Welsh Assembly can do more than simply modify existing laws on an ad hoc basis (Oliva and Lambert: 2010). Originally, the Welsh Assembly only enjoyed powers of executive devolution. This gave the Assembly powers which were generally the same as given to central government ministers in relation to England. These powers were limited to matters given in the list of Fields included in Schedule 2 to the *Government of Wales Act 1998*, including education. The Assembly had considerable powers under the various education statutes concerning religion in schools.[90] However, under the solely executive system of devolution the Assembly could not change these provisions because they were in primary legislation. They could only regulate their administration and the way in which the powers were exercised by advising on the scope and meaning of the provisions in issuing circulars, in making regulations[91] or issuing directions. In relation to religion in

---

89   However, it does not seem to be on the agenda for Westminster. The *Equality Act 2010* would have provided an obvious vehicle for reform. However, the exceptions in Schedule 11, Part 2 (discussed above) suggest that the current law is still considered to be acceptable.

90   For details of the powers of the Assembly, see the excellent Welsh Legislation Online website maintained by David Lambert, Marie Navarro and Manon George of the Welsh Governance Centre at Cardiff Law School [Online], available at: http://wwww.wales-legislation.org.uk [Accessed: 23 January 2011].

91   See for example *Education (Pupil Referral Units) (Application of Enactments) (Wales) Regulations 2007*; *Education (Information about Individual Pupils) (Wales)*

schools, the Assembly has power to make regulations in respect of sections 69 and 71 of the SSFA which concern religious education and worship.[92] Moreover, all of the ministerial functions under the *Religious Characters of Schools (Designation Procedure) Regulations 1998* are now exercisable solely by Welsh Ministers in relation to Wales.[93] However, executive devolution and the powers of the Assembly were limited: Cardiff Bay could modify the administration of English law but it could not start again from first principles. As Oliva and Lambert (2010) note, whilst the Assembly could alter rules as to the inspection of schools with a religious character and the creation of new schools with a religious character, the Assembly could not decide to discontinue the maintenance of schools with a religious character.

This also meant that, at times, the law in Wales lagged behind the law in England. An example of this can be found in the new right for sixth-formers to withdraw themselves from collective worship (a right that had previously been enjoyed at the request of their parents).[94] Section 55(8) of the *Education and Inspections Act 2006*, came into effect on 1 September 2007, amending section 71 of the *Schools Standards and Framework Act 1998* giving the right to sixth-formers in England to withdraw themselves from religious worship in accordance with their own wishes. However, this right was not extended to Welsh sixth-formers until December 2008. The change did not apply to Wales until an Assembly Minister exercised their power under sections 55 and 180 (as amended) of the *Education and Inspections Act 2006* to agree to a commencement order being made to bring into force Section 55 of the *Education and Inspection Act 2006*.[95] Although this example shows the scope for a divergent approach in Wales, it is worth noting that the powers of the Assembly were somewhat limited. The 'choice' was simply between following the new English law or not following it; for example, there was no power for the Welsh Assembly to decide that in Wales the right was to be enjoyed by all secondary school pupils rather than just by sixth-formers.

Regulations 2007.

92   As well as certain powers under section 396 of the *Education Act 1996*. See note 88 *supra.*

93   See The *Independent Schools (Religious Character of Schools) (Designation Procedure) (Wales) Regulations 2003* and the *Designation of Schools Having a Religious Character (Wales) Order 2007*.

94   The former law was clearly in line with Article 2 of the First Protocol of the ECHR which provides that the State must respect the right of parents to ensure for their children education conforming to the parent's own religious convictions. It is questionable whether the new law is in line with the letter of ECHR obligations, though it is in step with the tendency in English law to protect the rights of children, underscored by *the Children Act 1989* which states that the welfare of the child is paramount.

95   [Online], available at: http://wales.gov.uk/publications/accessinfo/drnewhomep-age/educationdrs2/educationdrs2009/6formrswithdrwreligsworshp/?lang=en [Accessed: 23 January 2011].

However, the competencies of the Welsh Assembly are growing. The *Government of Wales Act 2006* provides for the Assembly to have certain legislative powers in addition to its executive powers. The Act provided an interim system of legislative devolution[96] and also provided for further more comprehensive system[97] of legislative devolution which would only be in force following a favourable referendum of Welsh electors which took place in March 2011.[98] The interim system of legislative devolution on its own represents a significant strengthening of the powers of the Assembly. It bestowed upon Cardiff Bay the power to make laws called Measures within legislative powers contained in the 20 Fields defined in Schedule 5 to the *Government of Wales Act 2006*. Under each Field the Assembly could bid for Matters which set out the Assembly's legislative powers in the Field. Once a Matter is inserted by Parliament into a Field in Schedule 5 then the Assembly can create Measures within the description set out in the Matter. These Measures could create the same provisions as in an Act of Parliament.[99] And Cardiff Measures may repeal Westminster statutes.

The fifth field found in Schedule 5 is 'Education and Training'. It became open to the Welsh Assembly to request legislative powers in this field which could allow for the Assembly to pass Measures which fundamentally alter the laws on religion in schools. As Oliva and Lambert (2010) comment, the Assembly could now 'affect the financing of church maintained schools to the extent that they cease to be maintained by the State, the role of religion in state schools, inspections of church schools, training of teachers, the curriculum etc.'

The successful referendum vote in March 2011 resulted in the move to the further system of legislative devolution. This will further increase the likelihood of a different Welsh law on religion in schools. The difference between the interim and further systems of legislative devolution is that while under the existing interim system there is a continuous piecemeal addition by Westminster Parliament increasing the legislative powers of the Assembly; in the further system the Assembly's list of powers is comprehensively set out with some limits. Under the further system of legislative devolution, Schedule 7 of the 2006 Act becomes in force instead of Schedule 5.[100] The difference being that the powers expressed in Schedule 7 provides a settled list, though the list could be extended by Orders in Council.[101] Under the further system of legislative devolution the Assembly will be fully aware of the extent of all of its legislative powers by reference to the list of enabling powers in Schedule 7. The fifth field found in Schedule 7 is still be entitled 'Education and Training'. However, instead of including a range of specific powers added on an ad hoc basis depending upon Westminster's

---

96   *Government of Wales Act 2006*, Part III, Sch.5.

97   Ibidem, Part IV, Sch.7.

98   Ibidem, s.103.

99   Ibidem, s.94(1).

100   Ibidem, s.108.

101   s.109.

consent, there is an enabling power to create Acts of the Assembly on matters concerning:'Education, vocational, social and physical training and the careers service. Promotion of advancement and application of knowledge'.[102]

There has long been an opportunity for variation of the law on education in schools in Wales. However, the increasing powers of the Welsh Assembly provide the opportunity for a new Welsh law on religion in schools. The examination of the legal framework and the analysis of the empirical work undertaken by Buchanan suggest that reform of the law are needed. However, reform in this area will be controversial. The events of the 1980s and the different views of the head teachers surveyed show that reaching a compromise will be far from easy. However, at least now it is possible for Wales to start again from first principles. It will be interesting to see if the Welsh Assembly has the boldness to take on this challenge to develop a legal framework concerning religion in schools which is fit for the twenty-first century.[103] Although important changes undoubtedly occurred concerning the regulation of religion in the period around the First World War, it is to be hoped that suitable and important changes will also be enacted now, a century later.

References

Addison, N. 2006. *Religious Discrimination and Hatred Law*. Oxford: Routledge.

Barber, P. 2010. State schools and religious authorities: where to draw the line? *Ecclesiastical Law Journal* 12, 224.

Barnes, P.L. 2007. The disputed legacy of Ninian Smart and phenomenological religious education. *British Journal of Religious Education* 29(2), 157.

Buchanan, A. 2008. *The Law on Collective Worship in Welsh Schools – A Critical Study*. Cardiff University: unpublished LLB Dissertation.

Buchanan, A. and Sandberg, R. Forthcoming. The secret life of SACREs.

Cox, J.L. 2006. *A Guide to the Phenomenology of Religion*. Edinburgh: Continuum.

Cox, E. and Cairns, J.M. 1989. *Reforming Religious Education*. London: Kogan Page.

Cranmer, F. 2010. 'Who is a Jew? Faith schools and the Race Relations Act 1976. *Law & Justice* 164, 275.

Cumper, P. 1998. School worship: praying for guidance. *EHRLR* 1, 45.

Doe, N. 2002. *The Law of the Church in Wales*. Cardiff: University of Wales Press.

Garcia Oliva, J. and Lambert D. 2010. Regional ecclesiastical law: religion and devolution in Spain and Wales, in *Law and Religion: New Horizons*, edited by N. Doe and R. Sandberg. Leuven: Peeters, 279.

---

102   The only exception expressed in the field itself is 'Research Councils'.

103   The progress of the Assembly is best monitored using the Welsh Legislation Online website maintained by Cardiff Law School [Online], available at: http://wwww.wales-legislation.org.uk. [Accessed: 8 February 2011].

Petchey, P. 2008. Legal issues for faith schools in England and Wales. *Ecclesiastical Law Journal* 10, 174.

Rivers, J. 2010. *The Law of Organized Religions*. Oxford: Oxford University Press.

Sandberg, R. 2011. *Law and Religion*. Cambridge: Cambridge University Press.

Vickers, L. 2009. Religion and belief discrimination and the employment of teachers in faith schools. *Religion & Human Rights* 4 (2–3), 137.

Watkin, T.G. 1990. The vestiges of establishment: the ecclesiastical and canon law of the Church in Wales. *Ecclesiastical Law Journal* 2, 110.

Chapter 6

Religion and Education in Northern Ireland: Voluntary Segregation Reflecting Historical Divisions

Christopher McCrudden[1]

Since the foundation of Northern Ireland ('NI') in 1920, the issue of control over primary and secondary education has been a source of significant tension between its two main ethno-religious communities as well as between each and the NI government. Education in Northern Ireland is organized differently compared with the rest of the United Kingdom and several of its 'unique features' (McKeown and Connolly 1992: 211) arise out of the particular form of its political and religious sensitivities concerning education. This chapter is structured as follows. First, there is an outline of the features of the governance of education in the NI model. Secondly, there is an attempt to explain briefly why these features came about. Thirdly, consideration will be given to research that has attempted to understand the effects of the model on the religious background of pupils in different schools. Fourthly, the role of teachers in this model will be addressed. Fifthly, issues relating to curriculum and collective worship will be considered. Sixthly, the crucial issue of school funding will be examined. Finally, the prospects for the model in the future will be considered by examining pupil opinion on the structure of schooling, along with an explanation of how this model relates to political developments in Northern Ireland generally.

An important point should be made clear from the start. When 'religion' is discussed in the NI context, there is an important ambiguity in its use. It may be used in what is considered to be 'normal usage' in some other countries in signifying the religious beliefs and practices of a particular individual. However, 'religion' is also used as a way of describing the identity of the two main ethno-nationalist groups in Northern Ireland, 'Catholics' and 'Protestants'. 'Catholic', in this sense, describes the community that favours Irish nationalism and a greater identity within Ireland, whereas 'Protestants' favour Unionism and a greater identity within the United Kingdom. In this context, to describe the NI conflict as 'religious' is a shorthand way of describing a complex ethno-nationalist dispute in

1 I am most grateful to Professor Tony Gallagher, Queen's University Belfast, for extensive and helpful comments on an earlier draft, which have been significantly incorporated in the final chapter.

which religious beliefs play a relatively insignificant role. The armed conflict that dominated Northern Ireland until recently was, most definitely, not a dispute about transubstantiation or the Immaculate Conception. In the context of a discussion about the way in which 'religion' is involved with education in Northern Ireland, both senses of 'religion' are important but it is in the latter sense that 'religion' is more often used. For the communities of Northern Ireland, disputes over education are more often extensions of the ethno-nationalist conflict and seldom about religious beliefs or practices. The pattern of schooling both underpins, and is underpinned by, the strong bicommunalism that is generally reflected throughout much of NI social, political and economic life (Schmitt 1988). For Dunn (1989) the education system in Northern Ireland 'is not the result of casual or accidental processes, and is therefore both profoundly enduring and an almost perfect reflection of all the other major historical divisions in the society'.

Regulation of Education in Northern Ireland

Responsibility for Education

Primary and secondary education in Northern Ireland is a devolved matter in that the UK Parliament has devolved responsibility for it to the local administration (currently the NI Executive and Assembly). The Department of Education is the responsible ministry for primary and secondary education (for an overview of the administration of education, see Byrne and Donnelly 2006). Education has been a devolved matter since 1920 with the consequence that the features of the NI education system have been markedly influenced by local NI politics. In practice, however, the NI system has closely tracked some aspects of the model in England and Wales whilst also incorporating many significant differences. One difference relates to the role of local government below the central NI Executive and Assembly. Instead of a locally elected government being responsible for education in their jurisdictions (as is still substantially the case in England and Wales), the effective and efficient administration of schools at the local level in Northern Ireland is the responsibility of five Education and Library Boards ('ELBs'), each of which covers a particular geographical area of Northern Ireland larger than that of the local councils, although we shall see that funding arrangements for schools is divided between the ELBs and the Department of Education, depending on the type of school.

Types of School

There are several different types of school in Northern Ireland, mostly distinguished from one another by the type and level of public funding which the school receives and the extent of Departmental and ELB involvement in the management of the school. These two factors are intimately linked: the greater the extent of public funding, the greater the degree of governmental (Department or ELB) involvement in management. When the Department is the direct source of funding, it (rather than the ELB) is represented in the school's management. The main types of school are: Controlled Schools (operating under the ELBs and including primary, secondary and some grammar schools, and Controlled Integrated Schools); Maintained Schools (funded through the ELBs and in practice, mainly Catholic schools, but also Irish-medium Schools), and Voluntary Schools (funded directly from the Department and including Catholic grammar schools, other – mainly Protestant – grammar schools, and grant maintained integrated schools).

Controlled schools are owned and fully funded by the relevant ELB, both for running costs and capital expenditure. The ELBs are currently contracting authorities for capital projects in this sector and are the direct providers of maintenance and facilities management services to schools. The management of a 'controlled' school is the responsibility of the school's board of governors (composed of parents, teachers, representatives of the Department of Education, and nominees of the relevant ELB), which employs the school's teachers. Controlled schools are not permitted to have a particular denominational religious ethos. However, many 'controlled' schools originated as church schools established by one of the main Protestant denominations that transferred control of their schools to the State after 1920 on certain conditions. One of the conditions was that the transferor retained a degree of representation on the school's board of governors (Schedules 4 and 5 of the *Education and Library Board (Northern Ireland) Order 1986*). All 'controlled' schools are treated as if they had been transferred from one of the Protestant Churches. The transferors speak collectively to government through the Transferors' Representative Council, which includes representation from the three main Protestant denominations (Presbyterian, Church of Ireland and Methodist).

Maintained schools are funded by the ELBs for their full running costs and by the Department for capital building works. Schools may opt for either full or partial capital funding. Maintenance and facilities management services are provided by the ELBs. Maintained schools may have a particular denominational religious ethos. In the case of Maintained Catholic schools, which in practice dominate this sector, the management of the Catholic 'maintained' sector consists of two tiers of governance. The upper tier of governance is provided by the Council for Catholic Maintained Schools – established by the *Education Reform (Northern Ireland) Order 1989* – which has the statutory responsibility both to manage and employ the teachers in the Catholic schools in this sector. The Council also represents the Catholic Maintained schools to government more generally. The Council is composed of members appointed by the Department of Education, the Catholic bishops in Northern Ireland and parents' and teachers' representatives. Below the Council are the individual school's boards of governors, the majority of the members of which are directly or indirectly appointed by the Catholic Church. The Department and ELB are represented on the boards of all maintained schools, but the number of representatives is linked to its funding status. Where the school has opted for full capital funding, the Department is empowered to nominate more members of the board. The schools are owned by trustees and managed through boards of governors. The trustees are normally the bishops of dioceses and/or their nominees or senior members of the religious orders or congregations that have provided the school. The trustees are the contracting authority for capital projects in this sector.

The integrated education sector is the third significant sector. Integrated schools are established as a result of parental initiative. These schools aim to achieve a reasonable balance of Catholic and Protestant pupils. The first integrated school, Lagan College, was established in 1981. The legislation to fund integrated schools was introduced in 1989. Under different funding arrangements, the first integrated school received grant aid in 1984. There is an organization, the Northern Ireland Council for Integrated Education (NICIE) whose statutory role is to promote integrated education and support those wishing to establish integrated schools. In addition, an Integrated Education Fund (IEF) was established to manage a trust fund to be used to support new schools and, together with NICIE, it also seeks to represent the views of the sector to government. Once established and accredited, integrated schools receive full government funding. The Department of Education has the statutory responsibility to encourage and facilitate the development of such schools (*Education Reform Order 1989*). Grant Maintained Integrated schools are funded by DE for both running costs and capital building works. They are owned and managed by boards of governors. NICIE fulfils the role of contracting authority in the provision of accommodation to establish the school. The role of contracting authority for capital projects and services transfers to the board of governors once the viability of the school is established and it qualifies for capital funding. Legislation also exists to allow schools to transform to integrated status; a small number of schools, all controlled, have availed of this option.

The result of this system is that 'with few exceptions, boards of governors in Northern Ireland have a significant proportion of their membership drawn from the local clergy or from those whom they have chosen to represent them' (Gallagher and Lundy 2006: 173) and this is the case irrespective of whether the school is a Maintained (effectively Catholic) or a Controlled (effectively Protestant) school. The one major exception to this relates to the integrated sector, where a somewhat different practice operates, not least because the Catholic Church 'refuses to nominate representatives to serve on the boards of Integrated Schools' (Gallagher and Lundy 2006: 175).

Irish-medium education is the fourth sector. The legislation to fund Irish-medium schools dates back to 1998. Under different funding arrangements, the first Irish-medium school received funding in 1984. This sector provides education in an Irish-speaking school. The *Education (Northern Ireland) Order 1998* placed a duty on the Department of Education to encourage and facilitate the development of Irish-medium education. Irish language medium schools are eligible to achieve

Table 6.1   Number of schools by school type and management type 2009/2010[2]

School Type	Controlled	Catholic Maintained	Irish Medium	Other Maintained	Integrated[3]	Voluntary	Non-grant aided	Total
Nursery	65	33	0	0	0	0	0	98
Primary[4]	386	398	20	4	41	0	0	849
Post-primary	74	72	1	0	20	52	0	219
Independent	0	0	0	0	0	0	14	14
Total	525	503	21	4	61	52	14	1180

Based on information available at: http://www.equality.nisra.gov.uk/default.asp261.htm>.

---

2   Excluding special schools and schools in hospitals.
3   Integrated includes controlled integrated and grant maintained integrated schools.
4   Does not include 17 grammar school preparatory departments.

full government funding, if approved by the Department. Approved Irish-medium schools are funded by the ELBs for their running costs and by DE for capital building works. They are almost all owned and managed by boards of governors. The running costs of the schools are funded through the ELBs. *Comhairle na Gaelscolaíochta* fulfils the role of contracting authority in the provision of accommodation to establish a new school. The role of contracting authority for capital projects and services transfers to the school's board of governors when the school is recognized for capital funding. There are currently two types of Irish-medium schools: 21 stand-alone schools, and 12 Irish-medium units attached to English-medium host schools.

Voluntary grammar schools may (and do) select their pupils on the basis of academic aptitude. They may also have a particular denominational religious ethos; a significant proportion is Catholic. They are owned and managed by boards of governors or trustees. Voluntary grammar schools are funded by the Department for full running costs. Regarding provision of capital building costs, the position is complex. Since 1993, they have been allowed to opt for partial or full capital funding, accompanied by increased Departmental representation on the board depending on whether it is full or partial. In addition, two do not receive any capital costs. Voluntary grammar schools are thus divided into two groups. The two 'Voluntary B' schools receive support only to pay teachers and maintain buildings, are able to charge for tuition, and receive no capital costs. There are no 'public schools' (in the English sense) in Northern Ireland, and Voluntary B schools are the nearest equivalent. The remaining 'Voluntary A' schools receive government support for expenditure on buildings as well as running costs, and in return must accept a proportion of school governors appointed by the Department of Education; they may not charge for tuition, but may charge a capital fee.

Finally, outside the grant aided sector entirely, there is a small number of independent schools that do not receive any government funding with parents paying tuition fees to the school. In this small voluntary sector, the most interesting group of schools for the purposes of this chapter is the small group of explicitly Protestant faith schools, several of which were established by the Free Presbyterian Church. There are approximately eight of these. In addition, there are two independent schools teaching through the medium of Irish. All must be registered with the Department and are subject to inspection but in general there is significantly less government regulation of this sector.

Historical Development

The history of education in Northern Ireland is deeply entwined with the religious issue. (There are several excellent full length studies, in particular Akenson 1973, McGrath 2000, Dunn 1990.) The original, liberal vision of an education system that was non-denominational, integrated and secular held by the Marquess of Londonderry, the first Minister of Education in the early days of Northern Ireland failed due to opposition by both the Protestant and Catholic Churches to such an approach. From the 1920s to the 1980s, in a series of standoffs, the existing pattern of a highly segregated, denominational, and non-secular educational system emerged. On the Catholic side, this was driven by church doctrine that Catholic children should be educated in schools with a Catholic ethos and by the deep political suspicion that the Catholic population shared of the motives of the NI government – contributing initially to abstention from involvement with the new government and then to deep defensiveness. The Catholic Church persuaded the Government to fund the training of Catholic teachers in separate facilities. The Church's negotiations over the funding and management of Catholic schools in the 1940s and 1960s underpinned the segregated nature of the schools. During the 1980s, the Church successfully resisted a proposed amalgamation of the Catholic teacher training colleges with the state-run Stranmillis College (McMinn and Phoenix 2005).

For Catholics, as described by Gallagher, Cormack and Osborne (1994: 508):

> the importance of separate Catholic schools in Northern Ireland for Catholics was that they represented 'a haven of self-determination' in a society where the State was seen to be little interested in that community's values, traditions or beliefs. ... Apart from the Church itself, the Catholic school system represented the only significant social institution of civil society over which the Catholic community, through the Church, exercised a degree of control.

During the 1980s, however, the quality of Catholic education being provided was placed under much greater scrutiny and it was found not to be providing the standard of education required. The need to reform the sector from within was further stimulated by the link that was disclosed between the underperforming Catholic school system, in part due to inadequate funding, and problems that Catholics encountered in the employment market. In addition, the creation of the integrated schools, despite the opposition of the Catholic Church, led to concerns that parents might decide to leave the Catholic schools if they were not seen to be meeting their expectations for their children. These concerns led to the establishment of the Council for Catholic Maintained Schools, the creation of an increased number of Catholic grammar schools and the negotiation of significantly increased funding by securing the agreement of Government that capital costs should be paid in full – an issue to which I return subsequently (Flanagan and Clarke 2006: 150–54).

On the Protestant side, the fact that the state schools were often based on schools that had previously been Protestant and had agreed to transfer into the state system coupled with the fact that Catholics were to have their own schools contributed to a sense that the state schools should increasingly reflect a Protestant ethos. In exchange for the Protestant churches transferring almost all their schools to state control there was an understanding, enshrined in statute, that the Christian ethos of these schools would be maintained. The Protestant churches succeeded in securing their Churches' representation on the board of the first teaching training college. The original ban on providing religious education in state schools was overturned, initially in 1930 by a provision permitting Bible classes outside school hours and then in 1947 with a requirement that religious education be provided in all schools.

Pupils

Religion of Pupils in Different Types of Schools

Of the five 'sectors', the 'controlled' sector is substantially Protestant in its pupil composition whereas the second 'maintained' sector is substantially Catholic in pupil composition. Approximately 95 per cent of children in Northern Ireland attend a controlled or maintained school. The third, much smaller, 'integrated' sector is intentionally mixed in comprising significant numbers of both Catholic and Protestant pupils. The voluntary grammar school sector is also significantly segregated by religion, as is the independent sector.

As of 2009/2010, there were 525 controlled schools in Northern Ireland and there were 126,943 pupils registered as attending these schools. Approximately 5.4 per cent of the children attending these schools are Catholic. It is important to understand that the extent to which these schools are so significantly Protestant derives from the choice of parents (or from the perceived absence of other suitable alternatives) rather than from any religious test applied by the schools. There are 507 maintained schools, of which 503 are Catholic managed maintained schools and in 2009/2010, there were 119,917 pupils registered as attending maintained schools. Approximately 1 per cent of the children attending these schools are Protestant. As with 'controlled schools', the schools in this sector do not apply a religious test for entry; the Catholic nature of the school describes their ethos and management rather than their entry criteria. There are at present 61 controlled integrated and grant maintained integrated schools in Northern Ireland (with a total enrolment of over 20,582 pupils – over 5 per cent of total pupils), made up of 38 grant maintained integrated schools and 23 controlled integrated schools. Approximately 37 per cent of the children attending these schools are Catholic and 44 per cent are Protestant. Unlike in the controlled and maintained sectors, the religion of the pupils is highly relevant in entrance since the explicit aim of these schools is to have a balance of Catholic and Protestant children. As of 2009/2010, there were 47,559 children attending 52 voluntary grammar schools, of which 30 were under Catholic management. In the 30 under Catholic management, approximately 1 per cent of the pupils attending are Protestant. In the 22 not under Catholic management, approximately 10 per cent are Catholic. Further complicating the picture, it was noted earlier that some grammar schools are controlled schools and their pupils are mostly Protestant.

Table 6.2   Religion of pupils by school type and management type 2009/2010[5]

School Type	Management type	Protestant	Catholic	Other Christian	Non-Christian	Other	Total
Nursery/Reception	Controlled	2,150	1,155	119	30	607	4,061
	Maintained	63	1,563	53	11	106	1,796
Primary[6]	Controlled	54,953	4,102	3,210	583	13,456	76,304
	Maintained	855	75,136	248	270	97	76,606
	Integrated	3,404	3,171	441	90	1,380	8,486
Post-primary	Controlled	37,573	1,590	1,943	175	5,297	46,578
	Maintained	240	40,923	70	57	225	41,515
	Voluntary Grammar						
	(Catholic)	253	27,051	96	54	91	27,545
	(Other)	13,108	2,072	1,167	185	3,482	20,014
	Integrated	5,671	4,495	543	97	1,293	12,099
Total		118,270	161,258	7,890	1,552	26,034	315,004

Based on information available at: http://www.equality.nisra.gov.uk/default.asp261.htm>.

5   Excluding special schools and schools in hospitals.
6   Does not include 17 grammar school preparatory departments. Does include nursery classes and reception.

Anti-Discrimination Law and Schools Admissions

Until 1998, legislation prohibiting religious discrimination only extended to employment. In 1998, however, the legislation was extended to cover a much wider range of areas (*Fair Employment and Treatment Order 1998*). Importantly, however, this legislation did not extend to cover the admission of children to schools. Nor does Northern Ireland have the equivalent of the (British) *Equality Act 2010*, which prohibits religious discrimination in schools admissions. There is, therefore, no legal prohibition of religious discrimination in admissions to schools, and no equivalent exception for faith schools since this is unnecessary as they are not covered in any event. As we have seen, most 'state' schools in Northern Ireland principally attract Protestant children. There is, in addition, a large 'maintained' and 'voluntary' sector that mainly attracts Catholic children. Due to the effective self-segregation practised by most parents, there is no significant direct discrimination by either group of such schools in admission arrangements, though most such schools operate admission criteria that would be indirectly discriminatory. There is a small 'integrated' sector, which does, however, achieve a balance between Catholic and Protestant children by choosing explicitly on the basis of religion. None of this direct and indirect religious discrimination is 'caught' by the 1998 Order.

It will be seen, therefore, that there is a very clear attempt to insulate schools in Northern Ireland from being subject to claims of religious discrimination in the area of admissions. It would not be possible, therefore, to take a claim of direct or indirect religious discrimination in school admissions whether the claimant was alleging discrimination on the ground that the pupil or the teacher was Catholic, Protestant, Jewish or non-Jewish. The *EC Race Directive* and the *EC Employment Discrimination Directive* apply to Northern Ireland as they do to the rest of the UK. The Employment Directive applies only to employment and not to the admission of children to schools. The relevant NI legislation implementing these Directives consists of the *Race Relations Order (Amendment) Regulations (Northern Ireland) 2003* (implementing the Race Directive) and the *Fair Employment and Treatment Order (Amendment) Regulations (Northern Ireland) 2003* (implementing the religious discrimination provisions of the Employment Discrimination Directive).

Academic Selection and Gender Segregation

Two other features of the composition of schools and methods of admission must be noted. First, Northern Ireland chose to retain an extensive system of 'grammar' schools that describes those secondary schools that used a system of selection at age 11. There is no extensive system of comprehensive schools in Northern Ireland. Pupils used to sit a 'transfer test', organized by the Department of Education (commonly called the '11+'), which determined which school pupils entered after primary school; those who did well proceeded to a grammar school while others would go to a 'secondary' school. Selection has long been controversial (for a detailed account of the controversy up to the return of devolved government, see Gallagher 2006: 142–5). The debate over academic selection has gone on for over a decade following two official reports (Burns Report 2001, Costello Report 2003) which both recommended an end to academic selection. In the ensuing debate the two main nationalist parties (Sinn Féin, and the Social Democratic and Labour Party) have tended to favour abolition of academic selection, while the two main unionist parties (the Democratic Unionist Party, and the Ulster Unionist Party) have tended to oppose abolition. A draft Education Order published in 2006 included a clause to abolish academic selection, but this was rolled into the political talks to restore devolution which eventually resulted in the St Andrews' Agreement and the Democratic Unionist Party won a concession that the clause abolishing academic selection would be subject to approval by the NI Assembly. Since restoration of devolution in 2007, it appears that no consensus exists in the Assembly either to support the abolition of academic selection or to pass legislation establishing some alternative arrangements. The Sinn Féin Minister of Education attempted to force the issue by ending the system of official 11+ tests, but since academic selection itself is not unlawful, two unofficial groups have been established to run their own semi-regulated test systems. The Post Primary Transfer Consortium ('PPTC'), comprising mainly Catholic grammars, has developed its own unofficial post-primary entrance assessment in Mathematics and English. The Association of Quality Education (AQE), representing 34 mainly non-Catholic grammars, also sets a series of unofficial entrance tests. The second feature of the NI school system is that a majority of secondary schools are either boys' schools or girls' schools to a much greater extent than is the case in the state sector in England and Wales.

Teachers

Religion of Teachers

Not only are children significantly segregated by religion in where they attend school, they are also highly unlikely to be taught by a teacher who is a different religion from them. As Montgomery and Smith (2006: 52) argue:

it is extremely likely that students completing B.Ed courses in Northern Ireland have had quite separate experiences of schooling, teacher education and, indeed, employment. They will most probably have attended schools in either the controlled or maintained sector, enrolled in a university college where the majority of the intake is from the same religious tradition and then applied to teach in the school sector in which they themselves were educated.

Unlike with the religion of children in schools, there is no formal monitoring of the religion of teachers. In 2004, however, the Equality Commission conducted an investigation into the composition by religion of teachers in different types of schools. The Commission collected information from a 10 per cent sample of schools representing the key categories in the educational system. Eighty out of the 91 schools involved in the investigation provided compositional information. A known total of 1,629 teachers were employed in these schools. Approximately 85 per cent of teachers in 'controlled' schools were from the Protestant community, 5 per cent were from the Catholic community and 10 per cent were from neither community. A similar pattern was found in the Non Catholic Voluntary Grammar Schools. The opposite pattern was found in the Catholic schools. In maintained schools, 98 per cent of teachers were from the Roman Catholic community, less than 1 per cent of teachers were from the Protestant community and less than 1 per cent of teachers were from neither the Protestant nor the Roman Catholic community. A similar pattern to this was found in the two Catholic Voluntary Grammar schools for which information was collected. In the three Grant Maintained Integrated schools, 48 per cent of teachers were from the Protestant community, 43 per cent were from the Catholic community and 9 per cent were from neither the Protestant nor the Catholic community. This pattern was also reflected in the Controlled Integrated School for which information was collected. There is no reason to believe that this pattern of employment has changed significantly since 2004.

Teacher Training

Not only are Catholic and Protestant teachers likely to teach in separate schools, they are also likely to have been trained as teachers separately. As Montgomery and Smith (2006: 50) point out:

> Since the 1960s, students undertaking a one year PGCE [which most teachers in post primary education obtain] have attended one of the two universities in Northern Ireland [Queen's University, Belfast and the University of Ulster], both of which have mixed religious intakes. The two university colleges [Stranmillis, and St Mary's] offering the four year B.Ed programme [which most primary school teachers obtain], however, have continued to attract students from either the Protestant or the Catholic community.

Exception from Fair Employment Legislation for Employment of Teachers

There is a specific exception for employment as a schoolteacher in employment discrimination legislation (*Fair Employment and Treatment Order 1998*, Art 71). This exception has been subject to recurring scrutiny by the Fair Employment Commission (before 2000), and by the Equality Commission (since 2000). The latter has recommended repeal but this recommendation has not been implemented. When the EU's *Employment Discrimination Directive 2000* was being negotiated, the draft was amended in order specifically to protect the exception for the employment of teachers (Art 15).

Curriculum and Collective Worship

Research from the 1980s through to the first decade of this century has found that there are significant differences in the ethos of Catholic and 'controlled' schools. This contributes to pupils in segregated schools in Northern Ireland being 'worlds apart' (Murray 1985) from each other across a range of issues, including the more obvious religious and political issues but extending beyond these into issues such as attitudes towards obeying the law (Robbins and Francis 2008). Those attending integrated schools, on the other hand, were somewhat more likely to 'reject traditional identities and allegiances that those who had attended a segregated one' (Hayes et al. 2006: 4). There have been three sets of government initiatives attempting to address this, as identified by Dunn (1986: 235): 'the first has been to make attempts at curriculum change; the second has been to try to develop some form of school integration; the third has been to bring school children from opposite schools into contact with each other'. The second of these, namely the issue of integrated schools, has already been considered. In this section the first of these will now be considered. After some local resistance, Northern Ireland has followed the practice in England and Wales of having a core curriculum that all grant aided schools must follow. There are several distinctive aspects of this curriculum, however, which distinguish its content. In particular, NI schools are required to follow particular themes relating to 'Education for Mutual Understanding' and 'Cultural Heritage', though how successful they are in meeting their objective of bringing greater understanding of the other community to pupils remains highly contested (for a sceptical assessment in the late 1990s, see Dunn and Morgan 1999).

Religious education ('RE') is a compulsory part of the Northern Ireland curriculum and collective worship is required, though parents have the right to withdraw their child from part or all of RE or collective worship. Teachers may be required to conduct or attend collective worship; those in controlled schools may be excused on grounds of conscience whereas those in maintained and voluntary schools have no such escape route. For maintained and voluntary schools, there are no requirements as to the nature of this collective worship and will in practice be Catholic; for controlled schools the collective worship may not reflect any particular religious denomination and will, in practice, be broadly Protestant. Schools have to provide RE in accordance with a core syllabus drawn up by the four main churches (Catholic, Presbyterian, Church of Ireland and Methodist) and specified by the Department. An assessment of this in 2004 found that this 'tried to impose a particular non-denominational Christian uniformity on pupils and teachers' which contributed to a 'culture of "avoidance"' in relation to the teaching of differences between the Christian churches; this was in addition to the already well-known fact that the teaching of world religions had been 'seriously neglected' (Nelson 2004: 249).

The Department specified a revised core syllabus in June 2007, which was phased in from September 2007. The four main churches prepared a draft Revised Core Syllabus and the Department accepted these proposals. The revised RE core syllabus includes Christianity, morality and, for the first time, world religions with a requirement at Key Stage 4 for pupils to study the Christian Church from both a Protestant and a Roman Catholic perspective. It provides a common core for the teaching of RE that schools are free to build upon in a way that suits the needs of their pupils and the ethos of the school. This gives schools scope to include, for example, additional material on world religions or any other RE related subject matter. The revised core syllabus is supported by teaching materials to be developed with the support of an advisory group co-chaired by the Churches and the Council for the Curriculum, Examinations and Assessment ('CCEA').

Funding

For a significant period of its existence, there was a differential funding formula adopted for controlled, maintained, and voluntary grammar schools. The effect of this in practice was that the Catholic community bore a significant portion of the cost of the separate system. Originally, though state schools would receive funding for all salaries, running costs and capital costs, the types of schools that Catholic schools became were significantly less generously provided for (Smith 2001: 561) with the forerunners of maintained schools receiving only payment for salaries, half of running costs, and only a right to make a case for capital costs. The forerunners of the voluntary grammar schools were even worse off, receiving full salary costs, but only half of heating, lighting and cleaning and no capital costs. Although partially funded by the State, then, it was a source of considerable and continuing complaint that Catholic schools were not funded equally with the effectively Protestant state sector. The fact that the Catholic community made up the 'missing' funding for a significant period of time was a source of pride but was also a considerable financial burden. It was not until the 1990s that equality in resource allocation, gradually increased between the 1930s and the 1970s in exchange for Departmental representation on boards of governors, was achieved (for a detailed account of the decision to achieve parity in capital funding in 1993, see Gallagher 2006: 140–42).

Equality law and the development of a culture of equality in Northern Ireland has played a more significant role in challenging the actions of government in relation to school funding than in any other area of education. Taken together, section 76 and section 75 of the *Northern Ireland Act 1998* give rise to obligations on government not to directly discriminate on the grounds of religion, to have due regard to the need to promote equality of opportunity between the communities and to have regard to the need to promote better relations between the communities. Prior to the 1998 Act, however, the obligations on government were more limited. Sections 17 to 19 of the *Northern Ireland Constitution Act 1973* only prohibited direct discrimination on grounds of religion. These more limited provisions provided the basis for (unsuccessful) litigation by Catholic bishops against the funding formula that applied to integrated schools in the case of *In re Daly* (unreported judgment of the Northern Ireland High Court, 5 October 1990). Nor was it likely that challenging the funding formula through the European Convention on Human Rights 1950 would have been any more successful. The European Commission on Human Rights decided in 1978 that a challenge to the funding formula of integrated schools (before they were fully funded) was inadmissible on the ground that the difference in funding appropriate reflected the lesser degree of state control over the schools (*X v. United Kingdom* (1978) DR 179).

Although unsuccessful in the short run, *In re Daly* was an important step along the road to eventual change. The argument put by the Catholic bishops was that integrated schools were being unfairly advantaged to the detriment of those attending Catholic schools. In effect, the bishops argued that Catholic schools were subject to *in*direct discrimination, but this was not unlawful under the *1973 Constitution Act*, which prohibited only direct discrimination. Although Catholic schools may have been overrepresented in the disadvantaged category, they were not exclusive to it. It was held, therefore, that since (Protestant) voluntary grammar schools were subject to the same funding restrictions as Catholic schools then the latter were not subject to direct discrimination. For the Government, this was a pyrrhic victory, however, as it merely increased the pressure for full funding for Catholic schools as the concept of discrimination broadened to encompass indirect discrimination and the focus broadened from concern with discrimination (whether direct or indirect) to encompass also an obligation to ensure 'equality of opportunity', as can be seen in the expanded set of obligations on government in the *Northern Ireland Act 1998*, compared with the *Northern Ireland Constitution Act 1974*.

The next important step towards reform of funding was the review of inequality in the labour market between Catholics and Protestants that was conducted by a series of government bodies in the 1980s and 1990s. In particular, research commissioned by the Standing Advisory Commission on Human Rights discovered that the inequality in funding between Catholic and state schools contributed to lower qualifications of school leavers from Catholic schools compared with those from state schools and thus to the observable inequalities in the labour market which the government was under significant pressure to address (the research and the process of reform resulting from it are well described in Gallagher et al. 1994, Osborne 2004). The result, which followed swiftly on the heels of the published research, was that the funding mechanism was revised to ensure that the bulk of Catholic schools henceforth would receive equal funding to state schools. The same research also played a significant role in persuading government to increase the number of places in Catholic voluntary grammar schools after the Standing Advisory Commission on Human Rights reported that Catholic children had more difficulty in securing a grammar school place than Protestant children with the same grade in the transfer test (Lundy 2000).

Prospects for the Future

Public Opinion Regarding the Relationship Between Schools and Religion

Although the practice of sending children to highly segregated schools is clear, public opinion surveys have indicated that a significant proportion of the population appears to be in favour of more mixed religion schooling. In the 2009 Northern Ireland Life and Times Survey, those polled were asked: 'if you were deciding where to send your children to school, would you prefer a school with children of *only* your own religion, or a *mixed religion* school?' Of those responding, 62 per cent said they would prefer to send their children to a mixed religion school. Catholics were somewhat more likely to say they would choose a mixed religion school (63 per cent of Catholics, 54 per cent of Protestants) but those who identified as having no religion were most in favour (86 per cent). Gallagher and Lundy have identified a not insignificant unmet need for places in integrated schools: 'Approximately 800 children are turned away from integrated schools each year and these children are unlikely to find a place in any other integrated schools' (Gallagher and Lundy 2006: 186).

These findings do not capture the complexity of the situation, of course. It is unclear how much unmet need there is in practice. It is uncertain what *weight* those who have a preference for mixed schooling give to that preference, as compared to other preferences, such as the preference for local schools with a good academic reputation. A further complexity is that there may be generational differences in the level of support for mixed schools, even in the abstract. In the NI *Young* Life and Times Survey, those surveyed were much less enthusiastic with 45 per cent saying they would prefer a mixed school for their children. In this survey, young Catholic respondents were significantly less likely than young Protestants to prefer mixed schools with 32 per cent of Catholics expressing a preference for mixed schools as opposed to 47 per cent of Protestants. Indeed, 49 per cent of Catholic young people surveyed would prefer a school of their own religion for their children.

Education and Consociationalism in Northern Ireland

To complete the picture that education policy may play in Northern Ireland in the future, the current approach to governance in Northern Ireland more widely needs, briefly, to be considered. Since the *Belfast Agreement of 1998*, Northern Ireland has evolved to become something approaching a consciational democracy. I do not intend to argue further in support of the proposition that the Belfast Agreement has a strong consociational basis (see O'Leary 2004). Consociationalism is a term coined by Arend Lijphart (1977) to describe arrangements, utilized in several political systems with ethnic or other divisions involving the sharing of power between segments of society joined together by a common citizenship but divided by ethnicity, language, religion, or other factors. Countries adopting these arrangements at various junctures in their histories include Belgium, the Netherlands, Austria, Switzerland, Cyprus, the Lebanon, Macedonia and Bosnia-Herzegovina. Under such a system, some entitlements and responsibilities are given to communities rather than to individuals. Generally, the four key elements of consociationalism are said to be: (1) the sharing of executive power among representatives of all significant groups; (2) proportional representation and allocation of important resources and offices in society, such as positions in the civil service and judiciary; (3) an explicit minority veto on vital issues, resulting in practice in a mutual veto being able to be operated by both majority and minority community; and (4) communal autonomy, in which each group has a great deal of internal self-government coupled with equality between the divided communities. Education in Northern Ireland is one of the areas in which, in practice, significant autonomy is accorded to each of the two major ethno-national communities.

There are both positives and negatives to such 'group' entitlements, using the term 'group' loosely for the moment. On the positive side, they can ensure that all groups are represented and have access to political and economic power. On the negative side, they treat individuals as members of groups and confer benefits not on the basis of individual achievement but on group identity. There has long been a heated debate between proponents and opponents of consociationalism. Prominent among the critics are some in the liberal, left and feminist traditions (one famous 'liberal' critique is offered by Barry 1975). There are two elements of criticisms from these quarters that form an important part of the debate in Northern Ireland over the acceptability of such arrangements there. The first objection is that consociation 'freezes and institutionally privileges (undesirable) collective identities at the expense of more 'emancipated' or more 'progressive' identities, such as those focused on class or gender' (O'Leary 2005: 5, who rejects these arguments). The 'opportunities for transforming identities are more extensive' (O'Leary 2005: 5) than supposed by the unduly pessimistic proponents of consociation. Second, consociational arrangements 'jeopardize important values, principles, and institutions' (O'Leary 2005: 6, who rejects these arguments). One prominent critic asserts that 'consociational democracy *inevitably* violates the rights of some groups and the rights of some individuals' (emphasis added) (Brass

1991: 334 in O'Leary 2005: 6). Needless to say, these 'liberal' criticisms are met with equally robust defences by supporters of consociation (see for example O'Leary 2005). This debate echoes the debate in Northern Ireland over the relative autonomy of the communities regarding education and with that debate a move to attempt to develop alternative educational experiences, whether based on the formal model of 'integrated' schools, or based on other more fluid models in which Protestant, Catholic and integrated schools are encouraged to share pupils and teachers in mixed classes but within the existing plural pattern of control by the separate communities.

For O'Leary (2000: xix) this political context is highly relevant to the future of the Northern Ireland educational model described in this chapter. The 'principle of educational autonomy,' he writes, 'is part of all known consociational systems. It suggests a future for Catholic schools in Northern Ireland as part of the mechanism through which nationalists protect and express their identity …'. If this is an accurate prediction, then the Northern Ireland model is likely, perhaps, to retain a very similar structure in the future to that which it had in the past.

References

Akenson, D.H. 1973. *Education and Enmity: The Control of Schooling in Northern Ireland 1920–1950*. Newton Abbott: David and Charles.

Barry, B. 1975. The consociational model and its dangers. *European Journal of Political Research* 3, 393–411.

Brass, P.R. 1991. *Ethnic Conflict in Multiethnic Societies: The Consociational Solution and Its Critics*. New Delhi: Sage.

Burns, G. 2001. *Education for the twenty-first century: Report by the Post-Primary Review Body*. Bangor: Northern Ireland Department of Education.

Byrne, G. and Donnelly, C. 2006. The education system in Northern Ireland, in *Devolution and Pluralism in Education in Northern Ireland*, edited by C. Donnelly, P. McKeown and B. Osborne. Manchester: Manchester University Press, 13–24.

Costello. 2003. *Future Post-Primary Arrangements in Northern Ireland: Advice from the Post-Primary Review Working Group*. Bangor: Northern Ireland Department of Education.

Dunn, S. 1986. The role of education in the Northern Ireland conflict. *Oxford Review of Education* 12(3), 233–42.

Dunn, S. 1989. Integrated schools in Northern Ireland. *Oxford Review of Education* 15(2), 121–7.

Dunn, S. 1990. A short history of education in Northern Ireland 1920–1990, in *Fifteenth Report of the Standing Advisory Commission on Human Rights, Report for 1989–1990*. HC 459, London: HMSO.

Dunn, S. and Morgan, V. 1999. A Fraught path: education as a basis for developing improved community relations in Northern Ireland. *Oxford Review of Education* 25(1–2), 141–53.

Flanagan, D. and Clarke, J. 2006. The Council for Catholic Maintained Schools: policy and influence – a model for progress, in *Devolution and pluralism in education in Northern Ireland*, edited by C. Donnelly, P. McKeown and B. Osborne. Manchester: Manchester University Press, 150–54.

Gallagher, A.M., Cormack, R.J. and Osborne, R.D. 1994. Religion, equity and education in Northern Ireland. *British Educational Research Journal* 20(5), 507–18.

Gallagher, T. 2006. The impact of devolution on education policy: case studies, in *Devolution and Pluralism in Education in Northern Ireland*, edited by C. Donnelly, P. McKeown, P. and B. Osborne. Manchester: Manchester University Press, 139–48.

Gallagher, T. and Lundy, L. 2006. Religion, education and the law in Northern Ireland, in *Religious Education in Public Schools: Study of Comparative Law*, edited by J.L.M. López-Muñiz, J. De Groot and G. Lauwers. VI Yearbook of the European Association for Education Law and Policy (Springer), 171–95.

Hayes, B.C., McAllister, I. and Dowds, L. 2006. In search of the middle ground: integrated education and Northern Ireland politics. *Ark Research Update* (January), 42.

Lijphart, A. 1977. *Democracy in Plural Societies*. New Haven: Yale University Press.

Lundy, L. 2000. *Education Law, Policy and Practice in Northern Ireland*. Belfast: SLS Legal Publications.

McGrath, M., 2000. *The Catholic Church and Catholic Schools in Northern Ireland: The Price of Faith*. Dublin: Irish Academic Press.

McKeown, P. and Connolly, M. 1992. Education reform in Northern Ireland: maintaining the distance? *Journal of Social Politics* 21(2), 211–32.

McMinn, R. and Phoenix, É. 2005. The Chilver Report: unity and diversity. *Irish Educational Studies* 24(1), 5–20.

Montgomery, A. and Smith, A. 2006. Teacher education in Northern Ireland: policy variations since devolution. *Scottish Educational Review* 37, 46–58.

Murray, D. 1985. *Worlds Apart: Segregated Schools in Northern Ireland*. Belfast: Appletree Press.

Nelson, J. 2004. Uniformity and diversity in religious education in Northern Ireland. *British Journal of Religious Education* 26(3), 249–58.

O'Leary, B. 2000. 'Foreword', in *The Catholic Church and Catholic Schools in Northern Ireland: The Price of Faith*, edited by M. McGrath. Dublin: Irish Academic Press, xiii–xix.

O'Leary, B. 2004. The nature of the agreement, in *The Northern Ireland Conflict: Consociational Engagements*, edited by J. McGarry and B. O'Leary. Oxford: Oxford University Press, 260–293.

O'Leary, B. 2005. Debating consociational politics, normative and explanatory arguments, in *From Power Sharing to Democracy*, edited by S. Noel. Montreal and Kingston: McGill/Queen's University Press, 3–43.

Osborne, R.D. 2004. Education and the labour market, in *Fair Employment in Northern Ireland: a Generation On*, edited by B. Osborne and I. Shuttleworth. Belfast: Blackstaff Press, 65–87.

Robbins, M. and Francis, L.J. 2008. Still worlds apart: the worldviews of adolescent males attending Protestant and Catholic secondary schools. *Northern Ireland, Research in Education* 80(1), 26–36.

Schmitt, D.E. 1988. Bicommunalism in Northern Ireland. *Publius* 18(2), 33–45.

Smith, A. 2001. Religious segregation and the emergence of integrated schools in Northern Ireland. *Oxford Review of Education* 27(4), 559–75.

Chapter 7

The French Model: Tensions Between Laïc and Religious Allegiances in French State and Catholic Schools

Blandine Chélini-Pont

The educational system in France neither proscribes nor promotes religious education. Religious education in the French state system appears to play a marginal role in state education as a consequence of the progressive secularization of France. But is the situation any different in French private denominational schools? Logically, it should be. With the 31 December 1959 Act[1] on academic freedom, the French State integrated Catholic schools into the 'public service teaching mission' ('mission de service public') while acknowledging their 'distinctive character' ('caractère propre'). In so doing, the State guaranteed the exercise of academic freedom by allowing children from religious families to receive a religious education as part of their schooling. However, the religious ethos of Catholic schools, their 'distinctive character', despite being acknowledged in the law, has become diluted.

This chapter will explore the main features of the French model on religion at school, revealing an often unknown possibility of religious education in state secondary schools through chaplaincies (section 1) and a less surprising presence of religious education in Catholic private schools, thanks to the concept of 'distinctive character' which these schools enjoy (section 2). However, it will be shown that French Catholic schools struggle to maintain their Catholic ethos. Some difficulties in maintaining a strong religious ethos stem from internal problems (section 3): the attachment professed by the Catholic school system to freedom of conscience; the decision to be fully part of the – highly secularized – French 'public service' of teaching; and the laïcization of its staff and head teachers. Others are linked to the pupils and parents who choose to attend Catholic schools but do not necessarily have strong religious convictions, if at all (section 4).

---

1 Loi n. 59–1557 of 31 December 1959 sur les rapports entre l'Etat et les établisse mentsd'enseignementprivés, *JO* 1959, 57 (Act on the relationships between the State and private education institutions).

Religious Education in State Schools

Though often unfamiliar to parents and teachers, Article 2 of the *9 December 1905 Act* on the Separation between State and Churches,[2] founded on the religious neutrality of the State and its services, provides for the possibility of having chaplains in state secondary schools. Moreover, Article 1(3) of the *Act of 31 December 1959* or *Debré Law* (after the Prime Minister under President Charles de Gaulle) provides that national education authorities 'take all necessary measures so as to ensure freedom of worship and religious education for pupils of the state education system'.[3] On these textual grounds, as construed by the case law of the *Conseil d'Etat*, the *Décret of 22 April 1960* organized chaplains in French state schools.[4] The presence of chaplaincies in French state schools was later confirmed and inserted into the French Code of Education.

The Purpose of Chaplaincies: to Facilitate Religious Education

The possibility of a chaplaincy service was prompted by the need to allow access to religious instruction for those children whose parents wish it. The whole system is based upon this goal. Two requirements need to be satisfied for a chaplaincy service to be created in a given school: a request by parents and an established need for such a service in the school in question.

A chaplaincy service may be created in French state secondary schools upon the request of parents. The request for a chaplaincy service is a necessary precondition to its creation (Code de l'Education, articles R 141–1 to R 141–4, *Order of 8 August 1960*)[5]. The *Circular of 22 April 1988*[6] specifies that 'requests by parents, pupils' legal representatives or adult pupils must be submitted individually and bear the signature of interested parties'. These requests must be addressed to the head teacher of the school in question. They may be submitted by standard form or be handwritten on plain paper, as long as they mention the religion, family name, address, and signature of interested parties so as to clearly show the wishes of the interested family.

Under Article 2 of the *1905 Law*, the creation of a chaplaincy must be deemed necessary for pupils to practise their religion. The Conseil d'Etat makes it mandatory for the Minister of Education 'to create a chaplaincy service in schools where it is established that this institution is necessary for the free exercise of

---

2   Loi du 9 décembre 1905 concernant la séparation des Eglises et de l'Etat, *JO* 1905, 7205.

3   *JO* 1959, 57.

4   Décret relatif au contrat d'association à l'enseignement privé par les établissements d'enseignement privés, *JO* 1960, 3829.

5   *JO* 1960, 7964.

6   *Bulletin* 1988.

religion by students'.[7] For pupils at boarding schools, the creation of a chaplaincy service appears to be the only means for them to receive religious instruction and to worship. Declining to create a chaplaincy in a boarding school, when it corresponds to the desire of parents, would violate the principle of free exercise of religion. This is why, even before the Décret of 1960, the Conseil d'Etat had sanctioned a decision to abolish all chaplaincies created after 1939, because the decision 'could have the effect of depriving boarding students … of the possibility to freely practice their religion and receive religious instruction'.[8] Following this reasoning, Article R 141–2 of the Code of Education (former Article 1 of the *Décret of 22 April 1960*) requires a chaplaincy service to be created in boarding schools upon request by parents. It is the school head teacher's responsibility to organize this service but he must inform the rector (chief education officer) of the number of students per class and per religion who wish to receive religious instruction, the hourly schedule for each group and the location in which the teaching will take place.

For secondary schools not equipped with boarding capacity, there is no obligation. In state primary schools, there is no provision for chaplaincies at all. Freedom of religion is guaranteed by the provision of one day off school a week for pupils to receive religious instruction off school grounds, should they wish to.[9] In state secondary non-boarding schools, the decision to create a chaplaincy service is made by the rector.[10] Article 5 of the *Order of 8 August 1960* states that the decision 'is based on a report to be submitted by the head teacher within a maximum period of two weeks after the beginning of the school term'. The report must be exhaustive in order for the rector to make his/her decision.[11] Since Article 5 of the Order states that the decision must be taken by the rector before 1 November, the *Circular of 1988* suggests that 'the requests of families and

---

7   *Rec* CE 1955, 51.

8   *Rec* CE 1949, 161.

9   Article R 141–1 of the Code of Education (former Article 5 of the *Décret of 22 April 1960*), Conseil d'Etat case law: CE 24 December 1909 *Commune de Sarzeau*, *DP* 1911, 3rd part, 118.

10   Article R 141–4 of the Code of Education (former Article 3 of the *Décret of 22 April 1960*).

11   *JO* 1960, 7964. The *Circular of 22 April 1988* provides as well that the report must include the totality of the requests received, the distribution of the students interested by religion and classes, the conditions under which the teaching can take place, either inside or outside of the school, according to the following elements: the weekly school organization, with information on school activities or extra-curricular activities organized on Wednesday; distance to religious venues; characteristics of the students involved (age distribution between home students and half-boarders); external constraints such as schedules of school bus services, whether or not, inside the school, rooms can be used for religious teaching; the opinion of the school board on the operating conditions of the chaplaincy service. If the board could not be consulted on this issue in time, the opinion of the board is to be sent at a later stage within the timeframe given for the final decision to be taken by the rector (*Bulletin* n. 16, 28 April 1988).

the opinion of the school board be collected before the end of the school year preceding the one where the dossier is sent to the rector.' The decision to create a chaplaincy service or not in a given school is then left to the rector's discretion but the *1988 Circular* states that:

> The general rule should be to give satisfaction to the wishes of the requesting families, even if they represent only a very small percentage of the total number in the school. A refusal to create a chaplaincy service would in fact be hard to justify since the existence of such a service would not affect the convictions and the freedom of conscience of other school community members.

The possibility of having chaplains in French secondary state schools has not ensured widespread religious education in state schools.

The Relative Failure of Chaplaincies to Facilitate Religious Education

As one can see, the effectiveness of a religious education in French state secondary schools is difficult to guarantee because of its sheer legal complexity. No one, so far, has challenged the difficulty and vagueness of the procedure. This is because the majority of users, parents and children, are completely unfamiliar with the legal texts. Even when the possibility of requesting a chaplaincy service is known, it is not always used. The presence of chaplaincies varies greatly depending upon the geographical, religious and political context of the school in question. Generally speaking, they are more visible in Western and Northern parts of France which have remained more Catholic than other French regions.

More generally, the *laïc* legacy of the French Third Republic remains strong in French state schools. Except for some Muslim parents or pupils regarding the issue of the Islamic veil, no one in France really contests the absence of religion and of religious symbols – may they be worn by teachers or pupils – in French republican state schools. State secular schools are the gem of French *laïcité*. Despite the crisis that the school state system is undergoing, state schools remain the living symbol and the heart of *laïcité*. This symbolic status of schools explains why the Ministry of education receives priority in the state budget. It also explains why the state school system is part of the French psyche. The school timetable rather than the traditional religious calendar now rules people's lives with the two months of Summer holidays in July and August and the four shorter school holidays throughout the year. The *Baccalauréat*, the end of school national examination (at 'A' level stage) and notably its philosophy component, is celebrated every year by extensive coverage by national media. The state education system is, *par excellence*, the point of socialization for all generations, and its authority over the collective conscience remains strong. The notion of *laïcité* is largely tied to the state school system, to such a degree, states Yves Bruley, that 'public opinion is often tempted to conflate the two' (Bruley 2005: 154).

The existence of this state secular school system is the result of a long academic battle. The idea that the State should organize a public system of education for the population dates back to before the laws of the 1880s. The *Guizot law 1833*[12] and the *Falloux laws 1850*[13] had constructed the base for a state primary and secondary system under which bishops played an important role and sat on local academic councils (Mayeur 2004: 314–37). The education laws proposed by Republican Minister of Education Jules Ferry stripped the Catholic Church of this right of control, made attendance mandatory for all girls and boys aged between 7 to 13, proclaimed that state education was to be free, and erased and forbade any religious education – the apprenticeship of Catholic truth – from the syllabus of primary schools (Combes 1997). Instead, pupils were granted one day off a week so as to pursue religious activities outside school premises should they wish to. The message that stems from the Ferry laws and feeds French collective memory is twofold: (1) that open access to free schools for all French pupils without any discrimination[14] is owed to the school system created by Jules Ferry and (2) that the absence of religion at school is a precondition of the existence of this system.

After the Ferry laws (and throughout the decade that had preceded them), the Catholic Church fiercely attacked and criticized its exclusion from the state school system. The battle over schools divided the country into two camps. This 'war' was simultaneously the engine of anti-clericalism forces – the adepts of the new school order – and of clericalism forces – the adepts (Catholics and monarchists) of the old system (Rémond 2004, Lalouette 2004: 646–65). The construct in French national imagination of an opposition over school between clerical/anti-clerical enemies is rooted in these historical battles. But nowadays, the 'clerical forces' of this imaginary construct are no longer Catholics but can be sometimes confused with Muslims. In sum, Religious education is limited in French state schools. Presumably however, it should flourish outside of the French state system, in private denominational schools.

---

12   François Guizot (1787–1874) was a historian and a famous politician. He became Minister of Public Instruction during the first government of King Louis-Philippe's liberal regime, before receiving other responsibilities, including in the end the post of President of the Council in 1847. His education law made it compulsory for towns over 500 inhabitants to open a public school for boys. Thanks to this law, the number of French primary schools increased from 10,000 to 23,000 in 15 years.

13   Alfred de Falloux (1811–1886) was Minister of Public Instruction under the second French Republic. The law he initiated remained famous because of the insistence on freedom of education which allowed the Catholic Church to expand its own school system. Falloux also permitted some control of the state school system by the Catholic Church.

14   'Without discrimination' is the more contemporary term, the older one being 'without inequality'. The idea that before the Ferry laws, French children had no access to education is of course largely inaccurate.

Religious Education and Identity in Catholic Private Schools

Let us examine whether the Catholic educational system (which represents 98 per cent of private schools in France and educate 20 per cent of school pupils) is more effective in transmitting religious convictions. Since the Debré law of 1959 which set up the possibility for private schools to enter into a partnership contract with the State, Catholic schools under contract have been concerned about the 'doctrinal' preservation of their Catholic ethos. The Statutes of Catholic Schools of 1973 and of 1992, promulgated by the Conference of French Bishops at the time of the French decentralization laws, both begin in their preambles with a review of fundamental Catholic texts on this issue: the Declaration of 28 April 1965 (Gravissimum educationis momentum) and the texts of the Congregation for Catholic Education (Lay Catholics in School 1982, The Religious Dimension of Education 1988, The Catholic School System on the Threshold of the Third Millennium 1993 and, most recently, Educating together in Catholic Schools. Mission shared by the Ordained and the Laity Alike 2007).

The role of Catholic schools in the integral education of Man[15] is clearly acknowledged for both the good of the earthly realm and the extension of the Kingdom of God. Among all the passages cited in the Preamble to the Statutes of 1992, there is a symbolic one quoted from the Conciliar Declaration of 1965:

> The Catholic school system, by opening itself as befits the progress of time, teaches pupils to work effectively for the good of the earthly realm. At the same time, it prepares them to work on the extension of the Kingdom of God, so that in exercising an exemplary and apostolic life, they become a ferment of salvation for humanity.

Thus, the purposes of Catholic schools are to communicate the message of the Gospel, to transmit a precise faith ('the good news') around which an idea of Man is formed, taking into account all of Man's dimensions and potential. As to the exact nature of this teaching, the Preamble of the *Statutes of 1992* states, based on the *Conciliar Declaration* that it is designed:

> [to] create for the school community an atmosphere enlivened by the Gospel spirit of freedom and charity. It aims to help the adolescent in such a way that the development of his or her own personality will be matched by the growth of that new creation which is bestowed on him/her by baptism. It strives to relate all human culture to the news of salvation, so that the light of faith will illuminate the knowledge which pupils gradually gain of the world, of life and of the human race.

---

15   As expressed by the Congregation for Catholic Education 1982: n. 28 and in the *1973 and 1992 Statutes*: para. 1.

The 'distinctive character' (*'caractère propre'*) of Catholic schools in France is the term used in Article 1 of the *Debré law of 31 December 1959* to describe their Catholic ethos. This expression is also found in the *Conciliar Declaration of 1965 on Catholic education* (*propium autem illius est*, §8). It signifies the provision of a humane and intellectual education to each child stemming from the truths of the Catholic faith, a particularity that the *Debré law* protects in the name of freedom of conscience.

If freedom of conscience, for reasons we will discuss below, seriously limits the transmission and reception of the Gospel message in French Catholic schools, it nevertheless constitutes a constitutional protection for the distinctive character of Catholic schools in France.[16] In his preliminary speech to the Law, Michel Debré emphasized the 'fundamental principle of respect for freedom of conscience' and for freedom of education which implies the right of citizens to found and manage schools as well as the rights of parents to educate their children and to select their children's school:

> Private education is the expression of a fundamental freedom. We know it is not
> enough for a freedom to become a reality to proclaim it in a text. Expressions
> of the freedom must be allowed and those expressions must be guaranteed. It is
> not only a guarantee given to individuals; it is also a guarantee that is necessary
> for a balanced society, which would not really be a free society if freedoms were
> only theoretical.[17]

How then is the distinctive character of Catholic schools under state contract in France maintained? The system seems very efficient on paper. Article 4 of the Statutes of 1992 provides that 'in every Catholic school, the educational project explicitly refers to the Gospel and the teaching of the Catholic Church' or elsewhere 'each school is presented as a Christian community based on an educational project rooted in Christ and his Gospel (§1)'. The 'Catholic' label is only given if the school is built by the ecclesiastical authority of a diocese or otherwise with its approval and it is committed to follow the Statutes, their preambles, the texts of reference and canonical provisions. To implement these

---

16   The Conseil constitutionnel held that the preservation of the distinctive character of private denominational schools was a manifestation of the principle of academic freedom and added that freedom of conscience was a fundamental principle recognized by the laws of the Republic. Ccel 23 November 1977 n. 77–87, *Grandes décisions du Conseil constitutuonnel* 25. [Online] available at: http://www.conseil-constitutionnel.fr/conseil-constitutionnel.fr/conseil-constitutionnel/francaus/les-decisions/acces-par-date/decisions-depuis-1959/1977/77–87-dc-du-23-novembre-1977.7529.html [Accessed: 15 January 2010].

17   Speech of 23 December 1959 [Online] available at: http://www.assemblee-nationale.fr/histoire/Debre1959_bis.asp [Accessed: 6 December 2010].

requirements, each diocese establishes, under the bishop's pastoral responsibility,[18] two regulatory authorities assisted by a council body. These regulators act as the 'diocesan director' for diocesan schools and as the 'major superior' for schools under congregational trust. The regulators are 'guarantors before the bishop of the evangelical authenticity of the educational project' (§15) and the councils assisting them should help to 'maintain the vitality of the schools' educational community' (§16).

More generally, the diocesan director, appointed by the bishop is also the secretary general of the Diocesan Catholic Education Board which, under Article 28, has the primary responsibility to 'implement the pastoral guidelines of the Diocese in the Diocesan Catholic Education system'. These boards were at one time seconded to academic boards to adhere to the decentralization laws, but they were re-established as the principal regulatory bodies in 1996.

At the end of the chain, or first on the pastoral front, is the school head teacher. In the end, it is upon him that the development of the pastoral educational programme of the Catholic school depends. It is he who is responsible for both educational and spiritual activities (§8). The *Statutes of 1992* use the term 'Catholic schools of education' in order to show that it is not so much the teaching that is Catholic as it is the way in which schools continually reinvent the link between 'teaching, educating and revealing a sense of the person enlightened by the Gospel.' It is up to the head teacher to create this link and to make sure that the school does not become 'a private institution with a chaplaincy' but rather a place where the Gospel is the 'key to query all activities and directions' as stated in the document 'Keeping the Promise' sent to all Catholic schools in August 2005. The severance of this link would also be his responsibility and would mark the end of the distinctive character of the Catholic school in question.

Finally, since 1993, Catholic education 'Assizes' are held regularly to reflect upon the guiding principles of Catholic teaching. The first on 'Making sense of school to give meaning to life' focused for four years on the concept of 'distinctive character' and its articulation with the wider educational community, especially teachers.[19]

The Dilution of Religious Identity in Catholic Private Schools

Despite this coherent framework, the distinctive character of Catholic schools seems to have inexorably diminished since the 1970s so that the daily life of Catholic schools has largely been secularized. This situation provoked a strong

---

18   §15 of the *Statutes* states that 'Catholic schools are rooted in the diocesan church and are an important element of pastoral activity'.

19   *Les orientations de l'Enseignement catholique, la démarche des Assises de 1993 à 2006* (Guidelines of Catholic education, the approach of the Assizes from 1993 to 2006) [Online] available at: http://www.formiris2.org/medias/cle_219_1.pdf [Accessed: 6 December 2010].

reaction at the beginning of the school year in September 2006 by the Archbishop of Avignon, Mgr Cattenoz, which has echoed in several newspapers and sparked a rather lively internal debate.[20] Beyond the secularization of French society and the fact that Catholic schools accept this secularization and welcome all children, the difficulty of maintaining a religious identity within Catholic schools comes from the legal repercussions of the *Debré Law* and the Catholic educational culture itself in a country strongly influenced by 'secular education'. Three factors contribute to the dilution of the Catholic ethos within French Catholic private schools: (1) the constraints imposed by the necessary respect for the fundamental freedom of conscience; (2) the decision of Catholic schools to be integrated into the – highly secularised – 'public service' teaching mission; and (3) the *laïcization* of its staff and school head teachers.

The Constraints Imposed by Freedom of Conscience

Freedom of conscience is a fundamental principle for both the Catholic school system and the Republican law. On the Catholic side, the principle of free membership in a faith and school is seen as a fundamental requirement of freedom of conscience. The *Statutes of 1992* (para. 8) articulates the concept of 'respect for the religious freedom and conscience of pupils and families. Freedom is strongly defended by the Church'. It emphasizes the essential link between family and school as well as the vital role of parents as the first educators of their children who give their requisite consent to this education. One reminder of this was the speech given by Mgr Eyt, Archbishop of Bordeaux, during the First Assizes for Catholic Education in 1993 on the 'distinctive character of Catholic education in civil society and the Church', based upon the *Conciliar Declaration* and the *Familiaris Consortio encyclical* of John Paul II:

> Catholic teaching that does not respect freedom of conscience or that refuses to admit pupils on grounds of religious or philosophical opinions, would lose its distinctive character under the most solemn requirements of the Church … the rights and duties, primary and inalienable, to educate children belongs to parents. They must enjoy genuine freedom in their choice of school. This right precludes any schooling monopoly and postulates the freedom of education.

---

20   While the Bishop's Conference was reflecting on Catholic teaching, Mgr Jean-Pierre Cattenoz, Archbishop of Avignon, took position and delivered his views in a Diocesan charter written in June 2006. According to him, we are witnessing a 'distortion or sweetening of the distinctive character of our Catholic schools' and an 'abuse of the values of solidarity and inclusiveness.' Mgr Cattenoz therefore wishes to restore 'an integral catechesis based on the tradition of the Fathers of the Church and the Catechism of the Catholic Church.' To meet this goal, he hopes that 'all teachers be involved in the project or agree not to stay in the school' (Recentrer l'enseignement catholique, Elodie Maurot, *La Croix*, 28 September 2006, 10).

A monopoly in fact 'goes against the innate right of the human person, against progress and the transmission of culture itself, against harmony among citizens, and finally against pluralism that is now the norm in many societies'.[21]

It is obvious that, from the Catholic perspective, freedom of conscience is seen as the factor for the transmission of the Gospel. However, it is important to note that in the *Statutes of 1992* (para. 8), as in the speech of Mgr Eyt in 1993, 'freedom of conscience' did not entail abstention from transmitting the message of the Gospel to pupils:

> Catholic education is intended to be open to all who accept its educational project ... the positive definition of the distinctive character reflects the freedom of children, parents and teachers, but it also allows for the freedom of Christians and the Church to offer the message of the Gospel while respecting everyone's beliefs ... [a] Catholic education that would renounce offering faith, under any pretext whatsoever, would also lose its 'distinctive character'. Because, to present and offer does not amount to imposing.

However, this is not properly ensured by the *Debré Law of 1959*. Rather, Article 1 of that Law provides:

> In private schools under state contract as provided below, the teaching under the contract regime is subject to state control. The school, while retaining its distinctive character, must provide this education in full respect of freedom of conscience. All children, without distinction of origin, opinions or beliefs, have access to this education.

This Law clearly separates the 'public' content of educational programmes from 'non-state contractual activities', allowing both pupils and teachers to disregard the concept of 'distinctive character'. This means that, for the sake of their freedom of conscience, pupils cannot be obliged to attend catechism or be Catholic and teachers cannot not be required to participate in the school's educational project beyond teaching their own subjects.[22]

---

21   Mgr Eyt, Assizes of Issy-les-Moulineaux on 14–16 May 1993, Catholic Teaching documents: n. 1862, May 1993 [Online] available at: http://www.formiris2.org/medias/ cle_184_1.pdf [Accessed: 17 February 2011].

22   The Conseil d'Etat held that the obligations arising from the concept of 'distinctive character' cannot infringe on freedom of conscience and should be assessed with regard to the nature of the duties performed by staff employed within the private school in question: CE 20 July 1990, 3/5 SSR, 85429 [Online] available at: http://conseil-etat.vlex.fr/vid/ conseil-etat-ssr-juillet-recueil-lebon-40597849#ixzz11TEXZoIE [Accessed: 5 April 2011]. Similarly, the Conseil constitutionnel in its famous decision n. 77–87 – when asked to consider the provision in the *Debré law* whereby teachers who were entrusted the mission

To be recruited as primary or secondary private schools teachers, candidates need to pass an examination and undertake a motivational interview (which, if successful, grants them the right to access the exam). The motivational interview is designed to inform candidates on the distinctive character of Catholic education. The overall process of recruitment must abide by Article L 122–45 of the French Labour Code and be respectful of candidates' freedom of conscience. During this interview, candidates cannot be asked to commit to more than a duty of professional discretion and cannot be required to actively participate in the educational project.[23] The National Committee of Catholic Education states that the commitment in question is a matter of personal freedom: 'a Christian commitment is neither private nor public, it is the response of a person to a personal call discerned in the Christian community; it is of a vocational nature and can, as such, help to enrich all life and any professional status'.[24]

The Constraints Imposed by the Participation in the 'Public Service' Teaching Mission

What consequences does the integration of Catholic education into the public service mission entail? It should be noted that the educational service mission was a Catholic tradition before becoming a republican legal requirement. The Catholic school system is open to all and intended to be a 'social service' (expression of Mgr Eyt) aiming at achieving the common good. Welcoming everyone and participating in the future of a society seems as fundamental as the sustainability of the Catholic faith. The logic of Catholic education in France is therefore its integration into public education. It is not a logic imposed by the State, but a logic chosen by the Catholic school system. The choice is one of a massive presence rather than of a reduced denominational presence. In terms of territorial networking, this choice has a very large impact since one out of two pupils in France goes through his schooling between the two systems; a compensatory flow phenomenon-that prevents the marginalization of Catholic teaching. The Catholic education system considers itself to be both universal and national as well as non-

---

to teach in a private school under contract with the State were held to respect the distinctive character of the school – ruled that 'the obligation imposed on teachers to respect the distinctive character of the school, if it holds them to the duty of professional discretion, may not be interpreted as allowing to infringe on their freedom of conscience': note 18 *supra*.

23   The level of commitment may not be the same for everyone. 'Thus teachers on the educational project level have the freedom to adopt attitudes that go from respect – considered as a duty of professional discretion – to commitment in the implementation of the Christian offer.' National Committee of Catholic Education (CNEC), 18 October 1996, quoted on the webpage for the 'recruitment of private nursery and primary school teachers'. [Online]. Available at: http://www.crdp-nantes.fr/service/doc_admin/recrutement-enseignants-premier-degre-prive.pdf [Accessed: 6 December 2010].

24   Ibidem.

denominational and non-communitarian. Serving in a country in which 40 per cent of the population is self-described atheistical seems like an impossible challenge.

The Laïcization of Staff and Head Teachers

The process of replacement of clerics with lay staff and head teachers sharply accelerated in the early 1970s. According to André Blandin (Assistant Secretary for Catholic Education), Catholic teaching is experiencing:

> a sort of break from tradition for its school head teachers. The generation of those who are now retiring had directly succeeded a priest, a monk or a nun and had, in fact, by direct tradition, and sort of by osmosis, received basic training. Today's arriving generation has not been as lucky ... demand is therefore high and it is vital that teachers should have enough theological culture to understand the Church's mission at the time of their appointment. It is in this sense that the effort should be made rather than splitting the responsibility of the head teacher.[25]

Today, 88 per cent of primary school head teachers, 81 per cent of secondary school head teachers, 70 per cent of diocesan directors responsible for the Catholic character of the school and 97 per cent of all teachers are laypersons in the ecclesiastical sense of the term. In view of this cultural and intellectual laïcization, one may question whether laypersons have a different conception of faith, its transmission and its meaning, compared to priests and nuns of yesteryear who were subject to Canon-law and to the authority of their bishop or the superior of their congregation and who were personally committed to spreading the Christian faith. In the history of the Catholic Church, there has always been a distance between the laity and the clergy in terms of transmission procedures. Because of this gap and the perception of their own role within the Church, one might also ask whether the entire educational community, now composed of laypersons, feels 'dependent' upon the directions of the Church and the pastoral guidelines of the bishop, given that so many issues other than the service of the Church, such as academic excellence and results, are also at stake.

It is certain that a substantial effort is made to promote the identity of private school teachers and their integration into the school educational project, as one may see on the website of FORMIRIS ('The Federation of Associations for Training and Career Development in Catholic Education'). But the distance of teachers from the educational project is facilitated by their gradual affiliation into the (civil service) public teaching sector and the possibility for them to join

---

25   André Blandin was instrumental in the implementation of a charter for the training and recruitment of teachers in Catholic schools, prepared between 2002 and 2005; one of its primary objectives was to 'create a link between the project of Catholic education and teacher training'.

its unions alongside the traditional unions of the private sector. Lack of funding explains why the leaders of the Catholic educational system have fought for the State to provide complete financial support for their teachers with the same level of training and retirement conditions as public sector teachers. From the *Debré Law* to the *Censi Law of 2004*, the focus was on the conditions of recruitment and payment of teachers in the private sector (*Guermeur Law 1977*, the *Lang-Cloupet agreements* 1992). Likened to civil servants, private school teachers may go as far as to deny the distinctive character of the school that employs them and refuse any involvement in the school project. Unions such as the SUNDEP which fight against the participation of private sector teachers in any 'assizes' related to the 'distinctive character' of the school system is a surprising testimony to this fact. The SUNDEP claims to speak for the defence of secularism and to resist religious pressure, proselytism and radicalization in private education. In a similar vein, the Interprofessional union UNSA (formerly FEN, a union for state schools) criticizes the French Catholic educational system for having become over-subsidized by the State and accuses it of contributing to the decay of the public service of education with a policy of competition and of filling classrooms.

Catholic Private School Pupils

A final explanation for the rather diluted Catholic ethos displayed in French Catholic private schools as a whole – but with striking regional variations – lies with the pupils (and their parents) who attend Catholic schools. The last major challenge in maintaining the distinctive character of Catholic education comes from the key beneficiaries of the system, namely, its pupils. There are numerous sociological studies available concerning the public attendance of Catholic schools for the past 40 years and it is fairly easy to conclude that, after the 1960s, the incentive behind parents choosing a Catholic school has been less than before a religious one and that spiritual training for pupils has become increasingly trivial. We are therefore faced with a much contrasted picture on the users of the Catholic school today.

In terms of numbers, the proportion of children who attend Catholic schools has remained stable: 17 per cent since the 1970s. This stability is largely due to the capacity of the schools in question, which has not grown, and indeed has not been able to grow given that the *Law of 25 January 1985*, passed under the Ministry of Chevènement, limited the scope for opening or closing classes in private schools – using the criteria applicable in state schools. When the number of pupils decreases in state education, so does the number of teacher positions both in state and in private Catholic schools under contract (5,500 fewer positions in 2005). However, the drop in pupil numbers in state education is partly to be attributed to their transfer to the private sector. The number of pupils in Catholic schools therefore increased from 13,000 in 2004 to 23,000 in 2005 whereas the number of teachers dropped by 1,000. The result is that in some French Catholic schools, the number of pupils per class now reaches to 40 if not more. To avoid overcrowding, more and more prospective pupils are now being turned down by private Catholic schools: in September 2006, 30,000 pupil candidates were refused admission in the Catholic school system, amongst which 11,000 in the Ile de France alone.[26] Overall, the Catholic school system teaches 2 million pupils in the country, an enormous figure. In some regions, the proportion is particularly high; for example, the diocese of Lille is responsible for more than 377 schools and over 120,000 pupils.

To return to parental incentives, a survey by the French Institute of Public Opinion ('IFOP') for the 1978 Catholic weekly *La Vie* showed that 21 per cent of parents explained their choice for religious reasons (Tournier 1997: 560–88). They now represent 7 per cent. Meanwhile, according to a study published last year by CREDOC (research centre for the study and observation of the conditions of life) 33 per cent of parents turn to Catholic schools because of their disappointment with state schools aggravated by the upheaval of the educational world in 2003 and 2005 (Chauffaut 2005). Parents hope to find in the 'private' system a bandage for the wounds inflicted by the 'public' system and escape the rigors of the '*carte scolaire*' (distribution of pupils in state run schools according to residence) and the gigantic public secondary schools. Finally, Catholic schools are seen as a place of social selection and a safe haven where children are protected from frequenting other, 'ill bred' children of low socio-cultural background with violent or inappropriate behaviour. It is true that the Catholic teaching system is experiencing a recruitment contrast. Even though at primary level, the social background of pupils is comparable to that of state school pupils, even though efforts are made towards a broadening of the recruitment (towards pupils with disabilities as well as pupils from very disadvantaged backgrounds), children from higher social classes are overrepresented in secondary Catholic private education (21 per cent of adolescents) and the social differentiation gap widens as pupils rise in grade levels. Remaining to be measured is the low percentage of foreign pupils and the low number of pupils on scholarships in Catholic schools compared to state schools (Vasconcellos 2004: 56–63). Several researchers, working on the inequalities of the French educational system and its hidden system of 'favoured schools' (including private education), reveal that because of strong sociological pressure, Catholic schools are actually seen and sought after as places of academic excellence and protection for the more privileged (Oberti 2006: 320–43; Van Zanten 2006: 343–70).

Does this mean that parents who choose and succeed in enrolling their children to a Catholic school are devoid of any interest in the spiritual dimension of the school? Another researcher who studied six secondary schools in the Paris region points to the 'relative good will' of parents toward the religious dimension of the school while appreciating its only slightly religious character (Longeaux 2005). The less satisfied with the religious offer are a very small minority. These are parents that Longeaux calls 'assertive believers' while the 'cautious believers'

---

26 20,000 refusals counted in September 2007.

(somewhat or completely non-practicing), who form two-thirds of those who declare themselves Catholics, are satisfied alongside the parents who define themselves as 'non-believers'. For the latter group ('non-believers without prejudice'), religious identity is accepted as a good source of values for everyone. However, there is another category of parents, defined by Longeaux as 'assertive non-believers' who only accept the religious character of a school insofar as it respects strict secularism. These parents play on the concept of freedom of choice, which is also the means by which Catholics fought to maintain their schools; a freedom of choice that the Vatican II Declaration on Christian Education (para. 6) recognizes for all parents pursuant to a universal right to education for all children. To freedom of choice, they couple their own freedom of conscience and, as a result, feel entitled to reject any compulsory religious dimension within the Catholic school system.

Although the motivation of the majority of parents is rather cautious in religious terms, on the whole, parents who choose Catholic schools for their children highly rate the idea of Man that these schools convey, their attitude and view toward pupils and the transmitted sense that a person's behaviour can be 'universalized'. The experience of pupils who live in a society that is particularly insulated from the spiritual process and where religious transmission is often frowned upon, whether it is through catechesis, or through courses on religious culture, is also relevant. According to Longeaux, who interviewed a number of people, religion has never ceased to be a topic of interest to them but under very demanding conditions of freedom and critical distance. In his analysis of open comments from older pupils (to whom he devotes a chapter), the sociologist notes that private school pupils enjoy their school and recognize the good atmosphere and quality of education, especially if they have also experienced public schools. They recognize that they are well looked after and that there exists a communality that is very different from the indifference and individualism in state schools. On their relationship to Christianity, 42 per cent of them think Christianity will disappear and 36 per cent remain confident in Christianity but are not satisfied with its current state. In the overall student responses, the question of religion is addressed as an illuminator of truth. Four attitudes emerge. The first shows confidence in the truth of religion and engagement in some way that reinforces this sense – usually participation in large religious gatherings such as *World Youth Day*. This fringe insists on ownership and personal freedom of faith and openness to others. A second attitude appears in about 60 per cent of pupils, namely, those who deplore the irrelevance of the religious culture they receive, the obsolete nature of the rituals and celebrations and the refusal to take sexuality into account and to present it as a strong and positive ethic. A third attitude is to question the certitude of the Christian faith and criticize the rigidity of some believers. A final position, held by 10 per cent of pupils, condemns religion in general and Christianity in particular, considering them to be a form of obscurantism destined to disappear.

Conclusion: A Situation About To Change?

Given this paradoxical legal situation, which makes Catholic education an essential wheel of state education in France and allows it to welcome, thanks to its 'non-denominational' openness, all 'children of the Republic', how can the distinctive character of its teaching, recognized by French law, be preserved (Gire 1999, Salenson 1999)? It seems difficult to maintain a strong Catholic ethos in French Catholic schools when the population itself appears satisfied with a more tepid religiosity. As for state schools, how can the Republic pretend to be respecting religious education – a fundamental freedom – when in fact little is done to inform families of the possibility of its expression through chaplaincies? The answer certainly lies in the French population's lack of religious interest – itself a product of a strong republican orthodoxy transmitted in the twentieth century and a result of the general secularization of Western societies since the liberal sixties. But today, new religious trends have gained in popularity in French society and even if they have not had an impact yet on the inherited secular framework in which pupils in France are raised, it is likely that in future, the French system will be subject to changes.

References

Bruley, Y. et al. (eds) 2005. *Histoire de la laïcité à la française, loi de 1905: le livre du centenaire officiel*. (Paris: CLD).

Chauffaut, D., Olm, C. and Simon, M-O. 2005. Enquête. L'enseignement libre choix de conviction mais aussi de pragmatisme. *CREDOC, Consommations et mode de vie* 183, avril. Available at: http://www.credoc.fr/pdf/4p/183.pdf URL [Accessed: 1 January 2011].

Combes, J. 1997. *Histoire de l'école primaire élémentaire en France*. Paris: PUF.

Conciliar Declaration on Christian Education. 1965. *Gravissimum Educationis Momentum*, 28 April. Available at: http://www.vatican.va/archive/hist_councils/ii_vatican_council/documents/vat-ii_decl_19651028_gravissimum-educationis_en.html. URL [Accessed: 1 January 2011].

Congregation for Catholic Education. 1982. Le laïc catholique témoin de la foi dans l'école. Available at:http://www.vatican.va/roman_curia/congregations/ccatheduc/documents/rc_con_ccatheduc_doc_19821015_lay-catholics_en.html. URL [Accessed: 1 January 2011].

Dimension Religieuse de l'Ecole Publique. 1988, 7 April. Available at: http://www.vatican.va/roman_curia/congregations/ccatheduc/index_fr.htm. URL [Accessed: 1 January 2011].

Dossier Laïcité et Aumôneries. Aumôneries de l'Education Publiques.Available at: http://www.aep78.cef.fr/documentations/dossier-laicite-et-aumoneries.pdf. URL [Accessed: 1 January 2011].

(L')Ecole Catholique au Seuil du TroisièmeMillénaire. 1997. 28 December. Available at: http://www.vatican.va/roman_curia/congregations/ccatheduc/ documents/rc_con_ccatheduc_doc_27041998_school2000_en.html. URL [Accessed: 1 January 2011].

Eduquer Ensemble dans l'Ecole Catholique. 2007. 8 September. Available at: http://www.vatican.va/roman_curia/congregations/ccatheduc/documents/rc_ con_ccatheduc_doc_20070908_educare-insieme_en.html. URL [Accessed: 1 January 2011].

Eyt, P. (Mgr) 1993. Le caractère propre de l'enseignement catholique dans la société civile. *Assises de l'Enseignement Catholique*, Issy-les-Moulineaux 14–16 mai. Available at: http://cle.formiris.org/index.php?page=rubrique&ru bID=4&ssRubID=2 URL [Accessed: 1 January 2011].

Gire, P. 1999. La gestion du fait religieux dans un établissement catholique d'enseignement. *Chemin de Dialogue*, 14, December, 17–27.

Lalouette, J. 2004. Anticléricalisme et laïcité, in *Histoire des Gauches en France*, edited by J-J. Becker and G. Candar, vol. 2, *XXe siècle: à l'épreuve de l'histoire*. Paris: La Découverte, 646–65.

Longeaux, G. de 2005.*Christianisme et laïcité. Défi pour l'*école *catholique, Enquête en région parisienne*, Paris: L'Harmattan.

Mayeur, F. 2004. Histoire générale de l'enseignement et de l'éducation en France, vol.3, *De la révolution à l'ecole républicaine (1789–1930)*. Paris: Libraire Académique Perrin.

Oberti, M. 2006. La différentiation sociale et scolaire de l'espace urbain – ségrégation et inégalité scolaire, in *L'Epreuve des inégalités*, edited by H. Lagrange. Paris: PUF.

Rémond, R.1999. *L'anticléricalisme en France de 1815 à nos jours*. Paris: Fayard.

Salenson, G.1999. L'école catholique au seuil du troisième millénaire.*Chemin de Dialogue*, 14, December, 65–85.

Secrétariat Général de l'Education Catholique. 2006. Les orientations de l'enseignement catholique, la démarche des Assises de 1993 à 2006. Available at: http://medias.formiris.org/cle_219_1.pdf. URL [Accessed: 1 January 2011].

Statuts de l'Enseignement catholique en France 1973/1992/1999. Available at: http://www.scolanet.net/data_rec/pdf/656djcd6iq6s19.PDF and: http://cle. formiris.org/index.php?page=document&docID=85&rubID=4&ssRubID=2 URL [Accessed: 1 January 2011].

Swerry, J-M. 1995. *Aumôneries catholiques dans l'enseignement public*. Paris: Cerf.

Tournier, V. 1997. Ecole publique, école privée, le clivage oublié. Le rôle des facteurs politiques et religieux dans le choix de l'école et les effets du contexte scolaire sur la socialization politique des lycéens français. *Revue française de Science Politique* 47, 560–88.

Van Zanten, A. 2006. Les choix scolaires dans la banlieue parisienne – Un évitement aisé de la mixité par le choix du privé, in *L'Epreuve des inégalités*, edited by H. Lagrange. Paris: PUF.

Vasconcellos, M. 2004. *Le Système* éducatif. Paris: La Découverte, 4th edition.

Chapter 8

Religious Education in a Religiously Neutral State: The German Model

Heinrich de Wall

According to Article 7(3) of the *Grundgesetz* or German Basic Law[1] ('GG'), religion is part of the regular curriculum at state schools. Religious instruction in this context does not merely mean an information flow about religions and the doctrines of the various denominations but also education according to the tenets of a certain religious community. Accordingly, it is customary at German schools to provide Roman Catholic and Protestant religious instruction classes. This seems to contradict other articles and principles of the German constitution,[2] in particular the separation of Church and State and the principle of the State's neutrality in matters of religion and creed under Article 137(1) of the *Weimarer Reichsverfassung* or Weimar Constitution ('WRV').[3] There also seems to be a conflict between religious instruction at state schools and the right of parents to impart religious knowledge to their children in accordance with their right to educate children (Article 6(2) GG) and their freedom of religion (Article 4(1)-(2) GG). In this chapter, an outline will first be provided of the German system of religious instruction and the constitutional rules and principles in the Church/State relationship. Next, I intend to demonstrate how religious instruction appears to be a contradiction in terms but may be resolved. Finally, I will deal with current debates about religious education and on the introduction of Islamic religious instruction in Germany.

Religious Instruction as a Regular School Subject[4]

Article 7(3) GG, according to which religious instruction shall form part of the regular curriculum in state schools, implies that religious instruction is organized

---

1   An English version of the relevant provisions can be found at the end of this chapter.

2   For a concise summary of the German State/Church relation in English see Robbers (2005a). For more detailed commentaries in German, von Campenhausen and de Wall 2006: 39–148, Unruh 2009: 46–146.

3   Under Article 140 GG, most provisions of the Weimar Constitution on the Church/State relationship are retained within the Basic Law.

4   For details of the German Law on religious instruction, see Link 1995, Kästner 1998, Robbers 2005b.

and financed by the State. The 'State' in this context refers to the German states or *Länder* as well as local parishes and administrative units. Religious instruction classes are held by ordinary teachers who at the same time are employed by the State.[5] Being part of the regular curriculum, the subject of Religion is compulsory for pupils but there are two notable exceptions: first, it is obligatory only for members of the respective denomination and secondly, according to Article 7(2) GG parents or legal guardians have the right to decide whether children are to receive religious instruction. Parents retain the right to have their children opt out of religion classes even when they are members of the religious community on which doctrines the religious instruction is based. Catholic parents may thus decide that their children are not to attend Catholic instruction classes. The law guarantees that no one may be compelled by the State to take part and this optional character ensures that the provision of religious instruction in state schools does not conflict with freedom of religion. Usually, children who opt out of religious instruction are obliged to attend a religiously neutral Ethics class instead.

There are, of course, pupils whose parents have not formally taken them out of religious instruction who do not wish to attend these classes. The unwillingness of children to go to school or their opposition to the wishes of their parents is, however, not a problem which is exclusive to religious instruction but concerns all subjects and the school as a whole. In most German *Länder*, with the exception of Bavaria and Saarland, German law stipulates that at the age of 14 (when they reach majority in religious matters) it is up to pupils to decide whether they wish to continue attending Religion classes. Because of the option to drop Religion, and due to the fact that religious instruction is obligatory only for members of the respective religious community, it is obvious that not all pupils take part. Religious instruction is not required to be offered if only a handful of pupils of the respective denomination go to class or school. Instruction for individual pupils cannot be considered part of the regular curriculum. In the German *Länder*, rules differ concerning whether 7 or 12 pupils of a particular denomination constitute the minimum number required for a religious instruction class to be provided. At the same time, the option exists of putting together pupils of different classes and in some *Länder*, to merge pupils from different schools of the same city into one group.In accordance with the membership figures of the religious communities in Germany, usually only Roman Catholic and Protestant classes are offered. But religious instruction is not an exclusive privilege of the traditional Christian churches. There is Orthodox or Jewish religious instruction in some schools in Germany, Alevite religious instruction is about to be introduced in some places, and the introduction of Islamic instruction is a very topical public issue.

The exception for non-denominational schools mentioned in Article 7(3) of the Basic Law gives the State the opportunity to run individual schools whose

---

5   They customarily not only teach 'Religion', but other subjects as well. Special agreements, however, allow church clergymen to teach the subject for which the church is remunerated.

curriculum does not include Religion. Usually, German schools are not strictly non-denominational but rather inter-denominational schools which are open to pupils of all denominations and offer religious instruction. There is another exception to Article 7(3); according to Article 141 GG, the so-called 'Bremen clause', the first sentence of Article 7(3) does not apply in any *Land* in which another *Land* law was in force on 1 January 1949. This applies to Bremen and Berlin where there is a different tradition of religious education protected by the Basic Law.

The Denominational Aspect of Religious Instruction

The Role of Religious Denominations

The most important and characteristic feature of religious instruction in German state schools is its *Konfessionalität* or 'denominational character'. In religious instruction, students are not only given information about religion or the various denominations and their doctrines and practices but, as the Constitutional Court puts it, religion is seen as being a 'denominational commitment' (BVerfGE 74, 252). In Roman Catholic instruction, children are educated according to Church dogma which is considered to be binding and true. This is stipulated in the second sentence of Article 7(3): 'Without prejudice to the State's right of supervision, religious instruction shall be given in accordance with the tenets of the religious community concerned.' The question which arises is who should decide if and under what circumstances the instruction is in accordance with the tenets of the religious community. The answer is quite clear: because of the separation of Church and State and due to the right of religious communities to self-determination as guaranteed by Article 137(3) WRV, the State cannot pass judgement upon Catholic, Protestant, Jewish or Muslim teaching. This is the prerogative of the religious communities alone.

The Content of Religious Instruction

Deference to religious communities takes on three different aspects. Firstly, and most importantly, it means that the religious content of lessons may be determined by the respective religious communities. They decide which aspect of their teaching is to be presented in class and in which manner. The Catholic Church, for example, decides if the Assumption of the Virgin Mary shall be a subject of religious instruction and if it is to be regarded as truth. The Protestant Churches have to decide if this aspect is to be a topic of Protestant religious instruction, whether children need be taught about Protestant doctrine, and whether, according to that doctrine, the Catholic dogma on this issue is wrong. Despite the right of religious communities to determine the religious content of instruction, the delivery of the teaching remains under state supervision. It is thus up to the State to make sure that teachers are available to teach religious instruction classes and that the lessons are taught in accordance with the curriculum. 'State supervision' in this context also includes the right to determine the scientific and didactic standards of the lessons and to set up regulations determining the qualifications required of teaching staff. Therefore, in that sense, both churches and State are responsible for the contents of religious instruction: the State in respect of scientific and didactic standards and the relevant churches as regards religious contents. Consequently, the State and churches are forced to cooperate in this field. The curriculum of religious instruction is drafted by commissions consisting of both State and church experts and has to be approved by the respective church before it can be introduced by the state authorities.

Teachers and Pupils

The second aspect in which deference is shown to religious communities refers to teaching staff. The credibility of teachers is crucial for the success of the instruction. Again, only the religious communities can decide who is able to teach their respective religion authentically. Whether a teacher who claims to be a good Catholic is acceptable as a teacher of the Catholic religion cannot be decided by the state authorities. The State is not allowed to decide whether someone is a competent Catholic or Protestant teacher and it is equally unacceptable, as happened once in a case of illness that a Catholic teacher may fill in for a Protestant teacher simply because both communities are Christian ones. Therefore, every teacher, even if employed by the State, needs to be approved by the relevant church in question. This approval is called *missio canonica* in the Catholic Church and *vocatio* in the Protestant Churches. A third aspect is treated differently by the Protestant and the Catholic churches. According to the latter, pupils attending religious instruction classes must, except in rare exceptions, be Catholic. The Protestant churches are far more open towards pupils of other denominations. The denomination of pupils can have considerable influence on the character of the lessons. If students of different denominations take part, basic doctrines which are self-evident to believers will invariably have to be explained to non-believers. Discussions are also more likely to be controversial. The religious affiliation of pupils attending the class thus indirectly affects the content of the instruction and is consequently left under German Law to be decided by the relevant religious communities.

The Need for Cooperation between Church and State

Generally speaking, the Basic Law's rule whereby religious instruction in state schools 'shall be given in accordance with the tenets of the religious community concerned' demands cooperation between school authorities and religious communities. Due to the mutual obligation for Church and State to cooperate, religious instruction at state schools is often called a *res mixta* or 'common matter'. This is, however, merely a collective term for matters by which according to the law, State and churches both have individual legal standpoints. A matter is termed *res mixta* because State and Church have legal interests in it, not the other way round: churches cannot claim to have a legal say in a matter just because it is classified as being *res mixta*.

It must be emphasized that, according to German law, religious instruction cannot take place unless the respective denomination is organized as a religious community. The implementation of Article 7(3) GG depends, as prerequisites, on the existence of religious communities and their willingness to cooperate. The features which define a religious community are, however, not defined in the Basic Law and are therefore controversial.

Religious Instruction and the Rules and Principles of Religious Constitutional Law

This section will examine how the provisions on religious instruction in German state schools respects the fundamental freedoms of parents, pupils and religious communities as well as the constitutional principle of state religious neutrality. The possible conflicts and apparent contradictions between rules relating to religious education at state German schools and other rules and principles of the Basic Law can be solved: parents' right to educate their children, which is guaranteed by Article 6(2) GG, includes their right and duty[6] to have their children receive religious education. Article 7(2) GG clearly states that the decision whether children should participate in religious instruction or not is left to the discretion of the parents. Thus, religious instruction does not interfere with parental rights but can be understood as being its complement. The provision of religious instruction classes supports the religious freedoms of parents and children by helping pupils to develop an individual religious identity.It also respects parents' freedom not to believe (or to hold different beliefs) since parents are always free to decide whether their children should attend. This right to opt out from religious instruction classes is first and foremost vested in the parents but children's rights to religious freedom are not neglected either. Indeed, according to German law, once they have reached the age of religious majority children have the right to decide whether they want to participate in religious instruction. The German model is therefore respectful of pupils' right to freedom of religion.

Finally, it was shown above how deference is also shown to the rights of religious communities to freedom of religion and right to self determination. A controversial issue is, however, the question whether religious instruction comes in conflict with the principle of religious state neutrality. This principle is not explicitly mentioned in the Basic Law. The Constitutional Court has derived it from a number of Basic Law provisions, such as the principle of religious equality

---

6   Art 6 (2) GG states that 'The care and upbringing of children is the natural right of parents and a duty primarily incumbent upon them'.

(Article 3(3) GG), the separation of Church and State (Article 137(1) WRV) and the principle of freedom of religion (Article 4 GG, Article 136 WRV). What does 'neutrality' mean in this context? It implies not only that the State is obliged to treat all religions and creeds equally, but also that the state authorities are not allowed to comment on the truth or value of religions in general. The State must not favour one religion over another, but at the same time is not allowed to favour non-religious citizens either.However, religious neutrality does not mean that the State ought to ignore religion or that religion has to be kept out of the public sphere and state schools. This would severely harm religious communities since they appear in public and define themselves as important actors of public life. Like political parties and other organizations, churches and religious communities take part in the public debate over social and political issues. Religion is an important factor in the education of children, or is at least considered to be one by many parents and religious communities. Since the State has taken considerable responsibility in the field of education and has a virtual monopoly on schools, it would be a statement against religion if it were totally kept out of this sphere. Providing religious instructions in state schools for parents or children who wish to receive it, in cooperation with the relevant religious communities, does not interfere with the principle of the State's religious neutrality. Religious instruction is one example of the German understanding of 'positive' neutrality, by which the State is forbidden to express a preference or dislike for one particular religion or for religion in general but is allowed to accommodate religious people and religious communities who wish to manifest their religious beliefs in public. State religious neutrality in the German sense does not, therefore, entail keeping religion out of the public sphere.

This is the main difference between the French idea of *laïcité*, according to which religion must be kept out of the public sphere including state schools, and the German concept of neutrality. In the German view, *laïcité* leads to a denigration of religion which is incompatible with state neutrality. Religion ought not to be ignored, but every religious belief must be treated equally. It is thus permissible to wear a headscarf in German state schools if other religious dress codes are also observed. To ban headscarves among pupils would be a breach of religious freedom and neutrality unless there are just reasons for banning them such as safety reasons and that these (safety) reasons apply equally to all types of religious clothings. There are not only negative reasons for treating religions equally. Neutrality does not imply a ban on every form of support for religious communities.

However, the State is only allowed to support religious communities if other religions and non-denominational organizations are supported in a similar fashion. For example, if the State decides to subsidize hospitals, both religious and secular hospitals alike need to be subsidized. Against this background, religious instruction at schools cannot be considered a breach of neutrality but rather as an illustration of the German notion of state religious neutrality. Religious instruction, thanks to its non-mandatory nature, does not infringe on pupils or parents' individual rights nor can it be seen as an endorsement of religion in general. Moreover, because the State does not advantage a particular denomination over another (but merely demands that certain objective prerequisites are met such as the presence of a minimum number of pupils wishing to attend a particular class), it cannot be seen as supporting a particular religion over others either.

Public Debate about Religious Instruction

For decades now, people in Germany have been debating the issue of religious instruction. However, in the past few years new challenges have appeared which have altered the character of this discussion. Previously, it was commonplace to claim that it was no longer modern to offer denominational religious instruction. At the same time, it was not considered a sensible educational method, especially when imparting values to pupils, to separate a class according to denomination. In addition, the non-confessional parties considered religious instruction as a privilege of the churches. Following the reunification of Germany, these issues initially remained topical since, in the eastern part of the country, only a minority of pupils were members of a church and the majority did not belong to any religious body. Apart from that, school instruction in the former East Germany was decidedly anti-religious – a stance which was common among many of the teachers as well. On the other hand, church authorities were reluctant to cooperate with schools and administrative units whom they knew from the period of the East German regime to have been anti-religious.

Nonetheless, most of the *Länder* in the Eastern part of Germany introduced religious instruction in line with the Basic Law, with the exception of Brandenburg. Here, there is no religious instruction on denominational lines, but rather religion-free instruction in Lifestyle/Ethics/Religious Studies for all pupils. This has led to a heated debate as to whether or not this practice is unconstitutional. In accordance with a court proposal (BVerfGE 104, 305) the churches and the Brandenburg administration settled for the following arrangement: lessons in Lifestyle/Ethics/Religion are to continue but at the same time the churches are allowed to offer religious instruction on the school premises and pupils who take part in religious lessons are entitled to opt out of the course on Lifestyle/Ethics/Religion. For historical reasons, Article 7(3) GG, claiming that religious instruction is a regular subject in all schools, does not apply in Berlin and Bremen (Art 141 GG). For this reason, Berlin does not provide lessons in Religion but the churches are allowed to provide this on school premises (albeit as an extracurricular subject). Accordingly, many parents and both churches attempted in a referendum to introduce in Berlin the religious instruction model common to other *Länder*. Although enough signatures were gathered to stage the referendum, the initiative failed. This is not very surprising in view of Berlin's unique demographic situation, where the number of undenominational and anti-religious citizens is high and is not comparable to the rest of Germany.

The debate whether denominational religious instruction should be scrapped in favour of general lessons in Ethics has ebbed. This may be due to the fact that people increasingly value the role that denominational religious instruction plays in encouraging pupils to develop and maintain a religious viewpoint. Although church membership has dropped considerably in the last few decades in the western part of Germany, religious instruction is commonplace throughout and attendance in the subject is good and has generally remained stable.

Introduction of Islamic Religious Instruction

Recently, the matter of Christian religious instruction has taken a back seat, with demands by Muslims and Muslim organizations to introduce religious classes of their own in Germany coming to the forefront. This policy is supported by political parties as well as the assemblies of the *Länder* – who in decentralized Germany are responsible for education in their respective territory – because German-language religious education is considered a crucial integrative force for Muslim children in German society.[7] Until now, religious education frequently took place in the parents' language of origin within the Muslim communities – leading to a separation of Muslims from the rest of society and resulting in the formation of a parallel Islamic community. For this reason, many people are in favour of German-language religious instruction at state schools claiming, as outlined, that this policy is conform to the Basic Law.

Despite the fact that over the past 30 years a large number of Muslims (now approximately 4 million) have resided in Germany and that consequently the proportion of Muslims attending school is quite high, there have so far only been test runs in Islamic religious school instruction.[8] The reason why regular Islamic classes have not yet been implemented is that there are particular organizational and legal hurdles to overcome. For one thing, the Islamic community (unlike the regular churches and the Jewish community) does not have clear-cut membership rights. It is therefore difficult to ascertain which child belongs to a Muslim community and if he is expected to attend classes in Islamic religion. It is also unclear whether the respective community represents an ample number of school children or parents. In an attempt to resolve this issue, it was proposed that registration for religious instruction should be made compulsory and that whoever registered for a given type of religious instruction might be classified as belonging to the particular corresponding denomination.

---

7 At the first 'Deutsche Islamkonferenz' (German Islamic Conference), an official conference which took place between 2006 and 2009 and to which the federal Home Secretary invited Muslim delegates and representatives of the governments of the German Länder and local communities, Islamic religious instruction was also a major issue. All participants supported its introduction. See DIK 2009: 53–63.

8 Dietrich 2005: 121–31, Mohr and Kiefer 2009.

A more complicated problem is the fragmented nature of of German Muslim communities in which organizations do not exist or have only recently been founded. Apart from local Muslim communitie associations, there was until recently no such thing as an effective umbrella association of Muslims which could act as a spokesman on the issue of religious instruction. As mentioned already, there is no Islamic religious 'voice' that could speak up in favour of the implementation of Islamic religious instruction classes. Even though many Muslim umbrella organizations have been founded lately, but it is often unclear whether these are stable enough and whether they represent an ample number of Muslims. An additional problem is that under German law courts have not, so far, recognized umbrella organizations as being religious communities. The various Muslim communities are not divided along religious or denominational lines; in fact, Muslims in Germany point out that they are a unified religious force. This solves the problem to the extent that there is no need to introduce a multitude of different denominational subjects but the difficulty remains in that a large variety of individual groups has to be coordinated and that it is still hard to determine in each case which of these groups represent Islam. One must bear in mind that many Muslims do not belong to an Islamic group nor do they wish to join an Islamic organization and yet many at the same time would support the introduction of Islamic religious instruction. Some of the German *Länder* are now trying to solve the problem by founding specific advisory councils for religious instruction, of which representatives of many Islamic communities are members. These advisory councils fulfil the requirements needed for religious instruction within a particular community: laying the foundations for such classes, giving teachers permission to teach these subjects and so on. Lower Saxony, which set up an advisory board on 18 January 2011, has come furthest and there Islamic religious instruction is to be gradually introduced.

Conclusion

The implementation of Islamic religious instruction poses new challenges to the German system. It must prove that it also caters for the needs of pupils who are not part of the traditional, established religious communities. Additionally, problems have to be tackled that did not previously arise, such as defining organizational structures within the Islamic community. Any viable solution would have to comply with the tenets of religious freedom and the religious neutrality of the country, and at the same time protect the interests of Muslim school children. If such a solution may be found, it will prove that the German model of denominational religious instruction in a religiously neutral State is also a suitable foundation for a religiously pluralist society.

References

BVerfGE. *Entscheidungen des Bundesverfassungsgerichts* (Decisions of The Federal Constitutional Court), Tübingen: Mohr, 124 volumes.

Campenhausen (von), A. and de Wall, H. 2006. *Staatskirchenrecht*, München: C.H. Beck

DIK 2009. Verfassungsrechtliche Rahmenbedingungen eines islamischen Religionsunterrichts, Schlussfolgerungen der Arbeitsgruppe 2 der Deutschen Islamkonferenz, erarbeitet für deren Unterarbeitsgruppe, in *Drei Jahre Deutsche Islamkonferenz (DIK) 2006–2009*, Deutsche Islamkonferenz/ Bundesministerium des Inneren, Berlin, 53–63. Available at: http://gsb. download.bva.bund.de/BAMF/DIK/090616_DIK-Broschuere_gesamt_ ONLINE.pdf [Accessed: 9 February 2011].

Dietrich, M. 2006. *Islamischer Religionsunterricht*. Frankfurt am Main: Lang.

Kästner, K.-H. 1998. Religiöse Bildung und Erziehung in der öffentlichen Schule – Grundlagen und Reichweite der Verfassungsgarantie staatlichen Religionsunterrichts, in *Der Beitrag der Kirchen zur Erfüllung des staatlichen Erziehungsauftrags*, edited by H. Marré et al. Essener Gespräche zum Thema Staat und Kirche, 32. Münster: Aschendorff, 61–96.

Link, C. 1995. Religionsunterrich' in *Handbuch des Staatskirchenrechts der Bundesrepublik Deutschland*, edited by J. Listl and D. Pirson, vol. II, 2nd edition, Berlin: Duncker Humblot, 439–509.

Mohr, I. and Kiefer, M. 2009. *Islamunterricht – Islamischer Religionsunterricht – Islamkunde*, Bielefeld: Transcript.

Robbers, G. 2005a. State and Church in *State and Church in the European Union*. Edited by G. Robbers. Baden-Baden: Nomos, 77–94.

Robbers, G. 2005b. Art. 7 Absatz 3 in *Kommentar zum Grundgesetz*, edited by C. Starck, vol. I 5th edition. München. Franz Vahlen, 769–79.

Unruh, P. 2009. *Religionsverfassungsrecht*. Baden-Baden: Nomos.

Extracts from the Basic Law for the Federal Republic of Germany

Article 3

[Equality before the law]
1. All persons shall be equal before the law.
2. …
3. No person shall be favoured or disfavoured because of sex, parentage, race, language, homeland and origin, faith, or religious or political opinions. No person shall be disfavoured because of disability.

Article 4

[Freedom of faith and conscience]
1. Freedom of faith and of conscience, and freedom to profess a religious or philosophical creed, shall be inviolable.
2. The undisturbed practice of religion shall be guaranteed.
3. No person shall be compelled against his conscience to render military service involving the use of arms. Details shall be regulated by a federal law.

Article 6

[Marriage – Family – Children]
1. Marriage and the family shall enjoy the special protection of the state.
2. The care and upbringing of children is the natural right of parents and a duty primarily incumbent upon them. The state shall watch over them in the performance of this duty.

Article 7

[School system]
1. The entire school system shall be under the supervision of the State.
2. Parents and guardians shall have the right to decide whether children shall receive religious instruction.
3. Religious instruction shall form part of the regular curriculum in state schools, with the exception of non-denominational schools. Without prejudice to the State's right of supervision, religious instruction shall be given in accordance with the tenets of the religious community concerned. Teachers may not be obliged against their will to give religious instruction.

Article 140

[Law of religious denominations]
The provisions of Articles 136, 137, 138, 139 and 141 of the German Constitution of 11 August 1919 shall be an integral part of this Basic Law.

Article 141

['Bremen Clause']
The first sentence of paragraph (3) of Article 7 shall not apply in any *Land* in which *Land* law otherwise provided on 1 January 1949.

Extracts from the German Constitution of 11 August 1919 (Weimar Constitution)

Article 136

1. Civil and political rights and duties shall be neither dependent upon nor restricted by the exercise of religious freedom.
2. Enjoyment of civil and political rights and eligibility for public office shall be independent of religious affiliation.
3. No person shall be required to disclose his religious convictions. The authorities shall have the right to inquire into a person's membership in a religious society only to the extent that rights or duties depend upon it or that a statistical survey mandated by a law so requires.
4. No person may be compelled to perform any religious act or ceremony, to participate in religious exercises, or to take a religious form of oath.

Article 137

1. There shall be no state church.
2. The freedom to form religious societies shall be guaranteed. The union of religious societies within the territory of the Reich shall be subject to no restrictions.
3. Religious societies shall regulate and administer their affairs independently within the limits of the law that applies to all. They shall confer their offices without the participation of the state or the civil community.
4. Religious societies shall acquire legal capacity according to the general provisions of civil law.
5. Religious societies shall remain corporations under public law insofar as they have enjoyed that status in the past. Other religious societies shall be granted the same rights upon application, if their constitution and the number of their members give assurance of their permanency. If two or more religious societies established under public law unite into a single organization, it too shall be a corporation under public law.
6. Religious societies that are corporations under public law shall be entitled to levy taxes on the basis of the civil taxation lists in accordance with Land law.
7. Associations whose purpose is to foster a philosophical creed shall have the same status as religious societies.
8. Such further regulation as may be required for the implementation of these provisions shall be a matter for Land legislation.

Chapter 9

The Controversy Surrounding the Denominational Teaching of Religion in Spanish State Schools

Javier García Oliva[1]

In the last few decades, Spain has undergone an exceptional legal transformation. After many years under the dictatorship of General Francisco Franco (1939–1978), this southern European country experienced a successful transition towards democracy (1975–1978), which culminated with the enactment of the Constitution in late 1978.[2] Unsurprisingly, education was one of the most controversial areas during the democratic transition and it showed the different – and often antagonistic – views of the Spanish political parties. As observed by Palomino (2010), 'in Spain every change of Government goes alongside an in-depth reform of the education system. These ongoing reforms are the outcome of the inherent difficulty of Art 27 of the Spanish Constitution of 1978, towards which the two main parties of the constitutional stage – *Unión de Centro Democrático* and the Socialist Party – contributed with two very different approaches'.[3] Until 1975, the Catholic Church had been the official denomination of the State despite significant attempts by the former to severe its links with the Franco regime, mainly after the Vatican II Council with its impassioned defence of religious freedom. With the new democratic wave, the *Constituyente*[4] struggled to reconcile tradition with the

---

1   I am indebted to Dr Myriam Hunter-Henin (UCL), editor of this book, for her kindness and understanding throughout the writing of this chapter and I am extremely grateful to Dr Richard Caddell (Swansea University) for his invaluable comments on this paper. I would also like to thank Professor Javier Martínez Torrón, Dr Rafael Palomino, Dr Santiago Cañamares and Dr Irene Briones, all four of them at the Universidad Complutense de Madrid, and Dr Oscar Celador (Universidad Carlos III de Madrid) for their helpful observations on the first draft of this paper and for their guidance in relation to the relevant sources in Spanish Law.

2   García Oliva 2008.

3   Palomino 2010. The overwhelming majority of the sources which I have used are in Spanish and therefore I have translated them into English for the purposes of this chapter. Any errors remain my sole responsibility.

4   We are referring to the Seven Fathers of the Constitution, a group of wise men of the different political parties, including Gregorio Peces Barba, Manuel Fraga, Gabriel Cisneros and Miquel Roca.

recognition of a pluralistic society in which the Catholic Church was no longer the official faith of the Spanish State. As stated by Martínez Torrón (2006: IX), there is no doubt that the solution of the 'religious question' in the Spanish Constitution of 1978 was one of the key aspects behind the success of the democratic transition.

The analysis of religion in state schools will be the main focus of this work. The teaching of religion in private establishments, whether they are entirely run by private bodies – with sole financial autonomy – or partially subsidized by the State, responds to different premises and is beyond the scope of this chapter. From the outset, it will be highlighted that the teaching of religion in state schools in Spain is denominational as opposed to non-denominational, which, it could be argued, is the general rule in England and Wales.[5] The initial provisions concerning Catholicism have been, to an extent, extended to other denominations with which the public authorities signed agreements in 1992. The maintenance of a denominational model in Spain is legitimate, compatible with both constitutional provisions and international obligations and unfairly dismissed by some social sectors. Nevertheless, the desirability of such a framework in a modern democracy is a different matter.

In addition to the teaching of Catholic, Evangelical, Muslim and Jewish religion in state schools, this chapter will focus on 'Education for Citizenship and Human Rights',[6] a controversial subject which has been introduced by the Law of 3 May 2006,[7] and will finally consider the legal status of teachers of religion in Spanish state schools and the regulation of religious symbols in public education establishments. 'Education for Citizenship and Human Rights' has been highly contested and regarded by some as state indoctrination. However, there is no reason why students should not be reminded of the significance of key values such as tolerance and respect for others, provided that the crucial position of parents in the education of their children is scrupulously respected. As far as the position of teachers of religion is concerned, undoubtedly denominational religion is very different from other academic subjects, but the lack of renewal of a contract on grounds such as marital status or sexual orientation is bewildering to many sectors of the population and this seems to lead us, even further, towards a thorough reflection about the future ahead.

---

5   This is a generalization for the sake of this comparative analysis. There are also many faith schools in England and Wales, which are subsidized by the State, where denominational religion is taught.

6   *Educación para la Ciudadanía y los Derechos Humanos.*

7   *Ley Orgánica 2/2006, 3 May*, of Education. BOE núm. 106, 4 May.

The Model of Church/State Relations in Spain

From an ecclesiastical[8] point of view, Spain is a cooperationist system.[9] In such a model, there is an acknowledgement of the separation between the State and religious denominations, but at the same time this recognition is underpinned by a healthy cooperation between both institutions. It is a hybrid category, as it shares features with the two other general categories: separatist and national Church models. Alongside the separatist model,[10] there is no official recognition of one or more faiths in the public sphere but similarly to the national Church systems,[11] religion has an important role to play in the public arena. This obviously makes it different from the separatist model[12] and the non-recognition of a religious body as the official faith of the country, differentiates Spain from countries such as Denmark, Finland and Greece. As already indicated, it could be argued that a hybrid model of Church/State relationships is an attempt on the part of the public authorities to reconcile the traditional position of the Catholic Church with religious freedom as a non-negotiable feature of a democratic setting.

Crucially, the Constitution has embraced the principles of freedom of religion, thought and conscience[13] and of equality and non-discrimination.[14] Both are vital components of a democratic system, a view that has been endorsed in an ecclesiastical context. Indeed, it is clear that religious freedom cannot be considered in isolation to other fundamental freedoms. Instead, it may be considered a key component of the broader concept of freedom of belief, a notion that comprises in the view of Souto Paz (2003: 247–54) an array of legally protected privileges of thought, conscience and ideology. This perspective is endorsed by Llamazares (2002: 286) who argues that religious freedom must be understood as an important

---

8   Legal branch which deals with the relationships between public authorities and religious bodies.

9   This is a commonly accepted classification by European ecclesiastical lawyers (Robbers 2005). However, in the last few years some commentators have sharply questioned this divide into three categories (national Church/cooperationist/separatist) and have suggested that, broadly speaking, all European countries could be regarded as cooperationist models (Sandberg and Doe 2007).

10   For example, France or the Republic of Ireland.

11   For example, England, Scotland, Denmark or Greece.

12   It is very arguable that religion does not have a role in the public sphere in contemporary France. This is clearly the most striking example of a separatist country in Europe but, for instance, chaplains of religious bodies (who have access to prisons, hospitals and armed forces) are paid out of public funds.

13   Spanish Constitution 1978, Art 16.1: 'Freedom of ideology, religion and worship of individual and communities is guaranteed, with no other restrictions on their expression than may be necessary to maintain public order as protected by law.'

14   Ibidem, Art 14: 'Spaniards are equal before the law and may not in any way be discriminated against on account of birth, race, sex, religion, opinion or any other condition or personal or social circumstance.'

branch of the concept of freedom of conscience, as formulated by Articles 2 and 16.1 of the Constitution. In this manner, freedom of religion is not relegated to the status of an isolated and highly specific concept and must instead be viewed in a wider context of associated rights. Nevertheless, the substantive interpretation of Art 16 – at least, in the form of interpretive legislation – has tended to follow the more narrow approach. Religious freedom as contemplated by Article 16 has been developed by the Law on Religious Freedom (*la Ley Orgánica de Libertad Religiosa*) 1980. Strikingly, as Souto Paz (2003) argues, this key legislative provision ignored ideological freedom. This is in marked contrast to the wording of the Constitution and different international treaties such as the Universal Declaration of Human Rights 1948. Perhaps the individualized approach of the interpretive legislation demonstrates a trend towards state micro-management of sensitive rights viewed as fundamental to state identity and may explain to a degree the difficulties raised by the position of religion in state schools. In addition to the principles of freedom and non-discrimination, a contextual understanding of the model of Spanish Ecclesiastical Law requires a study of Art 16.3 of the Constitution. In compliance with this provision, public authorities have decided to maintain a special relationship with the Catholic Church – explicitly mentioned by the Highest Law – whilst rejecting the uniformity of the separatist system. This principle has been implemented by signing agreements with the Catholic Church in 1976, 1979 and 1994 and with other denominations/federations (Protestants, Jewish and Muslims) in 1992.

The Teaching of Religion in State Schools in Spain

With regard to the Catholic Church, the Agreement of 3 January 1979 between the Spanish State and the Holy See concerning Education and Cultural Affairs provides: 'Catholic religion shall be included in all educational centres, in conditions to those of the basic subjects … out of respect for freedom of conscience, this religious education shall not be compulsory for all students. However, the right to receive it is guaranteed.'[15] Moreover, this instrument declares that religious instruction 'shall be imparted by those persons who, each school year, shall be appointed by the academic authority from among those proposed by the diocesan authority'.[16] This statement brings both the State and the Catholic Church together as the latter is responsible for the appointment of the teacher whilst his/her remuneration is incumbent on public authorities. Under agreements – subsequently approved by

---

15   Instrument of Ratification, dated 4 December 1979, of the Agreement of 3 January 1979, between the Spanish State and the Holy See, concerning Education and Cultural Affairs, Art II.

16   Ibidem, Art III.

ordinary laws of Parliament[17] – signed between the Spanish State and authorities representative of religious minorities, Jews, Protestants and Muslims are entitled to teach their tenets in state schools, although teachers are not paid by public authorities. Therefore, four religious denominations have concluded pacts or agreements with the Spanish authorities, though their juridical nature varies. The agreements with the Holy See are international treaties whereas those with the three minority federations have been regulated by internal laws. As seen below, regardless of the legal position of these agreements, the teaching of religion in Spanish state schools is denominational, voluntary for parents and pupils and the contents of those subjects are decided by the denominations themselves.

Spain is certainly not alone in providing religious teaching in state schools in Europe.[18] Although there are very different responses to the teaching of religion in schools run by public authorities, the overwhelming majority of EU Member States provide it.[19] In Spain, in addition to the Agreements with the Catholic Church and the minority Federations the key provision in the 1978 Constitution is Article 27. Its first paragraph declares: 'Everyone is entitled to education. Freedom of instructions is recognized'. Crucially, as far as teaching of religion is concerned, the third paragraph provides: 'The public authorities guarantee the right of parents to ensure that their children receive religious and moral instruction that is in accordance with their own convictions'.[20] Nevertheless, as Rodríguez Blanco (2005: 5) has stated, the presence of classes of religion in state schools was only one of the possible models in order to implement the right of parents to have religious and moral instruction for their children in accordance with their own convictions but the legislature was not bound to adopt this pattern. The remaining

---

17 Law 24/1992, of 10 November, approving the Agreement of Cooperation between the State and the Federation of Evangelical Religious Entities of Spain; Law 25/1992, of 10 November, approving the Agreement of Cooperation between the State and the Israelite Communities of Spain and Law 26/1992, of 10 November, approving the Agreement of Cooperation between the State and the Islamic Commission of Spain.

18 The European Court of Human Rights ('ECtHR') has declared the lawful nature of the teaching of denominational religion in state schools, provided that such instruction is voluntary for the students. The alternatives provided by the state authorities (such as Ethics) are within the margin of appreciation of each Member State. See *Grzelack v. Poland 15 June 2010*, Application no. 7710/02 paras 104–5. For further analysis of the ECtHR jurisprudence in this field, see Navarro-Valls and Martínez Torrón 2011: 34–50. Furthermore, denominational religion has been accepted as a legitimate alternative by the Toledo Guiding Principles on Teaching about Religions and Beliefs in Public Schools [Online], available at: http://www.oslocoalition.org/documents/toledo_guidelines.pdf [Accessed: 28 February 2011].

19 France is the obvious exception.

20 See Celador Angón and Tejón Sánchez 2010: 105–13. This recognition is in compliance with the European Convention on Human Rights. In fact, Art 2 of its First Protocol declares the right of parents to ensure an education and teaching for their children in conformity with their own religious and philosophical convictions.

provisions of this key Article illustrate the serious attempt on the part of the *Constituyente* to reconcile the recognition of the right of education[21] – a traditional request by the left-wing parties in Spain – with 'the right of individuals and legal entities to set up teaching establishments … provided they respect Constitutional principles'.[22] The possibility for private establishments – many of which have a religious ethos – to receive the financial support of the State is recognized in the same provision: 'The public authorities shall give aid to teaching establishments which meet the requirements to be laid down by the law'.[23]

The significance of both right of education and freedom of teaching has been eloquently expressed by González Sánchez (2010: 402):

> Although freedom of information or expression are recent vehicles to express one's convictions or opinions, if the aim is to deepen views into a society, the two most important tools are the right of education and freedom of teaching, for the following two reasons: 1. Generally speaking, the addressees of those activities, children or teenagers, are easier to be influenced, as their scheme of human values is far less completed than an adult scheme. 2. As a consequence, when freedom of expression leads to the transmission of a message to the contemporary society, even to the extent of persuading it through teaching skills, in reality beliefs in a future society are being transmitted. Therefore, we can conclude that through efficient teaching, we are building up the future generations of our society.

As previously indicated, changes of political parties have usually been followed by substantial amendments of the model of teaching of religion. Commentators such as Ferrer Ortiz (2006) have rightly highlighted that this reliance on Parliament in an area like education is far from satisfactory:

> [P]roviding the ordinary legislature with the responsibility to develop the constitutional provision (Art 27), the problem was only apparently resolved. Education has become one of the most politicised questions in the country, completely dependent on the political party which holds power every single time. This becomes obvious when the different laws on education – reforms of other reforms – and the various pronouncements of the Constitutional Court and the Supreme Court, which aim to amend the excesses of both the legislature and the executive, are closely analysed.

Likewise, Moreno Mozos (2010: 359–60) has stated: 'We are witnessing, especially in some Autonomous Communities, an ongoing struggle or fight between the political powers and the civil society, having the latter experienced a rupture within

---

21   In addition to Art 27(1), see Arts 27(4) and 27(5).
22   1978 Constitution, Art 27(6).
23   Ibidem, Art 27(9).

itself, as well as an important process of judicialization of the education system.' Throughout the past few decades, religious instruction in schools – primarily in the Catholic faith[24] – has proved to be a controversial public issue in Spain. From the very outset, the Church claimed that the provisions of the 1979 Agreement had been breached, as the teaching of Catholic religion did not take place 'in conditions equal to those applicable to other basic subjects'. In fact, the relevant legislation, the LOGSE (*Ley Orgánica 1/1990 de Ordenación General del Sistema Educativo*), and the subsequent *Real Decreto* 2438/1995 declared that although the subject of Catholic religion would be examined it would have no bearing on university admission or grant applications. The other ongoing problem since the 1980s has been the existence of an alternative discipline which could meet with the approval (if not the satisfaction) of both the parents of children who followed Catholic religion and the parents who chose for their children an alternative course of instruction. Both pupils and parents were offered as an alternative to religious instruction a course on Ethics or a subject on 'additional academic support', but one way or another, a degree of frustration remained. Catholic parents regarded 'additional academic support' as a privilege granted to non-Catholic pupils and parents who did not want to pursue the Catholic teaching contested the compulsory nature of an alternative class, regardless of its content.

A few years later, the conservative Government (1996–2004) decided to address these concerns and, in 2002, enacted the LOCE (*Ley Orgánica 10/2002 de Calidad de la Educación*). As far as the teaching of religion is concerned, the LOCE set up a new subject, *Sociedad, Cultura y Religión*, which comprised two alternatives: (1) Denominational religion (Catholic, Protestant, Jewish or Muslim); or (2) Non-denominational religion, engaging the cultural, sociological and historical dimension of religion. Although this legislation was inevitably criticized, its non-confrontational nature was praised by some commentators (Esteban Garcés 2003: 109–41). In their view, this new settlement would, on the one hand, facilitate the solution of the traditional dichotomy between the subject of religion and its alternative and on the other, would leave behind all the anxieties created throughout the last few decades as the non-denominational subject *Sociedad, Cultura y Religión* was a fair acknowledgement of the socio-cultural dimension of religion and not just an imposition on those who did not choose Catholic religion. Furthermore, significant reforms were put forward by the LOCE, which emphasized that denominational religion (Catholic, Protestant, Jewish or Muslim) or its non-denominational alternative would be examined and the result considered for the purpose of university admission and grant applications. This way the controversial provisions of the LOGSE were successfully amended.

However, the situation changed remarkably under the new Socialist Government, which won the general elections of 2004 and 2008. Unsurprisingly,

---

24   It is important to bear in mind that the majority of Spanish parents choose Catholic religion for their children – [Online], available at: http://www.conferenciaepiscopal.es/ensenanza/ERE/ere2010.pdf [Accessed: 28 February 2011].

education was one of the areas where more important reforms were proposed and the *Ley Orgánica 10/2002 de Calidad de Enseñanza* was replaced by the LOE (*Ley Orgánica 2/2006 de Educación*), which declared that denominational religion would no longer be examined or graded. The LOE, in compliance with the provisions of the *Real Decreto 806/2006*, 30 June, came into effect the following academic year, in 2007/2008. This provision establishes the calendar of application of the educational system and it declares, in very wide terms, that schools will be entitled to provide those students who do not choose denominational religion with 'an appropriate educational attention'. Having said that, if the current legal framework concerning the teaching of religion (Palomino 2010: 347) is examined closely, the differences with the provisions contained by the LOCE are not so remarkable, at least as far as the teaching of religion in secondary schools is concerned. In fact, secondary schools are required to provide 'History and Culture of Religions' as an alternative. The differences are, however, striking, at the primary level of education, where the denominational teaching of religion is not supplemented by a non-denominational alternative. The contents of these programmes, with the exception of the subject 'History and Culture of Religions' are prepared and proposed by the denominations themselves.

At pre-school and primary levels, parents are entitled to make a choice for their children, whilst at secondary level students can make this choice, provided that they have reached the age of 18.[25] The legislation aims to avoid discrimination against those pupils who do not choose to study religion in secondary schools by providing:

> The teaching establishments will put in place the necessary organizational mechanisms in order to provide the required educational support to those pupils who have chosen not to follow teaching of religion and will guarantee that at all times either choice (to attend or not to attend religious instruction) will not imply any sort of discrimination. Alternatives to religious instruction classes will never include the learning of curricular contents, associated to the knowledge of the religious dimension … these organizational mechanisms must be included in the school's educational project in order to enable parents, tutors and students to know them beforehand.[26]

Furthermore, the *Real Decreto 1631/2006*, 29 December controversially declared that 'In order to make sure that the principle of equality and free coexistence of all pupils is guaranteed, the marks obtained in the subject of religion will not be taken into consideration in those procedures in which the different academic performances compete one with another or in those situations in which the future admission of students depends on the overall average mark'.[27] This response,

---

25 *Real Decreto 1631/2006, 29 December* (Disposición adicional segunda, paragraph 2).
26 Ibidem, para. 3.
27 Ibidem, para. 7.

which had already taken place under the LOGSE seems to be incompatible with the International Agreement signed with the Holy See, which provides that 'the teaching of Catholic doctrine and its delivery at the University Schools for Teacher Training, under the same conditions as the other basic disciplines, shall be voluntary'.[28] This should be regarded as a cause for concern, as the legislation of the State (whether primary or secondary) must comply with Spain's international obligations. As seen below in relation to the position of teachers of religion in state schools, however controversial some of these statements may well be in the light of recent social developments, the Spanish authorities must honour their commitments and cannot decide, unilaterally, to ignore or overlook the provisions contained in the Agreements signed with the Holy See.

Both the LOCE and LOE. provide a non-denominational alternative to the denominational teaching of religion and this is to be praised. It could be argued that the choices at the disposal of pupils and parents are inadequate and the fact that only denominations which have signed an agreement with the State can offer this teaching is not an ideal solution. Having said that, the most recent legislation should have addressed these issues and unfortunately, the lack of recognition of an alternative to denominational religion at pre-school and primary level, as well as the weaknesses which have already been identified with regard to the grading system of this subject and its alternative, could be regarded as a step in the wrong direction.

Although the alternative between a denominational and non-denominational model is appropriate and a very positive step in this development, it is also subject to ongoing changes, not necessarily for the better. This can be regarded as a powerful reason to embrace a non-denominational compulsory model.

Education for Citizenship and Human Rights:[29] Ongoing Controversy

In addition to the aforementioned disputes concerning the erosion of the fundamental nature of the subject of Catholic religion in state schools, as stated by the 1979 Agreement, the other controversial element in the LOE has been the inclusion of a new subject, 'Education for Citizenship and Human Rights', which has been further developed by subsequent legal provisions. This discipline deals with social and moral values which must be shared by citizens. Its contents are determined by the public education authorities and it is compulsory for all students.

The Royal Decree of 29 December 2006 has declared that the aims of this subject include '[r]ecognition of the human condition in its individual and social dimension whilst accepting pupils' own identities, characteristics and personal experiences through the respect of the differences with others and the development of their self-

---

28   *Instrument of Ratification, dated 4 December 1979, of the Agreement of 3 January 1979, between the Spanish State and the Holy See, concerning Education and Cultural Affairs*, Art IV(1).

29   Educación para la Ciudadanía y los Derechos Humanos.

esteem'.[30] This will be achieved 'by analysing the principles of personal and social Ethics'.[31] The same Decree declares: 'the subjects 'Education for Citizenship and Human Rights' and 'Education on Civil Ethics' will pursue ... [t]he development and expression of feelings and emotions, as well as communication and social skills, which will enable [the students] to take part in group activities with a tolerant attitude based on solidarity, by using dialogue and mediation in order to sort out all sorts of conflicts.'[32] Commentators are divided on the merits of this legislation. Llamazares (2006: 263–4) has passionately defended this new subject and has highlighted the fact that it concentrates on the teaching of human rights and democracy, whilst aiming to create citizens who are free, responsible, critical and uphold common values. In his view, this is necessary to respect people who are different and to emphasize the equality and freedom of all citizens, as well as the value of peace. Llamazares rejects criticisms of this new subject as state indoctrination, because the method is not dogmatic but critical and objective. Moreover, this author refutes suggestions that a conscientious objection to this subject could have succeeded on the basis that this discipline deals with commendable values which must necessarily be shared by citizens of a democratic society.

Unlike Llamazares, Moreno Mozos (2010: 362) has been particularly critical of the aims of this subject and has questioned whether the granting of such significant autonomy to pupils amounts to little more than an attempt to sever their links with their parents, by providing teachers with an important power to help pupils discover and guide their own feelings and emotions. In her view (Moreno Mozos 2010: 363), although minors are members of a society and are therefore holders of rights and obligations in a social group their moral education does not belong to the public authorities but to the parents in accordance with Article 27(3) of the Constitution. She believes that this new course on Ethics, which recognizes human rights as a pattern or model to follow, is a purely relativist morality as human rights are subject to changes or transformations in a society (Moreno Mozos 2010: 364). In her view, this law is based on 'an ideology of gender which is rooted in the denial of sexuality as a natural element of human nature, where human identity is no longer thought in terms of men and women but in terms of gender'. In compliance with this stance, the legitimate differences and reciprocity of the two sexes are regarded as an outdated socio-cultural choice' (Moreno Mozos 2010: 366).

Bearing in mind the controversy surrounding 'Education for Citizenship and Human Rights', Martín Sánchez (2010) has studied the different decisions of the Supreme Court,[33] which have labelled this subject as lawful. This commentator (2010: 383–4) opines that:

---

30   *Real Decreto 1631/2006, 29 December, B.O.E. n. 5. 5 January 2007*, 718.

31   Ibidem, 715.

32   Ibidem, 718.

33   *Sentencias de 11 de febrero de 2009, Recurso n. 905/2008; 11 de febrero de 2009, Recurso n. 948/2008; 11 de febrero de 2009, Recurso n. 949/2008; 11 de febrero de 2009,*

It is feasible to exercise a right of conscientious objection to the contents of *Educación para la Ciudadanía y los Derechos Humanos*, if parents consider that this subject is contrary to their convictions ... [i] n fact, if the educational process, in compliance with Art 27(2) of the Constitution, pursues the 'full development of the human personality' it is clear that this cannot be the exclusive competence of the State, not even at the school level. The right of parents recognized by Art 27.3 must also be respected because, amongst other reasons, the education model must serve the person and not the other way around.

The Supreme Court's acknowledgement of the possibility for parents to request the annulment of the legislation if there is an invasion in the powers recognized by Art 27.3 has met with the disapproval of Martín Sánchez (2010: 385). In this author's opinion, in the period of time from the request of annulment to its successful recognition, students have been bound to follow these classes and the prejudice or harm will already have been caused. Therefore, a simple objection procedure would be a more satisfactory solution to the religious instruction conundrum.

Regardless of the commendable nature of this discipline, which ultimately has been approved by the Spanish judiciary, it seems timely to highlight, following González Sánchez (2010: 402), that 'amongst the different possible models, from a theoretical point of view, which could have been found in our history, our Constitution unquestionably decided to entitle parents to choose the model of values which must be transmitted to the minors. Art 27.3 does not give rise to any sort of uncertainty'. Garcimartin (2007: 24) has also emphasized the entitlement of the parents to choose the type of moral and religious education that their children are to receive and has proposed an optional nature for this subject as a possible way forward.

The Legal Status of Teachers of Religion in Spanish State Schools

As far as the teachers of religion are concerned (Toscani Giménez 1999: 189–97, Castro Argüelles 2002: 291–305), a distinction must be made (Palomino 2010: 350) between those teachers who are civil servants and who wish to teach religion[34] and those other teachers, who are not civil servants and teach the subject of religion. For the latter category, the State demands the same academic requirements as for other teachers at non-university level. In fact, the legal framework concerning these teachers, regardless of the specific denomination, is uniform.[35]

Recurso n. 1013/2008; *11 de marzo de 2009, Recurso n. 4668/2008.*

34   See for instance *Convenio sobre designación y régimen económico de las personas encargadas de la enseñanza religiosa evangélica en los centros docentes públicos de educación primaria y secundaria, BOE de 4 de mayo de 1996* (claúsula quinta).

35   Some commentators (González Sánchez 2010: 407) have accurately criticized this uniformity put forward by the L.O.E. as it clearly ignores the provisions contained

The provisions of the LOE 2006[36] have been developed by *el Real Decreto 696/2007, 1 June*.[37] Teachers of religion must be proposed by the relevant authorities of the different religious bodies and must have obtained a certificate of suitability, issued by the latter.[38] Crucially, the employment position will be permanent.[39] In fact, the additional schedule of the Royal Decree provides: 'Those teachers of religion who, not being civil servants, were subject to a contract when this *Real Decreto* came into effect, will acquire a permanent contract'. Finally, this secondary source of law lists the causes of extinction of the contract, including '[w]ithdrawal, in compliance with the legal framework, of the certificate of suitability to teach religion, by the religious denomination which granted it in the first place'.[40] Undoubtedly, the most debatable situation, as seen below, is the position of teachers of Catholic religion.[41] This has given rise to social controversy and a response by the judiciary.

Teachers of Evangelical religion are selected by the Federation of Evangelical Religious Entities of Spain (FEREDE)[42] and they must have additional training which is provided by the Centre of Formation of Evangelical Religion (Palomino 2010: 351). In relation to the teachers of Islamic religion, the Agreement with the Islamic Commission of Spain declares that 'Islamic religious education shall be offered by teachers designated by the communities belonging to the Islamic Commission of Spain, in compliance with the respective Federation'.[43] As Palomino (2010: 351) observes:

> [A]t the beginning they faced a problem of competence to teach the subject. Currently, the title of teacher or *licenciado*,[44] as recognized by the Spanish State, is required in addition to the completion of the Certificate of Pedagogic Aptitude.

---

in the international agreements signed with the Holy See in 1979, when the Spanish legal framework must also be respectful of its international commitments.

36   See *Disposición adicional tercera*. Crucially this law states that the removal of teachers of religion must be in accordance with the Law.

37   In compliance with its Art 2, the contract of teachers of religion will be subject to the *Estatuto de los Trabajadores, disposición adicional tercera* of the LOE, the current *Real Decreto* and the norms which develop it, the 1979 Agreement on Education and the Agreements of Cooperation with other religious bodies, deeply rooted in the Spanish society.

38   *Real Decreto 696/2007, 1 June* (Art 3.1).

39   Ibidem, Art 4.1.

40   Ibidem, Art 7.1.

41   *Instrument of Ratification, dated 4 December 1979, of the Agreement of 3 January 1979, between the Spanish State and the Holy See, concerning Education and Cultural Affairs* (s.3).

42   *Law 24/1992, of 10 November, approving the Agreement of Cooperation between the State and the Federation of Evangelical Religious Entities of Spain.*

43   Law 26/1992, of 10 November, approving the Agreement of Cooperation between the State and the Islamic Commission of Spain, s.10(2).

44   A four-year degree.

More specifically, future teachers are required to participate in ongoing courses offered by the Centre of Teachers and Resources, in addition to the compulsory seminaries of the Union of Islamic Communities of Spain, and the conferences organized by the Islamic Organization for Education, Science and Culture.

With regard to the teachers of Jewish religion, the Agreement with the Israelite Communities of Spain declares that 'Jewish religious education shall be provided by teachers designated by the Communities belonging to the Federation of Israelite Communities, in compliance with this Federation'.[45]

As seen above, some of the provisions of the uniform legal framework put forward in 2006/2007 do not seem to be compatible with the international agreements signed with the Holy See in 1979. The implementation of this new settlement in the next few years remains to be seen, but a seminal decision of the Constitutional Court in February 2007[46] is bound to have an impact on this legislative development. The Court had to decide whether the decisions made by the bishops were exempted from any sort of intervention by the law of the State and whether it was possible to employ an individual in the public sector whilst following religious rather than secular criteria. As already indicated, teachers of Catholic religion at all different levels – pre-school, primary and secondary – must receive a certificate of suitability from the relevant ecclesiastical authority. Furthermore, they must be both competent and personally suitable. It goes without saying that the former is easier to verify, though the latter is, in the eyes of the Catholic Church, equally important.[47] Unquestionably, the teaching of religion goes beyond the mere transmission of contents and therefore the latter requirement met with the approval of commentators (Ferreiro 2004: 74) long before this landmark case:

> In our opinion, this is common sense. This subject does not simply aim to transmit contents, but more importantly, pursues the transmission of the particular values of the religious denomination. Consequently, it should not be surprising that the ecclesiastical authority, when deciding the persons in charge of the teaching of religion, takes into consideration not only academic aptitudes, but also their personal behaviour.

The Constitutional Court has emphasized the significance of the personal attitude on the part of the teacher of religion and the entitlement of the religious denomination to judge it, by stating:

---

45   *Law 25/1992, of 10 November, approving the Agreement of Cooperation between the State and the Israelite Communities of Spain* (s.10.2).

46   *STC 38/2007*, 15 February.

47   *Boletín Oficial de la Conferencia Episcopal Española*, n. 49: 60–1.

Religious bodies must be entitled to decide the suitability of the persons who are going to teach the tenets of each religious body. This evaluation does not exclusively focus on the theoretical or pedagogical knowledge of the teacher, but also on his/her personal conduct, provided that this personal conduct is a relevant element in the faith of that religious community. In other words, this personal conduct must have an effect on the suitability of the person to teach that faith, as that teaching is regarded as a mechanism of transmission of certain values. For this transmission, the personal example may be an instrument which the Churches may well consider non-negotiable'.[48]

This degree of autonomy on the part of the Catholic Church as far as the choice of the teachers of its religion is concerned – including the personal conduct of its staff – is compatible with Article 6 of the *Ley Orgánica de Libertad Religiosa* of 1980, which recognizes the internal autonomy of religious bodies. This internal autonomy is indispensable for the exercise of religious freedom and it is also in accordance with the Legal Agreement of 3 January 1979, which declares: 'The Spanish State recognizes the right of the Catholic Church to carry out its apostolic mission and guarantees the Church free and public exercise of those activities inherent to it, especially worship, jurisdiction and teaching'.[49] Moreover, the Constitutional Court clearly declared that 'the entitlement of religious bodies to decide the qualified persons who will teach their religious beliefs is a guarantee of the freedom of the Churches in order to transmit their doctrine without undue interference from public authorities'.[50] This emphasis on the collective dimension of religious freedom has been welcomed by some commentators (López-Sidro López 2007: 33). In his view, this collective dimension of the principle of religious freedom – or entitlement of the Catholic Church to appoint its own pastors – is compatible with the rights of parents to receive a moral and religious instruction for their children as provided by Art 27(3) of the Constitution. Both rights complement each other and are the two elements of the right of religious freedom: 'The person exercises his/her particular right in relation to a religious community and the denomination exercises its teaching authority towards its members, with their consent and with full control of the coherence of the teaching with its fundamental dogmas' (López-Sidro 2007: 19). According to this commentator, the combination between the collective and the individual dimensions of a fundamental right (religious freedom) must be given priority over other rights such as the right of teachers to fulfil their legitimate expectations to have a job. This is, in López-Sidro's opinion (2007: 22–3), a fictitious conflict, because we are not referring to two rights on an equal footing.

---

48   *STC 38/2007* (fj. 5).

49   *Instrument of Ratification, dated 4 December 1979, of the Agreement of 3 January 1979, between the Spanish State and the Holy See concerning Legal Affairs*, Art 1(1).

50   *STC 38/2007*, (fj.9).

Many of the controversial cases in which the positions of teachers of Catholic religion were not renewed, have referred to divorcees, cohabitees or persons in same sex relationships. These are, nowadays, lifestyles which are, to a considerable extent, accepted by the majority of Spanish society. Therefore, the powers provided to the diocesan bishop may be regarded as excessive, as they clearly contravene the mainstream tendency. However, the teaching of religion is very specific and has different features from other academic subjects.

The differences between the legal and moral fields have been pointed out by Otaduy Guerin (2007: 17):

> The fact that one particular conduct – such as abortion or same-sex marriage, for instance – is no longer a crime or it is even legalized, does not mean that it must be incorporated in all different social sectors. A sort of 'moral cure' should not be pursued, as if Parliament were a sort of purifying fire, so that those who dare to challenge the legislature will become socially stigmatized as if they were a potentially dangerous element for the peaceful development of social life. This sort of suggestions responds to a new moralism, which is diffused and certainly unacceptable, especially when they are used by those who have traditionally opposed any link between Law and Morality.

Navarro-Valls (2003) has defended the right of Churches to have their own identity and autonomy. Religious bodies may support a moral behaviour which is at odds with mainstream society, but this is, in this author's opinion, 'the natural reaction of an alive body which aims to maintain its own identity'.

In a humorous way, Bejarano (2001) declared:

> [W]hat I do not understand – perhaps one day somebody will be able to explain it to me – is the existence of as many types of Christianity as individual consciences and the fact that we all insist on teaching our religion in accordance with our conscience and without accepting the general rules of the Church. It may be preferable for a teacher of History of Religions to be atheist, or at least agnostic, rather than a believer. He or she will be more objective. However, a teacher appointed by the Church in order to transmit its teachings and its mysteries of faith, should logically be a believer and become an example or a model for his pupils with his own life. If this is not required, I understand nothing.

Bearing all this in mind, however, it must be emphasized that the entitlement of the diocesan bishop to decide who is capable and suitable to teach Catholic religion is not unlimited. Prudently, the Constitutional Court has stated as follows:

> The competent judicial bodies will have to decide whether the lack of proposal by the diocesan bishop is due to criteria of religious nature or morality, which are criteria the definition of which belongs to religious authorities in accordance with the right of religious freedom and religious neutrality of the State, or on the

contrary, it is based on other reasons which are alien to the fundamental right of religious freedom and therefore, not protected by it.[51]

This key distinction, as proposed by the Constitutional Court, is to be welcomed, as unlimited powers in the hands of the diocesan bishops would not be acceptable in a democratic State, but at the same time the powers at their disposal are a fair recognition of the legitimate autonomy of religious bodies in the Spanish legal framework.

Crucially, a recent decision of the Spanish Constitutional Court[52] represents a change with regard to the position of teachers of Catholic religion in state schools and the consequences of this outstanding shift remain to be seen.

Religious Symbols in Spain

Finally, some concise analysis of the role of religious symbols in state schools – one of the most controversial educational issues at present in Europe – should be advanced. In Spain, the use of portable religious symbols (such as the Muslim veil) in state schools has not received a response from the courts yet, though there have been some interesting cases concerning the use of religious garments which have been dealt with by the administrative authorities. In 2002, following a very heated social debate, the Minister of Education of the Regional Government of Madrid requested Juan de Herrera State Secondary School to allow a Muslim girl, Fátima Ledrisse, to wear the veil.[53] This politician stated that in the absence of legislation about the use of religious garments in state schools and out of respect for the religious identity of the girl, she should be allowed to wear the veil at school. Two years later, the presence of Muslim girls wearing the veil had become very frequent in Spanish state schools.[54] More recently, the Department of Education of the Regional Government of Catalonia ordered a school to admit a Muslim girl onto its premises after the school had denied her entry because she was wearing a veil. The Department of Education declared that despite internal secondary legislation prohibiting the use of external symbols – which could

---

51　*STC 38/2007* (fj.7).

52　*STC 51/2011,* 14 April. The highest Spanish Court considered that Resurrección Galera – a teacher of Catholic religion in a state school, whose contract was not renewed by the Church authorities because of her marital status – had been discriminated against on the grounds of her personal beliefs. Furthermore, the Constitutional Court stated that her ideological freedom (Art 16), in conjunction with her right to marry (Art 32) and her personal and family intimacy, had been breached.

53　[Online], available at: http://hemeroteca.abc.es/nav/Navigate.exe/hemeroteca/madrid/abc/2002/02/19.html [Accessed: 28 February 2011].

54　[Online], available at: http://www.elmundo.es/papel/2004/02/15/cronica/1588462. html [Accessed: 28 February 2011].

lead to discrimination on grounds such as gender – the entitlement of children to receive education must prevail over other considerations. During this controversy, the parents of the 8-year-old girl in question insisted on the voluntary nature of her decision. On the other hand, the governing body of a secondary school of Pozuelo de Alarcón (Madrid) decided to prevent a young Muslim girl from entering the school premises, as wearing the hijab breached the uniform policy of the school.[55] Setting these and several other very isolated cases aside, few significant problems have been experienced in practice in Spanish classrooms.

So far as static symbols (the crucifix) are concerned, in Spain, there have been several decisions at the regional level but so far this debate has not yet reached the highest judicial body. In 2007 the Superior Court of Castilla y León[56] took a permissive stance in relation to the controversial presence of crucifixes in state schools and declared that these establishments could decide whether the presence of the crucifix on their premises was adequate. In a very *solomonic* solution, the Court argued that the removal of the crucifix was not necessarily the most appropriate response to the well-being of the educational environment and that such situations required an *ad casum* solution. A year later, a lower court[57] remarkably regarded the presence of the crucifix in state schools as unconstitutional[58] and ordered the educational establishment, Macías Picavea School, to remove all crucifixes from the different classrooms. This decision was received by different organizations, not necessarily Catholic, with dismay[59] and the Government declared that they were not willing to make general decisions with regard to the presence of religious symbols in schools as these decisions had to be made *ad casum* by the governing bodies of the schools.[60]

The overall prohibition decided by this lower judicial body was appealed by the Regional Government of Castilla y León and the Association E-Christians before the Superior Court of Castilla y León.[61] Interestingly, this Court followed the first *Lautsi* decision, as stated in November 2009,[62] holding that the crucifix could violate rights to freedom from religion, whilst emphasizing that each jurisdiction

---

55   [Online], available at: http://www.elmundo.es/elmundo/2010/04/21/madrid/1271832161.html?a=720f08d30fb996825f8e8ccf6ad4a9f2&t=1271838241&numero= [Accessed: 28 February 2011].

56   *Sentencia del Tribunal Superior de Justicia de Castilla y León*, 27 February 2007.

57   *Sentencia del Juzgado Contencioso Administrativo de Valladolid*, 14 November 2008.

58   It should be taken into consideration that there is no principle of *stare decisis* in Spain and decisions of lower courts can contravene decisions of their higher counterparts.

59   [Online], available at: http://www.aciprensa.com/utiles/myprint/print.php [Accessed: 28 February 2011].

60   [Online], available at: http://www.elpais.com/articulo/sociedad/Gobierno/deja/centros/decision/crucifijo/elpepisoc/20081125elpepisoc_3/Tes [Accessed: 28 February 2011].

61   *Sentencia del Tribunal Superior de Justicia de Castilla y León*, 14 December 2009.

62   ECtHR *Lautsi* v *Italy* 3 November 2009, Application no. 30814/06. The Grand Chamber of the European Court of Human Rights reversed this decision on 18 March 2011

had its own specific features. Furthermore, it declared that the decision about the withdrawal or maintenance of the crucifix could not be a blanket decision but had to take into consideration the wishes of the parties involved. This eclectic decision on the part of the Court has been publicly acknowledged by the former Minister of Justice, Francisco Caamaño, who, however, stated that this was just a specific case.[63]

The highest judicial bodies of the State, both the Supreme Court and the Constitutional Court, have dealt, however, with the issues of the maintenance of an image of the Virgin Mary in the coat of arms and medal of the University of Valencia. The Supreme Court[64] regarded this symbolism as acceptable, stating that the coat of arms and medal with the image of the Virgin Mary did not only belong to the cultural and historical heritage of the institution but also to the Spanish people and, in particular, to the people of Valencia. This view was endorsed by the Constitutional Court,[65] which declared that the correct interpretation of the principle of religious neutrality of the State did not bind the university to withdraw the image of the Virgin Mary since respect for history and tradition had been the main factors taken into account by the academic authorities when deciding to retain, until then, the religious image in the university's emblems.

Likewise, on 3 December 2009, a bill was approved by the Lower Chamber of the Spanish Parliament (*el Congreso de los Diputados*) which, following the first decision of in the *Lautsi* case, requested the Government to remove all crucifixes from state schools. As the powers on education belong to both the regional and the national authorities in Spain, this request has an exclusively symbolic significance. The display of religious symbols in public places has met with the approval of leading commentators (Cañamares 2009: 193):

> The religious neutrality of the State does not require the elimination of any religious manifestations placed by individuals or groups in the public arena. On the contrary, such a principle is based on the free and equal exercise of the right to religious freedom for citizens and religious groups. What religious neutrality prohibits is any activity carried out on behalf of public bodies that can put the equal fulfilment of the free exercise of religion by individuals or communities at risk. Only under those circumstances can the practice be considered unconstitutional.

Cañamares is to be praised for the above distinction. In fact, the display of religious symbols in State schools does not put the free exercise of religion by individuals

---

and declared that 'it found no evidence that the display of such a symbol on classroom walls might have an influence on pupils'.

63   [Online], available at: http://www.20minutos.es/noticia/587935/ [Accessed: 28 February 2011].

64   *Sentencia del Tribunal Supremo*, 12 June 1990.

65   *STC 130/1991*, 6 June.

or communities at risk, whilst being an acknowledgement of the Spanish culture and the Christian tradition of Europe. It goes without saying, this display is only acceptable if compatible with a welcoming and respectful approach to non-Christians. The decision of the Grand Chamber in *Lautsi*[66] will shed light on this controversial issue.

Conclusion

In the last few decades, the divisive nature of the teaching of religion in state schools has been a cause of concern in the Spanish society. Although the Constitution is inconclusive and Article 27 is only one of the many examples of the hybrid nature of our highest Spanish Law, education should be a field of consensus rather than antagonism. The erratic legislative developments of the last 30 years and the continuous attempts on the part of the judiciary to address these ongoing problems are clear signs of the complicated nature of this field in Spain.

An alternative, non-denominational subject to the teaching of denominational religion –Catholic, Evangelical, Muslim or Jewish – is to be welcomed. This model is far more satisfactory than the absence of an alternative subject, which clearly places those students who choose to follow any of the four denominational paths in a disadvantageous position. That is why the solution adopted by both the LOCE (2002) and the LOE (2006) – in relation to secondary schools – is better than the framework of the latter with regard to pre-schools and primary schools. Understandably, under the current scenario, the teaching of denominational religion may concern small religious minorities that have not achieved the same degree of recognition from the public authorities. However, although a valid concern about the provision for minorities is expected, this cannot be the only criteria in law-making decisions or in the choice of the educational model for a contemporary society. Furthermore, there is no reason why denominational religion should be accused of bigotry or exclusionism. This is a prejudiced view and an unfair generalization. Nevertheless, this should not prevent us from discussing whether the school is the right venue for the teaching of denominational religion, or it should be provided exclusively by their families and their religious ministers.

Because of all the difficulties previously explained, the compulsory instruction of non- denominational religion seems to be far less problematic. Accordingly, the relevant question is not whether all citizens should be aware of the historical and the cultural elements of different religions, which is evident, but whether in the pluralistic and heterogeneous European society of the twenty-first century those students who choose denominational religion are deprived of an important component in their academic development. The combination of compulsory, non-denominational religion in schools and denominational teaching in religious establishments for those who want to pursue it would appear to be the most

---

66 Note 62 *supra*.

attractive option. In the meantime, however, and until the current framework is duly modified, the Spanish authorities must honour their duties and a scrupulous observance of their international obligations should be expected.

References

Bejarano, F. 2001. Profesores de Religión. *Diario de Jerez*, 22 September.

Castro Argüelles, M.A. 2002. Los profesores de religión y moral católica en centros públicos de enseñanza. *Actualidad Laboral* 1, 291–305.

Cañamares, S. 2009. Religious symbols in Spain: a legal perspective. *Ecclesiastical Law Journal* 11(2), 181–93.

Cañamares, S. 2009. El control jurisdiccional de la autonomía de la Iglesia católica en la designación de los profesores de religion. *Revista Española de Derecho Canónico* 66–166, 275–92.

Celador Angón, O. and Tejón Sánchez, R. 2010. El derecho de los padres a elegir la formación religiosa y moral de sus hijos, in *Educación e Ideología*, edited by D. Llamazares Fernández, R. Tejón Sánchez and O. Celador Angón. Madrid: Dykinson, S.L. 105–13.

Esteban Garces, C. 2003. *Enseñanza de la Religión y Ley de Calidad*. Madrid: PPC.

Ferrer Ortiz, J. 2006. Los derechos educativos de los padres en una sociedad plural. *Revista General de Derecho Canónico y Derecho Eclesiástico del Estado*, 10. [Online] Available at: http://www.iustel.com/v2/revistas/detalle_revista. asp?id_noticia+404982&d=1 [Accessed: 25 November 2010].

Ferreiro, J. 2004. *Profesores de Religión en la Enseñanza Pública y Constitución Española*. Barcelona: Atelier Editorial SL.

García Oliva, J. 2008. Religious freedom in transition Spain. *Religion, State and Society* 36(3), 259–81.

Garcimartín, M.C. 2007. Neutralidad y escuela pública: A propósito de la educación para la ciudadanía. *Revista General de Derecho Canónico y Derecho Eclesiástico del Estado*, 14. [Online] Available at: http://www.iustel. com/v2/revistas/detalle_revista.asp?id_noticia=400196&d=1 [Accessed: 20 November 2010].

González Sánchez, M. 2010. El profesorado de religion evangélica en los centros docentes públicos españoles, in *Religión en la Educación Pública. Análisis Comparativo de su Regulación Jurídica en las Américas, Europa e Israel*, edited by C. Asiaín. Madrid: Fundación Universitaria Española, 401–10.

López-Sidro López, A. 2007. Dimensión colectiva del derecho de libertad religiosa en los centros docentes públicos: la designación de los profesores de religión. *Revista General de Derecho Canónico y Derecho Eclesiástico del Estado*, 14. [Online] Available at http://www.iustel.com/v2/revistas/detalle_revista. asp?id_noticia=4001978&d=1 [Accessed: 1 December 2010].

Llamazares, D. 2002. *Derecho de la Libertad de Conciencia: Libertad de Conciencia y Laicidad*. 2nd edn. Madrid: Civitas.

Llamazares, D. 2006. Educación para la ciudadanía, laicidad y enseñanza de la religión, *Laicidad y Libertades: Escritos Jurídicos* 6, 219–66.

Martín Sánchez, I. 2010. Objeción de conciencia y educación para la ciudadanía, in *Religión en la Educación Pública. Análisis Comparativo de su Regulación Jurídica en las Américas, Europa e Israel*, edited by C. Asiaín. Madrid: Fundación Universitaria Española, 369–85.

Martínez Torrón, J. 2006. *Estado y Religión en la Constitución Española y en la Constitución Europea*. Granada: Comares.

Moreno Mozos, M.M. 2010. Los límites del Estado en la imposición de contenidos educativos. Caso español: la ley orgánica de educación de 3 de mayo de 2006, in *Religión en la Educación Pública. Análisis Comparativo de su Regulación Jurídica en las Américas, Europa e Israel*, edited by C. Asiaín. Madrid: Fundación Universitaria Española, 353–67.

Navarro-Valls, R. and Martínez Torrón, J. 2011. *Conflictos entre Conciencia y Ley: Las Objeciones de Conciencia*. Madrid: Iustel.

Navarro-Valls, R. 2003. La polémica sobre las clases de religión. *El País*, 3 November.

Otaduy Guerin, J. Idoneidad de los profesores de religión. Una revisión necesaria y urgente. A propósito de la sentencia 38/2007, de 15 de febrero, del Tribunal Constitucional. *Revista General de Derecho Canónico y Derecho Eclesiástico del Estado*, 14. [Online] Available at http://www.iustel.com/v2/revistas/detalle_revista.asp?id_noticia=400193&d=1 [Accessed: 17 November 2010].

Palomino, R. 2010. Algunas notas sobre el sistema educativo español, in *Religión en la Educación Pública. Análisis comparativo de su regulación jurídica en las Américas, Europa e Israel*, edited by C. Asiaín. Madrid: Fundación Universitaria Española, 345–52.

Robbers, G. 2005. *State and Church in the European Union*. 2nd edn. Baden-Baden: Nomos.

Rodríguez Blanco, M. 2005. La enseñanza de la religión en la escuela pública española. *Osservatio delle Liberta ed Istituzioni Religiose*, 5. [Online] Available at: http://www.olir.it/areetematiche/73/documents/RodriguezBlanco_Ensenanza.pdf [Accessed: 10 December 2010].

Sandberg, R. and Doe, N. 2007. Church-State relations in Europe. *Religion Compass* 1/5, 561–78.

Souto Paz, J.A. 2003. *Comunidad Política y Libertad de Creencias; Introducción a las Libertades Públicas en el Derecho Comparado Español*. 2nd edn. Madrid: Marcial Pons.

Toscani Giménez, D. 1999. La problemática judicial y la nueva regulación legal de los profesores de religión. *Revista de Derecho Social* 5, 189–97.

PART III
Case Studies:
The Influence of Religion on
Teaching Content and School Ethos

Chapter 10

Religious Education in Europe in the Twenty-First Century

Peter Cumper

It is significant that in her recent list of what constitutes 'responsible citizenship', one of the criteria identified by Martha Nussbaum (2010: 83–4) is the need to 'appreciate the complexities of the major world religions'. Her statement not only illustrates the increasing importance of religious belief today in the public sphere (Habermas 2006: 1–25), but also implies that it is incumbent on States to make appropriate provision for their citizens on such matters (Jackson 2002: 162–9, Ipgrave and Leganger-Krogstad in Jackson 2003: 147–68, 162–9). In other words, the State has a duty to provide classes on religion in schools – hereinafter referred to as 'religious education' ('RE') – so that young people have the skills to understand and relate to 'the other' in societies influenced by a diverse range of religious and secular values (Cassidy in de Souza et al. 2007: 869–84).

This chapter will focus on the challenges of teaching RE to school children in contemporary Europe. In particular, it will examine the contribution of European human rights law in seeking to ensure that young people are given fair and accurate information on an appropriate range of religious and equivalent philosophical beliefs. The chapter is divided into three sections: (1) RE and the European context, which identifies some of the reasons for teaching religion to children in school and examines certain differences between European States in this area; (2) RE and the jurisprudence of the European Court of Human Rights ('ECtHR'), which looks in particular at the recent case of *Grzelak v. Poland*[1] and then considers the principle of freedom *from* religion, the right of parents to withdraw their children from RE lessons and the aim of RE programmes; and (3) the chapter's conclusion, which offers a brief summary of some of the challenges facing law and policy makers in the formulation of the principles governing the provision of RE in Europe.

---

1   ECtHR 15 June 2010, Application no. 7710/02.

RE and the European Context

The Case for RE

In contemporary Europe, there is certainly little doubt that religious education programmes are (at least in principle) commonly associated with a number of benefits. For example, it has been claimed that lessons about religion may contribute to the promotion of moral values (Bell 1982–1983: 88, Barrow 1996: 243–6). Yet, even if this is not the case (White 2004: 151–64), there are clearly good educational reasons for studying RE as evidenced by the recent claim of a former Poet Laureate that some knowledge of holy books such as the Bible can contribute to a better understanding of English literature.[2] RE programmes can also play an important role in helping to foster a citizen's personal identity, especially in a cosmopolitan and religiously diverse society (Miedema in de Souza et al. 2007: 967–76, Gutmann 2003: 151–91).[3] Additionally, there is a widespread belief that RE can engender better relations between different faiths in post 9/11 Europe (Baratte in de Souza et al. 2007: 243–58), particularly given the widely acknowledged influence of religion in the contemporary political sphere (Westurland 1996, Berger 1999).

The potential contribution of RE as a way of helping to build bridges between people of different faiths in religiously diverse societies is probably the most compelling reason for its existence (Moore 2009, 139–45). Indeed, according to the theologian William Kay, the consequences of *not* offering RE lessons may be grave, for he claims that if the State fails to educate the young about the beliefs of other groups, 'the chances of future inter-religious disputes increase' (Kay 2005: 49). The suggestion that RE lessons may dispel myths and lead to better relations between people of different faiths or none, also explains why there is support for appropriate lessons on religion in the classroom from some rather unlikely sources, including the British Humanist Association (2006) and the prominent atheist Richard Dawkins (2007: 340) who claims that that a 'good case can indeed be made for the educational benefits of teaching comparative religion'. What is more, with bodies as diverse in composition and function as OFSTED (2010) and the OSCE (2007: 76)[4] in agreement that RE can help to reduce conflict and better promote community cohesion, lessons about religion in schools have increasingly become 'a vital task for public education' (Kamat and Mathew 2010: 359). Thus,

---

2   See 'Poet Laureate Andrew Motion's calls for all children to be taught the Bible', 17 February 2009 the *Daily Telegraph*.

3   The ECtHR has held that religious freedom 'is one of the most vital elements that go to make up the identity of believers and their conception of life': ECtHR *Buscarini and Others v. San Marino* [GC], Application no. 24645/94, ECHR 1999–I, para. 34.

4   'Knowledge about religions and beliefs has the valuable potential of reducing conflicts that are based on lack of understanding for others' beliefs and of encouraging respect for their rights'.

today, the most pertinent question in much of Europe is not *whether* but rather *how* RE should be provided in the classroom.

RE and Regional Differences in Europe

This chapter will focus mainly on the provision of RE in state funded non-denominational schools (Kamat and Mathew 2010: 359).[5] Thus, issues such as whether religious schools should teach the beliefs of other faiths will not be covered, given the constraints of space and the fact human rights law affords denominational schools considerable freedom in the area of curriculum design and delivery.[6] However, even by limiting the focus here to non-denominational public schools, it soon becomes clear that reaching agreement as to *how* religion should be taught in contemporary Europe is not an easy task. There are, after all, significant continent wide differences in terms of the approach – or indeed, lack of approach – taken by States to the provision of RE (Nipkon in de Souza et al. 2007: 577–90, Jackson in Skeie 2006: 11–28).

For a start, a handful of European countries – most notably France (Willaime 2007: 87–102, Estivalezes in de Souza et al. 2007: 475–86) as well as Albania and the former Yugoslav Republic of Macedonia[7] – choose not to provide formal lessons on religion in the classroom. But whilst such an approach is very much as exception to the norm, for Europe is a continent where religion is taught in the vast majority of States, common ground in terms of the *provision* of RE is nonetheless still very hard to find. It is worth noting that there are significant differences in regard to education generally, as opposed to religious education in particular, between European States (Brock and Tulasiewicz, 1994). There are, after all, many different models governing lessons on religion, ranging from a high level of ecclesiastical participation in some nations (Ireland, Italy, Greece and Cyprus) to a low degree of church involvement in others (the United Kingdom – Willaime 2007: 57–66). Indeed, the lack of uniformity is illustrated by the fact that there are not merely inter-state differences, but also significant intra state variations in how lessons on religion are provided. A case in point is the UK, where traditionally the syllabi upon which the teaching of RE has been based in English schools have been markedly different from those used in Scotland (Rodger 2003: 600–605) and Northern Ireland (Nelson 2004: 249–58).

---

5   In England there have been recent calls by Richard Dawkins for denominational schools to teach about different faiths and beliefs, as opposed to the present position where RE in such schools must be taught in accordance with the terms of school's trust deeds and the wishes of its governing body. See 'Teach RE in schools – but do it properly says atheist Dawkins', 18 August 2010, *The Times*. On the rules governing RE generally see DCSF (2010).

6   On this generally see Human Rights Committee *W. Dalgado Paez v. Colombia* 12 July 1990, Communication Number 195/1985, UN Doc A/45/40 vol. 2 (1990), 43, para. 5.7.

7   EtCHR *Hasan and Eylem v. Turkey* (2008) 46 EHRR 44, para. 31.

The moral from this is clear. In view of Europe's history, as well as a range of related social, political and religious factors, there is no single European model for RE (Heimbrock, Scheilke and Schreiner 2001). Indeed, given the nature of these differences, there is unlikely to be any significant continent wide agreement in the foreseeable future (Kuyk et al. 2007, Larsson and Gustavsson 2004). It is within this context that the ECtHR finds itself operating – a context that perhaps explains the Court's tendency to afford States a wide 'margin of appreciation' and its rather conservative view that: 'the setting and planning of the curriculum fall in principle within the competence of the Contracting States. This mainly involves questions of expediency on which it is not for the Court to rule and whose solution may legitimately vary according to the country and the era.'[8]

At first glance this statement would clearly militate against the ECtHR's intervention, by suggesting that RE is a matter essentially for Europe's governments and political institutions. On closer inspection, however, it soon becomes clear that the Court has an opportunity to bring about reform in this area (albeit slowly and incrementally) and there is perhaps some evidence to suggest that this is what it may (of late) have been doing.

RE and the Jurisprudence of the European Court of Human Rights

The history of the ECtHR reveals that RE is not an area that has traditionally been synonymous with radical judgments. Yet, since 2007, the ECtHR has found for applicants on three separate occasions: (1) *Folgerø and others v. Norway*;[9] (2) *Hasan* and *Eylem Zengin v. Turkey*;[10] and, most recently, (3) *Grzelak v. Poland*.[11] This chapter will focus primarily on the *Grzelak* case whilst making ancillary reference to the other two cases in order to analyse and assess the way in which the Court has responded to the challenges of teaching RE in a Europe that is today religiously diverse yet increasingly influenced by secular values.

Grzelak v. Poland

In *Grzelak*, a Polish boy (Mateusz Grzelak) who had refused to attend religious instruction lessons in school invoked (along with his agnostic parents) the European Convention on Human Rights 1950 ('ECHR'). He complained that, in the absence of the school acceding to his parents' request to offer him alternative classes to religious instruction (such as lessons on ethics), he had often been left unsupervised in the corridor and that, as a result, he had been forced to endure social ostracism and ridicule.

---

8   Ibidem, para. 51.
9   ECtHR *Folgerø and others v. Norway* (2008) 46 EHRR 47.
10   *Hasan*, note 7 *supra*.
11   ECtHR 15 June 2010 *Grzelak v. Poland*, Application no. 7710/02.

The applicants (the boy, and separately, his parents) relied upon Articles 9 and 14 of the Convention, arguing (1) that the school authorities had failed to organize an alternative class in ethics for Mateusz, and (2) complaining about the absence of a mark in the boy's primary school reports in the space reserved for 'religion/ ethics'.[12] There are two main parts to the European Court's judgment.

First, the Court held the fact that the school's failure to provide a mark for the subject 'religion/ethics' constituted a violation of Article 14[13] taken in conjunction with Article 9 of the Convention.[14] The Court found that the absence of a mark (and in its place the insertion of a straight line) in the section of a school report headed 'religion/ethics', would inevitably stigmatize a student in this position and effectively reveal much about his religious beliefs in an overwhelmingly Catholic country such as Poland:

> The Court considers that the absence of a mark for 'religion/ethics' would be understood by any reasonable person as an indication [that Mateusz Grzelak] was thus likely to be regarded as a person without religious beliefs ... The fact of having no mark for 'religion/ethics' inevitably has a specific connotation and distinguishes the persons concerned from those who have a mark for the subject.[15]

The Court concluded that, by effectively stigmatizing those students who lacked a mark in the 'religion/ethics' section of their school reports, Poland risked contravening the Court's long held principle that a person should not be compelled (even indirectly) to reveal their religious beliefs or the lack thereof.[16] Indeed, the Court, whilst acknowledging that its case law precluding an obligation to reveal

---

12   In the place reserved for a mark for 'religion / ethics' the boy's school reports just had a straight line.

13   Article 14 provides that 'The enjoyment of the rights and freedoms set forth in this Convention shall be secured without discrimination on any ground such as sex, race, colour, language, religion, political or other opinion, national or social origin, association with a national minority, property, birth or other status.'

14   Article 9 provides that:

(1) 'Everyone has the right to freedom of thought, conscience and religion; this right includes freedom to change his religion or belief, and freedom, either alone or in community with others and in public or private, to manifest his religion or belief, in worship, teaching, practice and observance.'

(2) 'Freedom to manifest one's religion or beliefs shall be subject only to such limitations as are prescribed by law and are necessary in a democratic society in the interests of public safety, for the protection of public order, health or morals, or the protection of the rights and freedoms of others.'

15   *Grzelak*, note 1 *supra*, para. 95.

16   ECtHR *Sofianopoulos and Others v. Greece* Applications nos. 1977/02, 1988/02 and 1997/02 ECHR 2002-X; and ECtHR 2 February 2010 *Sinan Işık v. Turkey*, Application no. 21924/05, para. 42.

information about oneself had traditionally only 'concerned identity cards [which are] documents of arguably greater significance in a person's life than school reports', nevertheless took the view that similar considerations would apply in relation to the production of school reports in this particular case.[17]

Another related matter which influenced the ECtHR was that, under an Education Ordinance which came into effect in 2007, marks that were obtained for a student's religious education (or ethics) class would be included in the calculation of the 'average mark' obtained by a pupil at the end of a given school year. The Court was concerned that this rule could adversely affect a student, such as Mateusz, who had not been afforded an opportunity to study for a course in ethics. The Court reasoned that students in this situation 'might feel pressurised – [to act] against their conscience [and] attend a religion class in order to improve their average'.[18] Thus, in rejecting the Government's argument that the absence of a mark for religion/ethics was 'entirely neutral',[19] the Court held that here had a been a violation of Article 14 taken in conjunction with Article 9 of the ECHR because the difference in treatment between non-believers wishing to take ethics classes and pupils attending religious instruction classes could not be objectively and reasonably justified.

Having found that Poland had 'infringed the very essence [of the boy's] right not to manifest his religion or convictions under Article 9',[20] in the second part of its judgment the ECtHR was less sympathetic to his parents' claims under Article 2 of Protocol No 1 ('Art 2 P. 1') that the school's failure to provide classes in ethics contravened the principle that children should be educated in conformity with the religious and philosophical convictions of their parents.[21] In rejecting this argument, the Court found it particularly significant that neither religious education nor ethics were compulsory subjects in Polish schools. Thus, since both were merely optional, the failure to offer Mateusz ethics lessons because of the Polish practice that there had to be a minimum of seven pupils before such classes could be offered was considered a reasonable requirement. For the Court, the rationale underpinning this decision was clear:

---

17   *Grzelak*, note 1 *supra*, para. 93. The Court was also concerned in *Folgerø* that for parents to obtain a partial exemption for their children to be excused from KRL (a single subject covering Christianity, religion and philosophy) they would have to give reasons for their request, and this could lead to them being put under pressure to reveal (to the school) otherwise private details of their own religious or philosophical convictions: *Folgerø*, note 9 *supra*, para. 98.

18   *Grzelak*, note 1 *supra*, para. 96.

19   Ibidem, para. 97.

20   Ibidem, para. 100.

21   Article 2, Protocol 1 provides: 'No person shall be denied the right to education. In the exercise of any functions which it assumes in relation to education and to teaching, the State shall respect the right of parents to ensure such education and teaching in conformity with their own religions and philosophical convictions.'

It remains, in principle, within the national margin of appreciation left to the States under Article 2 of Protocol No. 1 to decide whether to provide religious instruction in public schools and, if so, what particular system of instruction should be adopted. The only limit which must not be exceeded in this area is the prohibition of indoctrination.[22]

Accordingly, since the Court found that there had been no indoctrination in this case, it held that the Polish model of teaching religion and ethics came within the 'margin of appreciation' which is afforded to States in relation to the organization of the curriculum.

Although the *Grzelak* case (unlike *Folgerø*) was not decided by the Grand Chamber, it nevertheless provides a useful platform by which we can examine a number of the challenges facing the ECtHR in relation to the provision of RE in the classroom. In this respect, three issues are considered: (1) the duty of States to permit pupils to be free from religion or belief in the provision of RE programmes; (2) the scope of parental rights to withdraw their children from RE programmes; and (3) the extent that States are obliged to offer lessons on religion coupled with the complex issue of identifying and determining the proper aims of RE programmes.

Challenges Facing the European Court in Relation to the Provision of RE

The ECHR and non-believers: freedom from religion
In recent years, the European Court of Human Rights has strongly affirmed that Article 9 of the ECHR offers protection to non-believers in the field of education.[23] Such rhetoric was evident in *Grzelak*, when the Court restated its longstanding principle that the Convention affords rights not just to religious 'believers',[24] but also to 'atheists, agnostics, sceptics, and the unconcerned.'[25] In holding that Mateusz Grzelak had the right *not* to manifest religious convictions, the Court chose to distinguish his petition from a similar case that it had previously rejected as manifestly ill founded in 2001. In the earlier case of *Saniewski v. Poland*,[26] the Court had dismissed the applicant's claim that his future employment prospects

---

22 *Grzelak*, note 1 *supra*, para. 104.

23 ECtHR Grand Chamber *Lautsi v. Italy* 18 March 2011, Application no. 30814/06, para. 60. The Court has also expressed similar sentiments in relation to Article 11 of the EHCR: *Young, James and Webster v. the United Kingdom*, 13 August 1981, paras 52–7, Series A no. 44.

24 ECtHR *Kokkinakis v. Greece* (1994) 17 EHRR 397, 418.

25 Ibidem, 418. The ECtHR's approach is generally consistent with international human rights law. For example, the Krishnaswami Study suggested that the term 'religion or belief' should 'include, in addition to various theistic creeds, such other beliefs as agnosticism, free thought, atheism and rationalism': E/CN.4/Sub.2/200/Rev.1, 1.

ECtHR 10 February 1993 *X v. UK*, Application no. 18187/91.

26 ECtHR 26 June 2001 *Saniewski v. Poland*, Application no. 40319/98.

would be harmed because his school report, which had failed to record a mark for 'religion/ ethics', effectively revealed much about his beliefs/non-beliefs. In coming to a very different conclusion in *Grzelak*, the Court sought to distinguish *Saniewski* on three grounds:

> First, ... in the instant case [*Grzelak*] the allegations concern all the consecutive school reports of the third applicant [Mateusz Grzelak], including his leaving certificate for primary and lower secondary schools. Secondly, in the present case the Court has examined the issues raised in the light of Article 14 taken in conjunction with Article 9 (in its negative aspect). Thirdly, the relevant new factor for the Court is the amended Ordinance of 2007.

It is suggested that the reasons given by the Court for distinguishing *Grzelak* from *Saniewski* are rather unconvincing. This certainly was the view of David Thór Björgvinsson, the dissenting Icelandic judge in the case. Unlike the rest of the Court, he held that the differences between the two cases were essentially only 'quantitative', because the complaint in *Saniewski* involved only one school report, whereas the issue in *Grzelak* concerned all of the applicant's primary and secondary schooling.[27]

However, the real significance of *Grzelak* does not arguably lie in the technical niceties of any possible distinctions between it and another case but rather in the fact that the ECtHR missed an opportunity to have affirmed, in stronger terms, the protection of non-religious belief. After all, given that the Court has recognized the need for school curricula to keep pace with wider societal changes,[28] its judges might have used increasing social recognition of the viability and need to protect non-religious beliefs as the basis for overturning its previous ruling in *Saniewski*. However, the Court refrained from pursuing such a course of action and chose merely to distinguish *Saniewski* from *Grzelak* on the three rather tenuous grounds listed above.

It may be that one explanation for this more conservative approach was a desire to minimize controversy, especially given the potentially emotive nature of issues pertaining to RE.[29] Indeed, it is possible that such considerations explain why the Court made no reference to *Lautsi v. Italy*[30] (the Italian cross case) notwithstanding the seeming relevance of passages in that ruling, which had been

---

27   Partly dissenting opinion of Judge David Thór Björgvinsson, para. 9.

28   For example, the Court has accepted that school curricula 'may legitimately vary according to the country and the era': *Hasan* note 7 *supra*, para. 51.

29   Indeed, Mateus Grzelak had argued in his submission to the Court that "the entire education system in Poland was geared towards Catholicism and that those who did not share that faith were discriminated against". Perhaps unsurprisingly the Court conspicuously refrained from commenting on this particular claim. See ECHR *Grzelak v. Poland* 15 June 2010, Application no. 7710/02, para. 64.

30   ECtHR *Lautsi v. Italy* 3 November 2009, Application no. 30814/06.

handed down by the Court (in a Chamber ruling) eight months earlier. After all, the Court in *Lautsi* had noted that the 'negative right' of freedom from religion 'deserves special protection if … the State … expresses a belief and dissenters are placed in a situation from which they [can only] extract themselves … by making disproportionate efforts and acts of sacrifice'[31] – a state of affairs which effectively was the case in *Grzelak*, given the Court's recognition of the pressure placed on the boy to attend school RE classes. Thus, mindful perhaps of the politically sensitive nature of the issues at hand, particularly in a nation like Poland where there is a close correlation between the majority Catholic faith and national identity (Porter 2001: 289–99, Szaikowski 1983),[32] the Court in *Grzelak* chose to tread warily on the oft contentious terrain of religious education.

Irrespective of whether such an approach was justified – for an argument could be made that the Court was only being prudent in seeking to obviate the risk of potential criticism by being cautious in this area – the *effect* of the ECtHR's ruling in *Grzelak* was that non-religious pupils would be afforded greater protection in Poland than had been the case a decade earlier. What is more, in *Grzelak*, the Court clearly rearticulated the tenet of freedom *from* religion – an important principle that underpins the right of parents to withdraw their children from RE lessons, which will now be examined in more detail.

RE and the parental right of withdraw

Today, religious education is a compulsory subject in 25 of the 46 Council of Europe nations where religious education is taught in schools.[33] Yet the term 'compulsory' in this context is rather a misnomer. The ECtHR has itself expressly acknowledged that:

> In spite of the variety of teaching methods, almost all of the member States offer at least one route by which pupils can opt out of religious education classes by providing an exemption mechanism or the option of attending a lesson in a substitute subject, or by giving pupils the choice of whether or not to sign up to a religious studies class.[34]

In other words, the European Convention places States under an obligation to respect the wishes of parents who object to their children attending religious education classes. The rationale for this is Art 2 P.1 of the Convention, which imposes a duty on the State to ensure that information in the curriculum is 'conveyed in an objective, critical and pluralistic manner', without any 'aim of

---

31 Ibidem, para. 55.
32 See generally, Porter 2001, Bogdan Szajkowski 1983.
33 *Hasan*, note 7 *supra*, para. 33
34 Ibidem, para. 50.

indoctrination'.[35] In practice, this has been interpreted as meaning that parents retain the right to withdraw their children from RE lessons.[36]

The European Court of Human Rights has long recognized the correlation between parental opt-outs and the absence of indoctrination. For example, in *Folgerø*, where the applicants complained that changes to the Norwegian primary school curriculum had led to the replacement of two separate subjects (Christianity and philosophy of life) by a single subject covering Christianity, religion and philosophy ('KRL'), the Court upheld the complaint because, as a result of these changes, parents only have the power of a *partial* withdrawal of children from KRL. While the Court was satisfied that KRL's aim (which was for Christianity and other religions/philosophies to be taught together) was a commendable one, the fact there were a number of *qualitative* differences between the provision of Christianity and other religions/philosophies (including a 'Christian object clause' stipulating that a key aim of the law was to give pupils a Christian upbringing) meant that there had been a violation of parents' rights. Thus, the Grand Chamber of the Court held (9–8) that there had been a violation of Art 2 P.1, because parents could only request a *partial* exemption from KRL in order to counter the *qualitative* imbalance in the way it was taught and, as a result, material in the curriculum had not been conveyed in an objective, critical and pluralistic manner.[37]

A similar approach was taken by the ECtHR in *Hasan and Eylem Zengin v. Turkey*.[38] The applicants (Hasan Zengin and his daughter Eylem) had unsuccessfully requested that the girl be exempted from lessons in religious culture and ethics at her state school on the basis that the family were followers of Alevism (a faith with close ties to Islam, albeit one with beliefs that differ from the main Islamic schools of thought).[39] In response to the applicants' complaint of a violation of Art 2 P.1, the Court found that the teaching syllabus afforded greater priority to Islam than to other religions/philosophies and there was very little teaching about the Alevi faith. The Court held that the religious culture and ethics lessons in Turkish schools had failed to comply with the criteria of objectivity and pluralism which was necessary for a proper education in a democratic society and crucially, observed that unlike children from Christian or Jewish families, pupils from the Muslim tradition (including those of the Alevi faith) could not be withdrawn

---

35   ECtHR *Kjeldsen, Busk Madsen and Pederson v. Denmark* (1976) 1 EHRR 711, para. 53.

36   For example, in England and Wales the right of parents to withdraw their children from religious education is found in the *Education Act 1996* Part V, Chapter 3, s.389 and the *School Standards and Framework Act 1998* Part II, Chapter 6, s.71. The relevant law in Scotland is covered in the *Education (Scotland) Act 1980*.

37   The Grand Chamber also held that it was unnecessary to consider the case in relation to other ECHR Articles (Articles 8, 9 and 14).

38   *Hasan*, note 7 *supra*.

39   Under Turkish law, religious culture and ethics is a compulsory subject in primary and secondary schools and the applicants objected to the syllabus used in these classes because it was based solely on the Sunni interpretation of Islam.

from religious culture and ethics lessons. Thus, Turkey's failure to accede to that applicant's request that the girl be exempted from lessons in religious culture and ethics had constituted a violation of Art 2 P.1.

This power of parental withdrawal has long been the primary vehicle by which States avoid the charge of indoctrination in the classroom.[40] However, such parental 'opt outs' are a blunt and unsatisfactory way of maintaining religious freedom, being synonymous with a number of defects. For a start, they rest on the premise that parents always have a 'free' choice to withdraw their offspring from lessons but this is a questionable assumption, for peer pressure may preclude minority parents from choosing to remove their children from RE classes (Mawhinney 2006: 102–15). In addition, children who are withdrawn from RE lessons often risk being seen as different from their classmates[41] and this can in turn lead to bullying, because research has identified a link between bullying and religious difference. (Eslea and Mukhtar 2000: 207–17). And finally, adolescent pupils cannot lawfully withdraw themselves from RE lessons because Art 2. P.1 conspicuously affords rights to parents (and guardians) rather than to children themselves (Flutter and Rudduck 2004).

Perhaps unsurprisingly, given that a political forum would seem to be the most appropriate place for a detailed consideration of such issues, the ECtHR has refrained from any detailed discussion of the arguments for reform in this area. However, that said, the Court's recent jurisprudence provides a useful starting point from which a number of observations can be made in relation to the law governing the right of parents to withdraw their children from RE lessons.

First, there is no specific obligation upon States to provide alternative or equivalent lessons to children withdrawn from RE classes under Art 2 P.1. The ECtHR has made it clear that States retain a wide margin of appreciation in this regard and, even where there have been requests for such lessons, a potentially low take-up rate obviates any obligation on the part of States in this regard.[42] Indeed, the Court's deference to States was illustrated in *Grzelak* by its silence in response to the apparently shocking revelations that ethics (as an alternative to RE) was only taught in 1.03 per cent of Polish schools and that there were only 412 teachers of ethics in contrast to 21,370 teachers of religion.[43]

Secondly, the ECtHR's ruling in *Grzelak* – that the absence of a mark for 'religion/ ethics' on a school report could unfairly discriminate against non-religious pupils – appears to impose more rigorous obligations on States under

---

40   The UN Human Rights Committee also accepts that freedom of religion or belief 'permits public school instruction in subjects such as the general history of religions and ethics if it is given in a neutral and objective way': General Comment, no.22, para. 6.

41   As the late British Muslim scholar Zaki Badawi pointed out, withdrawing a child in such circumstances is akin to saying that s/he 'is not a member of the group' (Tames 1982: 154).

42   *Grzelak*, note 1 *supra*, para. 104.

43   Ibidem.

Articles 9 and 14 rather than Art 2 P.1. Thus, it is incumbent on schools to make an appropriate degree of provision for students who are removed from RE lessons because mere withdrawal on its own would appear to be insufficient. Whilst propriety may turn on the facts of a particular case, it seems clear that requiring an 'opted out' pupil to, for example, wait in the corridor for the duration of an RE lesson is almost certainly incompatible with the ECHR.

Thirdly, in States where there is a particularly close correlation between the majority faith and the nation's identity, the State should take account of the needs of *minority faith* pupils who have been withdrawn by parents from RE lessons.[44] In *Grzelak* the ECtHR acknowledged the potential vulnerability of minorities when it noted that the absence of a mark on a student's report for 'religion/ethics' was of 'particular significance', because Poland is a nation 'where the great majority of the population owe allegiance to one particular religion'. A similar approach was initially taken in *Lautsi*, when the Chamber of the ECtHR held that the risk of a crucifix on the wall being 'emotionally disturbing for pupils of other religions or those who profess no religion' was '*particularly strong* (author's emphasis) among pupils belonging to religious minorities'.[45] Even though the Grand Chamber subsequently rejected the view that the crucifix might have an influence on children in Italian classrooms,[46] it nonetheless refrained from commenting on the issue of *minority* faith pupils. Thus, it could be argued that ECHR case law puts schools under a specific duty to ensure that minority faith pupils (often clearly identifiable by their skin colour or dress) are neither stigmatized, nor put at risk of discrimination, if withdrawn from RE lessons (Kay and Francis 2001: 117–28).[47]

Fourthly, the parental opt out in the field of RE may have certain resource implications for States, because additional rooms and staff must be available to teach (or supervise at the very least) affected pupils for the duration of the lessons on religion. Yet any suggestion that the ECtHR's recent jurisprudence might lead to States radically improving the funding of RE programmes seems fanciful. After all, the Court has long taken the view that Art 2 P.1 does not require States to 'establish or subsidize, education of any particular type or at any particular level'.[48] Indeed, even if the Court were ever (conceivably) to deviate from this approach, the impact of any such change would be militated by the fact that several States have in place reservations to Art 2 P.1.[49] Thus, whilst there is undoubtedly a financial cost attached to parents being permitted to withdraw their children from

---

44   Ibidem, para. 95.

45   *Lautsi*, note 30 *supra*, para. 55.

46   *Lautsi* Grand Chamber decision, note 23 *supra*, para. 66.

47   In this regard it is perhaps interesting to observe that pupils from non-Christian backgrounds tend to have a much more positive view of RE than those from Christian families.

48   ECtHR *The Belgian Linguistic case* (No 2) (1968) 1 EHRR 252, 280–81.

49   [Online] available at: http://conventions.coe.int/Treaty/EN/v3MenuDecl.asp [Accessed: 19 February 2011].

RE lessons, the related obligations on States under the Convention are clearly less than onerous.

Finally, it is questionable whether the current 'parental withdrawal' model in respect of RE is actually sustainable in the long term. Europe is changing, and today finds itself being shaped by a combination of multi-faith and secular values (Koopmans, Statham, Giugni and Passy 2005). Accordingly, it is possible that, in the coming years, an increasing number of parents (of different faiths or none) will seek to remove their children from RE classes, not least because such lessons are often based primarily on Christianity (Ramadan 1999).[50] As minority faith communities come to have increasing economic, social and political influence in European public life, the number of requests may increase – not just for children to be withdrawn from (essentially 'Christian') RE lessons – but (perhaps even more significantly) for children to be in receipt of more inclusive forms of RE wherein a broader range of faiths and systems of belief are studied (Schreiner in Schreiner, Kraft and Wright 2007: 10–13). Thus, there are serious unanswered questions about the very feasibility of the opt-out model of RE for Europe in the longer term. Indeed, there is at the very heart of such matters the much wider question of what is or should be the aim of school programmes that teach religion – an issue that will now be examined in more detail.

The aim of RE programmes in Europe
The ECtHR has evidently taken the view that there is much to commend the provision of lessons on religion in schools, in citing with approval recommendations of the Parliamentary Assembly of the Council of Europe to this effect.[51] However, while the Court is supportive of religion being taught in theory it is less clear about how this should be done in practice, as illustrated by the fact that it sometimes refers to both religious instruction *and* religious education almost simultaneously in its judgments.[52] For example, in *Grzelak*, while the ECtHR primarily used the term 'religious instruction' to describe the Polish model of religion in schools[53] it

---

50 For example, with a new generation of what Tariq Ramadan (2005) has termed 'European Muslims' demanding the same citizenship rights as their 'Christian' neighbours, Muslim and other minority faith parents may increasingly withdraw their children from RE lessons.

51 See paragraph 13(ii) of Parliamentary Assembly Recommendation no. 1396 and paragraph 14 of Recommendation no. 1720, paragraphs 26 and 27, in *Hasan* note 7 *supra*, para. 69.

52 For example, in *Hasan*, note 7 *supra*, reference to 'religious instruction' is found in paragraphs 21, 28, 49, 71 and 84, whereas 'religious education' is used in paragraphs 30–34, 39 and 71. In contrast, in *Kjeldsen*, note 35 *supra* and *Folgerø*, note 9 *supra*, the Court only makes reference to 'religious instruction'.

53 See *Grzelak*, note 1 *supra*, paras 7–9, 11, 13–14, 17–18, 27–31, 36–8, 40–41, 45–6, 51, 53, 55, 59–60, 64–5, 77–8, 80–81, 83, 104 and 106.

also made frequent reference to 'religious education',[54] and, on some occasions, even appeared to use both terms interchangeably in the same sentence.[55]

At first glance, it might seem that this is only a matter of semantics but on closer inspection the consequences of using these different terms becomes apparent. A number of distinctions can be drawn between religious instruction ('RI') and religious education ('RE'). First, RI is usually synonymous with an education based on a particular faith whereas RE typically encompasses the study of a wider range of beliefs. Secondly, the teacher in RI is normally expected to adhere to a particular religious tradition or lifestyle in contrast to RE where the teacher's own religious beliefs (or lack thereof) are largely irrelevant. Thirdly, the term 'instruction' implies that the primary purpose of RI is one of directing students how to do something (for example, how to live a Christian life), and this gives it a much narrower focus than RE wherein students are typically encouraged to examine, critically, a range of values and opinions. Finally, the essentially prescriptive nature of RI is in marked contrast to the more liberal educational goals of RE, where matters such as creativity and personal reflection are actively encouraged. Thus, while accepting that one should be wary of making generalizations in this area (Schreiner in Schreiner, Kraft and Wright 2007: 15)[56] there are some significant differences in terms of tone and substance between RI and RE. As a result, RI is typically associated with the educational model that is intended 'to bring about commitment to a particular faith,' whereas RE programmes usually aim to foster an 'understanding of religion ... rather than [a] commitment to any specific faith'.[57]

The fact that the ECtHR has made several statements which could be interpreted as being endorsements of both RI *and* RE potentially muddies the waters even further. A case in point is *Kjeldsen, Busk Madsen and Pederson v. Denmark*[58] where, in distinguishing between 'religious' and 'sex' education, the Court suggested that the former primarily involves tenets of belief, whereas the latter is essentially based on knowledge.[59] Although there is some doubt as to whether

---

54   See *Grzelak*, ibidem, paras 10, 14, 32, 38, 47, 49, 55, 77, 95–7 and 104.

55   *Grzelak*, ibidem, paras 55 and 77. Indeed, in para. 104, 'religious education' is used to describe the Polish model, whereas elsewhere the term 'religious instruction' is employed in this context.

56   A degree of caution is of course always necessary when making such comments about models of teaching religion not least because, as Peter Schreiner points out, the term religious education has a number of 'different starting points, backgrounds and histories': Schreiner 2007: 15.

57   Hobson and Edwards 1999: 17–18.

58   Note 35 *supra*.

59   'Above all, the Court ... finds that there is a difference in kind between religious instruction and the sex education concerned in this case. The former of necessity disseminates tenets and not mere knowledge; the Court has already concluded that the same does not apply to the latter': *Kjeldsen*, ibidem, para. 56.

this distinction should be regarded as being of general application,[60] the Court in *Kjeldsen* took the view that religion is taught in the classroom primarily to provide 'subjective' information about beliefs (as in RI lessons) rather than to convey 'objective' knowledge about other faiths (as per RE).[61] Indeed, the Chamber's comment in *Lautsi*, that schools 'should be a meeting place for different religions and philosophical convictions, in which pupils can acquire knowledge about *their* (author's emphasis) respective thoughts and traditions',[62] rather than those of others, is perhaps a subtle nod in the direction of RI.

By way of contrast, however, the ECtHR has also made a number of statements which could be interpreted as an implicit endorsement of more comparative RE models. For example, the Court has spoken of the need for education to encourage 'pupils to develop a critical mind with regard to religious matters',[63] the philosophical premise underpinning multi-faith RE, and has highlighted the importance of 'educational pluralism [as being] essential for the preservation of 'democratic society' within the Convention meaning of that term'.[64] Yet, whilst the model of multi-faith RE sits neatly alongside the ECtHR's avowed conviction that the function of educating and teaching is to pass on 'knowledge … in an objective, critical and pluralist way',[65] this, crucially, is subject to the *caveat* that the State must respect the religious and philosophical convictions of parents.[66] Therefore, the Court's view is that programmes which provide for religion being taught in schools must be based upon both pluralistic values *and* the need to respect parents' wishes – with the latter being a particularly significant check on the ability of the Court to develop the law in this area.

Thus, is the ECtHR's interchangeable use of the terms RE and RI of any real significance? At first glance, it might seem not. After all, the bottom line for the Court is that parents' wishes have been respected so that all it need do, when adjudicating on cases in this area, is tailor its judgment in accordance with the

---

60 Perhaps rather confusingly, the Court in *Kjeldsen* also stated that 'Article 2 of Protocol No. 1 does not permit a distinction to be drawn between religious instruction and other subjects' (ibidem, para. 51). This comment was also repeated in *Folgerø and others v. Norway*, note 9 *supra*, para. 84(c) and *Hasan* note 7 *supra*, para. 49.

61 The Court is also open to criticism on pedagogical grounds. For example, the degree to which it is possible so clearly to distinguish between 'knowledge' and 'beliefs' is questionable, particularly given the observation of the educationalist, Andrew Wright that '[a]ll education, whether positively or negatively, implicitly or explicitly, by intention or by default, will end up passing on a set of values and cultural norms to pupils' (Wright 2000: 116).

62 *Lautsi v. Italy*, note 30 *supra* para. 47. The failure of the Chamber of the ECtHR to include the words 'and others' after 'their' in this statement would appear to be a significant restriction on its potential impact.

63 *Hasan*, note 7 *supra*, para. 69.

64 Ibidem, para. 5 6.

65 *Kjeldsen*, note 35 *supra*, para. 53.

66 *Lautsi*, Grand Chamber note 23 *supra*, para. 54, and *Hasan* note 7 *supra*, para. 68.

educational model (RE, RI or none) that is associated with the State against which a complaint has been brought. However, on closer inspection the Court's apparently random use of the terms RI and RE is significant because it not merely symbolizes a latent uncertainty as to how religion should be taught in the classroom (O'Grady 2005, Barnes 2007)[67] but also may (especially in the longer term) limit the Court's potential influence in relation to the effective setting of standards. The European Court knows what does *not* constitute proper religious education (indoctrination) but is much less certain about what *should be* the proper aim of such lessons on religion or equivalent forms of belief.

Conclusion

Commenting on the future of religion being taught in Europe's schools, a Norwegian academic, Geir Skeie (2006: 19–32), has said that: 'Europe has to choose between two alternatives. One is a secular vision expressed through the declaration of human rights, which is democratic. Another alternative is to identify Europe as being 'Christian', which means homogenization or at worst fundamentalism.'

Whilst possibly rather oversimplistic (Estivalèzes 2003),[68] this statement nonetheless illustrates the stark choice that many policy makers in Europe will have to make in the coming years. This choice is between retaining an essentially 'confessional' form of RE (grounded mainly in Christian values) whereby those who object to what is being taught about religion can remove their children from the classroom (Thompson 2004) or a more comparative form of RE, that is designed to take account of a broad range of different religious and beliefs (Erricker and Erricker 2000, Smart 1968).

With confident predictions that 'religion will play a larger role in the European public square' (Micklethwait and Woolridge 2009:138), the continent's political leaders will have to decide how Europe's schools – the vast majority of which have traditionally focused on Christianity when teaching RE – respond to increasing religious diversity and the growing influence of secularism. In this respect, the ECtHR will almost certainly be called upon to adjudicate between parties and, in so doing, the temptation may be to continue to grant States a wide margin of

---

67   In fairness to the European Court, many educationalists in Europe are themselves divided as to the proper aim and function of school programmes that teach religion. See O'Grady 2005 and Barnes 2007.

68   There is of course a third option, which is for States to adopt the French model, whereby they abandon formal RE lessons in public schools, and teach about religion exclusively under the auspices of other subjects (such as art, literature, history). However, with increasing calls in France for the nation's educational system to provide students with formal classes on religion, this model appears increasingly unlikely to be followed (Estivalèzes 2003).

appreciation – not least because there is little common ground between them in the provision of RE in schools. Of course, as noted above, there is potential for reform given the willingness of the Court in recent years to recognize the principle of freedom from religion. Yet, equally, the fear of displeasing powerful political and ecclesiastical forces may lead to judicial caution and restraint. Thus, it is hard to predict the extent to which the ECtHR will influence the decision-making process in the field of religious education in Europe in the years ahead.

What, however, can perhaps be said with some certainty is that today there are a number of striking anomalies in the field of religious education. First, the Council of Europe frequently passes resolutions affirming the need for bold and innovative RE programmes (Jackson 2010: 1121–51), but fine rhetoric is not always matched with hard cash, and RE remains an under-funded, low status subject in much of Europe. (Stern 2006: 5).[69] Second, the European Court maintains that Article 9 affords rights to non-believers as well as believers; yet States almost always prioritize the teaching of Christianity and (to a lesser extent) other major world religions, at the expense of equivalent 'non-religious' beliefs.[70] Third, there has been unprecedented recognition of the rights of young people in recent years, but RE continues to be an area where parents' rights take precedence, and those of children are generally ignored (Kilkelly 2001: 308–26). And finally, in spite of claims that religious education can help to strengthen communal ties, there has, as yet, been no clear evidence that RE programmes have to date created a new generation of more tolerant, or even religiously literate, Europeans. Even the prominent atheist Richard Dawkins (2007: 340) has written of being 'a little taken aback at the biblical ignorance commonly displayed by people'.

As noted at the beginning of this chapter, there is widespread support in principle for the provision of religious education in the classroom. However, in practice, a sense of realism is perhaps necessary. There is widespread disagreement throughout Europe as to whether school religious programmes should essentially instruct about religious faith (which tends almost invariably to be Christianity) or offer children a form of comparative education that covers a broad range of religions and systems of belief. The way in which such differences are ultimately addressed will tell us much about the role and place of religious (or equivalent) belief in the Europe of tomorrow, and in this regard the ECtHR will doubtlessly have a role to play. At best, RE may act as a positive bulwark against extremism and communal disharmony — and at worst it may become yet another battleground for disputes about faith and secularism in the public square.

---

69 For example, in the context of the UK, Julian Stern (2006: 5) has said that religious education is commonly regarded by pupils, parents and teachers 'as something of a backwater'.

70 For example, the UK has been criticized by the UN Special Rapporteur on the basis that the local bodies responsible for devising RE policies, which routinely include members of Christian and non-Christian traditions (SACREs), do not, as of right, include humanists (Asma Jahangir 2008: 20, para. 70).

References

Baratte, L. 2007. Religious education and peace education. A partnership imperative for our day, in *International Handbook of the Religious, Moral and Spiritual Dimensions in Education*, edited by M. de Souza et al. New York: Springer, 243–58.

Barnes, L.P. 2007. The disputed legacy of Ninian Smart and phenomenological religious education: A critical response to Kevin O'Grady. *British Journal of Religious Education* 29(2), 157–68.

Barrow, R. 1996. Moral education: the need for clearer thinking. *International Review of Education* 42(1–3), 243–6.

Bell, M.P. 1982–1983. Justification and multi-faith Religious education. *British Journal of Religious Education* 5(2).

Berger, P.L. 1999. *The Desecularization of the World: Resurgent Religion in World Politics*. Washington: Eerdman's Publishing Co.

British Humanist Association. 2006. *A Better Way Forward. BHA Policy on Religion and Schools*, [Online] available at: http://www.humanism.org.uk/_uploads/documents/Betterwayforward2006.pdf [Accessed: 9 February 2011].

Brock, C. and Tulasiewicz, W. (eds) 1994. *Education in a Single Europe*. London: Routledge.

Cassidy, E. 2007. Journeying toward the 'other'. A challenge for religion, spiritual and moral education, in *International Handbook of the Religious, Moral and Spiritual Dimensions in Education*, edited by M. de Souza et al. New York: Springer, 869–85.

Dawkins, R. 2007. *The God Delusion*. London: Transworld.

DCSF. 2010. Religious Education in English schools: Non-Statutory Guidance. [Online]. Available at: <www.teachernet.gov.uk/teachingandlearning/subjects/re/guidance/ [Accessed: 8 February 2010].

Erricker, C. and Erricker, J. 2000. *Reconstructing Religious, Spiritual and Moral Education*. New York: Routledge.

Eslea, M. and Mukhtar, K. 2000. 'Bullying and racism among Asian schoolchildren in Britain. *Educational Research* 42(2), 207–17.

Estivalèzes, M. 2003. Teaching about religion in the French education system. *Prospects* 33(2), 179–90.

Estivalèzes, M. 2007. Teaching about religion in the French education system, in *International Handbook of the Religious, Moral and Spiritual Dimensions in Education* edited by M. de Souza et al. New York: Springer, 475–86.

Flutter, J. and Rudduck, J. 2004. *Consulting Pupils: What's in it for Schools?* London: Routledge Falmer.

Gutmann, A. 2003. *Identity in Democracy*. Princeton: Princeton University Press.

Habermas, J. 2006. Religion in the public sphere. *European Journal of Philosophy* 14(1), 1–25.

Heimbrock, H.G., Scheilke, C. and Schreiner, P. (eds) 2001. *Towards Religious Competence: Diversity As A Challenge For Education In Europe*. (Münster: Lit Verlag).

Hobson P.R. and Edwards J.S. 1999. *Religious Education in a Pluralist Society: The Key Philosophical Issues*. London: Woburn Press.

Ipgrave, J. 2003. Dialogue, citizenship, and religious education, in *International Perspectives on Citizenship, Education and Religious Diversity*, edited by R. Jackson. London: Routledge Falmer, 147–68.

Jackson, R. 2002. Religious education and education for citizenship. *British Journal of Religious Education* 24(3), 162–9.

Jackson, R. 2009. Is diversity changing religious education? Religion, diversity and education in today's Europe in *Religious Diversity and Education: Nordic Perspectives*, edited by G. Skeie. Münster: Waxmann, 11–28.

Jackson, R. 2010. Religious diversity and education for democratic citizenship: the contribution of the Council of Europe. *International Handbooks of Religion and Education* 4(4), 1121–51.

Jahangir, A. 2008. *Report of the Special Rapporteur on Freedom of Religion or Belief to the United Kingdom of Great Britain and Northern Ireland*, A/HRC/7/10/Add.3, 7 February.

Kamat, S. and Mathew, B. 2010. Religion, education and the politics of recognition: a critique and a counter-proposal. *Comparative Education* 46(3), 359–76.

Kay, W. 2005. A non-statutory framework for religious education: issues and opportunities. *British Journal of Religious Education* 27(1), 41–52.

Kay, W. and Francis, L. 2001. Religious education and school assembly in England and Wales: what do religious minorities think in *Towards Religious Competence: Diversity As A Challenge For Education In Europe*, edited by H.G. Heimbrock et al. Münster: Lit Verlag; 117–28.

Kilkelly, U. 2001. The best of both worlds for children's rights? Interpreting the European Convention on Human Rights. *Human Rights Quarterly* 23(2), 308–26.

Koopmans, R., Statham, P., Giugni M. and Passy, F. (eds) 2005. *Contested Citizenship: Immigration and Cultural Diversity in Europe* (Minneapolis: University of Minnesota Press).

Kuyk, E. et al. (eds) 2007. *Religious Education in Europe. Situation and Current Trends in Schools*. Oslo: Iko and ICCS.

Larsson, R. and Gustavsson, C. (eds) 2004. *Towards a European Perspective on Religious Education*. Stockholm: Artos & Norma.

Leganger-Krogstad, H. 2003. Dialogue among young citizens in a pluralistic religious education classroom in *International Perspectives on Citizenship, Education and Religious Diversity*, edited by R. Jackson. London: Routledge Falmer; 169–90.

Mawhinney, A. 2006. The opt out clause: imperfect protection for the right to freedom of religion in schools. *Education Law Journal* 7(2), 102–15.

Micklethwait, J. and Wooldridge, A. 2009. *God is Back: How the Global Rise of Faith is Changing the World*. London: Allen Lane.

Miedema, S. 2007. Educating for religious citizenship: religious education as identity formation, in *International Handbook of the Religious, Moral and Spiritual Dimensions in Education*, edited by M. de Souza et al. New York: Springer, 967–76.

Moore, J. 2009. Why religious education matters: the role of Islam in multicultural education. *Multicultural Perspectives* 11(3), 139–45.

Nelson, J. 2004. Uniformity and diversity in religious education in Northern Ireland. *British Journal of Religious Education* 26(3), 249–58.

Nipkon, K.E., 2007. Religious education in Europe: comparative approach, institutions, theories, research in *International Handbook of the Religious, Moral and Spiritual Dimensions in Education*, edited by M. de Souza et al. New York: Springer, 577–90.

Nussbaum, M. 2010. *Not for Profit: Why Democracy Needs the Humanities*. Princeton: Princeton University Press.

O'Grady, K. 2005. Professor Ninian Smart, phenomenology and religious education. *British Journal of Religious Education* 27(3), 227–37.

OFSTED June 2010. *Transforming Religious Education. Religious Education in Schools*. Report 2006–09, Ref no. 090215.

OSCE 2007. *Toledo Guiding Principles on Teaching about Religion and Beliefs in Public Schools* [Online]. Available at: http://www.oscebih.org/documents/12567-eng.pdf [Accessed: 9 February 2011].

Porter, B. 2001. The Catholic nation: religion, identity, and the narratives of Polish history. *The Slavic and East European Journal* 45(2), 289–99.

Ramadan, T. 1999. *To Be A European Muslim*. Leicester: The Islamic Foundation, Leicester.

Rodger, A. 2003. Religious education, in *Scottish Education: Post-devolution*, edited by T. Bryce, T. and W.M. Humes. Edinburgh: Edinburgh University Press, 600–605.

Schreiner, P. 2007. Introduction in *Good Practice in Religious Education in Europe: Examples and Perspectives of Primary Schools*, edited by P. Schreiner et al. Munster: Munster Lit, 10–13.

Skeie, G. 2006. Diversity and the political function of religious education. *British Journal of Religious Education* 28(1) 19–32.

Smart, N. 1968. *Secular Education and the Logic of Religion*. London: Faber and Faber.

Souza, M. (de) et al. (eds) 2007. *International Handbook of the Religious, Moral and Spiritual Dimensions in Education*. New York: Springer.

Stern, J. 2006. *Teaching Religious Education*. London: Continuum.

Szajkowski, B. 1983. *Next to God-Poland: Politics and Religion in Contemporary Poland*. New York: St Martin's Press.

Tames, R. 1982. *Approaches to Islam*. London: John Murray.

Thompson, P. 2004. *Whatever Happened to Religious Education*. Cambridge: Lutterworth Press.

Westurland, D. (ed.) 1996. *Questioning the Secular State: the Worldwide Resurgence of Religion in Politics*. London: Hurst.

White, J. 2004. Should religious education be a compulsory school subject? *British Journal of Religious Education* 26(2), 151–64.

Willaime, J.-P. 2007. Different models for religion and education in Europe in *Religion and Education in Europe. Developments, Contexts and Debates*, edited by R. Jackson et al. Münster: Waxmann, 57–66.

Willaime, J.-P. 2007. Teaching religious issues in French public schools. From abstentonist laïcité to a return of religion in public education in *Religion and Education in Europe. Developments, Contexts and Debates* edited by R. Jackson et al. Münster: Waxmann, 87–102.

Wright, A. 2000. *Spirituality and the Curriculum*. Falmer.

Chapter 11

Religious Education and Religious Liberty: Opt-Outs and Young People's Sense of Belonging

Alison Mawhinney, Ulrike Niens, Norman Richardson and Yuko Chiba

The role of religion in Western societies has gained greater prominence in public discourse over the past decades. Concerns about social cohesion and peaceful intergroup relations have focused on growing religious and ethnic diversity due to global migration and changes in religious affiliations in Western societies (Bouma 2008). Since the 11 September 2001 attacks in New York, considerations about how to manage religious diversity most effectively have often centred on the integration of Muslims (and/or those from other non-Christian faith groups) into majority Christian societies (Bernard-Patel 2008). However, this perceived dichotomy between Christian/non-Christian communities (Leeman 2008) may overlook the diversity within the Christian community as well as agnostics, atheists, humanists and those indifferent to religion.

Debates about the effectiveness of liberal, plural and multicultural policies in promoting social cohesion have thus dominated policymaking and, within education, strategies to foster diversity and inclusion in their widest senses (including religiosity, ethnicity, disability, sexuality and so on) have often taken centre place in policies and curricula (Banks 2008). Consequently, the role of religious education has been reviewed and calls to broaden the often narrowly Christian-focused curricula have become louder.[1]

However, such changes in the public discourse are not reflected in the current law and policies of many countries which permit the teaching of confessional or doctrinal education in schools. National authorities can point to international human rights standards which permit such teaching in public schools provided that opt-outs are offered to those who do not wish to participate in such instruction. This chapter explores the impact of this position in terms of its effect on minority-belief students' attitudes to religious education in schools, their sense of belonging to their school, religious community and wider community and their religious liberty.

---

1   The term 'religious education' can be used to describe Religious Education ('RE') classes as well as other religious activities that occur during the school day, such as religious assemblies. However, this chapter focuses mainly on issues surrounding RE classes given their formal place in the school curriculum.

Teaching Religion: its Purpose and Impact

Despite having a place in the school curriculum of many countries around the world, RE has long been, and remains, a contentious area. Much work has been done in relation to providing philosophical and educational approaches to the teaching of religion in publicly-funded schools in religiously diverse societies, (Foster 2004, Hull 1990, Jackson 2004; 2009, Copley 2008). However, there remains considerable confusion as well as significant disagreement in the minds of many people about the purposes of RE. It is not difficult to see why there is significant unease or uncertainty on the part of some members of the public, including educational professionals, in relation to religious teaching in schools. There is a long history of involvement in the provision of public education on the part of faith communities, often predating the involvement of States. Many countries have evolved parallel systems of education with state-funded schools and religiously-founded schools working alongside each other; many schools in these contexts receive funding from both the State and their religious denomination. This dualism, or State-religion partnership, can be perceived as a representation of historical and cultural reality in reflecting the important place of religion in a particular society, though others may see it as an attempt by religious communities to exert undue influence on the young in an increasingly secular age.

International surveys of different approaches to RE in schools (such as Kuyk et al. 2007, in relation to Europe), demonstrate the range of responses to this situation. In many parts of the United Kingdom and some Scandinavian countries there has been significant movement away from Christian confessionalism towards multicultural content and pedagogies, focusing on the promotion of critical thought and mutual respect. In some other countries, RE is organized confessionally but includes significant teaching about a range of religions and beliefs. In other jurisdictions, such as Ireland and some Southern or Central European countries, the curriculum remains fixed on traditional Christian teaching though with significant debate at times about the need for a broader and more objective approach. Even in those countries where RE has long had no place in state schools (such as France, the United States and some former Soviet Bloc countries) there have been recent moves to introduce programmes for teaching about religions through history or social studies. The existence of legal provision for opting out of RE and other religious occasions in the legislation of many countries reflects both this diversity of approaches to RE and the confusion that still exists about its purposes.

In recent years, inter-governmental organizations such as the Council of Europe ('CoE'),[2] the Organization for Security and Cooperation in Europe ('OSCE') and the Oslo Coalition on Freedom of Religion and Belief have promoted multicultural RE, emphasizing objective study and the development of critical thought. Of particular interest are the *Toledo Guiding Principles* (OSCE/ODIHR 2007), which were drafted by the ODIHR Advisory Council of Experts on Freedom of Religion

---

2   See Keast 2007, CoE 2008; 2009.

or Belief. However, while offering practical guidance to States on how to adopt inclusive and impartial approaches to teaching about religions and beliefs, the document recognizes that there remain circumstances in which opt-out provisions may be the most satisfactory solution for some parents and pupils.

Religious Education and Identity Formation

While there has been an abundance of research into the impact of education on ethnic minorities and ethnic identity development, studies focusing on the experience of education (and RE in particular) from the perspective of young people from minority-belief backgrounds are relatively rare (Benson 2004).

The way in which RE is taught in schools, whether through confessional or multicultural teaching, may considerably impact on young people from minority-belief backgrounds and the development of their religious[3] and other social identities. Identity formation is an ongoing, complex and dynamic process among adolescents (Chaudhury and Miller 2008). Identity development, including religious identity, during adolescence is influenced by the social context, particularly the family, peers and community (Regnerus et al. 2004).

Schools represent one of the most significant social contexts for pupils; their culture and ethos may shape and influence young people's developing sense of self and religious identity. The desire to conform to the school's norms and to be accepted by their peers may consequently result in students from minority-belief backgrounds adopting the religious attitudes and behaviours of the majority (Barrett et al. 2008). Parents and religious minority communities may become concerned about their children being indoctrinated into another belief. However, young people may also experience tensions if school norms and RE teaching in particular are perceived as contradicting the values and norms held by themselves, their family and/or religious or secular community. Negotiating these tensions may then become crucial in their development of a secure identity and sense of belonging to their own religious or secular community as well as their school and society at large (Chaudhury and Miller 2008). Discussing issues relating to beliefs with peers may provide support in this negotiation process (Ipgrave and McKenna 2008).

Where young people are being opted out of RE, due to parental fears of indoctrination or perceptions of incompatibility of school and the individual's beliefs and norms, pupils may find it increasingly difficult to fit into the school community and may feel excluded and/or stigmatized due to their religious beliefs. For some, this may be compounded by an overlap between religious and ethnic minority categories (Brega 1999). This sense of stigmatization may, in

---

3   The term 'religious identity' is used in this chapter to include an identity which is secular or indifferent to religious beliefs.

turn, increase the importance of the young person's beliefs and alienation from or opposition to the majority norms and values (Verkuyten and Yildiz 2007).

A Human Rights Perspective

In order to protect the freedom of thought, conscience and religion of parents and children human rights enforcement bodies have held that doctrinal or confessional religious education cannot be taught in schools unless alternative provision is made for those not wishing to participate.[4] In other words, these bodies have relied upon opt-outs as a means of dealing with (or, perhaps more accurately, avoiding) the difficult question of whether faith formation classes should take place in schools.

Until recently, the mere existence of a right to opt out in domestic law was sufficient to satisfy human rights bodies that the right to freedom of religion of minority-belief individuals was protected in schools.[5] The manner of operation of opt-out clauses and the quality of the alternative provision offered by schools were not considered. However, the recent Norwegian cases brought before the United Nations Human Rights Committee[6] ('UNHRC') and the European Court of Human Rights[7] ('ECtHR') suggest a new willingness to explore these issues. Each organ concluded that the exemption scheme operated in Norwegian schools was deficient. It required parents to have detailed knowledge of the curriculum in advance so that they could identify the incompatible parts from which they would then need to request an exemption. In addition, there was concern that, in asking for an exemption, parents had to provide 'reasonable grounds' for their request. The Strasbourg Court found that this condition 'was capable of subjecting the parents concerned to a heavy burden with a risk of undue exposure of their private life and that the potential for conflict was likely to deter them from making such requests'.[8]

However, despite this more penetrating analysis of the operation of opt-outs the underlying assumption that this mechanism can ever protect and respect the right to freedom of thought, conscience and religion of minority individuals has rarely been assessed from the perspective of the minority-belief young person. Furthermore, the social impact of separating students in this manner has not been explored. The rest of this chapter reports on a research project that set out to seek an increased understanding of the role, impact and usefulness of opt-out provisions

---

4   *Hartikainen v. Finland*, Doc.A/36/40, p.147; ECHR 26 June 2001 *Saniewski v. Poland*, Application no. 40319/98, para. 2.

5   See, ECtHR *C.J. et al v. Poland*, Application no.23380/94, 84-A, Eur. Commission HR D&R 46. 1996.

6   ECtHR 23 November 2004 *Leirvag et al. v. Norway*, CCPR/C/82/D/1155/2003.

7   ECtHR Grand Chamber Judgment 29 June 2007 *Folgerø and Others v. Norway*, Application no. 15472/02.

8   Ibidem, para. 100.

in a religiously diverse society.[9] The chapter examines the project's findings with respect to minority-belief students' experiences of and attitudes to RE lessons, the influence of RE and opt-outs on their identity development and the usefulness of the right to opt out as a way to protect and respect religious freedom in the school from the perspective of young people, parents and community representatives from minority-belief backgrounds.

Research Project

Context

The research project took place in Northern Ireland ('NI'), a society with a high level of religious participation and traditionally low numbers of ethnic and religious minorities (though these have increased significantly in recent years). Numbers for religious and non-religious minorities are difficult to establish with certainty. The 2001 census figures,[10] the only official statistics available at the time of writing[11] are considerably out of date.

The school system (see McCrudden: this book, Chapter 6) is predominantly public, with very few private schools. Post-primary schools can be classified into the following types: (1) controlled, (2) Catholic-maintained, (3) voluntary, (4) integrated[12] and (5) independent. Except for independent schools, of which there are very few, all categories of school receive state funding to various degrees.[13] Controlled, Catholic-maintained and integrated schools all receive full state funding; voluntary schools receive partial state funding (all such schools are termed 'grant-aided'). To a greater or lesser extent all schools in Northern Ireland tend to follow a Christian ethos, though there are denominational differences that

---

9   The project, 'Opting out of Religious Education: The Views of Young People from Minority Belief Backgrounds', was funded by the Religion and Society Research Programme – a collaborative venture between the Arts and Humanities Research ('AHRC') and the Economic and Social Research Council ('ESRC'), award number AH/G016690/1.

10   According to the 2001 Northern Ireland Census the numbers for various communities at that time were: Islam 1,943; Hinduism (including Hare Krishna) 878; Judaism 365; the Bahá'í Faith 254; Humanism 40; Paganism 148; Atheism 106; Agnosticism 66; 'No religion or religion not stated' 233,853; Jehovah's Witness 1993; Church of Jesus Christ of Latter-Day Saints 1,414.

11   The most recent Northern Ireland census was conducted on 27 March 2011, but the results are not available at the time of writing.

12   An integrated school in Northern Ireland refers to a school that aims to take approximately similar numbers of Catholic and Protestant pupils as well as accommodating pupils from 'other' backgrounds, on an ideal ratio of 40:40:20.

13   Most independent school are associated with the Free Presbyterian Church (Dunn 2000). These schools receive no funding from the Department of Education and are funded by parents and charities.

are intertwined with ethno-political ideologies (Smith 2001). It may be noted that Northern Ireland, unlike other parts of the UK, has no faith schools serving religions other than Christianity. This context is significant given the lack of alternative schooling for minority-belief families and the challenges of making opt-out decisions in a mono-religious context.

Every grant-aided school must include provision for RE (*Education (NI) Order 2006*, s.5) according to the NI Core Syllabus for RE (see below) and must hold a daily act of collective worship (*Education (NI) Order 1986*, s.21.1). Schools are permitted to teach material that is not included in the Core Syllabus. In a controlled school, the RE provided must be non-denominational:[14] 'that is to say, education based upon the Holy Scriptures according to some authoritative version or versions thereof but excluding education as to any tenet distinctive of any particular religious denomination'(Education (NI) Order 1986, s.21.2). The collective worship in such schools 'shall not be distinctive of any particular religious denomination' (Education (NI) Order 1986, s.21.2). RE must be provided for all registered pupils, including those who do not take a General Certificate of Secondary Education ('GCSE'), the state exam normally taken at age 16, in the subject. Many schools also include non-examination RE for sixth-form students (aged 16 to 18) even though such students are currently beyond the official school-leaving age.

The Board of Governors is responsible for any inspection arrangements for RE in their schools. While schools may request inspection of RE by the Department of Education inspectorate (*Education (NI) Order 1996*, s.33.7), in practice very few of them do so. The task of inspection, therefore, remains mainly the responsibility of the Churches. In all grant-aided schools, including controlled schools, '[m]inisters of religion and other suitable persons ... to whom the parents do not object' are permitted to give RE to pupils. This education may include the teaching of 'tenets distinctive of a particular religious denomination' (*Education (NI) Order 1986*, s.21.7).

In 1989, the Education (NI) Order (s.13.1) stipulated that provision would be made for the Department of Education to specify a core syllabus for the teaching of RE in grant-aided schools. This core syllabus does not prevent the teaching of 'any other matter' during the period of RE (s.13.1.a). The legislation specified that the core syllabus is to be 'prepared by a group of persons ('the drafting group') appearing to the Department to be persons having an interest in the teaching of religious education in grant-aided schools' (s.13.4.a). In practice, the government offered the preparation of the core syllabus to the four largest Christian denominations: the Catholic Church in Ireland, the Presbyterian Church in Ireland, the Church of Ireland (Anglican) and the Methodist Church in Ireland. The Core Syllabus that emerged was mainly focused on Biblical material, with some aspects of Christian history and a Christian approach to morality. Only one

---

14   This does not, however, apply to integrated schools, where some denominational RE may be provided, for example in relation to sacramental preparation for Catholic pupils.

member of the early 1990s drafting group argued for the inclusion of non-Christian religions in the Core Syllabus but this point of view was not accepted by the group as a whole. As a consequence, the first Core Syllabus for Religious Education, which became official in 1993, was 'criticized for being exclusively Christian and confessional in tone' (Smith 2001: 573).

That the four denominations drafted the Core Syllabus signified their continuing influence on RE in schools and the lack of engagement with other religious and secular groups. Nonetheless, some argued that the development of the Core Syllabus also represented a major achievement. For example, the Core Syllabus was welcomed in some circles as a significant movement of inter-church (Catholic/ Protestant) cooperation. It also provided controlled schools with a structure for RE that had not previously existed. By contrast, Catholic schools considered the requirements of the Core Syllabus as fulfilled by their existing practices and therefore continued to use the existing materials (Richardson 2010: 221).

The Revised Core Syllabus for Religious Education was drafted in 2002–2003 and included a modest section on world religions at Key Stage 3 (ages 11 to 14).[15] An Equality Impact Assessment ('EQIA') on the proposed Revised Core Syllabus was conducted in 2006, involving public consultation on the document. The result revealed that the teaching of world religions as proposed was considered insufficient by many minority-belief people who suggested that world religions should also be taught at Key Stages 2 (ages 8 to 11) and 4 (ages 14 to 16) (Department of Education 2006). The Department of Education rejected this suggestion arguing that children learn to respect other faiths and cultures in other learning areas at Key Stage 2 and that schools are free to teach more world religions beyond the Core Syllabus if they so wish.

The Revised Core Syllabus, described by its authors as 'essentially Christian' (Churches' RE Core Syllabus Working Party 2003), came into effect in August 2007. It includes three Learning Objectives – *the Revelation of God*, *the Christian Church*, and *Morality* – at each of the five stages (namely, Foundation Stage and Key Stages 1, 2, 3 and 4). The fourth learning objective – *World Religions*, which applies at Key Stage 3 only[16] – is designed to introduce pupils to two religions other than Christianity 'in order to develop knowledge and sensitivity towards, the religious beliefs, practices and lifestyles of people from other religions in Northern Ireland' (Department of Education 2007: 29). Here, students are expected to learn about the selected 'two world religions other than Christianity' in terms of their

---

15   In the original introduction to the first draft of the Revised Core Syllabus that was published in 2003, the Churches' Working Party commented that the teaching of world faiths 'will require only a modest amount of teaching time in each year of key stage 3' (Churches' RE Core Syllabus Working Party 2003, Richardson 2010: 222).

16   Although the Core Syllabus does not prescribe the study of world religions at Key Stage 4, a world religions option has now been restored to the Northern Ireland GCSE exam in Religious Studies (normally taken at age 16). The first cohorts of pupils taking this option sat the exam in 2010 and 2011.

Origins, Beliefs, Sacred Writings and Symbols, Worship and Prayer, Feasts and Festivals, Family Life and *Ceremonies: Birth and Death*. Whether secular beliefs can be chosen is not specified in the Syllabus. Given the outline prescribed for the study of world religions, however, it would appear to exclude them.

Domestic law permits parents to opt their children out of RE and collective worship. Section 21.5 of the *Education and Libraries Order (NI) 1986* provides that: 'If the parent of any pupil requests that the pupil should be wholly or partly excused from attendance at religious instruction[17] or collective worship or from both, then, until the request is withdrawn, the pupil shall be excused from such attendance in accordance with the request.' The opt-out provision makes no reference to the right of the student to make the decision to opt out. This can be contrasted with other jurisdictions where the right to opt out is transferred to the child at a set age. For example, in Switzerland the age is 16 and in some German states it is 14 (Kuyk et al. 2007). In England, sixth-form pupils at mainstream schools and maintained special schools have the right to withdraw themselves from collective worship without the need for parental permission. This pupil right to withdraw does not extend to RE classes.[18] Moreover, domestic legislation in Northern Ireland provides no guidance as to the alternative arrangements to be offered to pupils who are opted out of religious activities and does not stipulate the grounds upon which a parent may choose to withdraw their child. By contrast, the provision dealing with the right of teachers to be excused from conducting or attending collective worship or teaching RE notes that the request to opt out must be 'made solely on grounds of conscience' (*Education (NI) Order 1986*, s.22.2).

The findings of the EQIA on the Northern Ireland Revised Core Syllabus acknowledged that information provided to parents about opt-out provisions was inadequate and concluded that '[s]chools should ensure that parents are aware that they have the right to withdraw their child from some or all of RE classes and collective worship on the grounds of conscience if they so wish.' (Department of Education 2006: 32). However, the Department of Education did not set out how it intended to assist schools in increasing awareness of the right or how it intended to monitor the performance of schools in this task.

---

17   The subject was called 'Religious Instruction' in Northern Ireland until 1989, when the term was changed to 'Religious Education'.

18   Joint Committee on Human Rights, Nineteenth Report, Session 2007–2008, HL 107/HC 553, para. 1.45. The Joint Committee on Human Rights has recommended to the Government that the legislation be amended to replace 'sixth form pupil' with 'competent pupil' which should be defined as a pupil with sufficient maturity, understanding and intelligence to make an informed decision about whether to withdraw themselves from Collective Worship. It also argues that this opt-out should be extended to Religious Education in order to be compliant with the rights of a child to freedom of thought, conscience and belief under Article 9 ECHR and to Article 12 of the UNCRC.

Methodology

The research design of the project was based on a general fundamental principle of the UN Convention on the Rights of the Child, namely that young people should be consulted on all matters which directly affect them. A qualitative research approach was selected to maximize the opportunity to develop an understanding of the complexity of this issue from the perspectives of those most likely to be affected by it. Central to the data collection were semi-structured individual interviews with young people (aged 13 to 18) who come from minority-belief backgrounds. In addition, with the right to opt out of religious education being a parental one, minority-belief parents with a child aged 13 to 18 were interviewed. Furthermore, representatives of religious and humanist organizations were approached in order to elicit their views about the effectiveness of current opt-out legislation in respecting their members' right to freedom of religion or belief and their community's identity.

Research participants were recruited based on the prescribed four categories: (1) religious minority beliefs other than Christian, (2) Christian-related minority beliefs, (3) non-religious beliefs and (4) non-belief. The purpose of this categorization was to assure the coverage of different types of belief systems. In the process of identifying research participants, religious and non-religious (for example, minority-ethnic and youth-related) organizations were initially contacted. Personal networks and contacts were also made use of in order to facilitate access to minority-belief people. Once contacts were established and initial participants identified, the snowball sampling technique was employed. Thus the sample is by no means statistically representative: when carrying out our data analysis, the researchers considered 'What does this represent?' rather than asking 'How representative is this?' (Cowie 2006).

A total of 26 students and 24 parents participated in the research. Five community representatives were also interviewed and another answered the interview questions by email. Care was taken to develop a rapport with research participants, to highlight the voluntary nature of the research and to ensure privacy and confidentiality.

Research Observations

As the research did not aim to provide a representative analysis of minority belief communities' views on religious education and opt-outs, the results cannot be generalized. However, the flexible approach to this qualitative research with regard to the sampling strategy and data collection enabled an in-depth exploration of key issues raised by young people from minority belief communities.[19]

---

19   Data triangulation based on the interviews with parents and community leaders corroborated the findings from the research with young people and provided validation of

Three fundamental issues emerged with respect to the students' experiences of and attitudes to RE lessons, the influence of RE and opt-outs on their identity development and the sufficiency of opt-outs in protecting and respecting religious liberty in schools.

Challenges for Religious Education

Despite a range of experiences in relation to the attitudes encountered in schools and the practicalities involved, one of the clearest messages to come from pupils, parents and community representatives alike was dissatisfaction with the current RE curriculum in Northern Ireland. The feelings on this were strongest where parents and pupils felt that teachers were promoting a particular (usually strongly Christian) viewpoint: 'I started doing the course. It was all about the life of Jesus and … Christian morality and it was focused on the one religion. And we were being taught it as if this was what we were meant to believe' (S4).[20] Some respondents commented on the sense of Christian superiority that they sometimes encountered in RE lessons, referring to '[t]he fact that Christianity is just pushed on you …' (S3) and '… it was just like putting Christians above everything else' (S1).

Where it was clear that teachers were genuinely trying to be more inclusive and considerate of a range of views and backgrounds, however, then the attitudes of the respondents were much more moderate and sympathetic:

> I think my teacher is quite good in that way … when he talks about it he doesn't say 'So what do we do?' because he knows his class is majority Christians … even so he wouldn't say, you know, 'What do we think'. He goes in general 'What would Christians think' so I can write the same thing, I don't have to change it and say 'Oh well okay if I was a Christian I would sort of think'. He doesn't single anyone out, he says 'What would Christians in general think?' (S17).

Another minority religion student noted that her teacher 'speaks to the class saying, 'It is okay if somebody doesn't believe this, they are not to be disrespected or put down or anything" (S3). A Muslim student expressed particular enthusiasm for RE as she had experienced it and indicated that she would even consider becoming an RE teacher because she had enjoyed it so much. While many of the respondents felt that their beliefs were respected by teachers in their schools, there was also a feeling among some that their position was tolerated rather than respected and in some cases it was suggested that teachers were unintentionally disrespectful.

---

the findings.

20   This refers to the interview transcript from which the quotation was obtained. The students, parents and community representatives interviewed were coded as 'S1, S2 … S26', 'P1, P2 …P24' and 'C1, C2 … C6', respectively.

Some respondents expressed concern that not all RE teachers seemed to be trained specialists and a parent commented generally on the issue of training to teach RE:

> I think there are certainly gaps in there where their training could be better ...
> I do think that it's very difficult for people to think outside the Christian box
> ... And I think that part of the training of RE teachers should be actually to
> think and to experience something outside the box that you were born into or
> whatever (P8).

It was, however, the RE curriculum that came in for most criticism. Many of the students, parents and community representatives interviewed expressed support for the idea of teaching about religion in schools, including several of those from non-religious and humanist backgrounds. Very few of those interviewed for this study expressed the view that religion should not be taught at all in schools. This support for RE included recognition by many of the value of learning about Christianity as the most frequently encountered religion in Northern Ireland. The concerns expressed related to the heavily Christian content of the Core Syllabus and the approach that many teachers seemed to adopt in relation to it: 'I expected it to be much more valuing of different religions, religious backgrounds and of humanists or people of no religion, but I haven't found any of that. I have found it very dogmatic' (P10). Preference was expressed by many for a more balanced and inclusive content and for an approach that would encourage critical thought and debate. Other concerns related to the almost total absence of religions other than Christianity from the Northern Ireland GCSE Religious Studies exam syllabus.

Social Inclusion and Religious Identity

Findings clearly highlighted the dialogical relationship between pupils' religious identities and their perception of school culture, including teacher-peer interactions as well as the way in which RE was taught.

Identity Development

Religion was seen as central in the lives of pupils from minority religious background and defined how they saw themselves. For young people from minority ethnic communities, religious identity was also seen as closely interlinked with their ethnic identity. As one student said: 'I feel it's [faith] a part of my identity, cultural identity' (S6). While this link appeared to be unproblematic for some students, it was more fraught with difficulties for others; for example, where religion was not the majority culture in their country of origin or where it did not play a major role in their family. In contrast to the central role of religion for minority religious students, respondents who described themselves as 'atheist' and/or 'non-religious' did not attribute much significance to the influence of religion on their lives, except for the imposition of religious values through society. As one student related: 'You end up accepting that Northern Ireland is a very Christian place' (S1). This Christian influence was clearly acknowledged by student interviewees and they appeared to be resigned to it rather than resisting it.

There was a strong sense of self-sufficiency and independence in pupils' accounts of the development of their religious identity and they frequently emphasized that the decision about their religious beliefs lay with them, which was equally reiterated by parental interviewees. While learning about other faiths mainly took place in school, it was also reaffirmed, expanded upon and/ or re-evaluated at home through questions and conversations. One of the students explained: 'there is something that came up in RE and I didn't quite understand or I didn't agree with it, I would say to my Mum or Dad ... I don't know, I don't understand it, can you explain it?' (S3).

Student interviewees of the Bahá'í, Hindu and Jehovah's Witness faiths frequently referred to same-faith peers and highlighted the religious and social elements of these friendships. For example, one student said:

> People of my age and the junior youth would still meet a lot kind of in our free
> time and sometimes that would be for like eh devotionals or sessions with, you
> know, religious themes or content and sometimes it would just be to like hang
> out, have fun, go to the cinema, whatever (S6).

Other interviewees regretted the small size of their respective communities, which did not offer them the opportunity to make such friends close to home. Friendships with peers who belonged to the same religion appeared to be important to enable the development of a secure identity and to re-evaluate faith in the face of a society with differing beliefs.

There was little evidence of direct pressure to conform for most pupils though a few reported being questioned or criticized by peers or teachers about their beliefs. Parents and community representatives expressed concerns that Christian school culture and confessional RE teaching in particular could indoctrinate their children and may lead to the assimilation of students into the majority culture. One of the community representatives explains: 'Just as if somebody is teaching politics, you don't expect them to try to brainwash all the pupils into being socialists or conservatives or whatever. You expect them to teach politics in a neutral way. So it should be the same in Religious Education' (C3).

The expectation that RE should be taught in a neutral way in order to be inclusive for all pupils in the school was voiced with conviction by many of the interviewees.

General Sense of Inclusion/Exclusion in School

Student interviewees described the prominence of religion in their school culture very differently, with some rating it as highly important while others saw it having little importance. All of the student interviewees reported to have friends in school who held different religious beliefs from them and most considered these relationships to be unaffected by religious differences. In these mixed-religion friendship contexts, identities and understandings of the other appeared to be negotiated through discussions about religious differences or avoidance of them whereby talking about religion was seen as irrelevant or too controversial.

The role of such conversations about religion changed with the age and maturity of the pupil interviewees. Younger interviewees showed more concerns about fitting in with their peers which, for some and in some contexts, could entail the denial of their own beliefs. As a non-belief pupil explained: 'I just say "I am a Christian, too." They never ask [me anything further]' (S2). This desire to conform to their peers' norms also influenced the decision to participate in RE; as one student said: 'because none of my friends would [drop out], well, because I just like to be normal like everyone else' (S2). This reluctance to opt out of RE classes for fear of appearing different was reflected in a number of student interviews and very clearly highlighted by community representatives and parents. One parent said: 'I think opting out is quite, it's quite a difficult thing for children to cope with, so I think it creates a lot of tensions and problems for the child within the school system' (P22). One of the older students explained the change in relationships with peers in terms of religious identity gaining greater stability and significance over the years in adolescence: 'When we were younger it wasn't as important but now it is – it's quite a sensitive topic to a lot of people so it is best to just leave it alone and not impose your views on anyone else, because they don't like it' (S4). A few respondents recalled past episodes of being bullied in school which they saw rooted in religious and ethnic prejudices whereby these could not be disentangled. The attribution of such behaviour to some individuals only, and friendships in schools and family back-up appeared to provide support in dealing with such incidents.

The sense of double stigmatization as a result of religion and ethnicity was also echoed by immigrant parents who showed concerns that opting their child out of RE could add to their sense of otherness. In order to support their children, parents of immigration background appeared to straddle a balance between acceptance of a degree of assimilation for their children and a potential sense of estrangement from them. As one of them illustrated: 'We feel that to make them different may be difficult for them yeah just for their sake. So they are basically very much like locals compared to ourselves … being different from other people surrounding could make you feel very … lonely and disadvantaged' (P1). The presence of other pupils from religious and/or ethnic minority communities within the school was regarded as particularly helpful in promoting a sense of belonging to the school community, as one of the younger respondents explained:

Because just all of us can be together … Yeah, like in another school, school of Protestants, they just fight them [students from minority backgrounds] and all

> that. [So] just go to [School Name] and all the friends are there. And I have got
> my ... four cousins who go to [School Name] as well (S10).

If it was coupled with a perceived interest in pupils' beliefs, teachers' and peers' acknowledgement of religious differences and minor modifications to everyday practices in school – for example, the celebration of different religious festivals during assembly – appeared to foster a sense of belongingness to the school community. A student related: 'The attention to detail kind of made a difference and meant there was a greater sense of inclusion, you know' (S6). This attention to detail was also highlighted as important to promote inclusion in RE lessons.

Overall, while some interviewees expressed a sense of alienation from the majority norms, the findings provided little evidence of opposition to them. On the contrary, many student interviewees, parents and community representatives appeared to be highly engaged in negotiating such norms in the light of their own beliefs. However, the interviews clearly revealed the challenges for young people in negotiating their divergent religious identities in the context of a majority Christian school culture and RE curriculum and the extent to which the latter may promote or hinder a sense of inclusion to the school community and wider society.

Sufficiency of Opt-Outs

The research clearly reveals that young people and parents from minority-belief backgrounds are not necessarily aware of opt-out rights in relation to religious education and, in particular, to other religious occasions in school. In fact, interviews revealed that some minority-belief families requested an opt-out without knowledge of their legal entitlement. The majority of parents stated that schools did not inform them of this right, neither in the school literature nor through the school website or other formal communication:

> Well I was kind of aware that it [the right] was there, but no, no information
> is provided to you, I mean when, when you get information from the school
> about all the different things that the school is providing and so on, they did not
> provide you with any information about the opt-out ... it was extremely difficult
> to actually get that information (P22).

Many parents and community representatives interviewed admitted that they knew rather little about the content of the RE curriculum taught in their children's school. Some went on to suggest that schools should provide information on what was taught so that parents would be in a position to make an informed choice on whether to opt their child out of RE class:

> There are I suppose a lot of parents who don't know what's taught. They don't
> know it, you know. So is there an obligation then for a school to sort of provide
> some sort of curriculum content ... I think that would be important so then they

can make a better informed decision. Hard to make a decision about stuff if you don't have enough information, you know (P20).

In addition to the clear lack of knowledge on the part of parents and students regarding the existence and use of opt-outs, the research revealed that many teachers, including senior management, appear to have little awareness of the legal situation. In some cases, teachers reacted in an emotional and negative way when parents raised the question of opt-outs. In some instances, parents were provided with inaccurate information and advice:

> She [the teacher] was as rude to me and she says … it is compulsory she can't opt out of RE … she didn't insult me but she was very patronizing. She said to me it is important for them for their upbringing it is important for their moral upbringing for them to learn these things (P5).

For those that knew of the opt-out provision and remained in RE lessons, the decision to do so was based on a range of different reasons. First, perceptions of religious education in their school were a key factor: positive relationships with the RE teacher and classmates, inclusive approaches taken by the school to RE in terms of content and pedagogy and the belief that religious education as taught in their school was not doctrinal or that the child would be immune to potential indoctrination because of the exposure to their own or other faith in the home and community environment. Second, individual considerations relating to a fear of appearing different, the individual's interest in learning about other religions as well as academic considerations played a role in the decision to remain in RE. Some pupils were persuaded to stay in RE lessons by their parents who believed that it would be in their best interest to gain an understanding of the dominant religion of the country. For those parents who did withdraw their children from RE, the decision was related to the curricular content which they felt conflicted with their own belief system. This occurred most frequently when the teaching focused on doctrinal or confessional Christianity and was unsympathetic to other beliefs. Often the decision posed a dilemma for parents and was reached after the child had been attending the class for some time and had become uncomfortable with what was being taught.

Opt-Outs and Respect for Beliefs

In general, pupils recognized and accepted the underlying rationale for the right to opt out of religious education. However, the existence of this right – whether used or not – did not necessarily lead them to feel that their religion or beliefs were acknowledged and respected in the school. While many felt supported by their peers and, at times, by their teachers the lack of attention given to their beliefs in the RE curriculum caused them to feel that these beliefs were not valued or respected by the school nor indeed more widely by the education system. In addition, the lack of accessible and transparent policies and procedures dealing with opt-outs as well as the lack of consultation relating to alternative arrangements for opted-out pupils led to a sense amongst many minority-belief students that their beliefs were not of interest or concern to their school.

While opt-out clauses were seen as sufficient by some interviewees, several parents and community representative expressed dissatisfaction with the overall concept that the opt-out clause could protect and respect minority-beliefs in schools:

> I don't think it's a good system at all. It marginalizes kids that are from minorities.
> I mean it makes you be obvious. You *have to* opt out, you know, that's wrong
> … You shouldn't have to opt out of something like religious study. They could
> probably change it quite easily. I would say that nobody would want to opt out
> of it if they were taught differently (P5).

It was suggested that the right to opt out was not so much a protection mechanism for minority-belief individuals but an 'exclusion clause' and that it was damaging to a child's self-esteem if her or his beliefs were not recognized within the school and the curriculum. One community representative remarked: 'I wouldn't put it like a safeguard. I would say [it is an] exclusion clause' (C2).A parent whose son opted out noted that opting out made him and his son feel as if they were 'somehow disruptive' and 'causing trouble' for the school. Furthermore, this parent stated that the process did not value the child or their beliefs:

> Every child's self-esteem should be enhanced, their beliefs valued and so on,
> there was none of that … I didn't see any of that … Their own beliefs are not
> being recognized. Simply that their lack of belief in the dominant religion is
> being accepted and 'Well if you don't want to hear that you don't have to' or
> 'If you don't want to participate in the class you don't have to'. Well that is not
> protecting other children's beliefs or their self-esteem (P10).

In order for pupils to feel respected and protected in their right to freedom of thought, conscience and religion, young people expected schools to move beyond merely offering a poorly executed opt-out clause. However, some pupils felt that the opt-out clause had been effectively implemented in their school and as a result did not feel that their beliefs had been marginalized or ignored by the school management.

Conclusion

The right to opt out is considered fundamental in protecting and respecting religious liberty when doctrinal religious education is taught in schools. However, while the existence of an opt-out mechanism appears to be appreciated by many of those interviewed in this study it was not generally perceived to be an effective means towards respecting the right to the freedom of religion and belief of minorities. Members of such groups, from a diversity of religious and non-religious positions, clearly felt that more was required than the right to be absent from a particular period in the school timetable, irrespective of whether they themselves took up the opt-out route. Some, indeed, felt that opting out actually made things worse by marginalizing them and perhaps even by providing an excuse for inaction by those who appeared to care little about including minorities in relation to Religious Education.

The overwhelming view coming from this study was that in order for religion and belief minorities to achieve a greater sense of respect and to feel more included it would require significant changes in the content of, and approach to, RE in the schools they or their children attended. This presents particular challenges for many schools where curriculum and staff development in RE are not normally high on the list of priorities, and also to those responsible for defining the RE syllabus.

In Northern Ireland, the unique role of four Christian denominations defining curriculum content in RE without any reference to any other faith communities is questionable in the light of findings such as these. When the Syllabus itself is presented as 'essentially Christian' and even the limited Key Stage 3 section on world religions was written without input from members of 'other faiths' then it is not surprising that many teachers are unaware of, or insensitive or indifferent to, the concerns of religion and belief minorities. Change in relation to this particular status quo will not come easily, but it is hard to see how an exclusively Christian-Churches-controlled RE Syllabus can meet the concerns of minorities and others without a significant change of direction.

Teacher development is also a crucial factor and the concerns expressed by some respondents about lack of awareness and 'unintentional disrespect' can only be improved if training at initial and in-service levels is taken seriously. In addition to improving the awareness and understanding of teachers about the beliefs, practices and concerns of members of minority faith communities, the research indicates that this needs to be broadened out to include other beliefs such as humanism and similar non-religious life-stances. Furthermore, such improved awareness needs to be developed in all school types, including faith schools.

Negotiating their religious identities can be particularly challenging for young people from minority-belief backgrounds. As suggested by Barrett et al. (2007), this research clearly emphasized the influence of the school, and RE in particular, on minority-belief young people's development of religious identity. Researching the experiences of young people from mixed religious backgrounds in England, Arweck and Nesbitt (2010) found that school and home learning relating to religious beliefs complemented each other. By contrast, the findings from the research presented in this chapter clearly highlight the pressure that young people from minority-belief backgrounds may experience due to the perceived divergence of the values and norms transmitted through their home upbringing and school life and RE in particular. For many young people the desire to conform with majority peer norms, to be seen as 'normal' and to participate in RE lessons the same as everybody else was juxtaposed against their opposition against confessional teaching and a strong Christian influence in school life as a whole.

A sense of stigmatization resulting from the perceived impossibility to fit into the majority norms and the subsequent experience of exclusion pervaded many of the interviews. In line with previous research indicating an increasing sense of coherence between identity and meaning with age (for example, Furrow et al. 2004), this appeared to be particularly challenging to negotiate for younger pupils while some older pupils seemed to navigate more confidently the sometimes conflicting expectations of home, community and school contexts. Schachter (2005) highlights the complex processes of identity development in such contexts of conflicting norms and identifications. She suggests that these may not necessarily be uniformly integrated into one coherent image of identity as generally assumed by modern developmental theorists (for example Erikson 1968) but instead may be more flexible and vary depending on context, which appeared to be reflected in the accounts of students participating in this research. As suggested by Schachter and Ventura (2008), the research highlights the considerable role that parents and communities play in mediating and helping young people from minority-belief backgrounds to interpret various social influences and pressures. Furthermore, parents from minority-belief communities may compromise their own beliefs and values to enable their children to integrate better into their school and society.

While some pupils in our research did express a sense of exclusion or alienation from majority norms as experienced in RE, the school community and wider society, there was no evidence of the development of reactive religious identities, which would be defined by their opposition to the majority culture and 'disidentification' (Verkuyten and Yildiz 2007). The teaching of doctrinal RE in schools poses a complex challenge for human rights law. Its concern is to protect the right to freedom of thought, conscience and religion in the school environment and it attempts to do so through demanding the provision of opt-outs in order to prevent children becoming indoctrinated with beliefs which are contrary to the religious and philosophical convictions of their parents. However, this research demonstrates that the right to opt out may be ineffective in certain situations, for example, if individuals are not made aware of this right, if schools lack clear and well-publicized policies for handling opt-out requests and if quality alternatives are not made available to students who wish to withdraw from RE. Findings from this research suggest that when doctrinal or confessional religious education is taught in schools, the right to freedom of religion and belief of minority-belief individuals would be better protected by requesting schools to operate an opt-in rather than an opt-out mechanism. This approach would remove many of the dilemmas and difficulties typically encountered by minority-belief individuals when considering whether to exercise their right to opt out of RE.

However, more fundamentally, the research suggests that even if properly executed, an opt-out/opt-in mechanism cannot constitute respect for the beliefs of minority-belief individuals. As has been argued, from a minority student perspective respect for religious liberty should be protected through the teaching of a range of belief systems within the RE curriculum and the wider school curriculum. Furthermore, it was noted that an opt-out decision can have a detrimental impact on young people's identity development and lead to difficulties in reconciling their belief system with that of their peers and their school.

It is not the job of human rights law to declare how RE should be taught in schools; rather its focus is properly centred on the challenge of protecting the right to freedom of thought, conscience and religion in educational establishments. If its attempts to do so generate concerns such as those highlighted in this chapter, then it is for educators and public policy-makers to take responsibility for the development of programmes which make good these deficiencies. In this task, the research presented here demonstrates the importance of considering the wide range of religious diversity in schools, beyond simplified dichotomies between us and them, to facilitate a sense of inclusion to the school community, and ultimately wider society, for all students.

References

Arweck, E. and Nesbitt, E. 2010. Religious education in the experience of young people from mixed-faith families. [Online: Warwick Research Archive Tool.] Available at: http://wrap.warwick.ac.uk/3730/ [Accessed: 5 February 2011].

Banks, J.A. 2008. Diversity, group identity and citizenship education in a global age. *Educational Research* 37(3), 129–39.

Barrett, J.B., Pearson, J., Muller, C. and Frank, K.A. 2007. Adolescent religiosity and school contexts. *Social Science Quarterly* 88(4), 1024–37.

Benson, P.L. 2004. Emerging themes in research on adolescent spiritual and religious development. *Applied Developmental Science* 8(1), 47–50.

Bernard-Patel, S. 2008. Interdit de porter le foulard ... But I can wear my headscarf! *The International Journal of Diversity in Organizations, Communities & Nations* 8(4), 213–20.

Bouma, G.D. 2008. The challenge of religious re-vitalization to multicultural and multifaith Australia. *The International Journal of Diversity in Organizations, Communities & Nations* 8(4), 1–4.

Brega, A.C. and Coleman, L.M. 1999. Effects of religiosity and racial socialization on stigmatization in African-American adolescents. *Journal of Adolescence* 22(2), 223–42.

Chaudhury, S.R. and Miller, L. 2008. Religious identity formation among Bangladeshi American Muslim adolescents. *Journal of Adolescent Research* 23(4), 383–410.

Churches' RE. Core Syllabus Working Party 2003. *Proposals for a Revised Core Syllabus in RE in Grant-Aided Schools in Northern Ireland.* Bangor: The Department of Education.

Copley, T. 2008. *Teaching Religion: Sixty Years of Religious Education in England and Wales*. Exeter: University of Exeter Press.

Council of Europe. 2008. *White Paper on Intercultural Dialogue: Living Together as Equals in Dignity*. Strasbourg: Council of Europe Publishing.

Council of Europe. 2009. *Dimensions of Religions and Non-Religious Convictions within Intercultural Education*. Recommendation CM/Rec(2008)12 and explanatory memorandum. Strasbourg: Council of Europe Publishing.

Cowie, F. 2006. Dressing the part: gender, performance and the culture of law schools. *Northern Ireland Legal Quarterly* 57(3), 557–76.

Department of Education. 2006. *The Result of the Equality Impact Assessment of the Proposal for the Revised Core Syllabus*. [Online] Available at: http://www.deni.gov.uk/results_doc._eqia-6.pdf [Accessed: 2 February 2011].

Department of Education. 2007. *Revised Core Syllabus for Religious Education*. [Online] Available at: http://www.deni.gov.uk/re_core_syllabus_pdf.pdf [Accessed: 11 February 2011].

Dunn, S. 2000. Northern Ireland: education in a divided society, in *The Education Systems of the United Kingdom*, edited by D. Philips. Oxford Studies in Comparative Education. Oxford: Symposium Books.

Erikson, E.H. 1968. *Identity: Youth and Crises*. New York: Norton.

Foster, C.R. 2004. Religious education at the edge of history. *Religious Education* 99(1), 72–8.

Furrow, J.L., King, P.E. and White, K. 2004. Religion and positive youth development: Identity, meaning and prosocial concern. *Applied Developmental Science* 8(1), 17–26.

Hull, J.M. 1990. Religious education in the state schools of late capitalist society. *British Journal of Educational Studies* 38(4), 335–48.

Ipgrave, J. and McKenna, U. 2008. Diverse experiences and common vision: English students' perspectives on religion and religious education, in *Encountering Religious Pluralism in School and Society: A Qualitative Study of Teenage Perspectives in Europe*, edited by T. Knauth et al. Muenster: WaxmannVerlag.

Jackson, R. 2004. Intercultural education and recent European pedagogies of religious education. *Intercultural Education* 15(1), 3–14.

Jackson, R. 2009. Is diversity changing religious education? Religion, education and diversity in today's Europe, in *Religious Diversity and Education: Nordic Perspectives*, edited by G. Skeie. Münster:Waxmann, 11–28.

Keast, J. (ed.) 2007. *Religious Diversity and Intercultural Education: A Reference Book for Schools*. Strasbourg: Council of Europe Publishing.

Kuyk, E., Jensen, R., Löh Manna, E., Schreiner, P. (eds) 2007. *Religious Education in Europe: Situation and Current Trends in Schools*. Oslo: IKO Publishing House and Intereuropean Commission on Church and School.

Leeman, Y. 2008. Education and diversity in the Netherlands. *European Educational Research Journal* 7(1), 50–9.

OSCE/ODIHR. 2007. *Toledo Guiding Principles on Teaching about Religions and Beliefs in Public Schools*. Warsaw: The Office of Democratic Institutions and Human Rights of the Organization for Co-operation and Security in Europe.

Regnerus, M.D., Smith, C. and Smith, B. 2004. Social context in the development of adolescent religiosity. *Applied Developmental Science* 8(1), 27–38.

Richardson, N. 2010. Division, diversity and vision: religious education and community cohesion in Northern Ireland, in *Religious Education and Social and Community Cohesion: An Exploration of Challenges and Opportunities*, edited by M. Grimmitt. Great Wakering: McCrimmons.

Schachter, E.P. 2005. Context and identity formation: a theoretical analysis and a case study. *Journal of Adolescent Research* 20(3), 375–95.

Schachter, E.P. and Ventura, J.J. 2008. Identity agents: parents as active and reflective participants in their children's identity formation. *The Journal for Research on Adolescence*, 18(3), 449–76.

Smith, A. 2001. Religious segregation and the emergence of integrated schools in Northern Ireland. *Oxford Review of Education* 27(4), 559–75.

Verkuyten, M. and Yildiz, A.A. 2007. National (dis)identification and ethnic and religious identity: A study among Turkish-Dutch Muslims. *Personality and Social Psychological Bulletin* 33(10), 1448–62.

Chapter 12

History Textbooks within the Framework of French *Laïcité*

Anna Van den Kerchove

In France, schools have been the forum *par excellence* for French *laïcité*, ever since its first implementation in the nineteenth century. Two laws indeed separated the French school state system from the Roman Catholic Church. Article 1 of the *Ferry Law of 28 March 1882* prescribed a compulsory curriculum for primary school education in which the previous course on 'religious and moral instruction' was replaced by a new course on 'moral and civic instruction'. Article 3 of the same Law abolished the right of priests to inspect, supervise and manage primary schools (whether public or private).[1] Article 17 of the *Goblet Law of 20 October 1886* provided that education in state schools had to be taken over by lay, that is 'non-clerical' teachers.[2] However, due to the principle of religious freedom, Article 2 of the *Ferry Law* also granted one day off school in the week in order for parents to give their child religious instruction should they wish to;[3] this was reinforced by Article 1 of the *Debré Law of 31 December 1959*.[4] The separation of the educational state system from the Catholic Church was extended to the rest of

---

1 'Sont abrogées les dispositions des articles 18 et 44 de la loi du 14 mars 1850, en ce qu'elles donnent aux ministres des cultes un droit d'inspection, de surveillance et de direction dans les écoles primaires publiques et privées et dans les salles d'asile, ainsi que le paragraphe 2 de l'article 31 de la même loi qui donne aux consistoires le droit de présentation pour les instituteurs appartenant aux cultes non catholiques.' [Online]. Available at: http://www.senat.fr/evenement/archives/D42/mars1882.pdf [Accessed: 10 December 2010].

2 'Dans les écoles publiques de tout ordre, l'enseignement est exclusivement confié à un personnel laïque.' [Online]. Available at: http://dcalin.fr/textoff/loi_goblet_1886.html [Accessed: 10 December 2010].

3 This day off was originally on Thursdays until a decree in 1972 replaced it by Wednesdays.

4 *Debré Law*, Art. 1(3): 'The State shall take all necessary steps to ensure freedom of religion and religious instruction for pupils receiving public education.' ('il (l'État) prend toutes les dispositions utiles pour assurer aux élèves de l'enseignement public la liberté des cultes et de l'instruction religieuse'). [Online]. Available at: http://www.legifrance.gouv.fr/jopdf/common/jo_pdf.jsp?numJO=0&dateJO=19600103&numTexte=&pageDebut=00066&pageFin= [Accessed: 10 December 2010].

state services and bodies with the *Law of 9 December 1905*.[5] Since then, the State has been separate from religions by virtue of the so called principle of *laïcité* or 'de-clericalization'.[6]

Since 1882, neither religious education nor proselytism has been permitted in the public school system though religious instruction may be provided by families and religious communities outside school. The implementation of *laïcité* does not mean, however, that 'religious issues' (*'faits religieux'*) (Borne and Willaime 2007: 37–57)[7] have entirely disappeared from the French curriculum and textbooks. For example, the history collection known as *Malet et Isaac* which has been used by generations of French history teachers and of French pupils did not leave religious issues aside.[8] However, the tone was at times critical of religion. One famous example is the story concerning Joan of Arc and the voices she had heard according to medieval sources. The famous textbook by Ernest Lavisse, known as 'Le Petit Lavisse', thus described this episode in the following terms: 'she thought she could see a great brightness to the right side of the church. And it seemed to her that she could hear a voice saying ...'.[9] This way of writing carries value judgments and could no longer be used nowadays.

After tracing the evolution of History French national programmes and illustrating the link between the syllabus and the textbooks, some general remarks concerning six History textbooks will be made. First, I will show that religious issues are more prominent in the new textbooks than in previous ones and that authors also pay more attention to the way religious issues are approached. Secondly, I will compare what is said about Christianity and what is said about other religions. This analysis will lead to two general observations. On the one

---

5   The 1905 Law does not apply to the Alsatian and Moselle *départements* because they were at that time under German rule. In 1918, when these territories went back to France, they were exempted from the 1905 Law. These *départements* are still under the 1801 Concordat, a derogation which is no longer controversial today. The 1905 Law does not apply either to the French overseas territories known as 'overseas territories' (*'Territoires et collectivités d'Outre-Mer'*) or to Guyane, which used to be colonies in 1905.

6   The word *laïcité* is absent in the law but the concept is expressed in its first two provisions: 'The Republic guarantees freedom of conscience. It guarantees the free exercise of religions under the exclusive limitations provided below pursuant to law and order' and 'the Republic adopts, employs or subsidizes no religion'.

7   The expression 'religious issues' (*'faits religieux'*) (Willaime 2007: 37–57) was first proposed by Régis Debray in his Report and was later adopted by French National Education authorities. It is employed in a durkheimian sense with implied social, material and symbolic dimensions.

8   This collection was initiated by Albert Malet following a new history national syllabus in 1902. First published by Hachette, this collection was taken over by Jules Isaac in 1923. The whole collection has been regularly republished and the last new edition dates back to 1960.

9   'Elle crut voir une grande clarté du côté de l'église à droite. Et il lui sembla qu'elle entendait une voix qui lui parlait' (Lavisse 1954: 70–1).

hand, there is a positive evolution in France with a greater awareness of the importance of religious issues. On the other hand, more can and should be done – in particular in the way non-Western Christian religions are presented.

The Evolution of the History National Syllabus in French State Schools

During the second half of the twentieth century, there was an awareness of the cognitive loss of religious subjects. Various initiatives stressed the need to expand upon religious topics within French state schools, including in the curriculum and the training of teachers. In 1989, the historian Philippe Joutard submitted a report to Lionel Jospin (then Minister of National Education). The report stated that 'knowledge of religious cultures is necessary for the understanding of our societies, their past and present, their artistic and cultural heritage, their juridical and political system'. To attain this goal, the report recommended promoting religious topics within existing subjects of the national curriculum. Three reasons were put forward for this option of incorporating religious issues within existing subjects rather than creating a new separate subject on religious issues. First, pragmatic considerations were invoked: creating a new discipline from scratch and a body of teachers to teach it would be difficult; moreover, adding a subject to an already saturated syllabus would unduly burden pupils' timetable. Secondly, ideological reasons, linked to the respect of the principle of *laïcité*, prevented the creation of a separate subject linked to religious issues in state schools. Thirdly, intellectual pedagogical convictions whereby religion should best be taught through its historic, social and cultural impacts seemed to reinforce the chosen option.

Under the influence of this report, the History school syllabus of the mid-nineties placed more emphasis on religious issues. For instance, in the History curriculum for pupils aged between 15 and 16 – at year 10 level ('*classe de seconde*', first level of the French upper secondary school, the '*lycée*')[10] – two of the six topics were directly connected to religious topics: 'the beginnings and expansion of Christianity' and 'the Mediterranean world in the twelfth century at a crossroad of three civilizations'; one might also add the chapter related to 'Humanism and Renaissance' where teachers were invited to discuss the Reformation. In 1995 and 1997, the programmes for the first two levels of the first French secondary schools (*collèges*) also gave greater priority to religious issues with the Egyptian religion, the Hebrews, the Greek mythology, the beginnings of Christianity, the

---

10   A brief presentation of the French school system may be useful. It is divided up into three levels: (1) Primary schools ('*écoles primaires*') for five years (for 6–11-year-old children); (2) Lower level of secondary schools ('*collèges*') for four years (for 11–15-year-old children) and (3) Upper level of secondary schools ('*lycées*') for three years (for 15–18-year-old children). The first year of the *lycée* is called '*classe de seconde*'.

Muslim world, Medieval Christianity and Reformation.[11] In 2000, the History curriculum for the class of *seconde* was rewritten and the topic on 'the beginnings and diffusion of Christianity' became compulsory.[12]

In the aftermath of 9/11, Régis Debray submitted a new report to Jack Lang, Minister of National Education. He recalled Joutard's comments and asked for a transfer of the mission of teaching about religious issues from the private to the public sphere (Debray 2010)[13] and for an enhanced inclusion of religious issues within existing subjects. He concluded with 12 recommendations concerning the initial and ongoing training of teachers (with an initiative for collaboration between secondary school teachers and researchers) as well as the national curriculum.

In 2010, the curriculum of the *seconde* was amended.[14] By contrast to the previous syllabus, the new (and current) History curriculum provides very little space to religious issues. A proposal for a new History curriculum was publicly submitted in February 2010 and reviewed by History teachers and academic historians. The *Institut européen en sciences des religions* ('IESR') regretted the disappearance of some topics (such as 'the Mediterranean world in the twelfth century at a crossroad of three civilizations') and the general loss of 'the religious dimension' which was only 'explicitly present in topic three' of the curriculum and only appeared marginally in other topics.[15] On 29 April 2010, the final version of the new History curriculum was published in the *Bulletin officiel*[16] and came in force in September 2010. Some optional topics with a religious dimension were made mandatory such as 'the study of a Reformer'. Despite these last-minute modifications, the final version of the History curriculum dedicates little place to religious issues as shown by the following table which details the content of the French national History curriculum for year 10 pupils (*'classe de seconde'*) as applicable in 1996 (first column), in 2010 (second column) and as interpreted in the latest textbooks – published in 2010 – (third column).

---

11   *BO*, 21 December 1995, in force in September 1996 and *BO*, 30 January 1996, in force in September 1997.

12   *BO Hors-série* no. 6, 31 August 2000, in force in Septembre 2001. [Online]. Available at: http://www.education.gouv.fr/bo/2000/hs6/default.htm [Accessed: 10 December 2010].

13   Debray 2002: 15. [Online]. Available at: http://www.iesr.ephe.sorbonne.fr/docannexe/file/3739/debray.pdf [Accessed: 10 December 2010].

14   The programmes for the *collèges* were amended in 2008: *BO Spécial* no. 6, 28 August 2008, in force in September 2009 until September 2012. [Online]. Available at: http://www.education.gouv.fr/cid22116/mene0817481a.html [Accessed: 24 January 2010].

15   *IESR* (*Institut européen en sciences des religions*), latest update on 21 February 2010, [Online]. Available at: http://www.iesr.ephe.sorbonne.fr/index6111.html [Accessed: 10 December 2010].

16   *BO Spécial* no. 4, 29 April 2010. [Online]. Available at: http://media.education.gouv.fr/file/special_4/72/5/histoire_geographie_143725.pdf [Accessed: 10 December 2010].

Table 12.1   French national History curriculum for Year 10 pupils

History curriculum (1996)	History curriculum (2010)		Textbooks (2010)
	Topic one. Europeans and the settlement of the world's population.		
	Main topics	Sub-topics	
	The place of European populations within the settlement of the world's population.	*Phases of population growth from Antiquity to the nineteenth century; *European emigration to other continents, mainly during the nineteenth century.	*Chapter one.* The place of European populations within the settlement of the world's population.
Topic one. An example of citizenship in the ancient world: citizens in Athens during the fifth century BC.	*Topic two.* The invention of citizenship in the ancient world.		
*Being a citizen in Athens; *A strict conception of citizenship.	Main topics	Sub-topics	
	Citizenship and democracy in Athens (fourth and fifth centuries BC).	*The participation of citizens to the institutions and life of the city; *democracy viewed and criticized by the Athenians.	*Chapter two.* Citizenship and democracy in Athens (fourth and fifth centuries BC).
	Roman Citizenship and empire (first to third centuries).	Extension of the citizenship to Roman Gaul; extension of citizenship to the whole Empire: *Caracalla's Edict.*	*Chapter three.* Roman Citizenship and empire (first to third centuries).
Topic two. The birth and diffusion of Christianity. *The religious and historical context to the birth of Christianity; *Expansion of Christianity until the end of the fourth century.			

History curriculum (1996)	History curriculum (2010)		Textbooks (2010)
Topic three. The Mediterranean world in the twelfth century at a crossroad of three civilizations.	*Topic three.* Societies and cultures in Medieval Europe, from the eleventh century to the thirteenth century.		
*The Christian Western world, the Byzantine Empire and the Muslim world; *Relations between the three civilizations: exchanges, wars and cultural influences.	Main topic	Sub-topics	
	Medieval Christianity	The study of the fundamental place of Christianity in Medieval Europe. One example to be studied out of the two below: *an element of the religious heritage (church, cathedral, artwork …) or *an aspect of the multiple dimensions of the conversion to Christianity in Europe (evangelization, integration, exclusion, repression …).	*Chapter four.* Medieval Christianity
	One of the two following topics		
	Rural societies and culture	*Life of peasant communities; *Feudality.	*Chapter five.* Rural societies and culture.
	Urban societies and cultures.	*Urban growth; *study of two European towns, chosen from two different cultural areas.	*Chapter six.* Urban societies and cultures.
Topic four. Humanism and Renaissance	*Topic four.* New geographic and cultural horizons of Europeans in the Modern Times		
* A new vision of human beings and of the world.	Main topic	Sub-topics	
	Discovery of a larger world (fifteenth and sixteenth centuries).	Contacts between Europeans and other worlds and widening of European's geographical horizons. * From Constantinople to Istanbul: a place of contact between different cultures and religions (Christians, Muslim and Jewish).	*Chapter seven.* Discovery of a larger world (fifteenth and sixteenth centuries).

History curriculum (1996)	History curriculum (2010)		Textbooks (2010)
		*an additional topic out of the two following case studies: a Pre-Columbian city confronted to European conquest and colonization; or Beijing, a forbidden city?	
	One of the two following topics:		
*Artistic Renaissance	Men of the Renaissance (fifteenth and sixteenth centuries)	*Study of a Reformer's life and his role in the expansion of Protestantism. *A case study chosen out of the following two: study of a publisher's life and his role in the diffusion of Humanism; or Study of an artist in the society of his time.	*Chapter eight.* Men of the Renaissance (fifteenth and sixteenth centuries).
	The development of a new scientific spirit.	Two questions out of the following three: *Study of a sixteenth- or seventeenth-century scholar's life and work; *The diffusion of Science in the eighteen century; *The invention of steam: technological revolution.	*Chapter nine.* The development of a new scientific spirit.
Topic five. The French Revolution and French politics until 1851.	*Topic five.* Revolutions, liberties and nations in the dawn of the modern era.		
	Main topic	Sub-topics	
The break from the '*Ancient Régime*' *Implementation of revolutionary principles; *Tensions between conservatism and modernity.	The French Revolution: the advent of a new political universe.	The emergence of the ideas of liberty before and in the early days of the French Revolution, political events until the French Empire.	*Chapter ten.* The French Revolution: the advent of a new political universe.

History curriculum (1996)	History curriculum (2010)		Textbooks (2010)
Topic six. Changes in Europe during the first half of the nineteenth century. *Economic and social changes *Liberal and national aspirations until the revolutions of 1848; *Europe in the middle of nineteenth century.	Freedom and nations in France and Europe during the first part of the nineteenth century.		*Chapter eleven*. Freedom and nations in France and Europe during the first part of the nineteenth century.

In this context, it is interesting to study how History textbooks introduce religious issues within the curriculum. In analysing the six History textbooks which were published during the Summer of 2010 (Colon 2010, Billary 2010, Bourel and Chevallier 2010, Cote 2010, Lambin 2010, Le Quintrec 2010), this chapter takes into account both the text and the documents contained in the textbooks.

Role of the Textbooks

First, some brief remarks about the role of textbooks and their link to the curriculum may be useful. For French teachers, the national curriculum, issued by National Education authorities and published in the *Bulletin officiel*, is the unique reference: 'it is the national framework within which every teacher organizes his own teaching'.[17] Each teacher should construct his lessons in accordance to the curriculum related to the subject he teaches. However, because the curriculum is often brief, French National Education authorities also issue explanatory notes called '*Ressources pour le lycée/la seconde*' ('Resources') which give details as to the spirit of the curriculum, the tools to use to draw up the lesson plan (in particular in relation to the new school topic 'History of Arts')[18] and highlights

---

17   *Code de l'Éducation*, Art L 311–13: "Les programmes définissent, pour chaque cycle, les connaissances essentielles qui doivent être acquises au cours du cycle ainsi que les méthodes qui doivent être assimilées. Ils constituent le cadre national au sein duquel les enseignants organisent leurs enseignements." [Online]. Available at: http://www.legifrance. gouv.fr/affichCodeArticle.do?idArticle=LEGIARTI000006524740&cidTexte=LEGITEX T000006071191&dateTexte=20090125 [Accessed: 10 December 2010].

18   "History of Arts" is a new discipline with a curriculum of its own. However, as religious issues, it has no specific hour. It is a transdisciplinary topic which has to be implemented by many teachers, including History teachers. "Organization de l'enseignement de l'histoire des arts", *Encart – Bulletin officiel*, no. 32, 28 August 2008. [Online]. Available at: http://media.education.gouv.fr/file/32/09/0/encart_33090.pdf [Accessed: 10 December 2010].

possible pitfalls to avoid. The 'Resources' give more place to religious issues than the curriculum; for example, when giving details about topic two on 'The invention of citizenship in the ancient world', the 'Resources' recommend that teachers discuss the religious and cultural dimensions of political life in Athens. Similarly, in respect of the fourth topic on 'Europeans in the Modern Times', the 'Resources' begin by stating that: 'the period from the sixteenth to the eighteenth centuries witnessed a real shift in the frame of thought of science and technology. New scholarly practices and technical changes emerged and their propagation, by gradually replacing medieval spiritualism by a new rational view of the world, challenged Christian traditions.'[19] The 'Resources' go on by recommending that these changes be put into its geographical and historical context. 'It is difficult', they add, 'to understand the shift triggered by Copernicus' or Galileo's ideas without referring to medieval science or without describing the cultural and religious context of the modern era.'[20]

Contrary to the national curriculum and the 'Resources', textbooks are not issued by National Education authorities or supervised by them. They do not therefore contain any mandatory rules or official guidelines. Written by teachers and/or researchers employed by private publishers, they offer one possible interpretation of the national curriculum. They respond to a commercial strategy and try to meet teachers' expectations. Despite their non-mandatory and non-official character, textbooks are often better known to teachers than official documents and guidelines. One may add that the six textbooks were written quickly (within six months) and do not always take into account the 'Resources' that were published later, in June 2010.

The Pervasiveness of Religious Issues in History Textbooks

All of the 6 textbooks are usually divided into 11 chapters corresponding to the 11 topics listed in the curriculum. The curriculum only explicitly mentions religious issues in four topics: 'Medieval Christianity', 'The discovery of a larger world (fifteenth and sixteenth centuries)', 'The men of the Renaissance (fifteenth and sixteenth centuries)' (as an optional topic to be chosen as an alternative to the topic on 'The development of a new scientific spirit' and 'The French Revolution'. Textbooks however go further. Half of them (Colon 2010, Cote 2010, Le Quintrec 2010) provide information about religious issues in nine topics. The two chapters that do not refer to religion at all are the first and last chapters on the settlement of the world's population and the emergence of nations in nineteenth century Europe respectively. The three remaining textbooks discuss religious issues under 10

---

19   [Online]. available at: http://media.eduscol.education.fr/file/lycee/77/9/LyceeGT_Ressources_HGEC_2_Hist_10_T4NvEspritScienTech_148779.pdf [Accessed: 10 December 2010].

20   Ibidem.

topics, and especially in the last chapter relating to the 'fights for freedom' in the first half of the nineteenth century (Lambin 2003: 318–9, Bourel and Chevallier 2010: 292–3). Elsewhere, the authors point to a connection between the Black Death and religion. They show how this dramatic event modified the relation to death and how this modification became more visible with the increase of religious processions (Billard 2010: 18–19). This way of presenting historical events reveals how religion and religious practices enlightens our understanding of social events and reciprocally how religious practices cannot be fully understood without referring to non-religious events.

This record of the Black Death is really symptomatic of a mutation: it is now acknowledged that the discussion of religious issues may be relevant to the teaching of non-religious topics. Religion is thus viewed as an integral aspect of society among others (cultural, economical, political, and so on). The other chapters of this textbook and all of the other textbooks bolster this observation. Religious issues regularly appear throughout the various chapters. Remarks about religious issues are sometimes brief[21] but they nevertheless show that textbook authors no longer hide the role of religious issues in history. For instance, in the chapter relating to 'the Great Discoveries', five of the textbooks mention (besides technological, economic and political reasons) religious motivation, namely, the desire to expand Christianity at a time when Eastern Europe had to resist the Muslim Ottoman invasion.

Moreover, religious issues can now be included in French state school teaching through the new subject of 'History of Arts'. The History of Art curriculum, for the *seconde*, dedicates a topic on 'the arts and the holy'. All of the six textbooks devote many pages to the history of the arts and most of these pages refer to religion whether it be Greek statuary and the figuration of Greek Gods (Lambin 2010: 60–61); the square house in the city of Nîmes (Le Quintrec 2010: 76–7); an example of a new painting technique with a reproduction of the wedding of the Virgin by Raphael (Cote 2010: 200–201) or the Aztec religion (Cote 2010: 175–6).

The analysis of these six textbooks reveal that the discussion of religious issues is now seen in France – at least by textbooks authors – as falling within state school teachers' mission.

---

21   Billard 2010: 224 thus merely states about the Concordat: 'the religious question is resolved by the Concordat of 1801.' In their last chapter, Bourel and Chevallier (2010: 292) mention that the Restoration in France 'guaranteed some of the 1789 principles, such as religious freedom'. In a whole chapter dedicated to the citizenship in Rome, Lambin 2010: 86 merely alludes to religion: 'the differences between the Latin West and the Greek East, tenuous in the legal sphere, were more noticeable and long-lasting in the political, cultural and religious spheres' (author's translation).

A Specific Deontology?

However, beyond the question of the quantity of information given, there is also the question of its quality. Teaching *about* religious issues is not the same as teaching *from* religion – it is not religious education. Teaching about religious issues within existing core subjects implies to respect the methodology appropriate to these core subjects. Teachers who cover religious issues in class must be careful to avoid any formulation expressing faith. In the above-mentioned textbooks, the discourse is less doctrinal than in the past and adopts a more distanced and objective point of view. Textbook authors distance themselves from religious truths by making more use of the conditional tense 'Jesus would have said …' or of expressions such as 'according to …'. In the chapter on 'Medieval Christianity', most authors refrain from using the Christian title of 'Saint' when referring to Francis of Assisi or to Bernard of Clairvaux.[22] They now seem aware that this title is not a natural way of speaking, but is rooted in a specific cultural and religious context. However, there are inconsistencies and within the same textbook, the honorific title of 'Saint' may be used in some chapters and omitted in others, depending on the author of the specific chapter.

Christianity and Other Religions

Christianity and other Monotheistic Religions

Due to the brevity of the national curriculum (even if complemented by the guidelines provided in the 'Resources'), textbook authors have a wide discretion in the interpretation of the topics. There are important differences between textbooks and within each of them in the way that religious issues are presented, depending on the general policy adopted by the publisher and on the views of the author(s) of the chapter in question. But in all textbooks and in all chapters, Christianity is predominant. Latin Christianity from the Middle Ages to the Modern Age is the religion that features most often. It is understandable that given the focus of the curriculum upon Western Europe, other Christian faiths and non-Christian religions are less explored. Most textbooks devote a full chapter on Latin Christianity during the Middle Ages, usually chapter five, with detailed information about Christian beliefs and practices at the time and do not differ greatly in their content.

For non-Christian religions, textbooks do not usually contain a chapter equivalent to the one dedicated to Medieval Latin Christianity. Latin Christianity is the only religion studied for its own sake. Details concerning other beliefs, rituals and organization are very rare. The curriculum focuses on the Greek and Roman legacy in Western Europe, in particular citizenship in Athens and in the

---

22   The teacher should not have to conceal the fact that some persons were and are still considered as 'Saints'.

Roman Empire. All textbooks mention the religious dimensions of citizenship. The link between religious life and political life is thus well established – more so than in previous textbooks. However, the political dimension of civic religious life (the cohesion and hierarchy within the community) is less evoked. Overall, Roman polytheism is neglected. The Roman religion appears through the religious titles of the emperor and through the imperial cult which is mentioned but not fully explained. The importance of religious life in the Roman Empire is hardly discussed. These lacunae are due to the fact that Greek and Roman cults are discussed with a view to enhance pupils' understanding of ancient citizenship rather than studied for themselves. Some aspects of the ancient cults are thus given preference over others. Moreover, the citizenship is mainly approached from an institutional perspective.

For religions which developed alongside Christianity, the data provided in the textbooks mainly illustrates their relationship with Christian Europeans. Non-Christian traditions are perceived from a Western and a Christian point of view. Thus, only two or three aspects of non-Christian religions are usually discussed – often, with a narrow somewhat distorted point of view. Three examples may be given. The first concerns Judaism. In the curriculum and in the 'Resources', Jews are only mentioned under the topic on Constantinople: this topic, say the 'Resources' are an opportunity for teachers to show the dynamism of Muslim societies; 'it is at Istanbul and in the Ottoman Empire that some of the Jews expelled from Europe took refuge'.[23] It is an implicit invitation to speak of the contrasted situation of Jews in Western Europe and in the Ottoman Empire. Most of the textbooks follow this invitation and go even further. Indeed, not only do they mention Jews in the chapter on Constantinople – as recommended by the 'Resources' – but also in the one on Medieval Christianity (for which neither the curriculum nor the 'Resources' raise the question of Jews). In the former, Jews appear as an illustration of the liberal attitudes towards religious minorities in the Muslim world; Jewish beliefs and rituals are not explained. In the latter, Jews are presented as 'an example of the multiple dimensions of the conversion to Christianity in Europe (evangelization, integration, exclusion, repression ...)'. The Jews embody the way the Latin Church and the royal power used to repress the 'religious dissidents' alongside the Christians who were considered to be heretics. This narrow focus contributes to a 'victimization vision' (*'vision victimaire'*) of Jewishness and does not allow pupils to understand the full reality of Judaism at the time. Only one textbook (Le Quintrec 2010: 108–9) adds to this aspect of Jewish life during Medieval times. Out of five documents selected to illustrate the question of Jews in Western Europe, four (three texts and one image) deal with the issue of Jews' discrimination by the Catholic Church but one – an extract of a Hebraic Bible – concerns Jewish religion itself and its symbols. In the accompanying text, an introductory paragraph explains that Jewish communities were quite few and

---

23	[Online]. Available at: http://media.eduscol.education.fr/file/lycee/77/5/LyceeGT_
Ressources_HGEC_2_Hist_08_T4ElargistMonde_148775.pdf [Accessed: 10 December 2010].

were only tolerated in exchange for a special tax; it then shows how the situation changed since the twelfth century with the Crusades and the growing perception of Jewish people as deicide. One may regret the absence of any mention of Jews in the chapter entitled 'urban societies' where Jews' integration into medieval towns and their economic, architectural, social and religious presence could have been explored. Only one textbook (Billard 2010: 116–7) devotes two pages of this chapter to non-Christian religious presence in medieval towns by presenting 'places of prayer in medieval societies'. However, whereas for Christians and Muslims the authors present photographs and plans of a cathedral and a mosque, for Jews, the selected document is picture of a rabbi reading a book. Synagogues are only mentioned in the caption accompanying the document. The absence of a photograph and plan of a synagogue is unfortunate as it may give pupils the false impression that Jews did not leave any visible architectural traces in medieval cities and prevents a fruitful comparison between the three religious temples.

Islam features even less than Judaism in the textbooks. The 'Resources' mention Islam in the chapter on 'Constantinople' and recommend that teachers highlight 'the dynamism of societies of Islam'. Following the 'Resources', textbooks discuss the Muslim conquests and underline Muslim tolerance towards Jews and Christians. One textbook goes further and devotes two pages to the beginnings of Islam but one may actually wonder whether these two pages – out of their historical context – may not give pupils the misleading impression that Islam has remained static since its beginnings. It would have been better to give more information about the Muslim faith and Muslim cultural dynamism of the time. Only one textbook, as already mentioned, deals with Muslim religious issues more directly in two pages devoted to places of prayer in medieval towns (Billard 2010: 116–7). Obviously, this is not sufficient to enable pupils to grasp the significance of Muslim religious issues in the Middle Ages and the Modern Era but it is assumed in the curriculum, 'Ressources' and textbooks alike that pupils build on knowledge acquired on this topic in the first two years of secondary schools (in classes of *sixième* and *cinquième*).

Christianity and Other Religions

What about the other religions discovered by the Europeans at the beginning of the Age of Sail when they conquered new territories? Pupils never learnt about them at school before so that reliance on assumed acquired past knowledge is not possible. The curriculum offers teachers an option between two topics: either the analysis of 'a Pre-Columbian city confronted to European conquest and colonization' – such as, suggest the 'Resources', the Aztec city of Tenochtitlan/Mexico or the Inca city of Cuzco – or 'Beijing, a forbidden city?' The 'Resources' recommend that the chosen Pre Columbian city be studied in light of the evangelization and the Christian acculturation of the Aztec and the Inca. Under the heading of the suggested study of Beijing, the 'Resources' advise teachers to show pupils how 'Confucianism and

Taoism increased the hostility of the Chinese towards merchants and the foreign world'.[24] As for the textbooks, they all rightly mention the religious motives behind the great discoveries. All of them refer to the evangelization and missions conducted in America and the Far East (China and Japan). However, the picture they give is often distorted and at times inaccurate: most of the textbooks omit to mention the resistance that these missions encountered and, in some places, their lack of success, preferring to put the emphasis upon tolerance (Bourel and Chevallier 2010: 168–9). None of the textbooks really exploits the reference in the 'Resources' to 'Confucianism and Taoism, possibly because the 'Resources' were not published until after the textbooks. Only two textbooks speak of the difficulties that the missionaries met in Asia: in China (Le Quintrec 2010: 164–5) and in Japan (Cote 2010: 180–81). A third one mentions the resistance (albeit low) to the conversion to Christianity in America, saying that the new converted Christians kept some scraps of their previous religion (Bourel and Chevallier 2010: 165).

It is thought that more information about religions other than Christianity – even if not called for by the official national curriculum nor the 'Resources' – would have helped pupils understand better the trends of evangelization and acculturation and resistance to it. None of the textbook explains in relation to China what Confucianism and Taoism are. Five textbooks mention the Aztec religion whether in the lesson only (Bourel 2010: 163), in the selected documents (Cote 2010: 175–6) or in both (Lambin 2010: 184–5). All of these textbooks highlight a unique aspect of this religion, the one which was criticized at that time and which partly justified the conquest and the evangelization: the practice of human sacrifices (and the number of its victims).[25] Human sacrifices are indeed an important aspect of the Aztec religion but this information would have its whole pedagogical value if explained in context, in light of other aspects of the religion. Only two textbooks (those which state the number of victims sacrificed) also (briefly) give an explanation by referring to the Aztec 'flowery wars'[26] (Bourel and Chevallier 2010: 164, Lambin 2010: 184).

The approach is therefore the same as for Judaism and Islam: no religion other than Christianity is studied for its own sake but is only mentioned from the Christian point of view. Even from a Christian point of view, more could be said. Most of the textbooks thus do not evoke how the conquests changed the European view of the world. All of the textbooks open the chapter on 'Renaissance' by an introductory paragraph describing the shift in Europe from a religious to a

---

24   [Online]. Available at: http://media.eduscol.education.fr/file/lycee/77/5/LyceeGT_ Ressources_HGEC_2_Hist_08_T4ElargistMonde_148775.pdf [Accessed: 10 December 2010].

25   Bourel and Chevallier (2010: 164): 'every year, nearly 20,000 prisoners were sacrificed'. See also Lambin (2010: 185 (in a caption to a document): 'For the inauguration of the Great Temple of Mexico, begun by Moctezuma 1st, thousands of victims were sacrificed in four days; some sources speak of 80,400 victims.'

26   A codified and ritualized practice in which both sides clashed in order to proceed with the capture of prisoners to sacrifice to the gods. See Hassig 1988.

humanist perspective of the world. This shift in mentalities is rightly attributed to the new intellectual movements of the Renaissance. However, the impact of the Great Discoveries, the contact with previously unknown cultures and religions could also have been mentioned. Two of the textbooks make the connection to some extent: one, with a map showing the division of the world according to Genesis (Colon 2010: 162); the other, stating that Jerusalem was no longer the 'centre of the world' and that, consequently, the whole medieval conception of the world collapsed (Lambin 2010: 182).

Conclusion

Many in France say that nothing is done in order to introduce religious issues in schools. Others say that a lot has changed in French state schools since the Joutard and the Debray reports. France certainly is not comparable to countries where a specific hour and subject is allocated to religion. However, positive steps can be noted. The study of these six history textbooks aimed at year 10 pupils (class of *seconde*) reveals a situation which is symptomatic of the present French situation.

On the one hand, a lot still needs to be done. It is important to adopt a less subjectively Christian and European point of view. Other religions and other beliefs should be studied for themselves and not merely through the eyes of Christian Europeans or through their relations with Europeans. Even if the national curriculum is centred on Europeans, there is scope for introducing non-European perspectives and for doing so properly. There is still a trend (albeit less acute than in the past) to insist on factual events. For instance, the 'Great Schism' between Orthodoxy and Catholicism is mentioned but the reasons that prompted it and the differences between the two religions are not discussed. More space should be given to beliefs, to the symbolic, so as to avoid being too superficial. More should also be said about Islam and Judaism. Since teenagers learn of these two religions mainly in the first two years of secondary school, in classes of *sixième* and *cinquième* (in lessons addressing the beginnings of each religion) they may be left with the false impression that these religions, contrary to Christianity, have remained static. They may also fail to see how Judaism and Islam are part of European history and European heritage. Without entering into the sensitive debate about the Christian roots of Europe, it would be useful to show pupils the positive interaction between Christians and non-Christians within Europe.

On the other hand, textbook authors do no longer hesitate to speak about religious issues, even if not prompted to do so by the curriculum. This testifies that the discussion of religious issues at school is now left to teachers' discretion and that religious issues are no longer a taboo problematic topic. Religious issues now appear as one dimension of society amongst others, to which they are related.

Overall therefore a real progress is to be noted, even if more could be done. Each of the six school textbooks examined contained some very good pages. The aim is not to unduly criticize textbooks because writing a textbook is not an easy task, particularly in a short period of time. Rather, it is to suggest that teachers make use of the 'Resources' alongside textbooks and keep a critical eye at all times. The national curriculum may be criticized for its brevity but this concision allows for many interpretations of which the textbooks only offer a few.

References

Billard, H. (ed.) 2010. *Histoire 2e. Programme 2010*. Paris: Magnard.

Bourel, D. and Chevallier, M. (ed.) 2010. *Histoire 2de*. Paris: Hatier.

Colon, D. (ed.) 2010. *Histoire 2e. Collection David Colon. Programme 2010*. Paris: Berlin.

Cote, S. (ed.) 2010. *Histoire 2de. Programme 2010*. Paris: Nathan.

Debray, R. 2002. *Rapport à Monsieur le Ministre de l'Éducation nationale. L'enseignement du fait religieux à l'école laïque*. Paris: Odile Jacob. [Online]. Available at: http://www.iesr.ephe.sorbonne.fr/docannexe/file/3739/debray.pdf [Accessed: 10 December 2010].

Hassig, R. 1988. *Aztec Warfare: Imperial Expansion and Political Control*. University of Oklahoma Press, 'Civilization of the American Indian Series' (2nd edition 1995).

Lambin, J.-M. (ed.) 2010. *Histoire Seconde*. Paris: Hachette Éducation.

Lavisse, E. 1954. *Histoire de France, Cours élémentaire*. Paris: Armand Colin, 48th edition.

Le Quintrec, G. (ed.) 2010. *Histoire 2de. Programme 2010*. Paris: Nathan.

Willaime, J.-P. 2007. Qu'est-ce qu'un fait religieux?, in *Enseigner les faits religieux. Quels enjeux?* Edited by D. Borne and J.-P. Willaime. Paris: Armand Colin, 37–57.

Chapter 13

Teaching Evolution, Creationism, and Intelligent Design in US Schools (With Some European Comparisons)

Eric Barendt

The teaching of evolution and competing theories concerning the origins of life and man has aroused enormous controversy in the United States of America, particularly during the 1920s and more recently from the 1960s and 1970s (Greenawalt 2005). Partly, this is a manifestation of the continuing 'cultural' wars between, on the one hand, scientists and liberal rationalists who fully accept Darwin's theory of evolution and, on the other, fundamentalist Christians who regard this theory as incompatible with the teachings of the Bible and as destructive of the view that human beings are unique, morally responsible persons created in the image of God (Dixon 2008). For many periods of United States history the conflict has remained dormant but it has revived during the past 50 years. From the 1960s, education authorities encouraged the teaching of evolution in state ('public') schools to enhance general scientific knowledge, widely thought to be deficient in the United States at a time when it was facing challenges from the Soviet Union – especially after the launch of the Sputnik rocket in 1957. In response, fundamentalists organized to promote the teaching of creationism, in particular the view that the account of the origins of life in Genesis was supported by scientific data.[1]

The conflict has an important legal, indeed a constitutional, dimension because of the interpretation of the First Amendment by the courts. That Amendment provides, inter alia: 'Congress shall make no law respecting the establishment of religion, or prohibiting the free exercise thereof'. Since some landmark decisions in the late 1940s, the Establishment Clause has been interpreted by the US Supreme Court ('the Court') to preclude not only an established church as exists in England, Scotland and a few other European countries (on which see García Oliva 2010) but also any state provision for, or promotion of, religion.[2] The states must remain neutral towards different religions as well as between religious beliefs and non-

---

1   See the judgment of Overton, Dist Judge in *McLean v. Arkansas Board of Education* 529 F Supp 1255, 1258–64 (1982).

2   The First Amendment, like other provisions in the Bill of Rights, limits state governments as well as the federal Congress and executive government (Greenawalt 2005).

religious, secular beliefs (Greenawalt 2005). As the Court put it in the first of its important rulings on the Clause, '[T]he clause ... was intended to erect 'a wall of separation' between Church and State.'[3] As the following section of this essay shows, these principles have had an enormous impact on public schools quite apart from their repercussions for the teaching of evolution, creationism, and 'Intelligent Design' ('ID').

It should be noted that, like the other provisions in the Bill of Rights (for example, the limbs of the First Amendment guaranteeing freedom of speech and of the press, and the Fourth Amendment protecting the freedom from unreasonable searches and seizures), the Establishment Clause binds the states (as well as federal government) but not private institutions and persons. In the United States, constitutional rights are only directly effective against 'state action' and so they do not limit private freedom of action (Barendt 2007). Thus, parochial church, Jewish or Muslim schools are perfectly free to teach what they like about evolution and the origins of life or to begin each day with prayers. The Establishment Clause limits only what public, or 'state', schools may do in these respects.

The Religion Clauses and Education

There are two clauses in the First Amendment concerning religion (the Establishment Clause and the Free Exercise Clause) precluding any state interference in the free exercise of religion. This second limb of the First Amendment resembles Article 9 of the European Convention on Human Rights 1950 and equivalent provisions in national constitutions in Europe. Its scope has frequently been the subject of litigation in the United States, notably in cases concerning claims to exemption from general criminal or other laws, on the ground that their application would infringe religious freedom. In a major decision, in 1990 the Court held that Native Americans could not rely on the Free Exercise guarantee to claim immunity from observance of drug laws in Oregon after they had been dismissed from employment for ingesting peyote (a hallucinogenic drug) during sacramental worship.[4] The Court has only rarely been prepared to grant religious groups exemption from what on their face appear to be religiously neutral laws. One case in which it did uphold the Free Exercise Clause in the education context is *Wisconsin v. Yoder*[5] in which the Amish community claimed exemption from the state requirement to ensure that its children attend public schools until the age of 16. The Court accepted the argument that enforcement of this requirement against one of its members, who had withdrawn his 15-year-old daughter from school after she

---

3 *Everson v. Board of Education* 330 US 1, 16 (1947). By a 5–4 majority, the Court upheld the provision of free bus transport for school children attending non-profit (including church) schools.

4 *Employment Division, Department of Human Resources v. Smith* 494 US 872 (1990).

5 406 US 205 (1972).

had completed the eighth grade, would undermine the Amish community as the community prefers to teach teenage children at home to ensure maintenance of its traditional ethos and practices. Further, the Court did not think that the exemption would amount to any endorsement or sponsorship of religion, so its grant did not infringe the Establishment Clause. But, after the ruling in the Oregon drugs case, it is doubtful whether the Court would now be sympathetic to an argument that a parent is entitled under the Free Exercise Clause to withdraw a child from attendance at science classes where evolution is taught because, say, she objected to Darwinian theory (Greenawalt 2005).

The Free Exercise limb of the First Amendment has played relatively little part in the context of public school education. By contrast, the Establishment Clause has been of enormous significance – even beyond its implications for what may be taught in science lessons. Schools may not conduct religious instruction classes if they are held on school property[6] nor may they start the day with prayers[7] or a Bible reading.[8] An attempt in Alabama to circumvent the school prayer ruling by providing for one minute's meditation or voluntary prayer at the beginning of the school day was ruled incompatible with the First Amendment in *Wallace v. Jaffree*.[9] Although, on its face, the requirement might appear to have been neutral between religious and secular beliefs it was clear that the intention of the state legislation had been to endorse religion by encouraging voluntary prayer. The Court has also struck down a state requirement to display the Ten Commandments on school classroom walls.[10]

The Court has adopted two principal tests for determining whether a state law infringes the Establishment Clause. Under the *Lemon* test,[11] it asks whether there was a valid *secular purpose* for the requirement imposed by the state, and whether its *effect* advanced or restricted religion. The state must show both that it had a valid secular purpose for imposing the requirement and that its effect was neither to promote nor to inhibit religion. Otherwise, the law will be invalid under the First Amendment. In practice, courts usually now prefer to apply what is known as the 'endorsement' test formulated by O'Connor J in her separate concurring judgment in *Wallace*. The courts will strike down any challenged provision if it is found to endorse, or provide support for, religion. It is this test which was applied by a federal District Court in Pennsylvania in the important *Dover Area School District* case (considered later in this chapter) when it invalidated a school board decision promoting the theory of ID in local public schools. But it does not seem

---

6   *McCollom v. Board of Education* 333 US 203 (1948).

7   *Engel v. Vitale* 370 US 421 (1962).

8   *Abington Township v. Schempp* 374 US 203 (1963).

9   472 US 38 (1985).

10 *Stone v. Graham* 449 US 39 (1980).

11 So named because it was formulated by the Supreme Court in *Lemon v. Kurzman* 403 US 602 (1971).

particularly important which test is used as it is virtually impossible to envisage a requirement which would satisfy one but not the other.

The Teaching of Evolution

The controversy concerning the teaching of evolution in American public schools dates back to the 1920s. A number of states proscribed it during this decade. Matters came to a head with the famous 'Monkey Trial' of 1925 in Dayton, Tennessee as fully described by Larson (1997) and briefly related by Dixon (2008). Scopes, a science teacher, was convicted for the offence of teaching a theory which denied the story of Divine Creation as taught in the Bible and taught that man had descended from animals. The case itself is best known for the confrontation between the two lawyers: William Jennings Bryan acting for the prosecution and Clarence Darrow, a leading member of the American Civil Liberties Union ('ACLU'), who represented the accused.[12] However, Scopes' appeal to the state Supreme Court was allowed on a technicality so that court did not even consider the constitutional arguments (Dixon 2008). The state law was upheld.[13] As a result of this case and pressure from fundamentalists, evolution was rarely taught in public schools until the 1960s when the United States became concerned at the low level of scientific knowledge among high school graduates (Greenawalt 2005).

The issue came before the courts again in the late 1960s when Susan Epperson (a young, liberal-minded biology teacher) challenged, with the support of the ACLU, an Arkansas statute similar in its terms to the Tennessee law that had been upheld in the *Scopes* case. Out of concern that if she taught evolution from a new biology textbook she would be dismissed from employment or even face prosecution, she applied for a declaration that the state legislation infringed the First Amendment. The Arkansas courts upheld the law as a valid exercise of the state's authority to determine the school curriculum but the US Supreme Court unanimously struck it down as unconstitutional. Seven members of the Court held that it infringed the Establishment Clause, which in their view did not allow a state to require teaching and learning tailored to the principles of any religious sect or dogma.[14] It was clear beyond doubt that fundamentalist sectarian convictions were the reason for the law's existence because it lacked any secular educational purpose. On the other hand, the Court added that studies of religion and the Bible from a literary or historical perspective, presented objectively as part of a secular programme, would not infringe the First Amendment.

---

12   The confrontation destroyed the political ambitions of Bryan, who had stood three times without success for nomination as the Democratic candidate for the US Presidency (Dixon 2008).

13   *Scopes v. State* 393 US 97 (1927).

14   Fortas J in *Epperson v. Arkansas* 393 US 97, 106–8 (1968). Two members of the Court, Black and Stewart JJ, concurred with the decision but on the ground that in their view the Arkansas law was too vague to be enforced.

The Court pointed out that the law was not neutral between religion and non-religion; rather, it attempted to blot out a particular theory concerning the origins of man because it conflicted with a literal reading of the account in Chapter I of Genesis.[15] On one reading of this particular passage in the judgment, there would have been no constitutional objection to a simple ban on any teaching in the school classroom of the origins of life and man; the state would then, it might be said, be acting neutrally between evolutionary and creationist theories by ignoring both of them. However, the better view is that such a ban would infringe the Establishment Clause because it would be motivated by religious reasons of hostility to evolutionary theory. As Greenawalt (2005) argues, even the presentation in high schools of evolution as 'merely a scientific theory' would also infringe the First Amendment by suggesting that Darwinian theory is less reliable than other scientific theories; evolution would be subject to special treatment for the reason that it runs counter to the creationist account of the origins of life.

The Teaching of Creationism

In the wake of the decision in *Epperson*, fundamentalists changed their tactics and promoted the teaching of creationism in science classes. Schools should be required to teach creationism as part of a balanced treatment of the differing accounts of the origins of life and man. Creationism assumes a variety of forms, some of them more fundamentalist than others. But all deny the common ancestry of plants and animals and assert that the complexity of life cannot be attributed to the gradual process of natural selection (Dixon 2008). Human beings and other species must have been created separately, a process which evidences the hand of a creator invariably identified as God. Some creationist theories contend that the world is only between 6,000 and 20,000 years old as suggested by the Old Testament, a view which evolutionary scientists regard as ludicrous; they estimate the age of the earth as between 4.2 and 4.8 billion years (Kitcher 1982). For them, creationism should either not be regarded as science at all or should be treated as very bad science because its claims have been refuted by the evidence from fossils and other pointers to the evolutions of forms of life over millions of years.

Balanced treatment laws have been rejected by the courts in two leading cases. In the first, a District Court in Arkansas granted an injunction to stop the enforcement of a state statute requiring public schools to provide balanced treatment of creation science and evolutionary science.[16] Interestingly, the application for the order was made by Bishops of the Episcopalian, Roman Catholic, United Methodist and African Methodist Episcopalian Churches as well as other church and Jewish leaders; opposition to creationism is not confined to secular scientists. In the court's view, the state law, based on a Model Act drafted by fundamentalist leaders, was

---

15   *Epperson*, note 14 *supra*, 109.

16   *McLean v. Arkansas Board of Education* 529 F Supp 1255 (1982).

clearly motivated by religious, not secular, purposes and so failed the first prong of the *Lemon* test that a law impinging on religion must have a valid secular purpose.[17] District Judge Overton also found that 'creation science' could not be regarded as a proper science. It could not point to a single academic journal article in support of its claims and it was dogmatic and absolutist in that it did not admit the existence of doubt or that it could be falsified on discovery of incompatible evidence. Since the *effect* of the law was therefore to advance religion, not scientific knowledge, it also infringed the second limb of the *Lemon* test.

In a few paragraphs towards the end of its judgment, the court added that evolution is not itself a 'religion' for the purposes of the Establishment Clause. This point is important. If Darwinian theory were regarded as religious in character, pupils (in practice, parents on their behalf) would have been able to claim that they were entitled to exemption from attending science (or other) classes discussing its principles. Otherwise, their Free Exercise rights would have been infringed as they would have been compelled to consider religious teaching incompatible with their own beliefs. Judge Overton was right to reject this argument; its acceptance might have had serious implications for the teaching of a variety of secular topics that fundamentalists regard as misconceived – for example, climate change or birth control.

The second case is the decision of the Court in *Edwards v. Aguillard* (1987).[18] By a 7–2 majority, it invalidated a Louisiana statute forbidding the teaching of evolution in public schools unless it was accompanied by instruction in 'creation science'. Schools were not required to teach either evolution or creation science but, if they did, they had to provide balanced teaching. The theories of evolution and creation science were defined in the law as 'scientific evidences for evolution or creation science and inferences from those evidences'. The state courts upheld challenges to this law brought by parents, Louisiana teachers, and religious leaders. The majority judgment of the Court was given by Brennan J, who found the state's argument that there was a valid secular purpose for the law a complete sham. Its stated purpose was to protect academic freedom, understood to refer to the academic freedom of teachers to teach what they wanted during science classes. But the Court was rightly unimpressed by the argument that this was the real purpose of the legislation. In the first place, there was nothing to prevent science teachers from presenting creationist theories along with Darwinian theory if they thought that both should be discussed in the classroom as credible alternative explanations for the origins of life.[19] The Act did not, in short, give teachers a flexibility they did not already have. Moreover, the legislation appeared to give

---

17   See text at note 11 *supra*.

18   482 US 578 (1987).

19   It is also unclear that school teachers have individual rights to academic freedom under the First Amendment to teach what they wish in the classroom. Constitutional academic freedom is generally understood in the United States as an institutional right for universities and perhaps schools (Barendt 2010).

preferential treatment to creationist theory because it required curriculum guides to be developed for it but not for evolution and provided research services for the former but not the latter. Even more significantly, the background documents to, and the debates on, the legislation plainly showed that its purpose was to alter the science curriculum to the advantage of creationism and to discredit the theory of evolution. That aim amounted to an endorsement of religion or showed a purpose of advancing it.

There was a strong dissent from Scalia J joined by Rehnquist CJ, then the two most conservative members of the Court. In their view, the Louisiana legislature was acting for a valid secular purpose in that it accepted the view that a body of scientific evidence supported creationism. As Greenawalt (2005) admits, that is a good point but it is rather undermined by the legislature's apparent acceptance that teachers need not provide any instruction in either creationism or evolution. An omission to teach evolution altogether could only be explained by hostility to religion.

The dissenters also thought it wrong to go behind the stated aim of the legislation to promote academic freedom within schools by presenting balanced treatment of both evolution and creationist theories. There was therefore a valid secular purpose for the legislation, though Scalia J explicitly made plain his dislike for the *Lemon* secular purpose test and the Court's jurisprudence on the Establishment Clause. For him, it did not matter whether the state legislature had also been motivated by a wish to protect the religious feelings of the children who might have been offended by the teaching of evolution – though sensitivity to that group hardly seems compatible with the state's concern for academic freedom. That freedom surely does not require teachers to put forward ideas they consider nonsensical just because they are congenial to the views of students or their parents.

In response to this decision, a few states have encouraged or required the teaching of other alternatives to evolutionary theory or discussion in science classes of how that theory does not always succeed in providing a complete explanation for the complexity of life. In a further attempt to disparage evolutionary theory, Louisiana required teachers to issue a disclaimer to the effect that its teaching was not intended to dissuade acceptance of the Biblical version of creation in Genesis. The disclaimer was held incompatible with the Establishment Clause by a Circuit Court of Appeals.[20] Kansas adopted standards in 1999 under which teachers were no longer required to teach major aspects of evolutionary theory, leaving the decision whether to teach them up to individual teachers, but these standards were apparently withdrawn following changes in the composition of the school authorities (George 2001). In 2001, the US Senate amended President George W. Bush's Education Bill to ensure that school students are told in science classes why evolutionary theory arouses fierce controversy but the amendment was subsequently retracted by the Joint House of Representatives and Senate

---

20   *Freiler v. Tangipahoa Board of Education* 185 F 3d 337 (5th Cir 1999).

Conference Committee. As Wexler (2003) explains, for once scientists and other defenders of evolutionary theory had won the educational argument.

The most common tactic of fundamentalists has been to promote the teaching of ID in science classes. To some extent they have relied on an observation in the majority judgment in *Edwards* to the effect that the decision in that case should not be taken to imply that a state could not require the teaching of scientific critiques of prevailing theories such as neo-Darwinism, the modern version of evolutionary theory.[21] On one view ID is quite different from creationism. It is not, for example, based on a religious text such as the Book of Genesis. Nor does it assert that the Earth is only a few thousand years old. Some proponents of ID may even accept the common ancestry of human beings and other forms of life (De Wolf, Meyer and De Forest 2000). Unlike creationism, ID accepts many of the conclusions of neo-Darwinism. But it argues that the complexity of life cannot be entirely explained by the process of natural selection and suggests the inevitability of ID, though proponents of ID theory for understandable reasons are reluctant to identify the designer as God.

Admitting that ID theories are in some respects quite different from creationism, the question remains whether these differences are sufficiently significant to distinguish them for the purpose of high school teaching. One court has given a legal reply to this question that is considered in the next section of this chapter. After discussion of that decision, we consider whether there is any room in principle for the teaching or discussion of ID in American public schools and whether it could even be mentioned in science classes as filling the gaps in evolutionary theory.

The Dover School District Case

The Dover Area School District Board in Pennsylvania issued a policy which required a statement to be read to 9th grade pupils (aged between 14 to 15) in biology classes.[22] The text began by saying that the state Academic Standards required pupils to study Darwin's theory and to take a standardized test, of which that theory was part. It went on:

> Because Darwin's Theory is a theory, it continues to be tested as new evidence is discovered. The Theory is not a fact. Gaps in the Theory exist for which there is no evidence ... Intelligent Design is an explanation of the origins of life that differs from Darwin's view. The reference book, *Of Pandas and People*, is available for students who might be interested in gaining an understanding of what Intelligent Design actually involves.

---

21   *Edwards*, note 18 *supra*, 593.
22   For the whole of the statement, see Nagel 2008.

The last paragraph of the statement encouraged students to keep an open mind on all theories but left discussion of 'the Origins of Life to individual students and their families.' By implication, it was not a subject for classroom discussion.

A number of parents and a member of a high school science department challenged the policy, arguing that it infringed the Establishment Clause of the First Amendment. The federal District Court accepted their arguments, ruling in a long and careful judgment that the policy amounted to an endorsement of religion contrary to the Establishment Clause.[23] It also violated the Clause under the older *Lemon* test, for it was clear from a detailed examination of the change to the School Board policy that its real purpose was to promote religion and that any secular purpose advanced for it was a sham.

Much more time was spent on an analysis of the implications of the 'endorsement' test for the School District policy. District Judge John E. Jones rejected the defendant Board's objection to use of that alternative test; he pointed out that the Court had used it in a number of cases, including its decision in *Edwards* on the teaching of creationism. Applying this test, he found that the ID policy conveyed a message of endorsement of religion both to objective observers in the position of the pupils to whom the statement was to be read and also to reasonable, objective adult observers. The judge found that ID theory was the progeny of creationism. Evidence was given by a theologian, Dr John Haught, to the effect that its arguments were essentially those of Saint Thomas Aquinas: that the complexity and richness of the world pointed to the existence of God as the intelligent designer. It was the same argument as that advanced by the Anglican clergyman, William Paley, in his classic work *Natural Theology*, first published in 1802. The complete ban on classroom discussion of the theory in conjunction with evolutionary theory conveyed a strong message of endorsement of religion. Furthermore, the statement singled out evolution as worthy of special scepticism; no equivalent statements were to be read out about mathematical theorems or the laws of physics. It therefore misrepresented the status of neo-Darwinian theory among members of the scientific community.[24] Finally, pupils were directed to a specific book, the pedigree of which showed that it was originally written as a creationist textbook as the words 'creationism' and 'creationist' in early drafts of the book were replaced by ID. Both pupils and adult observers would inevitably treat the policy as endorsing fundamental religious belief about the origins of life.

District Judge Jones also found that ID could not properly claim to be a science. It did not employ scientific methodology and departed from the scientific assumption that physical or biological phenomena have natural, rather than supernatural, causes or explanations. It neither advanced propositions which it then tested or researched nor was it supported by peer reviewed literature. Like creationism, it employed an illogical dualism: if evolutionary theory does not provide a wholly convincing explanation for some biological development, the explanation *must* lie

---

23   *Tammy Kitzmiller v. Dover Area School District* 400 F Supp 2d 707 (MD Pa 2005).
24   *Dover School District*, 727–8.

in the existence of an intelligent designer (or creator). It excluded the possibility that science might eventually answer the questions left open in the present state of scientific knowledge. The *Dover School District* decision therefore repeats for ID theory many of the arguments made by the District Court in the earlier Arkansas case with regard to creationism: it is a religious, not a scientific, theory of the origins of life, which may not be taught in science classes without infringing the First Amendment.

Is there any Room for Discussing ID in State Schools?

There are a number of questions here. One is whether ID theories are properly characterized as 'religious' so that their teaching amounts to an infringement of the Establishment Clause as found by the District Court in the *Dover School District* case. We have seen that ID theories are not identical to creationism, in that they do not on their face refer, say, to the first book of Genesis and they may accept that the Earth is several billion years old. Beckwith (2003) has argued that ID is neither a religion with comprehensive creeds or dogma nor an institutional church with a distinctive liturgy or other forms of worship. This point has some merit. ID would probably not have any place in the curriculum of a religious seminary committed to the teaching of theology. But Wexler (2006) has rightly argued that the criteria suggested by Beckwith are irrelevant. The question is whether ID theories are advanced in support of religious belief or whether they are put forward for a proper secular purpose. On that test, it is clear that ID theories 'sound in religion'.[25] That is how they would be understood by reasonable pupils and observers conversant with the background to their introduction as legislation or high school policy and with the relevant debates in the state legislature or at school board meetings.

That does not mean, however, that there is no room at all for discussion of ID (or, for that matter, creationist) theories in state schools. They could, for example, be usefully discussed in general civics or philosophy classes in the course of an examination of the political controversy surrounding the teaching of evolution or of the philosophical underpinnings of the sciences in which the limits of empirical knowledge might be explored. Wexler (2002) and Greenawalt (2005) have both argued that public schools should teach more *about* religion, a phenomenon of enormous importance in the United States (as well as in other liberal societies) whether or not its claims to state fundamental truths are accepted. Indeed, the study of comparative religion has perhaps never been as important as it is today; yet US schools apparently devote relatively little time to it (Wexler 2002, Greenawalt 2005). Moreover, there is no constitutional objection to teaching about religion in public schools, provided that it is not done in a manner which amounts to its endorsement. The Court expressly stated in *Schempp* that it is permissible to

---

25   Wexler 2006: 68.

discuss the Bible and religious beliefs in the classroom.[26] Indeed, in his concurring opinion in that case Brennan J added that meaningful teaching of many subjects in the humanities and social sciences would be incomplete without some treatment of religion.[27]

Moreover, on the *Lemon* test there is clearly a valid secular purpose for teaching about religion in that it informs students about matters of fundamental importance to many of their contemporaries and should promote a better understanding of the beliefs and creeds of minorities within the community and by people in other countries. What is wrong, and constitutionally invalid, is teaching in support of religious beliefs in science classes because that does amount to an endorsement of religion and so infringes the Establishment Clause of the First Amendment.

Thomas Nagel's argument

In a recent article, the distinguished political and moral philosopher (and self-avowed atheist) Thomas Nagel (2008) has made an impressive argument for permitting at least some discussion of ID theory in public schools, even in biology classes. Nagel regards the theory not as an argument for the existence of God but a claim about what to believe about biological evolution: 'if one independently holds a belief in God that is consistent both with the empirical facts about nature that have been established by observation, and with the acceptance of general standards of scientific evidence.'[28] Nagel challenges the assumption commonly shared by scientists (and many others) that science can never provide evidence for something which cannot be explained by science itself. It is not, in his view, inconceivable that there could be scientific arguments against Darwinian theory. The rejection of ID as a possible explanation for phenomena which are not (as yet) fully explained by that theory is not itself based on science but rather rests on the assumption that supernatural intervention in the world is impossible. Now, that assumption may be a perfectly reasonable one (it is held by atheists and many agnostics) but it is a belief about a religious question – not a scientific conclusion which is supported by empirical evidence.

Nagel therefore distinguishes ID theory from creationism. While empirical evidence precludes any discussion of the latter in a biology class, the same cannot be said of ID. The decision to either include it in such a class or to exclude it altogether rests on religious assumptions, not on scientific evidence. The best position, according to Nagel, would be for relevant school authorities to admit that the empirical evidence (at least for the time being) allows for different explanations of biological phenomena, explanations which are dependent on religious beliefs held for reasons independent of science. That position would seem to allow

---

26   See Justice Clark for the Court in *Abington Township v. Schempp*, note 8 *supra*, 225.

27   *Schempp*, note 8 *supra*, 300.

28   Nagel 2008: 188.

the possibility of some mention of ID theory in a biology class as one possible explanation for the order and complexity of life, as yet unexplained by evolutionary theory. This is also Greenawalt's conclusion (2005), though he advocates caution in this area: 'Science teachers should *not* get far into the question of whether any as yet undiscovered principles of evolution … are likely to have proceeded from a creative intelligence.'[29] Otherwise, students with religious convictions may infer far too much from the gaps in current evolutionary theory.

Nagel's argument is important. It is shared by other philosophers like John Cottingham (2009) who argue, that science does not, and perhaps cannot, preclude the possibility of divine intervention. It is possible that we live in a totally closed universe without any supernatural realm or intervention but that cannot be established by science itself. All that science can do is to narrow the range of phenomena for which no natural explanation has been established and for which divine intervention (or ID) remains a possible cause. ID perhaps has something in common with miraculous recoveries from life threatening conditions, which cannot be easily explained by the present state of medical knowledge; if a natural explanation cannot be provided, the intervention of a saint may be invoked to explain an otherwise inexplicable recovery to full health. So ID theories could be used to fill the gaps in evolutionary theory.

But it is doubtful whether an acceptance of Nagel's theory would have led to a different result in the *Dover School District* case. School pupils were referred to a book (*'Of Pandas and People'*) which they were invited to read if they were interested in understanding ID theory. But it was not to be discussed in the classroom where the limits of that theory might have been explained by the biology teacher and in which evolutionary theory could have been defended. Moreover, the clear implication of the text read to pupils was that evolution is special in that it is 'not a fact'. Evolution, it seems, was singled out because it is considered uniquely threatening to fundamental religious beliefs. The Dover Area policy went far beyond the limited mention of ID as a possible explanation for gaps and uncertainties in evolutionary theory which the arguments made by Nagel and Greenawalt allow. The constitutional question in the United States is whether teaching or other reference to ID (or creationism) amounts to an endorsement of religion. The Dover Area policy did amount to such an endorsement so the District Court was right to strike it down. But Nagel's argument shows that a different, more modest, reference to ID (even in the science classroom) need not infringe the First Amendment.

Are these Difficulties Unique to the United States?

A final question is whether the difficulties explored in this essay are unique to the United States of America. There have been reports that creationists have attempted

---

29   Greenawalt 2005: 115.

with some success to infiltrate UK science teaching; in particular, a state funded school academy, the Emmanuel College, was established in Gateshead in 2002 with, among its aims, the goal of teaching creation science in biology classes (Williams 2008). These moves have led to the establishment by Richard Dawkins (the well-known biologist and author of *The God Delusion*) of a foundation to stop the teaching of creation science in science classes. He has been supported not only by other leading scientists such as Professor Steve Jones but also by Richard Harries, the former Bishop of Oxford and a noted liberal theologian (Dawkins 2006). So the evolution v. creationism/ID conflict has, to some extent, been replayed in the United Kingdom.

But there are at least two reasons to believe that any conflicts of this kind will be much more modest in the UK and in other European countries than those which have broken out periodically in the United States. The first is the constitutional background. European constitutions do not generally contain clauses similar to the Establishment Clause of the First Amendment (but see García Oliva 2010). Freedom of faith, conscience and religion may be guaranteed (for example, Basic Law of Germany, Article 4) and the discriminatory treatment of individuals on the basis of their religious or other opinions may be proscribed (Basic Law of Germany, Article 3). However, these provisions do not forbid the teaching of creation science (or evolution, for that matter) which is left to the judgment of the relevant state authorities. Indeed, Article 7 of the Basic Law provides for religious instruction in state schools in accordance with the beliefs of the particular community. In England, there is a legal requirement for public schools to provide for collective worship[30] to which there is no constitutional objection (Ahdar and Leigh 2005).

Thus, the conflict would not assume a legal or constitutional dimension in the United Kingdom, Germany, and presumably most other European jurisdictions as it has in the United States. Indeed, it is far from certain that the constitutional questions would now be resolved in the same way as they were by the Court in its landmark ruling in *Edwards v. Aiguillard* discussed in this chapter.[31] The character of the Court has changed radically over the last 20 years so that Scalia J, who dissented in *Edwards*, might conceivably be able to lead a majority for a more limited view of the scope of the Establishment Clause. It is a much more conservative Court, though that does not mean of course it would necessarily diverge from a jurisprudence on this aspect of the First Amendment that has been consistent since the end of the 1940s.

The second reason for believing that conflicts between scientists and creationists in Europe will be much more moderate than they have been in the United States is a matter of sociology. Put simply, there are very few fundamentalists in the UK and other European countries and they have relatively little political influence on educational policy. Despite the formal separation of Church and State in the United States, religious belief and observance is much more significant there than

---

30   *Schools Standards and Framework Act 1998*, s.70.
31   Note 18 *supra*.

it is in any major European country; it is, for example, unlikely that a candidate for a state Governorship, let alone the Presidency, could admit to being agnostic while English politicians now feel no inhibitions about revealing their lack of religious belief.[32] So cultural clashes between religious believers (in particular, fundamentalists) on the one hand and empirical scientists on the other have been much fiercer in the US than they are likely to be on this side of the Atlantic. That means, perhaps, that the US experience is most unlikely to be reproduced in the same way in the United Kingdom or in other European countries. But it does not mean that this experience has nothing to tell us about the complex interplay of religion, education and the law.

References

Ahdar, R, and Leigh, I. 2005. *Religious Freedom in the Liberal State*. Oxford: Oxford University Press.

Barendt, E. 2007. State action, constitutional rights and private actors, in *Human Rights and the Private Sphere*, edited by D. Oliver and J. Fedtke. Abingdon: Routledge-Cavendish, 399–426.

Barendt, E. 2010. *Academic Freedom and the Law*. Oxford: Hart Publishing.

Beckwith, F. 2003. *Law, Darwinism, and Public Education: The Establishment Clause and the Challenge of Intelligent Design*. Lanham, Maryland: Rowman and Littlefield.

Cottingham, J. 2009. *Why Believe?* London: Continuum.

Dawkins, R. 2006. *The God Delusion*. London: Bantam Press.

De Wolf, D.K., Meyer, S.C, and De Forest, M.E. 2000. Teaching the origins controversy: science, religion, or speech. *Utah Law Review* (1), 39–110.

Dixon, T. 2008. *Science and Religion: A Very Short introduction*. Oxford: Oxford University Press.

García Oliva, J. 2010. Church, state and establishment in the United Kingdom: anachronism or idiosyncrasy? *Public Law* (3), 482–504.

George, M. 2001. Comment: and then God created Kansas? The evolution/ creationism debate in American public schools. *University of Pennsylvania Law Review* 149(3), 843–72.

Greenawalt, K. 2005. *Does God Belong to Public Schools?* Princeton NJ: Princeton University Press.

Kitcher, P. 1982. *Abusing Science: The Case Against Creationism*. Cambridge MA: MIT Press.

Larson, E.J. 1997. *Summer for the Gods: The Scopes Trial and America's Continuing Debate over Science and Religion*. New York: Basic Books.

---

32   At the time of writing (2010), the leaders of the Labour Party (Ed Miliband) and of the Liberal Democrat Party (Nick Clegg) are self-declared agnostics.

Nagel, T. 2008. Public education and intelligent design. *Philosophy and Public Affairs* 36(2), 187–205.

Paley, W. 2006. Natural theology, or evidence of the existence and attributes of the deity, collected from the appearance of nature, edited by M.D. Eddy and D. Knight. Oxford: Oxford University Press.

Wexler, J.D. 2002. Preparing for the clothed public square: teaching about religion, civic education, and the constitution. *William and Mary Law Review* 43(3), 1159–1263.

Wexler, J.D. 2003. Darwin, design, and disestablishment: teaching the evolution controversy in public schools. *Vanderbilt Law Review* 56(3), 751–858.

Wexler, J.D. 2006. Intelligent design and the First Amendment; a response. *Washington University Law Review* 84, 63–98.

Williams, J.D. 2008. Creationist teaching in school science; a UK perspective. Evolution: education and outreach. (1) 87–95. Available at: http://www.springerlink.com/content/4103235r16308112/fulltext.html [Accessed: 2 December 2010].

Chapter 14

Beating People is Wrong: *Campbell and Cosans*, *Williamson* and their Aftermath

Frank Cranmer[1]

In 1982 two Scottish mothers, Grace Campbell and Jean Cosans, objected successfully to the teachers at their children's schools threatening to belt their children with a tawse: a heavy leather strap whose continued use for corporal punishment had been authorized, though only as a last resort, by the code of practice of the Scottish Liaison Committee on Educational Matters (Scottish Office 1968). In *Campbell and Cosans*[2] the European Court of Human Rights ('ECtHR') decided by six votes to one – Evans J, the United Kingdom judge, dissenting – that, in permitting Scottish teachers to use the tawse, the UK had failed to respect the applicants' 'philosophical convictions' about the use of corporal punishment within their children's education contrary to their right to education as guaranteed by Article 2 of Protocol 1 of the European Convention on Human Rights 1950 ('ECHR'). Crucially, at paragraph 36 of its judgment the Court set out the test against which beliefs and convictions are to be judged: the Convention protects 'views that attain a certain level of cogency, seriousness, cohesion and importance'.[3]

Corporal punishment in maintained schools was subsequently abolished in England and Scotland by sections 47 and 48 of the *Education (No. 2) Act 1986* and in Northern Ireland by the *Education (Corporal Punishment) (Northern Ireland) Order 1987*. The ban also applied to children attending independent schools that received public money – for instance, under the Assisted Places Scheme – but not to children who were privately funded and who were attending schools that were

---

1   I must thank Russell Sandberg both for his perceptive comments on an early version of this chapter and for permitting me to draw upon a draft of Chapter 5 of his book (Sandberg 2011 – which at the time of writing was awaiting publication) and Norman Doe for his helpful observations on *McFarlane*. An early version of the *McFarlane* material was presented to the June 2010 Humanist Philosophers' Conference held under the auspices of the British Humanist Association and benefited greatly from the subsequent discussion.

2   *Campbell and Cosans v. United Kingdom* (1982) 4 EHRR 293 Series A no. 48.

3   Subsequently, in *Costello-Roberts v. United Kingdom* (1993) 19 EHRR 112, the Court held that a 7-year-old boy who had been 'slippered' at a private boarding-school had not suffered degrading punishment contrary to Article 3 ECHR nor interference with private and family lifecontrary to Article 8 – but the issue of compliance with Article 2 of Protocol 1 was not raised.

independent both of the state system and of public funding. In England the ban was made general by section 131 of the *School Standards and Framework Act 1998*, which inserted a new section 548 ('no right to give corporal punishment') into the *Education Act 1996*. Corporal punishment was finally abolished in Scotland by section 16 of the *Standards in Scotland's Schools etc. Act 2000* and in Northern Ireland by article 36 of the *Education and Libraries (Northern Ireland) Order 2003*.[4]

When in 1999 the issue of corporal punishment *within the family* was tested at Strasbourg in *A*[5] it was held that caning a 9-year-old boy severely enough to cause bruising violated the prohibition on degrading treatment under Article 3 of the ECHR. Although the Department of Health subsequently carried out a consultation (2000) on the issue, officials decided not to legislate because they believed that the common law defence of 'reasonable chastisement' complied with Article 3 (Parsons 2007: 311).

Williamson in the Court of Appeal

Not everyone agreed with the outcome of *Campbell and Cosans*[6] and, in a sense, *Williamson* was *Campbell and Cosans* in reverse. The claimants were Evangelical Christian parents and teachers at four independent schools who argued that corporal punishment, far from being cruel and degrading, was an essential element of their faith. They cited biblical passages such as Proverbs 13:24: 'He who spares the rod hates his son, but he who loves him is diligent to discipline him'.[7] Before the Court of Appeal in *Williamson*[8] they contended that the statutory ban contravened

---

4   Perhaps surprisingly, though Regulation 5 of the *Day Care and Child Minding (National Standards) (England) Regulations 2003* subsequently banned childminders in England from smacking children, the prohibition was not applied to those teaching in part-time educational settings and out-of-hours faith schools. On 30 March 2010, following recommendations from its Chief Adviser on Child Safety, Sir Roger Singleton, the then Government announced that it intended to ban physical punishment of children in England in any form of tuition or care outside the family. At the time of writing it remained to be seen whether or not the Coalition Government elected in May 2010 would take this forward, especially in light of the serious allegations about beatings in out-of-hours Muslim religious classes raised in a BBC radio programme, *File on 4*, on 23 October 2011 and the subsequent press comment (Wardrop 2011).

5   *A v. United Kingdom* (1999) 27 EHHR 611.

6   In the wake of *A v. United Kingdom* Paul Diamond (1999: 51) argued that corporal punishment might not be contrary to the ECHR *in principle*, suggesting that Article 2 of Protocol 1 might '… give rise to an obligation on the State to respect religious and philosophical views in favour of corporal punishment'.

7   New International Version 1984.

8   *R v. Secretary of State for Education and Employment & Ors ex parte Williamson & Ors* [2002] EWCA Civ 1926, [2003] QB 1300 on appeal from *Williamson v. Secretary of*

parents' rights to freedom of thought, conscience and religion under Article 9 ECHR to administer what they described as 'loving corporal correction' to their children in accordance with their religious beliefs.

That right, they argued, was a right at common law. It had been acknowledged, for example, by Lord Mustill in *Brown*[9] that:

> [i]t is probably still the position at common law that a parent or someone to whom the parent has delegated authority may inflict physical hurt on his or her child, provided that it does not go too far and is for the purpose of correction and not the gratification of passion or rage.

Their contention was that the prohibition in section 548(1) of the *Education Act 1996*, as amended, applied only to teachers *as teachers* and had not overridden the common law rights of parents to delegate to their children's teachers the authority to administer corporal punishment on their behalf. The claimants lost both at first instance and in the Court of Appeal.

In her detailed analysis of *Williamson*, Sylvie Langlaude (2006: 340) points out that the Court of Appeal decided the case on narrow Article 9(1) grounds. Buxton LJ concluded (Judgment: para. 19) that neither teachers nor parents were manifesting beliefs 'in the sense of that expression as it is used in Article 9(1) of the Convention' and concluded that Article 9 was not, therefore, engaged. Rix LJ was prepared to accept that a complete ban on corporal punishment interfered with the appellant parents' right to manifest their beliefs and would have to be justified under Article 9(2); however, he concluded (Judgment: para. 206) that, on the evidence, section 548 had not '... materially interfered with a Christian scheme of corporal punishment in school in circumstances where the actual application of the punishment can be performed by the parents themselves'. In the view of Arden LJ, the beliefs of the parents did not require that they should send their children to any particular school nor, save in the case of one school in Liverpool, that chastisement should be carried out *by teachers*. Therefore, section 548 of the *Education Act 1996* as amended did not infringe their freedom to manifest under Article 9. As to the appellant teachers, Arden LJ concluded (Judgment: para. 212) that their rights to manifest could not have been violated because they could not have any better rights than the parents had.

State for Education & Employment [2001] EWHC Admin 960, [2002] ELR 214.
  9   *R v. Brown* [1994] 1 AC 212, 266.

Williamson in the House of Lords

On appeal,[10] the House of Lords agreed that the applicants' rights under Article 9 had been interfered with. Lord Nicholls of Birkenhead, for example, (Judgment: para. 40) rejected the Secretary of State's submission that section 548 still gave the parents several adequate alternative courses of action: that they could '... attend school on request and themselves administer the corporal punishment to the child; or ... administer the desired corporal punishment when the child comes home after school; or, if the need for immediate punishment is part of the claimants' beliefs, ... educate their children at home'. The Secretary of State's proposed solutions were both unrealistic and significantly different from the administration of corporal punishment by teachers; moreover, Lord Nicholls (Judgment: para. 41) could see no reason to suppose that, in general, the claimant parents had either the personal skills to educate their children at home or the financial means to employ home tutors. Nevertheless, he concluded (Judgment: paras 48–9) that the interference with their right to manifest was justified under Article 9(2) since it was 'prescribed by primary legislation in clear terms', it was necessary in a democratic society to protect the rights and freedoms of others and it had the legitimate aim of protecting children as a vulnerable group and promoting their well-being. Moreover, he concluded (Judgment: paras 9 and 13) that it was not necessary to examine the claim that the teachers should be able to stand in the place of the parents and administer physical punishment on their behalf. Since the purpose of the ban was to prohibit the use of corporal punishment by all teachers in all schools, parents could not merely opt in or out of the ban at will.

Possibly because Baroness Hale of Richmond had formerly been a member of the interdepartmental review of childcare law (whose report of 1985 had led to the *Children Act 1989*), the Law Commissioner in charge of family law reform and a judge in the Family Division, she began from the position that the case was as much about the rights of the child as the rights of the parents and drew a sharp distinction between belief and manifestation (Judgment: para. 71). She conceded (Judgment: para. 77) that the rightness or wrongness of corporal punishment were '... essentially moral beliefs, although they may be underpinned with other beliefs about what works best in bringing up children. Both are entitled to respect'. However, she concluded (Judgment: para. 78) that '[r]espect is one thing. Allowing them to be practised is another'.

She also expressed concern (Judgment: para. 74) that earlier argument had largely ignored the issue of justification: in the High Court, 'the possible justification for the ban was dismissed in a single paragraph ... In the Court of Appeal it did not feature at all'. Article 37 of the United Nations Convention on the Rights of the Child provides, inter alia, that 'States Parties shall ensure that ...

---

10   *Williamson & Ors, R (on the application of) v. Secretary of State for Education and Employment & Ors* [2005] UKHL 15.

[n]o child shall be subjected to torture or other cruel, inhuman or degrading treatment or punishment ...' and Article 19.1 provides that signatories should:

> ... take all appropriate legislative, administrative, social and educational measures to protect the child from all forms of physical or mental violence, injury or abuse, neglect or negligent treatment, maltreatment or exploitation, including sexual abuse, while in the care of parent(s), legal guardian(s) or any other person who has the care of the child.

Lady Hale concluded (Judgment: para. 82) that the ultimate justification for the ban was that it conformed with the UN Convention – not least because the UN Committee on the Rights of the Child had already commented adversely on the UK's general approach to compliance with the Convention.

It should be said that not everyone agrees with Lady Hale on this point. Rosalind English (2005) comments:

> ... opinions on corporal punishment are strong and irreconcilable, and there is no reason to believe that the debate would have been resolved in the House of Lords any more decisively than anywhere else, as is amply demonstrated by [Lady Hale's] extensive citations from high-sounding but unhelpful sources like UN Committee and Council of Europe Recommendations, government and Commission of Inquiry reports and conclusions of various Working Groups, all of which add much heat but no light to this controversial matter.

Belief and Manifestation

Although the issue in *Williamson* was fairly narrow, its importance goes far beyond the simple question of whether or not the ECHR gave parents the right to delegate to teachers the power to beat their children. In addition, their Lordships looked more generally at the application of Article 9 and the wider issue of the degree of toleration that should be extended to religious belief. At paragraphs 22 and 23 of his Judgment, Lord Nicholls of Birkenhead put the test like this:

> [I]t is not for the court to embark on an inquiry into the asserted belief and judge its 'validity' by some objective standard such as the source material upon which the claimant founds his belief or the orthodox teaching of the religion in question or the extent to which the claimant's belief conforms to or differs from the views of others professing the same religion. Freedom of religion protects the subjective belief of an individual ... [R]eligious belief is intensely personal and can easily vary from one individual to another. Each individual is at liberty to hold his own religious beliefs, however irrational or inconsistent they may seem to some, however surprising. Everyone, therefore, is entitled to hold whatever beliefs he wishes. But when questions of 'manifestation' arise, as

they usually do in this type of case, a belief must satisfy some modest, objective minimum requirements ... Manifestation of a religious belief, for instance, which involved subjecting others to torture or inhuman punishment, would not qualify for protection.

At paragraph 57 Lord Walker of Gestingthorpe doubted whether it was right except in extreme cases for the courts to impose an evaluative filter at the stage of identifying whether or not there was a belief, '... especially when religious beliefs are involved' on the grounds that to do so would to take the Court beyond its legitimate role. Moreover, though he agreed (Judgment: para. 60) that the appeal should be dismissed, in doing so he expressed serious doubts about the practical feasibility of the test in *Campbell and Cosans*:

> The court is not equipped to weigh the cogency, seriousness and coherence
> of theological doctrines. ... Moreover, the requirement that an opinion should
> be 'worthy of respect in a democratic society' begs too many questions ...
> [I]n matters of human rights the court should not show liberal tolerance only to
> tolerant liberals.

Furthermore, in order to qualify for protection a particular manifestation would normally have to be something actually enjoined by the doctrines and practice of the religion in question rather than a matter merely of pious opinion or personal devotion.

Lord Walker also drew a crucial distinction between 'manifestation' and 'motivation' (Judgment: paras 62–3);

> [m]ost religions require or encourage communal acts of worship of various sorts,
> preaching, public professions of faith and practices and observances of various
> sorts (including habits of dress and diet). There will usually be a central core of
> required belief and observance and relatively peripheral matters observed by
> only the most devout. These can all be called manifestations of a religious belief.
> ... not every act which is in some way motivated or inspired by religious belief
> is to be regarded as the manifestation of religious belief.

That, in a nutshell, is the problem: where to draw the line. Lord Walker seemed to be acutely aware of this when he cited with approval (Judgment: para. 67) the conclusion of Sachs J in *Christian Education South Africa*[11] – a case on almost identical facts – that '... the State should, wherever reasonably possible, seek to avoid putting believers to extremely painful and intensely burdensome choices of either being true to their faith or else respectful of the law'. In the passages cited above, his Lordship was distinguishing, in effect, between the *forum internum* and

---

11   *Christian Education South Africa v. Minister of Education* [2000] ZACC 11, 2000
(4) SA 757, 2000 (10) BCLR 1051.

the *forum externum* – and Langlaude (2006: 341) contrasts his liberal approach with that of Strasbourg in *Refah Partisi*[12] and *Leyla Şahin*.[13]

Lord Nicholls took a similar position, pointing out (Judgment: para. 31) that in *Arrowsmith*,[14] even though Pat Arrowsmith had been motivated by her well-known pacifist views when she had handed out leaflets to soldiers urging them to decline service in Northern Ireland, neither the content of the leaflets nor the act of distributing them had actually *expressed* those pacifist views – so in handing them out she had not, in fact, been 'manifesting' her pacifism. Lord Nicholls noted (Judgment: paras 32–3) that if 'the belief takes the form of a perceived obligation to act in a specific way then, in principle, doing that act pursuant to that belief is itself a manifestation of that belief in practice' since 'in such cases the act is "intimately linked" to the belief'. However, that did not mean 'that a perceived obligation is a prerequisite to manifestation of a belief in practice'. Moreover, he pointed out (Judgment: para. 38) that '[w]hat constitutes interference depends on all the circumstances of the case, including the extent to which in the circumstances an individual can reasonably expect to be at liberty to manifest his beliefs in practice'.

In *Kalaç*[15] a judge-advocate in the Turkish Air Force had been compulsorily retired on the grounds of his adherence to a fundamentalist sect, membership of which was regarded as contrary to the constitutional principle of secularism. It was held that his rights under Article 9 had not been violated since, in choosing to join the Air Force, he had voluntarily accepted a code of military discipline that involved restrictions on his freedom which did not apply to civilians. The ECtHR declared (Judgment: para. 38) that 'Article 9 does not protect every act motivated or inspired by a religion or belief'. Moreover, in exercising his freedom to manifest his religion an individual may need to take his specific situation into account': the so-called 'specific situation rule'. However, Lord Nicholls concluded (Judgment: para. 39) that the specific situation rule could not apply to the facts in *Williamson* since there was 'no comparable special feature affecting the position of the claimant parents'.

Given that both Lord Nicholls and Lord Walker seemed to be supporting a somewhat reformulated version of the causative relationship between belief and manifestation, what can we deduce from their opinions in particular? Their propositions seem to be something along the following lines:

1. people are entitled to hold whatever beliefs they wish; but
2. not every act motivated or inspired by religion or belief is protected by Article 9; and
3. the freedom to manifest may depend on the specific situation of the individual.

---

12   *Refah Partisi (The Welfare Party) & Ors v. Turkey* [2003] (Application nos 41340/98, 41342/98, 41343/98, 41344/98).

13   *Leyla Şahin v. Turkey* [2005] (Application no. 44774/98).

14   *Arrowsmith v. United Kingdom* [1978] ECHR 7.

15   *Kalaç v. Turkey* (1997) 27 EHRR 552, 564.

However:

4. the courts are not equipped to weigh the cogency, seriousness and coherence of theological doctrines; and
5. they will not attempt to judge the 'validity' of an asserted belief by standards such as its source material or the extent to which other adherents hold the same belief; but
6. when questions of 'manifestation' arise, in order to be protected a belief must satisfy some modest, objective minimum requirements.

Taken together, the last three points seem slightly at odds with each other: in effect, 'we are not really competent to engage with matters of theology or the validity of a belief but sometimes, in order to decide whether or not a particular manifestation is to be protected, we may well have to do exactly that'.

Williamson, its context and its aftermath

Williamson was decided during a period when the courts were already becoming increasingly reluctant to involve themselves in deciding what was or what was not a 'religion or belief' for the purposes of Article 9. Rastafarianism is a case in point, particularly concerning the ritual use of cannabis. Both the cannabis cases themselves (including those that predate the *Human Rights Act 1998*) and the wider issues surrounding them have been the subject of extensive recent analysis by Gibson (2010).

In *Taylor*,[16] an appeal by a Rastafarian against a conviction for possessing cannabis with intent to supply, the prosecution had conceded in the Crown Court that Rastafarianism was a religion and that all the cannabis was for Rastafarian religious purposes but the trial judge had nevertheless concluded that the *Misuse of Drugs Act 1971* could not be read as incorporating a Rastafarian religious defence under Articles 8 or 9. In the Court of Appeal, the Vice-President (Rose LJ) rejected the argument that the case engaged Article 9 on the facts: 'Even if (which we doubt, but for present purposes it is unnecessary to decide) simple possession of cannabis by a Rastafarian for religious purposes in a private place raises different considerations, that is not this case' (Judgment: para. 17). Parliament had provided a religious defence in certain circumstances to the charge of carrying a bladed weapon[17] but had not done so for the possession and use of cannabis. Similarly, in *Andrews*[18] a claim by a Rastafarian that his conviction for importing cannabis

---

16   *R v. Taylor* [2001] EWCA Crim 2263.

17   *Criminal Justice Act 1988*, s.139(5)(b). *The Carrying of Knives etc. (Scotland) Act 1993* s.1(5), consolidated as s.49(5)(b) *Criminal Law (Consolidation) (Scotland) Act 1995*, made parallel provision.

18   *R v. Andrews* [2004] EWCA Crim 947.

violated his Article 9 rights and that the *Customs and Excise Management Act 1979* was incompatible with the ECHR was dismissed, applying *Taylor*.

Neither in *Taylor* nor in *Andrews* did the courts apply a restrictive definition of 'religion' as a filtering device; instead, they left the question of definition on one side, relying on the 'prescribed by law' limitations under Article 9(2). More radically, in *Joseph*[19](in which a Rastafarian appealed successfully against a Crown Court conviction for refusing to supply a blood sample for reasons of religion and offering a urine sample instead) Woolf CJ simply refused to take 'any view as to whether Rastafarianism is or is not a religion'(Judgment: para. 13) on the ground that the answer to that question was not necessary for the determination of the appeal.

At the same time, the courts were also displaying an increasing lack of enthusiasm for determining the religious status of individuals because to do so would tend to engage doctrinal matters beyond their professional and technical competence. In *Blake*[20] the claimant had been consecrated as a bishop in the 'Province for Open Episcopal Ministry' and contended that two articles in the *Daily Mail* impugning his episcopal status were defamatory. Gray J stayed the action on the grounds that, were it to proceed, the court would be drawn into what he described (Judgment: para. 33) as 'substantive doctrinal questions including the canon law of the catholic apostolic churches [and] questions of ecclesiastical procedure' which were not justiciable.

The judgment of the House of Lords in *Williamson*, therefore, reflected the general attitude of the lower courts to questions of belief and manifestation. Since then, the courts' reluctance to become involved in matters of religion has become, if anything, even more marked. Lord Hope began his judgment in the *JFS* case[21]by stating that it '… has long been understood that it is not the business of the courts to intervene in matters of religion' (Judgment: para. 157) and cited in support of that contention Simon Brown J's *dicta* in *Wachmann*.[22]

Similarly, in *Eastern Media Group*[23] Eady J followed the same course as that taken by Gray J in *Blake* by staying a libel action on the grounds that the respondent's suggestion that the claimant was a religious impostor could only be determined by examining the doctrines of Sikhism. To do so, said his Lordship (Judgment: para. 5), would be contrary to:

> … the well known principle of English law … that the courts will not attempt to rule upon doctrinal issues or intervene in the regulation or governance of

19   *Joseph v. DPP*[2003] EWHC 3078 (Admin).

20   *Blake v. Associated Newspapers Ltd* [2003] EWHC (QB).

21   *E, R (on the application of) v. Governing Body of JFS & Anor* [2009] UKSC 15.

22   *R v. Chief Rabbi of the United Hebrew Congregations of Great Britain and the Commonwealth, ex parte Wachmann* [1992] 1 WLR 1036, 1042–3.

23   *HH Sant Baba Jeet Singh Ji Maharaj v. Eastern Media Group & Anor* [2010] EWHC 1294 (QB).

religious groups. That is partly because the courts are secular and stand back from religious issues while according respect to the rights of those who are adherents or worshippers in any such grouping. It is also partly because such disputes as arise between the followers of any given religious faith are often likely to involve doctrines or beliefs which do not readily lend themselves to the sort of resolution which is the normal function of a judicial tribunal. They may involve questions of faith or doctrinal opinion which cannot be finally determined by the methodology regularly brought to bear on conflicts of factual and expert evidence. Thus it can be seen to be partly a matter of a self-denying ordinance ... and partly a question of simply recognizing the natural and inevitable limitations upon the judicial function.

Sir Charles Gray did the same in *Shergill*,[24] a case on similar facts to those of *Eastern Media Group*.

That said, however, the courts have not always been entirely comfortable either with the specific situation rule or with the non-interventionist approach to questions of manifestation. In *Copsey*,[25] an unfair dismissal claim brought by an employee obliged to work on Sundays contrary to his religious convictions, the Court of Appeal applied the specific situation rule but with some reluctance. In finding for the employers, Mummery LJ commented that the Strasbourg rulings were 'repeated assertions unsupported by the evidence or reasoning that would normally accompany a judicial ruling' and were 'difficult to square with the supposed fundamental character of the rights' (Judgment: paras 35–6). Had it not been for those rulings, he 'would have regarded this as a case of material interference with Mr Copsey's Article 9 rights'.

Disputes over religious dress have depended largely on the facts in the instant case.[26] In *Begum*,[27] in which Ms Begum, a Muslim, had been refused permission to wear the *jilbab* coat at school, the House of Lords held unanimously on the facts that there had been no interference with her right to manifest. At para. 50 of his opinion Lord Hoffmann cited with approval the *obiter dicta* of Lord Nicholls at paragraphs 15–19 and 38 of *Williamson* as to the fundamental importance of the right to manifest and what constituted interference with that right but concluded that Ms Begum's rights were not infringed '... because there was nothing to stop her from going to a school where her religion did not require a *jilbab* or where she was allowed to wear one. Article 9 does not require that one should be allowed to manifest one's religion at any time and place of one's own choosing'. In so saying, Lord Hoffmann seems to have gone somewhat further than the approach adopted in *Williamson*; while Lord Nicholls himself agreed with Lord Hoffmann that the

---

24   *Shergill v. Purewal & Anor* [2010] EWHC 3610 (QB).

25   *Copsey v. WBB Devon Clays Ltd* [2005] EWCA Civ 932, [2005] ICR 1789.

26   For helpful recent analyses of religious dress issues, see Hill and Sandberg 2007, Lewis 2007, Bacquet 2009 and Hill's and Sandberg's chapters in this book.

27   *Begum, R (on the application of) v. Denbigh High School* [2006] UKHL 15.

school's refusal to allow Ms Begum to wear the *jilbab* was objectively justified, he suggested (Judgment: para. 41) that Lord Hoffmann's proposed remedy might 'overestimate the ease with which Shabina [Begum] could move to another, more suitable school and underestimate the disruption this would be likely to cause to her education'. Presumably, a school in which Ms Begum did not feel obliged to wear the *jilbab* would have had to be a single-sex establishment with an entirely female staff. Moreover, on the basis of Lord Nicholls's earlier statements in *Williamson* (*Williamson* Judgment: paras 22–3) that 'freedom of religion protects the subjective belief of an individual' and that 'a belief must satisfy some modest, objective minimum requirements' for its manifestation to be protected, it is at least arguable that her views on modesty in dress for Muslim women might have deserved protection under those heads.

Nevertheless, Lord Hoffmann's argument was developed further in *Playfoot*[28] by Michael Supperstone QC (sitting as a Deputy High Court Judge). He considered whether or not the refusal of the Governing Body to let Ms Playfoot wear a silver 'purity ring' at school as a symbol of her religiously-motivated commitment to chastity before marriage infringed her Article 9 rights and, in so doing, he derived five principles from *Begum* and *Williamson* (Judgment: para. 21) as follows:

1. Article 9 does not require that one should be allowed to manifest one's religion at any time and place of one's own choosing (Lord Hoffmann in *Begum* at 50).
2. Article 9 does not protect every act motivated or inspired by a religion or belief (Lord Nicholls in *Williamson* at 30).
3. In deciding whether a person's conduct manifests a belief and practice for the purposes of Article 9 one must first identify the nature and scope of that belief (Lord Nicholls in *Williamson* at 32).
4. If the belief takes the form of a perceived obligation to act in a specific way, then, in principle, acting pursuant to that belief is itself a manifestation of that belief in practice: in such cases the act is 'intimately linked' to the belief (Lord Nicholls in *Williamson* at 32 and Lord Walker in *Williamson* at 63).
5. By the time that the Court has reached the stage of considering the manifestation of the belief, it must have regard to the implicit (and not over-demanding) threshold requirements of seriousness, coherence and consistency with human dignity (Lord Nicholls in *Williamson* at 23 and Lord Walker in *Williamson* at 64).

Supperstone QC concluded, inter alia, that Ms Playfoot's desire to wear the ring was not 'intimately linked' to her belief in premarital chastity because she was not compelled to wear it as an obligation of her Christian faith. Moreover, just as in

---

28   *R (on the application of Playfoot) v. Governing Body of Millais School* [2007] EWHC Admin 1698.

Begum Lord Hoffmann had noted that there had been no evidence that Ms Begum would have found it difficult to go to another school, Supperstone QC pointed out (Judgment: para. 31) that '… in the present case there is no evidence that the claimant attempted to transfer to any other school or even made any enquiries in that regard'.

Whether or not Supperstone QC's interpretation of *Williamson* was correct is at least debatable. Sandberg (2011) points out that although Lord Nicholls recognized (*Williamson* Judgment: para. 33) that acting in pursuance of a perceived religious obligation would be a manifestation of that religion, in the following paragraph he rejected the contention that '… a perceived obligation is a prerequisite to manifestation of a belief in practice. It is not'. And there is a further point. While there is nothing in the Christian religion (certainly within the mainstream historic denominations) that obliges unmarried adherents to wear a 'purity ring', Supperstone QC did not consider whether or not a belief in premarital chastity might *itself* represent a philosophical belief, rather than a religious one, that met the *Campbell and Cosans* test of 'a certain level of cogency, seriousness, cohesion and importance' and was therefore worthy of protection under Article 9. Had he come to *that* conclusion, he would then have had to consider whether or not the 'purity ring' was intimately linked with Ms Playfoot's 'philosophical' belief in premarital celibacy rather than with her religious convictions.

The court had no such difficulty in *Watkins-Singh*.[29] In yet another school uniform case, Silber J cited with approval (Judgment: para. 58) the *obiter dicta* of Lord Nicholls in *Williamson* (*Williamson* Judgment: para. 22) on judging the genuineness of belief and concluded that wearing the *kara* bangle was of sufficient importance to Ms Watkins-Singh's religious identity as a Sikh to merit protection – even though, since she had not yet been baptized, she was under no formal religious obligation to wear it. It should be noted, however, that the claim in that case was based mainly on the provisions of the *Race Relations Act 1976* as amended and the *Equality Act 2006* rather than on Article 9 ECHR and the *Human Rights Act 1998* because it had been held in *Mandla*[30] that Sikhs constituted a racial group for the purposes of the 1976 Act.

Conversely, in *Eweida*[31] the Court of Appeal concluded that preventing the appellant, a devout Christian, from wearing a small, visible cross with her uniform was not unjustifiable indirect discrimination on the grounds, inter alia, that there was no evidence that the visible display of a cross was a requirement of the Christian faith. A similar line was recently taken in *Chaplin*[32] in which it was held, applying *Eweida*, that a nurse who had been moved to a desk job for refusing on religious

---

29   *Watkins-Singh, R (on the application of) v. Aberdare Girls' High School & Anor* [2008] EWHC 1865 (Admin).

30   *Mandla v. Dowell Lee* [1982] UKHL 7.

31   *Eweida v. British Airways Plc* [2010] EWCA Civ 80.

32   *Chaplin v. Royal Devon and Exeter Hospital NHS Foundation Trust* [2010] ET 1702886/2009.

grounds to stop wearing a crucifix with her uniform, contrary to the Trust's health and safety policy, had not been unfairly dismissed. In coming to the conclusion that a Christian was not obliged to wear a crucifix, the Employment Tribunal had taken the trouble to consult Ms Chaplin's minister, The Reverend John Eustice of the Free Church of England, who was reported (Judgment, para. 17) as stating that wearing a crucifix was not a mandatory requirement for members of his Church.[33]

All that is not to say, however, that the courts have consistently refused to take a view as to whether or not a particular belief meets the *Campbell and Cosans* test; indeed, recent decisions suggest that the range of beliefs which may meet that test is being extended rather than curtailed. In *Grainger*,[34] Burton J held that a belief in man-made climate change and its alleged resulting moral imperatives was capable, if genuinely held, of being a philosophical belief for the purpose of the *Employment Equality (Religion or Belief) Regulations 2003* – always provided that it was of a similar cogency or status to a religious belief. In doing so, however, he concluded (Judgment: para. 32 applying Lord Nicholls in *Williamson*, para. 23) that 'in the light of the unusual nature of the asserted belief and of its alleged manifestation [there would] need to be evidence and cross-examination directed to the genuineness of the belief'. In the event, however, the case was settled and there was no further examination of the issue. Similarly, in *Power*[35] HHJ Clark upheld the finding of the Employment Tribunal judge that belief in spiritualism and a philosophical belief in life after death and psychic powers met the criteria of Article 9 ECHR and were together capable of constituting a belief for the purpose of the 2003 Regulations, while in *Maistry*[36] a similar view was taken of an avowed belief that public service broadcasting had the higher purpose of promoting cultural interchange and social cohesion.

McFarlane

The issue of the protection of belief and of its manifestation arose recently in *McFarlane*[37] and was subjected to rigorous analysis of its underlying principles by Laws LJ. In that case, the applicant for leave to appeal against the decision of an Employment Appeal Tribunal was a Christian who believed that same-sex sexual activity was sinful. He had entered into a contract of employment with Relate as a paid counsellor and, in doing so, had signed up expressly to Relate's equal opportunities policy. He experienced no difficulties of conscience in counselling same-sex couples where no sexual issues arose but, at length, he sought to be

---

33   At the time of writing *Eweida* and *Chaplin* had been appealed as conjoined cases to the ECtHR.

34   *Grainger Plc & Ors v. Nicholson* [2009] UKEAT 0219/09/0311.

35   *Greater Manchester Police Authority v. Power* [2009] UKEAT 0434/09/DA.

36   *Maistry v. British Broadcasting Corporation* [2011] ET 1313142/2010.

37   *McFarlane v. Relate Avon Ltd* [2010] EWCA Civ B1.

exempted from any obligation to work with same-sex couples in cases involving psychosexual therapy. He was ultimately dismissed on the grounds that he evidently had no intention of complying with Relate's equal opportunities and professional ethics policies in relation to work with same-sex couples and same-sex sexual activities. His claim for unfair dismissal was rejected both at first instance and by the Employment Appeal Tribunal.[38]

As part of his case, McFarlane had entered a witness statement by the former Archbishop of Canterbury, Lord Carey of Clifton (2010), the tone of which was intensely critical of the way in which the courts had handled previous cases involving issues of religion and belief: in particular, of *Eweida* and *Chaplin*. At paragraph 20, Lord Carey concluded by calling on the Lord Chief Justice to establish a specialist multi-faith panel of judges with 'a proven sensitivity and understanding of religious issues' to hear cases engaging religious rights: a kind of Religious Division of the High Court.

Laws LJ dismissed McFarlane's petition for leave to appeal from the decision of the EAT, largely because he regarded himself as bound by the decision of the Court of Appeal in *Ladele*[39] – in which it had been held that a local authority registrar could not refuse to officiate at civil partnership ceremonies on religious grounds because the obligation on public authorities not to discriminate on grounds of sexual orientation extended to their employees and officeholders who were to be considered 'public authorities' in their own right.[40] However, the consequence of Lord Carey's rather curious and, dare one say it, inept intervention was that in the course of his judgment Laws LJ addressed the general issue of what he described as 'Religion and Law' and revisited some of the matters dealt with in *Williamson*.

Given its general nature and importance, the judgment is worth quoting at length:

> 22. In a free constitution such as ours there is an important distinction to be drawn between the law's protection of the right to hold and express a belief and the law's protection of that belief's substance or content. The common law and ECHR Article 9 offer vigorous protection of the Christian's right (and every other person's right) to hold and express his or her beliefs. And so they should. By contrast they do not, and should not, offer any protection whatever of the substance or content of those beliefs on the ground only that they are based on religious precepts. These are twin conditions of a free society.

> 23. The first of these conditions is largely uncontentious. I should say a little more, however, about the second. The general law may of course protect a particular social or moral position which is espoused by Christianity, not because

---

38   *McFarlane v. Relate Avon Ltd* [2009] UKEAT 0106 09 3011.

39   *Ladele v. London Borough of Islington* [2009] EWCA Civ 1357.

40   At paragraph 16 Laws LJ rejected the contention of Paul Diamond QC, for the applicant, that *Ladele* had been decided *per incuriam*.

of its religious *imprimatur*, but on the footing that in reason its merits commend themselves. So it is with core provisions of the criminal law: the prohibition of violence and dishonesty ... But the conferment of any legal protection or preference upon a particular substantive moral position on the ground only that it is espoused by the adherents of a particular faith, however long its tradition, however rich its culture, is deeply unprincipled. It imposes compulsory law, not to advance the general good on objective grounds, but to give effect to the force of subjective opinion. This must be so, since in the eye of everyone save the believer religious faith is necessarily subjective, being incommunicable by any kind of proof or evidence. It may of course be true; but the ascertainment of such a truth lies beyond the means by which laws are made in a reasonable society. Therefore it lies only in the heart of the believer, who is alone bound by it. No one else is or can be so bound, unless by his own free choice he accepts its claims.

24. The promulgation of law for the protection of a position held purely on religious grounds cannot therefore be justified. It is irrational, as preferring the subjective over the objective. But it is also divisive, capricious and arbitrary. We do not live in a society where all the people share uniform religious beliefs. The precepts of any one religion – any belief system – cannot, by force of their religious origins, sound any louder in the general law than the precepts of any other. If they did, those out in the cold would be less than citizens; and our constitution would be on the way to a theocracy, which is of necessity autocratic. The law of a theocracy is dictated without option to the people, not made by their judges and governments. The individual conscience is free to accept such dictated law; but the State, if its people are to be free, has the burdensome duty of thinking for itself.

25. So it is that the law must firmly safeguard the right to hold and express religious belief; equally firmly, it must eschew any protection of such a belief's content in the name only of its religious credentials. Both principles are necessary conditions of a free and rational regime.

Does *McFarlane* Reopen the Issues Decided in *Williamson*?

What Laws LJ seems to be saying is that the law protects particular values not because they are religious but only because they are perceived as having wider benefits to society as a whole. On his analysis:

1. The common law and Article 9 ECHR protect the right to hold and express beliefs but they do not protect the substance or content of beliefs merely because they are religious. They may therefore protect a particular social

or moral position based on religion only if that position is in the interests of society at large.

2. It would be wrong to protect a particular social or moral position merely because it was based on religion. The state must therefore hold the ring between different opinions and make its own judgments about the merits or otherwise of particular moral stances.

3. Though the law must safeguard the right to hold and express religious beliefs it must not seek to protect religious beliefs as such.

But if that be the case, on what basis *does* the law protect 'religion'?

In a democratic society, as opposed to a theocratic one, the basis of any law protective of religion seems to rest on three possibilities. First, the lawmaker may regard religion (that is, its content and its practice) as intrinsically valuable and worth protecting in its own right as a 'Good Thing'. Secondly, society at large may acknowledge that religious belief is such an important part of the self-identity of the individual believer that it should not be impugned except in circumstances where the 'greater good' of that society dictates that the interests of believers must be overridden: the 'extremely painful and intensely burdensome choices' referred to by Sachs J in *Christian Education South Africa*. Thirdly, a particular moral or religious position may be regarded by society at large as being of general social benefit and therefore worthy of protection for the good of society as a whole rather than because of its moral or religious content: the position of Laws LJ. Or perhaps it depends on any or all of those things to a greater or lesser degree according to circumstance.

The motives for the second of these possibilities – the importance of religion for the self-identity of the believer – would appear to be rather contrary to the position adopted by Laws LJ which, suggests Russell Sandberg (2010: 369), goes too far in asserting that laws to protect positions held purely on religious grounds are unjustifiable and irrational. Moreover, practical examples of such protections are not hard to find.

When the Farm Animal Welfare Council recommended that slaughtering animals without prior stunning should be banned – a move which, for all practical purposes, would have ended the *halal* and *kosher* meat trades – the then Government rejected that advice in relation to ritual slaughter. Ben Bradshaw (2004), at the time Parliamentary Under-Secretary of State for Environment, Food and Rural Affairs, described the decision as having been taken out of 'respect for the important beliefs of minority religions in this country' and the current exemption is still that set out in the Welfare of Animals (Slaughter or Killing) Regulations 1995.[41]

---

41   In June 2010 the European Parliament voted by 559 to 54 for a compulsory measure requiring meat from animals slaughtered without stunning to be labelled as such. The proposal did not, however, find favour with the Council of Ministers and the draft regulation on food information to consumers (16555/10) agreed by the Council on 7 December 2010 makes no mention of it.

Commenting on *Williamson*, Graham Zellick (2005) distinguishes between ritual slaughter and corporal punishment like this: '*shekhitah* engages a fundamental tenet for many Jews, whereas beating children is at best marginal and peripheral to Christian doctrine and practice … [i]ndeed, most Christians would probably say that beating children formed no part of Christian doctrine, practice or belief at all'.

Similarly, Part 6 of Schedule 3 to the *Equality Act 2010* permits clergy with a conscientious objection to marrying two people of the same chromosomal sex to opt out of conducting such a ceremony notwithstanding the fact that, under section 9(1) the *Gender Recognition Act 2004*, '[w]here a full gender recognition certificate is issued to a person, the person's gender becomes for all purposes the acquired gender'. Even though the Commons debates on section 9(1) of the 2004 Act were not entirely without expressions of unease, since it arrived on the statute book unscathed one can only assume that section 9(1) had the overall support of society at large – or at least the support of society at large as moderated through the views of its elected representatives.[42] Yet the conscientious opt-out flatly contradicts the position adopted in 2004.

In *Sulaiman*,[43] where the issue was the validity of a 'bare *talaq*' Islamic divorce pronounced in England but effective in Saudi Arabia and registered there, Munby J characterized the stance of the secular law towards religion as '… an essentially agnostic view of religious beliefs and a tolerant indulgence to religious and cultural diversity' (Judgment: para. 47). Both the conscientious opt-out from the marriage provisions of the *Gender Recognition Act* and the saving for ritual slaughter look remarkably like examples both of Munby J's 'tolerant indulgence' and of what Laws LJ described as '[t]he promulgation of law for the protection of a position held purely on religious grounds'. As to the conscientious opt-out, neither is it easy to see what wider benefit it could possibly have for society at large nor is it incontrovertible 'that in reason its merits commend themselves'. Indeed, the Government Equalities Office was so unsure as to those merits that though the Equality Bill started in the Commons the opt-out was inserted into Schedule 3 to the Bill as a new Part 5A only at a very late stage in the Lords.[44] As to ritual slaughter, like the prohibition against pork it was no doubt a very important public health measure when originally formulated; but now that we have refrigeration and meat hygiene inspectors, surely its purpose can only be religious.

---

42 See, for example, the Standing Committee debate in the Commons: HC Deb (2003–2004) St Co A 11 March 2004 cc 124–43. Though Clause 9 was subjected to very close scrutiny, it was agreed to without amendment or division. Section 9(1) of the Act is identical with Clause 9(1) of the Bill as printed in the Commons.

43 *Sulaiman v. Juffali* [2002] 2 FCR 427.

44 See HL Deb (2009–2010) 19 January 2010 cc 907–13.

Conclusion

The judgment in *McFarlane* seems to call into question some of the reasoning behind the judgments of the House of Lords in *Williamson* or, at any rate, to impose a slightly more rigorous test for what might in future qualify for protection. The step in the argument assembled from *Williamson* and *Begum* by Supperstone QC which Laws LJ appears to have downplayed is the link between belief and action: that an act based on a belief may *itself* be a practical manifestation of that belief and, therefore, 'intimately linked' to it as suggested by Lord Nicholls at paragraph 32 and by Lord Walker at paragraph 63 of *Williamson*. The devout Jew or Muslim who will eat only *kosher* or *halal* meat or the Sikh motorcyclist who refuses to remove his turban in order to don a helmet or the nurse who refuses to take part in a termination of pregnancy on grounds of conscience would all regard that link as crucial.

As noted above, in *Williamson* Lord Nicholls declared (Judgment: para. 22) that '[f]reedom of religion protects the subjective belief of an individual ... Each individual is at liberty to hold his own religious beliefs, however irrational or inconsistent they may seem to some'. If what Laws LJ is now saying is, in effect, that the law should not seek to protect the content of religion at all and ought only to protect its manifestation in fairly limited circumstances, does that represent a radical departure from previous judicial pronouncements? Or is he merely acknowledging that the *forum internum* is, by definition, internal?

As to the influence of *McFarlane*, only time will tell. Sandberg (2010: 370), for example, goes so far as to suggest that '[i]t may be inferred from the judgment that there is no reason to protect religion as such'. For the moment, however, *Williamson* continues to be enormously significant in cases involving religious manifestation and its influence can be detected in various ways in *Begum*, *Playfoot*, *Watkins-Singh* and *Grainger* – and in *McFarlane* itself. Even in *Eweida*, though *Williamson* was not cited in the Court of Appeal it was still referred to by Elias J in the Employment Appeal Tribunal.[45]

The basic tension at the core of *Williamson* – the extreme reluctance to judge the validity of a particular belief coupled with the recognition that, on occasion, such reluctance will have to be overcome in order to decide whether or not a particular manifestation is sufficiently fundamental as to merit protection – has meant, for example, that the subsequent series of decisions on religious dress appears to be inconsistent: 'yes' to a *kara* bangle in *Watkins-Singh*, 'no' to a cross or crucifix on a chain in *Eweida* and *Chaplin*. But that inconsistency is surely an inevitable consequence of the common law method of adjudication. Their Lordships in *Williamson* did not make any attempt to set down an absolutely objective and reliable tick-box test for what should be protected – nor, realistically, could they have done so had they tried. Ultimately, when issues of belief and manifestation arise every court has to make what is sometimes a difficult value-judgment on the

---

45 *Eweida v. British Airways Plc* [2008] UKEAT 0123 08 2011, paras 26–9.

particular facts of the case before it, 'without fear or favour, affection or ill-will'. And that is why Lord Carey's proposal simply cannot be countenanced.

References

Books and Articles

Bacquet, S. 2009. Manifestation of belief and religious symbols at schools: setting boundaries in English courts, *Religion and Human Rights* 4, 121–35.

Bradshaw, B. 2004. European Standing Committee A (2003–2004) 20 April: *Protection of Animals during Transport*, London, House of Commons.

Carey, G. 2010. Witness Statement of Lord Carey of Clifton 9 April 2009 in the Court of Appeal A2/2009/2733 between Mr G. McFarlane Claimant and Relate Avon Ltd Respondent. [Online: *Thinking Anglicans*]. Available at: http://www. google.co.uk/url?sa=t&rct=j&q=witness%20statement%20of%20lord%20 carey%20of%20clifton&source=web&cd=2&ved=0CCsQFjAB&url=http%3A 2F%2Fthinkinganglicans.org.uk%2Fuploads%2FOn%2520behalf%2520of% 2520Gary%2520McFarlane.doc&ei=iBCtToK9KITh8AOjtLSKCw&usg=AF QjCNEt_G-6evgWn3XsFBAtmX97bRnk2w&cad=rja [Accessed: 30 October 2011].

Department of Health. 2000. *Protecting Children, Supporting Parents: A Consultation Document on the Physical Punishment of Children*, London: Department of Health.

Diamond, P. 1999. Is corporal punishment contrary to the European Convention of Human Rights? *Education and the Law* 1, 43–52.

English, R. 2005. Williamson. [Online: *1 Crown Office Row Resources*]. Available at http://www.1cor.com/1315/?form_1155.replyids=419 [Accessed: 30 October 2011].

European Union. 2010. *Proposal for a Regulation of the European Parliament and of the Council on the provision of food information to consumers*, 16555/10, Brussels, 1 December 2010.

Gibson, M. 2010. Rastafari and cannabis: framing a criminal law exemption. *Ecclesiastical Law Journal* 12, 324–44.

Hill, M, and Sandberg, R. 2007. Is nothing sacred? Clashing symbols in a secular world. *Public Law* 3, 488–506.

Langlaude, S. 2006. Flogging children with religion: a comment on the House of Lords' decision in *Williamson*. *Ecclesiastical Law Journal* 8, 339–45.

Lewis, T. 2007. What not to wear: religious rights, the European Court, and the margin of appreciation. *International & Comparative Law Quarterly* 56, 395–414

Parsons, S. 2007. Human rights and the defence of chastisement. *Journal of Criminal Law* 71:4, 308–17.

Sandberg, R. 2010. Laws and religion: unravelling *McFarlane v Relate Avon Limited*. *Ecclesiastical Law Journal* 12, 361–70.

Sandberg, R. 2011. *Law and Religion*. Cambridge: CUP.

Scottish Office, 1968. *Elimination of Corporal Punishment in Schools: Statement of Principles and Code of Practice*, Edinburgh: Scottish Office.

Wardrop, M. 2011. More than 400 claims of physical abuse on children attending British madrassas. *Daily Telegraph* 18 October.

Zellick, G. 2005. Is ritual slaughter a human right? *Manna* 88 3 August 2005. [Online]. Available at: http://news.reformjudaism.org.uk/manna-magazine/is-ritual-slaughter-a-human-right.html [Accessed:30 October 2011].

Cases

A v. United Kingdom (1999) 27 EHHR 611.

Arrowsmith v. United Kingdom [1978] ECHR 7.

Begum, R (on the application of) v. Denbigh High School [2006] UKHL 15.

Blake v. Associated Newspapers Ltd [2003] EWHC (QB) unreported. Transcript available at http://www.5rb.com/docs/Blake%20v%20ANL.pdf [Accessed: 30 October 2011].

Campbell and Cosans v. United Kingdom (1982) 4 EHRR 293 Series A no 48.

Chaplin v. Royal Devon and Exeter Hospital NHS. Foundation Trust [2010] ET 1702886/2009.

Christian Education South Africa v. Minister of Education [2000] ZACC 11, 2000 (4) SA 757, 2000 (10) BCLR 1051.

Copsey v. WBB Devon Clays Ltd [2005] EWCA Civ 932, [2005] ICR 1789.

Costello-Roberts v. United Kingdom (1993) 19 EHRR 112.

E, R (on the application of) v. Governing Body of JFS & Anor [2009] UKSC 15.

Eweida v. British Airways Plc [2008] UKEAT 0123 08 2011; [2010] EWCA.Civ 80.

Grainger Plc & Ors v. Nicholson [2009] UKEAT 0219/09/0311.

Greater Manchester Police Authority v. Power [2009] UKEAT 0434/09/DA.

HH Sant Baba Jeet Singh Ji Maharaj v. Eastern Media Group & Anor [2010] EWHC 1294 (QB).

Joseph v. DPP [2003] EWHC 3078 (Admin).

Kalaç v. Turkey (1997) 27 EHRR 552.

Ladele v. London Borough of Islington [2009] EWCA Civ 1357.

Leyla Şahin v. Turkey [2005] ECtHR (No 44774/98).

Maistry v. British Broadcasting Corporation [2011] ET 1313142/2010.

Mandla v. Dowell Lee [1982] UKHL 7.

McFarlane v. Relate Avon Ltd [2009] UKEAT 0106 09 3011: [2010] EWCA Civ B1.

R v. Andrews [2004] EWCA Crim 947.

R v. Brown [1994] 1 AC 212.

R v. Chief Rabbi of the United Hebrew Congregations of Great Britain and the Commonwealth, ex parte Wachmann [1992] 1 WLR 1036.

R v. Secretary of State for Education and Employment & Ors ex parte Williamson & Ors [2002] EWCA Civ 1926: [2003] QB 1300.

R v. Taylor [2001] EWCA Crim 2263.

R (on the application of Playfoot) v. Governing Body of Millais School [2007] EWHC Admin 1698.

Refah Partisi (The Welfare Party) & Ors v. Turkey [2003] ECtHR (Nos. 41340/98, 41342/98, 41343/98 and 41344/98).

Shergill v. Purewal & Anor [2010] EWCH 3610 (QB).

Sulaiman v. Juffali [2002] 2 FCR 427.

Williamson v. Secretary of State for Education & Employment [2001] EWHC Admin 960: [2002] ELR 214.

Williamson & Ors, R (on the application of) v. Secretary of State for Education and Employment & Ors [2005] UKHL 15.

Watkins-Singh, R (on the application of) v. Aberdare Girls' High School & Anor [2008] EWHC 1865 (Admin).

Conventions

Council of Europe. 1950–2004. *Convention for the Protection of Human Rights and Fundamental Freedoms*, as amended by the provisions of Protocol No. 14 as from its entry into force on 1 June 2010. Strasbourg: European Court of Human Rights.

United Nations. 1989. *Convention on the Rights of the Child*, adopted and opened for signature, ratification and accession 20 November 1989, entered into force 2 September 1990. New York and Geneva: Office of the United Nations High Commissioner for Human Rights.

Statutes and Statutory Instruments

Carrying of Knives etc. (Scotland) Act 1993 (c. 13), London: HMSO.

Children Act 1989 (c. 41), London: HMSO.

Criminal Justice Act 1988 (c. 33), London: HMSO.

Criminal Law (Consolidation) (Scotland) Act 1995 (c. 39), London: HMSO.

Customs and Excise Management Act 1979 (c. 2), London: HMSO.

Day Care and Child Minding (National Standards) (England) Regulations 2003, SI 2003/1996, London: HMSO.

Education Act 1996 (c. 56), London: HMSO.

Education and Libraries (Northern Ireland) Order 2003, SI 2003/424 (NI 12), London: HMSO.

Education (Corporal Punishment) (Northern Ireland) Order 1987, SI 1987/461 (NI 6), London: HMSO.

Education (No. 2) Act 1986 (c. 61), London: HMSO.

Employment Equality (Religion or Belief) Regulations 2003, SI 2003/1660, London: HMSO.

Equality Act 2006 (c. 3), London: HMSO.
Equality Act 2010 (c. 15), London: HMSO.
Gender Recognition Act 2004 (c. 7), London: HMSO.
Human Rights Act 1998 (c. 42), London: HMSO.
Misuse of Drugs Act 1971 (c. 38), London: HMSO.
Race Relations Act 1976 (c. 74), London: HMSO.
School Standards and Framework Act 1998 (c. 31), London: HMSO.
Standards in Scotland's Schools etc. Act 2000 (asp. 6), Edinburgh: HMSO.
Welfare of Animals (Slaughter or Killing) Regulations 1995, SI 1995/731, London: HMSO.

PART IV
Case Studies:
Religious Symbols at School

Chapter 15
Bracelets, Rings and Veils: The Accommodation of Religious Symbols in the Uniform Policies of English Schools

Mark Hill

This chapter is a critical analysis of the emergent – and, in many ways, self-contradictory – English case law in its approach to freedom of religion under Article 9 of the European Convention on Human Rights and its application to school uniform policies. The specific cases to be discussed deal with the wearing of the *jilbab* and the *niqab*, the Sikh *Kara* bracelet and a purity ring. These cases, however, need to be interpreted within the social context in the United Kingdom and the general law of religious liberty. The first part of this chapter addresses the social context (relying upon Hill, Sandberg and Doe 2011, Hill and Sandberg 2007). Before turning to the details of the specific cases determined by the courts in recent years, certain general observations will serve to contextualize this jurisprudence.

The English Social and Legal Context

A word must be said about the nature of schooling in the United Kingdom. The state educational system is largely non-elective, government-funded and follows a national curriculum. The wearing of a prescribed uniform for school children of all ages is a near-universal feature of its educational system, whether in state schools or in private (fee-paying) schools. This is not a matter of primary or secondary legislation or of local governmental regulation but rather reflects a widespread and long-standing social practice. It is exceptional for a school not to have a policy on uniform for its pupils. The uniform (traditionally black or grey trousers, jumpers and jackets in the coloured livery of the school and ties for boys) serves to identify individuals as members of a specific institution and to encourage and promote the corporate, collective ethos of the school. More subtly, by insisting upon identical clothing (often from a designated manufacturer) it ensures that all school children dress the same and appear equal: thus, differences of social and economic background that would be evident from the nature and extent of personal wardrobes are eliminated. It is an effective levelling feature – particularly in comprehensive secondary schools whose catchment areas may include a range of school children drawn from differing parental income brackets and social classes.

Second, I think it is inconceivable that the UK government would ever impose a statutory prohibition on the wearing of religious headscarves or other faith-based dress. The social and constitutional context could not be more different from the model of *laïcité* in France where a legal ban is less controversial. The approach to religion and religious liberty in the United Kingdom has differed over time and the current human rights era marks an abrupt shift from passive religious tolerance to the active promotion of religious liberty as a basic right (Hill and Sandberg 2007: 488–506). Religious tolerance is a hallmark of a liberal State. Following the Reformation and the establishment of the Church of England as a state Church, limited and piecemeal toleration was afforded to the practices of dissenters. In time, religious liberty developed at common law as a broad and largely negative freedom rather than a positive right (Hill 2005: 1131–2). No general right to wear religious symbols or dress was prescribed but a broad freedom existed at common law whereby individuals could wear what they pleased unless they were obliged to conform to a dress or uniform code at work or school (Rivers). This common law position was supplemented by specific statutory exceptions designed to mitigate the effect of other legal provisions. Sikhs are exempt from the requirement to wear a safety hat on a construction site and from the law relating to the wearing of protective headgear for motor cyclists (Poulter 1998: chapter 8)[1] while Jews and Muslims enjoy exemptions from rules on animal slaughter methods.[2] More commonly, particular provision is occasionally afforded on grounds of religion.[3] Traditionally, these privileges were rare and hard fought. For instance, the law provides no special protection for Rastafarians for their use of cannabis on religious grounds[4] nor would a defence grounded in divine law be sustainable.[5] The seminal decision of the House of Lords nearly 20 years ago in *Mandla v. Dowell Lee*[6] declaring that a Sikh school boy should be permitted to wear a turban at school, as an exception to a strict school uniform policy, was determined on the basis that denial constituted a breach of race discrimination legislation.[7]

---

1   *Employment Act 1989*, s.11; *Road Traffic Act 1988*, s.16. For a full account, see Poulter 1998: chapter 8.

2   *Welfare of Animals (Slaughter or Killing) Regulations 1995*, SI 1995/731, Reg 2.

3   For instance, it is a defence to charge of having a blade in a public place if the blade is carried 'for religious reasons': see the *Criminal Justice Act 1988*, s.139. Section 1 of the *Adoption and Children Act 2002* and various other statutes regarding the care of children recognizes the right of children to have 'due consideration' given to their 'religious persuasion'.

4   *R v. Taylor* [2001] EWCA Crim 2263, *R v. Andrews* [2004] EWCA Crim 947.

5   *Blake v. DPP* [1993] Crim L.R 556.

6   [1983] 2 AC 548.

7   The broad interpretation of 'race' in the context of this decision was to become central to a more recent decision of the Supreme Court (as the House of Lords has since been reconstituted) which concerned admission to Jewish schools, in which the court

Such provisions owe more to the tradition of religious tolerance and accommodation than to any sophisticated notion of religious liberty as a widespread positive right (Vickers 2006: 598).[8] However, by the closing decades of the twentieth century international human rights treaties and the ideals they embodied began to influence the law.

The Human Rights Act 1998

The Human Rights Act 1998 ('HRA') has changed this approach and the current jurisprudential debate now focuses on the precise reach of positive legal rights. Whereas previously the ECHR merely had the status of a treaty obligation under international law,[9] Convention rights (including freedom of religion under Article 9) are now part of domestic law and directly justiciable in UK courts. Article 9 of the ECHR provides:

1. Everyone has the right to freedom of thought, conscience and religion; this right includes freedom to change his religion or belief, and freedom, either alone or in community with others and in public or private, to manifest his religion or belief, in worship, teaching, practice and observance.
2. Freedom to manifest one's religion or beliefs shall be subject only to such limitations as are prescribed by law and are necessary in a democratic society in the interests of public safety, for the protection of public order, health or morals, or the protection of the rights and freedoms of others.

Article 9 provides a positive right to both the freedom of thought, conscience and religion and the manifestation of that religion or belief. The right to freedom of thought, conscience and religion is absolute. By contrast, the right to manifest one's religion or belief is limited by Article 9(1) in that the manifestation must be 'in worship, teaching, practice and observance' and, more importantly, by the qualifications in Article 9(2) which permit the State to interfere with the right if three tests are met: the interference must be 'prescribed by law', have one or more of the legitimate aims listed and be 'necessary in a democratic society'. Individuals claiming violation of their Article 9 rights need to show that there has been an interference with the manifestation of their religion or belief under Article

---

declined to give effect to the Chief Rabbi's strict definition of matrilineal Jewishness: see *R (on the application of E) v. Governing Body of JFS* [2010] 2 WLR 153.

8   This is illustrated by the fact that Sikhs injured as a result of wearing a turban instead of a safety hat are denied certain forms of legal redress: see *Employment Act 1989*, s.11. For a discussion of the legal requirements of tolerance within a modern setting, see Vickers 2006: 598.

9   However, individual petition to the European Court of Human Rights in Strasbourg had been permitted since 1966.

9(1), following which the onus is on the State to show that such interference was justified under Article 9(2).

Interference under Article 9(1)

The European Court of Human Rights ('ECtHR') in Strasbourg generally takes a formulaic approach to Article 9 cases. The Court invariably begins by stressing the importance of the right, citing the leading case of *Kokkinakis v. Greece*[10] which declared that 'freedom of thought, conscience and religion is one of the foundations of a "democratic society" within the meaning of the Convention'.[11] The Court then asks whether there has been an interference with Article 9(1) and if there has been, whether that interference is justified under Article 9(2). The question of whether there has been an interference is often a formality: it is sometimes expressed as asking whether Article 9 has been engaged. Strasbourg has employed three 'filtering devices' to exclude claims under the question of interference: the definition of belief, the manifestation/motivation requirement and the specific situation rule (Sandberg 2009: 267–82).

Definition of belief[12]
The European Court of Human Rights has taken a liberal approach to the definition of religion. Strasbourg institutions have considered claims concerning scientology,[13] druidism,[14] pacifism,[15] communism,[16] atheism,[17] pro-life,[18] Divine Light Zentrum,[19]

---

10   (1994) 17 EHRR 397.

11   The *Kokkinakis* justification is twofold, stressing both the social and personal functions of religion. The European Court of Human Rights permits a 'margin of appreciation' allowing States to differ from each other in relation to their laws and policies to some extent to allow for their different cultures. While previously Strasbourg has spoken of the existence of a wide margin of appreciation in the sphere of morals and religion (especially in relation to attacks on religious convictions), recent decisions suggest a degree of inconsistency in the deference which the Strasbourg Court will afford to national legislatures on matters of religion: see *Sahin v. Turkey* (2005) 41 EHRR 8 and EctHR Grand Chamber *Lautsi v. Italy* 18 March 2011, Application no. 30814/06.

12   See Sandberg 2008: 1–23.

13   *X and Church of Scientology v. Sweden* (1978) 16 DR 68.

14   *Chappell v. United Kingdom* (1987) 53 DR 241. Although the existence of Druidism as a religion was questioned, the case was decided purely on the grounds that state restrictions on the celebration of the summer solstice at Stonehenge were justified under Article 9(2).

15   *Arrowsmith v. United Kingdom* (1978) 19 DR 5.

16   *Hazar, Hazar and Acik v. Turkey* (1991) 72 DR 200.

17   *Angeleni v. Sweden* (1986) 51 DR 41.

18   *Plattform 'Ärtze für das Leben' v. Austria* (1985) 44 DR 65.

19   *Omkarananda and the Divine Light Zentrum v. Switzerland* (1981) 25 DR 105.

the Moon Sect,[20] as well as 'splinter' groups within larger traditions,[21] and have invariably done so without questioning whether the objects of such claims are protected (Ahdar and Leigh 2005: 124, Taylor 2005: 207). Strasbourg case law tends to revolve around the definition of 'belief' rather than that of 'religion'. The term 'belief' is considered in its jurisprudence to require a worldview rather than a mere opinion.[22] However, Strasbourg has only been prepared to use the belief filter in exceptional cases.

The Strasbourg approach has been replicated at the domestic level. In the House of Lords decision of *R v. Secretary of State for Education and Employment and others ex parte Williamson*,[23] Lord Nicholls noted that the protection of 'religion or belief' meant that the question of 'deciding whether a belief is to be characterized as religious ... will seldom, if ever, arise under the European Convention' because it does not matter whether the belief is religious or non-religious.[24] Moreover, Lord Nicholls noted that 'freedom of religion protects the subjective belief of an individual'.[25] Lord Walker of Gestingthorpe, in particular, doubted whether it was right for courts, except in extreme cases, 'to impose an evaluative filter' at the stage of identifying whether there was a belief 'especially when religious beliefs are involved'.[26] Generally, however, United Kingdom domestic courts have not relied upon the definition of belief as a filter in their interpretation of Article 9.[27]

The manifestation or motivation requirement
The second filter used in relation to Article 9(1) is the manifestation/motivation requirement, which requires that the claimant's actions actually express his or her religion or belief and area a manifestation of that religion or belief as opposed to being merely motivated by it.[28] It is not surprising, therefore, that this filter is

20 *X v. Austria* (1981) 26 DR 89.

21 For example, *Serif v. Greece* (1999) 31 EHRR 561 (Mufti elected by Mosque congregations in opposition to the Mufti appointed by the Government).

22 It was defined in *Campbell and Cosans v. United Kingdom*, (1982) 4 EHRR 293, para. 36 as denoting 'views that attain a certain level of cogency, seriousness, cohesion and importance'.

23 [2005] UKHL 15, [2005] 2 AC 246.

24 Ibidem para. 24.

25 Ibidem para.22.

26 Ibidem para. 57.

27 This is shown by two cases concerning religious drug use. In *R v. Taylor* [2001] EWCA Crim 2263 and *R v. Andrews* [2004] EWCA Crim 947, cases concerning the possession and import of cannabis by Rastafarians, the Court of Appeal held that drug prohibition laws could be justified under Article 9(2). It was assumed without comment that Rastafarianism was a religion and that drug-taking was capable of being a manifestation of that religion under Article 9(1).

28 *Arrowsmith v. United Kingdom* (1981) 3 EHRR 218. This rule has been criticized on the basis that the presence or absence of religious motivation may actually serve as a good indicator of whether a belief should be protected and that a rigid adherence to

not always employed by the court (Knights 2007, Sandberg 2009). At Strasbourg, the test has often been rephrased as requiring, for example, that the action is 'intimately linked' to the claimant's religion or belief[29] or 'give expression' to his religion or belief.[30]

In *R v. Secretary of State for Education and Employment and others ex parte Williamson*,[31] though Lord Nicholls did note the motivation requirement in stating that 'Article 9 does not "in all cases" guarantee the right to behave in public in a way "dictated by a belief"',[32] he nevertheless held that this should not exclude the claim. He also noted that if 'the belief takes the form of a perceived obligation to act in a specific way, then, in principle, doing that act pursuant to that belief is itself a manifestation of that belief in practice' and that 'in such cases the act is 'intimately linked' to the belief'.[33] However, he added this did not mean 'that a perceived obligation is a prerequisite to manifestation of a belief in practice'.[34] That a belief was obligatory was simply good evidence that the exercise of that belief was manifestation protected by Article 9; a belief did not have to be obligatory to be protected by Article 9.

The specific situation rule

The third 'filtering device' may be styled the specific situation rule. It recognizes that a person's Article 9 rights may be influenced by the particular situation of the individual claiming that freedom. This principle is not of universal application: it only applies where a person voluntarily submitted to a particular system of rules. Strasbourg has recognized that the application of this rule in specific situations such as in relation to detainees,[35] non-compulsory military service,[36] employment,[37] and enrolment at university.[38] However, in *Jewish Liturgical Association Cha'are Shalom Ve Tsedek v. France*[39] Strasbourg seemed to go further by imposing an 'impossibility test': the Court commented that an 'alternative means of accommodating religious beliefs had … to be "impossible" before a

---

the manifestation requirement 'would seem to discriminate against religions without an established cultural base in European States' whose devotions 'take different forms, such as sexual intercourse, ritual violence, or refusal to pay taxes to a centralised state hostile to their beliefs'. See Edge 1996: 45–7.

29   *C v. UK* (1983) 37 DR 142, 144; *Hasan and Chaush v. Bulgaria* (2002) 34 EHRR 55.
30   *Knudsen v. Norway* (1985) 42 DR 247.
31   [2005] UKHL 15, [2005] 2 AC 246.
32   Ibidem para. 30.
33   Ibidem paras 32–3.
34   Ibidem paras 32–3.
35   *X v. United Kingdom* (1974) 1 D& R at 41–2.
36   *Kalaç v. Turkey* (1997) 27 EHRR 552.
37   *Stedman v. United Kingdom* (1997) 5 EHRLR 544; *Ahmad v. United Kingdom* (1981) 4 EHRR 126.
38   *Karaduman v. Turkey* (1993) 74 DR 93.
39   (2000) 9 BHRC 27.

claim of interference under Article 9 could succeed.' This broader approach has not been consistently followed in subsequent Strasbourg cases and in *Sahin v. Turkey*,[40] concerning a university regulation banning a student from wearing a headscarf at enrolment, lectures and examinations, although the specific situation rule was referred to by the Court,[41] the Court proceeded 'on the assumption that the regulations in issue, which placed restrictions of place and manner on the right to wear the Islamic headscarf in universities, constituted an interference with the applicant's right to manifest her religion'.[42]

The early decisions of UK domestic courts recognized the specific situation rule but echoed the later Strasbourg jurisprudence in noting its limited scope and refrained from enthusiastically applying the rule.[43] The House of Lords decision in *Williamson* also recognized the existence of the specific situation rule but did not apply it to the facts of the case. As Lord Nicholls noted: 'What constitutes interference depends on all the circumstances of the case, including the extent to which in the circumstances an individual can reasonably expect to be at liberty to manifest his beliefs in practice', meaning that an individual 'may need to take his specific situation into account'.[44]

Justification under Article 9(2)

In Strasbourg jurisprudence, the focus invariably shifts from the question of interference under Article 9(1) to the Article 9(2) qualifications that are used to determine whether the interference by the State was justified. The same is also true of domestic decisions – though for the reasons discussed above in most cases the consideration of Article 9(2) by a domestic court is often *obiter*, the court having rejected the claim on the question of interference under Article 9(1). Nevertheless, the vast majority of decisions address the three tests laid out in Article 9(2) applying them sequentially: to be justified, the interference must be 'prescribed by law', have a 'legitimate aim' and be 'necessary in a democratic society'.

---

40   (2005) 41 EHRR 8.

41   Ibidem para. 66.

42   Ibidem para. 71.

43   This was epitomized by the Court of Appeal decision in *Copsey v. WBB Devon Clays Ltd* [2005] EWCA Civ 932 concerning an employee dismissed after he had refused to agree to a contractual variation in his working hours to introduce a rotating shift procedure which included some Sunday working. Although the Court of Appeal dismissed the employee's appeal on the basis of domestic employment law, the judges were extremely critical of Article 9 and the Strasbourg specific situation rule questioning whether it enhanced the protection afforded by domestic law.

44   Ibidem para. 38.

Prescribed by law

This first test requires that the interference must have some basis in domestic law. This test has not proved problematic for the domestic judiciary: for instance, the House of Lords has held that both a rule 'prescribed by primary legislation in clear terms'[45] and a school uniform policy[46] were, respectively, prescribed by law. In relation to the latter, emphasis was given to the fact that schools and their governors were permitted under statutory authority to make rules on uniform and those rules had been very clearly communicated to those affected by them.[47]

Legitimate aim

The second test is that the interference fulfils one of the aims listed in Article 9(2). These overlap substantially (Taylor 2005: 301–2).[48] At Strasbourg, this requirement is often a formality: Taylor has noted that the margin of appreciation adopted by European institutions means that they 'tend to accept rather than challenge the aim claimed by the State, and accordingly pass over this precondition with little detailed analysis'. The same appears to be true at a domestic level. Although in most cases the legitimate aim is protecting the Convention rights and freedoms of others,[49] a wide range of legitimate aims have been cited by courts.[50]

---

45   *R v. Secretary of State for Education and Employment and others ex parte Williamson* [2005] UKHL 15, [2005] 2 AC 246.

46   This was accepted by all of the appellate committee in *R (on the application of Begum) v. Headteacher and Governors of Denbigh High School* [2006] UKHL 15, the full judgment in which is discussed in greater detail below.

47   Lord Bingham in *Begum*, Ibidem para. 26.

48   Evans 2002.

49   See *Begum*, note 46 *supra per* Lord Bingham at para. 26, Lord Hoffmann at para. 58 and Baroness Hale at para. 94.

50   The question of how narrow a legitimate aim may be was addressed by the Court of Appeal in *R (on the Application of Swami Suryananda) v. Welsh Ministers* [2007] EWCA Civ 893 concerning the decision by the Welsh Assembly Government to order the slaughter of Shambo, a bullock at the claimant's Hindu temple which had tested positive for the bacterium that causes bovine tuberculosis (TB). The claimant applied for judicial review, contesting that, since the sacredness of life was a cornerstone of Hindu beliefs and bovines played an important part in Hinduism, the decision breached his rights under Article 9 ECHR. The High Court ([2007] EWHC (Admin) 1736) granted the application for judicial review and quashed the decision by the Welsh Ministers, holding that the Welsh Assembly Government had defined this legitimate object too narrowly to be a proper public interest objective for the purposes of Article 9(2), namely the elimination of any risk of a particular animal transmitting TB may be appropriate in the pursuit of some wider public health objective but cannot be a public health objective in itself. The Court of Appeal unanimously allowed the appeal and on the question of the legitimate aim held that although there was a risk that an objective may be framed so narrowly that it becomes coincident with the results sought, in the instant case the Welsh Ministers had a public health objective – the eradication or at least control of bovine tuberculosis and so the Minister was entitled to make the decision she did.

Necessary in a democratic society

The third test has been the subject of clarification by the ECtHR. It is understood that the requirement that the interference be necessary in a democratic society requires two tests to be met: the interference must correspond to a 'pressing social need' and it must be 'proportionate to the legitimate aim pursued'.[51] This requires a 'balancing exercise' whereby the court asks 'whether the interference with the right is more extensive than is justified by the legitimate aim' (Feldman 2002: 57). Since 'the notion of proportionality will always contain some subjective element and depend significantly on the context' (Evans 2002: 145), it is not surprising that different judges have taken differing approaches to this test.

Discrimination in the Enjoyment of Convention Rights

The enjoyment of all Convention rights is subject to Article 14. While Article 9 may be said to be concerned with positive religious freedom (the liberty to believe and manifest one's belief), Article 14 is concerned with negative religious freedom – the liberty from discrimination on the grounds of belief (Ahdar and Leigh 2005: 100). Article 14 forbids discrimination on, inter alia, grounds of religion but only does so in regard to 'the rights and freedoms set forth in this Convention'. Article 1 of Protocol 12 extends this to 'any right set forth by law' but this has not been ratified in the UK. This does not mean that a 'violation of a substantive Article need to be established at all in cases involving discrimination' under Article 14 (Taylor 2005: 182–3). Strasbourg has confirmed that 'a measure which in itself is in conformity with the requirements of the Article enshrining the right or freedom in question may, however, infringe this Article when read in conjunction with Article 14 for the reason that it is of a discriminatory nature',[52] that is, if the distinction has no objective and reasonable justification.[53] Other provisions will often interact with Article 9; for instance, where freedom of expression clashes with freedom of religion. Strasbourg has held that the freedom to manifest religion does not include a right to be exempt from all criticism[54] and freedom of expression contains 'a duty to avoid expressions that are gratuitously offensive to others and profane'.[55]

---

51   *Serif v. Greece* (2001) 31 EHRR 20.

52   *Case Relating to Certain Aspects of the Laws on the Use of Languages in Education in Belgium* (1979–1980) 1 EHRR 252 at 282.

53   Infringement of Article 14 may be justified if it pursues a 'legitimate aim' and if there is a 'reasonable relationship of proportionality between the means employed and the aim sought to be realized': *Darby v. Sweden* (1991) 13 EHRR 774.

54   ECtHR 13 September 2005 *İA v. Turkey*, Application no. 42571/98, para. 28: 'Those who choose to exercise the freedom to manifest their religion, irrespective of whether they do so as members of a religious majority or a minority, cannot reasonably expect to be exempt from all criticism. They must tolerate and accept the denial by others of their religious beliefs and even the propagation by others of doctrines hostile to their faith.'

55   Ibidem para. 24.

Although the reasoning of the ECtHR in some respects may be suspect, the UK domestic courts are nevertheless under a statutory duty[56] to take it into account.[57] In the cases concerning religious liberty heard in England since the enactment of the HRA, some judgments have been delivered without reference to Article 9 or to freedom of religion at all.[58] In other cases, detailed reference to and the application of the Article 9 rights have reinforced the common law position, not necessarily changing the outcome of the case but augmenting and, on occasion, improving the reasoning upon which the decision was made.[59] Recent cases on the use of drugs for a religious purpose are a clear example of this: the HRA has allowed judges to use the limitations under Article 9(2) as the process by which to determine the matter.[60] This seems preferable to the approach used by the American District Court, which excluded a similar claim by relying instead upon a restrictive definition of religion as a filtering device.[61] The English interpretation of the Article 9 right and its limitations seems more satisfactory than the American approach which effectively assesses the legitimacy of a religious belief and crudely manipulates its definition of religion.

Religious Dress

In common with many civic freedoms, the legal regulation of religious matters has been affected by the HRA. No longer are restrictions on religious symbols and religious dress merely governed by *Wednesbury* unreasonableness,[62] as Poulter (1997: 68–9) had previously suggested. There is now an alternative cause of action under Article 9 itself. As already discussed, the ECtHR has determined that wearing religious dress or displaying religious symbols is a manifestation of one's religion or belief and is thus protected by Article 9(1), but has consistently upheld limitations upon the exercise of the right. In *Dahlab v. Switzerland*,[63] the Court held that a ban preventing a teacher of small children from wearing her headscarf at school was justified as it had the legitimate aim of protecting the rights and

---

56   Section 2(1) of the *Human Rights Act 1998* prescribes that a UK 'court or tribunal determining a question which has arisen in connection with a convention right must *take into account* any … judgment, decision, declaration or advisory opinion of the European Court of Human Rights' (emphasis added).

57   Though not necessarily follow it: *Copsey v. WWB Devon Clays Ltd* [2005] ICR 1789.

58   See, for example, *Gallagher v. Church of Jesus Christ of the Latter-Day Saints* [2006] EWCA Civ 1598.

59   See, for example, *Re Durrington Cemetery* [2000] 3 WLR 1322 *per* Hill Ch, concerning the exhumation of the remains of a Jew from a graveyard consecrated in accordance with the rites of the Church of England.

60   *R v. Taylor* [2001] EWCA Crim 2263.

61   *United States v. Kuch* 288 F Supp 439 (1968).

62   *Associated Provincial Picture Houses v. Wednesbury Corporation* [1948] 1KB 223.

63   ECtHR 15 February 2001, Application no. 42393/98.

freedoms of others, public order and public safety and there was a pressing social need given the impact that the 'powerful external symbol' conveyed by her wearing a headscarf could have upon young children and by the possible proselytising effect. In *Sahin v. Turkey*,[64] the court held that a university regulation banning a student from wearing a headscarf at enrolment, lectures and examinations was justified as being prescribed by law, having the legitimate aim of protecting the rights and freedoms of others and of protecting public order and being necessary in a democratic society.[65]

The jilbab

The most substantive discussion of the law affecting religious dress for school pupils is to be found in the decision of *R (on the application of Begum) v. Headteacher and Governors of Denbigh High School*,[66] both at first instance and in two subsequent appeals. Shabina Begum, a Muslim, stopped attending Denbigh High School when the school refused to allow her to wear the jilbab[67] which she described as the only garment that met her religious requirements since it concealed the contours of the female body, including the shape of her arms and legs.[68] At first instance,[69] Bennett J gave little prominence to Begum's alleged Article 9 right to manifest her religion by wearing the jilbab. He held that although her refusal to respect the school uniform policy was 'motivated by religious beliefs', there had been no interference with her Article 9(1) right since even if Begum had been excluded (which he held she was not) she would have been 'excluded for her refusal to abide by the school uniform policy rather than her beliefs as such'.[70] This approach was not in conformity with Strasbourg jurisprudence. The bold assertion that insistence on wearing religious dress does not constitute a manifestation of one's religion or belief is wrong.

---

64   (2005) 41 EHRR 8.

65   The Court held that the interference had a pressing social need given the existence of extremist political movements in Turkey and 'the impact which wearing such a symbol … may have on those who choose not to wear it'. The interference was also proportionate since the authorities 'sought throughout that decision-making process to adapt to the evolving situation through continued dialogue with those concerned, while at the same time ensuring that order was maintained on the premises'.

66   [2006] UKHL 15, [2006] 2 WLR 719.

67   An item of clothing that was variously described by the House of Lords as 'a long coat like garment'; 'a long shapeless back gown'; and 'a long shapeless dress ending at the ankle and designed to conceal the shape of the wearer's arms and legs': [2006] UKHL *per* Lord Bingham at para. 10, Lord Hoffmann at para. 46 and Lord Scott at para. 79.

68   See the Court of Appeal judgment of Brooke LJ, [2005] EWCA Civ 199 paras 8 and 14.

69   [2004] EWHC 1389.

70   See paras 72–4.

The subsequent Court of Appeal judgment, which reversed the decision of Bennett J, was subject to much academic criticism (Poole 2005: 685).[71] The flaw was not the treatment of Article 9(1), which was undoubtedly correct, but rather the application of Article 9(2). The Court of Appeal followed Strasbourg jurisprudence to hold that Article 9(1) was engaged but, as Poole has pointed out, in deciding that the limitation of the right was justified under Article 9(2) Brooke LJ's interpretation of the Strasbourg jurisprudence was predicated upon a basic mistake (Poole 2005: 689–90). Rather than deciding whether the limitation could be justified as being necessary in a democratic society, he outlined the decision-making structure and process which the school should have used since, on his findings, the onus lay on the school to justify its interference with the Convention right.[72] This is a legally unsupportable approach. Whilst courts adopt a procedural analysis in the Administrative Court when subjecting the decisions of public authorities to judicial review, there is nothing in the HRA, the ECHR or Strasbourg jurisprudence requiring public authorities themselves to adopt a proportionality approach to the structuring of their own decision-making (Poole 2005: 689–90).

The further appeal to the Judicial Committee of the House of Lords (now reconstituted as the UK. Supreme Court) led to a decision[73] that was welcomed in that it corrected the Court of Appeal's overly formulaic approach to Article 9(2), and held, correctly in my view, that there was no breach of Article 9. However, the majority of their Lordships repeated and compounded the error originally made by Bennett J in relation to Article 9(1). Lords Bingham of Cornhill, Hoffmann and Scott of Foscote properly held that there had been no interference with Begum's rights under Article 9(1) but their confused, and not always consistent, understanding of Convention case law evidences defective reasoning: Lord Scott even spoke of an Article 9(2) right to manifest one's religion.[74] Their Lordships applied the 'specific situation' rule as if it were of general effect.[75] Lord Bingham correctly elucidated the rule but proceeded to apply it to the facts of the *Begum* case without explanation. He quoted selectively from numerous Strasbourg and domestic cases which had addressed the rule but omitted to mention references to the specific limits to its scope and extent. No reason was given why the 'specific situation' rule ought to be applied to school pupils. Lord Bingham seemed to think that the application of Strasbourg case law to university students was justification enough but this is to ignore the fact that unlike a university student, a school pupil has not voluntarily accepted an employment or role which might legitimately limit

---

71   [2005] EWCA Civ 199. See for example Poole 2005: 685.

72   Ibidem paras 75–6.

73   Note 66 *supra*.

74   Ibidem para. 85. This is erroneous in that the right is contained in Article 9(1); Article 9(2) simply contains the limitations to the exercise of the right.

75   As discussed above, the 'specific situation' rule is derived from and has been elucidated by the European Court of Human Rights' determinations in the cases of *Dahlab v. Switzerland* and *Sahin v. Turkey*.

his Article 9 rights. In state schools there is no contractual relationship between school and pupil and, not infrequently, little choice as to the school which a child must attend.

The reasoning in the opinions of Lord Nicholls and Lady Hale (differing from the other three Law Lords but concurring in the ultimate disposal of the appeal) is correct in law and more consistent with Strasbourg jurisprudence in that they both recognized that Begum's right under Article 9 had been engaged but that this was justified under Article 9(2). Lord Nicholls noted that he would prefer to state that there was interference with Article 9 and then to consider whether that interference was justified since this would require the public authority to 'explain and justify its decision'.[76] However, his Lordship did not find it necessary fully to elucidate this approach, which had it been adopted by the whole House, would have produced a fuller and more satisfactory analysis.[77] The restriction of Article 9(1) by the majority was unnecessary given that legitimate limitations on the right are routinely justified under Article 9(2).

Although the ultimate disposal of the case in the House of Lords was undoubtedly correct, restoring as it did the dismissal of the claim by Bennett J, the reasoning is not entirely satisfactory in common with many of the early cases brought to the appellate courts in the altered legal landscape of the HRA. Lord Bingham stated that:

> The Strasbourg institutions have not been at all ready to find an interference with the right to manifest religious belief in practice or observance where a person has voluntarily accepted an employment or role which does not accommodate that practice or observance and there are other means open to the person to practise or observe his or her religion without undue hardship or inconvenience.[78]

He concluded that the Strasbourg case law indicated that 'interference is not easily established'[79] before applying the 'specific situation' rule to the case without explanation. The House of Lords conceptualized the question largely in terms of proportionality, giving scant attention to identifying a pressing social need.[80] Lady Hale concluded that the school's uniform policy was a thoughtful and proportionate response to reconciling the complexities of the situation. This is demonstrated by the fact that girls have subsequently expressed their concern that if the *jilbab* were to be allowed they would face pressure to adopt it even though

---

76   Note 66 *supra*, para. 41. Albeit not in the formulaic manner which had influenced the flawed reasoning in the Court of Appeal, discussed above.

77   It is significant that Lords Bingham and Hoffmann still felt it necessary to consider Article 9(2) in depth anyway.

78   Note 66 *supra*, para. 23.

79   Ibidem, para. 24.

80   Ibidem, paras 26 and 94.

they might not wish to do so.[81] The analysis of the House of Lords would have been far more satisfactory had it adopted the classic Strasbourg approach without recourse to the 'specific situation' rule:

1. Was the wearing of the *jilbab* a manifestation of the applicant's religion? – yes
2. Was its prohibition an interference? – yes
3. Could the prohibition be justified? – yes

The niqab

In *R (on the application of X) v. Y. School*,[82] Silber J considered the *Begum* precedent to be 'an insuperable barrier' to a claim for judicial review by a school girl who wished to wear a *niqab* veil while she was being taught by male teachers at school or was likely to be seen by men. The claimant, a 12-year-old Muslim girl, refused to attend school on the basis that the school would not permit her to wear a niqab veil, which covered her entire face save her eyes. Silber J held that there had been no interference with the claimant's Article 9 rights and, even if there had been, it would have been justified under Article 9(2). He implicitly accepted Lord Bingham's assertion in *Begum* that the 'specific situation' rule applied in the case of schools. Further, unlike Lord Bingham, Silber J stated that there would be no interference with the Article 9 right simply because 'there are other means open to practise or observe [one's] religion without undue hardship or inconvenience'.[83]

The four reasons for dismissing the claim given by Silber J, in my assessment, are based upon a questionable reading of the Strasbourg jurisprudence and fail to explain why the 'specific situation' rule should be given general effect. His first reason amounted to nothing more than a recitation of Lord Scott's proposition in *Begum* that there is no infringement of the right to manifest 'where other public institutions offering similar services' are available. Similarly, the second reason was a quotation of Lord Hoffmann's assertion in *Begum* that 'Article 9 does not

---

81   Ibidem, para. 98. Drawing upon the Strasbourg decision in *Sahin*, Lord Bingham concluded that that the interference with the Article 9(1) right was proportionate since the school 'had taken immense pains to devise a uniform policy which respected Muslim beliefs but did so in an inclusive, unthreatening and uncompetitive way': para. 34.

82   [2006] EWHC (Admin) 298.

83   This arose from Silber J's (mis)interpretation of Lord Bingham's elucidation of the 'specific situation' rule. Lord Bingham had said that 'The Strasbourg institutions have not been at all ready to find an interference with the right to manifest religious belief in practice or observance where a person has voluntarily accepted an employment or role which does not accommodate that practice or observance *and* there are other means open to practise or observe his or her religion without undue hardship or inconvenience'. Silber J interpreted this as meaning that there would be no interference either: (a) where a person has voluntarily accepted an employment or role which does not accommodate that practice or observance; *or* (b) where there are other means open to practise or observe his or her religion without undue hardship or inconvenience. He appears to dilute Lord Bingham's test.

require that one should be allowed to manifest one's religion at any time and place of one's choosing'. The third, derived from Strasbourg jurisprudence, was that 'the Strasbourg case law shows that there is no interference with an Article 9 right where there is an alternative place at which the services in question can be provided without the objectionable rule in question'.[84] The fourth reason was that Strasbourg had imposed 'a high threshold before interference can be established'.[85] Quoting Lord Bingham, Silber J found no interference with the claimant's rights under Article 9 and interpreted Lord Bingham's elucidation of the specific situation rule in *Begum* as meaning that there would be no interference whenever a person had voluntarily accepted an employment or role that does not accommodate that practice or observance or where there are other means open to practise or observe that religion without undue hardship or inconvenience. In other words, since it was open to the girl to move to another school (as was the case in *Begum*) where she would be permitted to wear the garment in question there was no interference in the manifestation of her religion.

The weakness of the approach of English law post *Begum* was underlined by Silber J's comments commending the school on having in place a well thought out policy. Ironically, the approach now taken by English law makes the quality of the policy irrelevant. Provided that the right to manifest can be exercised elsewhere, it seems that the court will be entitled, or even obliged, to find that there had been no interference. Surely, the better approach would have been to require schools to provide a balanced policy weighed against the factors enumerated in Article 9(2). In his admirable treatment of Article 9(2), Silber J unwittingly showed the inadequacy of the approach now taken by English courts applying the reasoning in *Begum*. By giving general effect to a filtering device which had hitherto been used only by the ECtHR in a limited class of specific cases, and consequently closing down the reach of Article 9(1), the domestic courts are applying too broad an approach.[86] This seems contrary both to the spirit of the Convention as previously interpreted by the House of Lords in *Williamson*[87] and by the ECtHR.[88] This is particularly concerning given that Strasbourg has started to take a less

---

84   For this proposition, Siber J cited the *Jewish Liturgical Association Cha'are Shalom Ve Tsedek v. France* (2000) 9 BHRC 27, the authority of which he later questioned by repeating Lord Hoffmann's comment in *Begum* that use of the term impossible 'may be setting the test rather high'.

85   Silber J stated that he had not been shown or found any case where 'it was held that there would be an infringement of person's Article 9 rights when he or she could without excessive difficulty manifest or practise their religion as they wished in another place or in another way': para. 38.

86   The analysis of Article 9(2) by Silber J is entirely *obiter*, he having determined that Article 9(1) was not engaged in the first place.

87   *R v. Secretary of State for Education and Employment and others ex parte Williamson* [2005] UKHL 15, [2005] 2 A.C 246.

88   Strasbourg has recognized that "The State's role as the neutral and impartial organizer of the practising of various religions, denominations and beliefs is conducive to

restricted approach. Collins (2006: 619–43) notes that recent years have witnessed a 'profound reorientation' in interpretation towards an 'integrated approach' which 'involves an interpretation of Convention rights with reference to the rights contained in social and economic charters'. This wider mechanism as employed by the ECtHR contrasts sharply with the increasingly narrow approach taken by English courts.

The purity ring

In *R (on the Application of Playfoot (A Child)) v. Millais School Governing Body*,[89] an application for judicial review of a decision by a school to prevent a school girl from wearing a 'purity' ring on grounds of Articles 9 and 14 of the ECtHR was refused by the High Court on the question of interference. The judge held that Article 9 was not engaged since, although the claimant held a 'religious belief' in that she had made a decision to remain a virgin until marriage because she was a Christian, the wearing of the ring was not 'intimately linked' to the belief in chastity before marriage because *Playfoot* was under no obligation, by reason of her faith, to wear the ring. The judge correctly cited Lord Nicholls in *Williamson* as stating that if 'the belief takes the form of a perceived obligation to act in a specific way, then, in principle, doing that act pursuant to that belief is itself a manifestation of that belief in practice' but incorrectly said that this meant that the reverse was also true: if there was no such obligation then the act cannot be a manifestation of that belief.[90] The judge further commented that even if he had found that the purity ring was a manifestation of religion then, there would have been no interference with Article 9 since the claimant had voluntarily accepted the school's uniform policy and there were other means open to her to practise her belief without undue hardship or inconvenience. Thus, he relied upon the slightly crude 'specific situation' rule rather that a more nuanced analysis of the Article 9 formulaic approach.

The Sikh Kara bracelet

In *R (on the application of Watkins-Singh) v. The Governing Body of Aberdare Girls' High School*,[91] a school girl who was an observant though non-initiated Sikh sought to wear her Kara bracelet to school. Silber J heard expert evidence that although the Kara was often worn it was only compulsory in the case of initiated Sikhs. Silber J stated that disadvantage would occur – but would not only occur –where a pupil is forbidden from wearing an item where 'that person genuinely believed for reasonable grounds that wearing this item was a matter of exceptional importance to his or her racial identity or his or her religious belief'and where

---

religious harmony and tolerance in a democratic society': ECHR 31 July 2001 *Refah Parts i v. Turkey*, Application no. 41340/98.

89　[2007] EWHC Admin 1698.
90　Ibidem para. 23.
91　[2008] EWHC (Admin) 1865.

'the wearing of the item can be shown objectively to be of exceptional importance to his or her religion or race, even if the wearing of the article is not an actual requirement of that person's religion or race'.[92] This approach, though related to religious discrimination law, is in line with the most recent Strasbourg jurisprudence on the manifestation/motivation requirement discussed above. According to some commentators (Sandberg 2009: 267, Leigh 2009), the success of the claim in *Watkins-Singh*) means that litigants are now best advised not to pursue claims under Article 9 but to invoke the detailed anti-discrimination provisions under the Equality Act and its accompanying secondary legislation.[93]

Conclusions

The accommodation of religious symbols in school uniform policies is but one aspect of the dynamic of legal regulation of pluralistic societies. It is difficult to draw meaningful conclusions from isolated, fact specific cases. Certain general conclusions can be drawn. One starts with the prevailing ethos of liberal tolerance towards all faiths, against which the social need for school children to identify themselves – regardless or religion or race – as members of a particular school. There is obviously a tension between these competing virtues and a tolerable degree of discretion is afforded to individual schools to declare and enforce their uniform policies in keeping with the particular social, racial and religious demography of the catchment area. With informed cooperation, reasonable accommodations can be reached with which the vast majority of staff, children and parents will be content. It follows that the cases which fall to be litigated are examples of extreme positions: either in the form of the demands made by the pupil, being animated by political considerations often extraneous to the religion or by implacable rigidity on the part of the school to what would be a modest and unobjectionable departure in a very minor respect to the uniform policy, as in the case of the virtually invisible Sikh bracelet.

There has been a clear change in the legal regulation of spiritual concerns over the last decade. The effect has been the recasting of protection by means of universally framed but qualified rights. It is somewhat regrettable that the courts have sought artificially to limit the universal application of such rights rather than systemically developing an exposition of the qualifications to those rights. These early incongruities will doubtless settle over time. The judiciary is struggling to find a vocabulary to articulate a consistent and predictable jurisprudence in a context whereby the common law inheritance of centuries of benevolent liberalism will not be lost.

---

92   Ibidem paras 56–7.

93   However, *dicta* from *Begum* have been influential in a number of religious discrimination decisions, such as *Ladele v. London Borough of Islington* [2009] EWCA (Civ) 1357, paras 54–61.

This changing legal response may have its origins in legitimate concerns which have increased in importance since the seismic events of 9/11, and their real and perceived ramifications. We are living in an age of multiculturalism, pluralism and religious resurgence. This necessarily results in a sustained debate as to the place of religion in public life as well as its legal regulation. There has been a shift in dynamic – from the indulgence of permissive tolerance to the more militant exercise of a specific right. Where the right to religious freedom is becoming the universal tool of the litigator, whether fundamentalist or moderate, the State can no longer merely be benign and instead is compelled to intervene to define, clarify and occasionally enforce (or prohibit the enforcement of) the individual's right.

In the current age of uncertainty, the law relating to religion does not exist in isolation from societal trends. That is why it is vital that critical attention is paid not only to individual legal developments but also to their collective effect and to general questions concerning law, religion and society in what Sandberg (2010) styles 'banal religiosity'.[94] In the current climate, it is imperative that the legal parameters be clearly defined by the legislators and coherently enforced by the judiciary. Convincing evidence and coherent legal argument must be deployed to help delineate the outermost borders of general accommodation rather than simply denying the protection which the law intended. Lawmakers and law enforcers must ensure that each and all of the qualifications to the right are clearly understood and applied transparently and consistently.

With these principles in mind, there can be little doubt that most elements of religious dress can be accommodated sensitively and appropriately without disturbing the laudable ethos of individual schools. An outright ban on religious symbols in state schools in the United Kingdom is unthinkable but toleration and accommodation, whilst hallmarks of a liberal democracy, still require long-stop boundaries. The mechanism for describing the extent of such boundaries is to be found within the qualifications set out in Article 9(2). In time, the English judiciary will become more confident to engage in the policy matters that Article 9(2) brings into play and the sooner the 'specific situation' rule is abandoned as blunt and ineffective instrument for determining these cases the better.

---

94 The concept of 'banal religiosity' denotes a post-Christian mindset that clings on to religion simply as a vague moral source of identity. Like Billig's (1995) concept of 'banal nationalism', banal religiosity is constantly perpetuated by everyday habits. It is a civic religion based upon basic ethical principles traditionally aligned with religious traditions which has grown as a response to religious difference. In the same way that banal nationalism can be contrasted with 'hot nationalism' which occurs at time of 'social disruption' banal religiosity can be contrasted with fundamental religiosity. Whilst such dramatic but peripheral displays of religiosity dominate the debate regarding the role of religion in society, the concept of banal religiosity allows us to draw attention to the powers of an ideology which is so familiar that it hardly seems noticeable. See also Sandberg 2010.

References

Ahdar, R. and Leigh, I. 2005. *Religious Freedom in the Liberal State*. Oxford: Oxford University Press.

Billig, M. 1995. *Banal Nationalism*. London: Sage.

Collins, H. 2006. The protection of civil liberties in the workplace. *Modern Law Review* 69(4), 619–43.

Edge, P.W. 1996. Current problems in Article 9 of the European Convention on Human Rights. *Juridical Review*, 42.

Evans, C. 2002. *Freedom of Religion under the European Convention on Human Rights*. Oxford: Oxford University Press.

Feldman, D. 2002. *Civil Liberties and Human Rights in England and Wales*. 2nd edn. Oxford: Oxford University Press.

Hill, M., Sandberg, R. and Doe, N. 2011. *Religion and Law in the United Kingdom*. The Netherlands: Kluwer Law International.

Hill, M. and Sandberg, R. 2007. Is nothing sacred? Clashing symbols in a secular world. *Public Law* 66(2), 488–506.

Hill, M. 2005. The permissible scope of legal limitations on the freedom of religion or belief in the United Kingdom. *Emory International Law Review* 19(2), 1129–86.

Leigh, I. 2009. Recent developments in religious liberty. *Ecclesiastical Law Journal* 11, 65.

Poole, T. 2005. Of headscarves and heresies: the *Denbigh High School* case and public authority decision making under the Human Rights Act. *Public Law*, 685–95.

Poulter, S. 1998. *Ethnicity, Law and Human Rights*. Oxford: Oxford University Press.

Poulter, S. 1997. Muslim headscarves in school: contrasting legal approaches in England and France. *Oxford Journal of Legal Studies* 17(1), 43–74.

Knights, S. 2007. *Freedom of Religion, Minorities and the Law*. Oxford: Oxford University Press.

Rivers, J. Religious dress: British perspectives and OSCE developments (Strasbourg Conference) [Online]. Available at: http://www.strasbourgconference.org/ papers [Accessed: 8 February 2011].

Sandberg, R. 2009. The changing position of religious minorities in English law: the legacy of *Begum*, in *Legal Practice and Cultural Diversity*, edited by R. Grillo et al. Aldershot: Ashgate, 267–82.

Sandberg, R. 2008. Defining religion: towards an interdisciplinary approach. *Revista General de Derecho Canonico y Derecho Eclesiástico del Estado* 17, 1–23.

Sandberg, R. 2010. *Religion, Society and Law: An Analysis of the Interface Between Law on Religion and the Sociology of Religion*. Doctoral thesis: Cardiff University.

Taylor, P.M. 2005. *Freedom of Religion: UN and European Human Rights Law and Practice*. Cambridge: Cambridge University Press.

Vickers, L. 2006. Is all harassment equal? The case of religious harassment. *Cambridge Law Journal* 65(3), 579–605.

Chapter 16

A Uniform Approach to Religious Discrimination? The Position of Teachers and Other School Staff in the UK

Russell Sandberg

On 1 October 2010, the majority of the provisions of the *Equality Act 2010* came into force. This was greeted with mass hysteria in the newspapers. The *Daily Mail* splashed with the questionable assertion that the Act meant the end of office jokes whilst the *Daily Telegraph* ran a column declaring the Act to be the 'worst law in English history'. The Act draws together, and further strengthens, nine separate pieces of anti-discrimination legislation including the law designed to protect against discrimination on the grounds of religion or belief. It also outlines a number of exceptions afforded to religious groups (Sandberg 2011). Provisions previously found in the *Employment Equality (Religion or Belief) Regulations 2003* and Part 2 of the *Equality Act 2006* can now be found in the *Equality Act 2010*. These provisions have led to numerous cases and tribunal decisions, particularly in employment law. Moreover, the hyperbole in the press reaction of October 2010 suggests that further litigation is inevitable. These, still rather new, rights are not generally well understood.

The first decade of the twenty-first century witnessed numerous social and political developments surrounding the place of religion in the public sphere. The shadow of the terrorist attacks in New York on 11 September 2001 and in London on 7 July 2007 loomed large in debates concerning the extent to which religious difference should be accommodated. These concerns led to a plethora of new laws concerning religion in the United Kingdom. The *Human Rights Act 1998* ('HRA') encouraged discussion of religious freedom as a human right, religious discrimination became prohibited for the first time and the *Racial and Religious Hatred Act 2006* criminalized the stirring up religious hatred (Sandberg 2011: chapters 5–7). These legal changes transformed the legal framework concerning religion. There is now more 'religion law' – national and international law affecting religion – than ever before (Sandberg 2008: 336–40, Sandberg 2011). There now exists a new legal framework concerning religion. The novelty of these legal provisions and the general hullaballoo concerning religion in the public sphere are the main reasons for the plethora of cases concerning religious dress and symbols which have taken place in recent years in Britain and across the globe and the amount of column inches they have consumed in the media. This chapter seeks to explore the case law that has developed in relation to the position of teachers and other school staff in the United Kingdom.

The chapter is divided into two parts. The first part will seek to provide the sociological and legal context in which the case law is to be found, exploring the main social changes concerning religion and introducing the legal responses which have been made. The second part explains the current law protecting the religious freedom of staff in schools in more depth. It will elucidate the protection under education law for those who are employed in different types of school as well as the application of general pieces of religion law found in human rights and discrimination law statutes. Focusing particularly upon the effect of discrimination law provisions now found in the *Equality Act 2010*, this part will explore the findings and effect of four significant cases: the Employment Tribunal ('ET') decisions in *Noah v. Sarah Desrosiers (t/a Wedge)*[1] and *Chaplin v. Royal Devon & Exeter NHS Foundation Trust*,[2] the Employment Appeal Tribunal ('EAT') decision in *Asmi v. Kirklees Metropolitan Council*[3] and the Court of Appeal decision in *Eweida v. British Airways*.[4] The conclusion will then seek to draw together these findings, not only concerning the extent to which the wearing of religious dress and symbols by school staff is accommodated under English law but also in relation to what this suggests about the sociological place of religion in the public sphere.

Rewriting the Narrative

Until fairly recently, there was a cosy consensus surrounding the place of religion in the public sphere. It was widely considered that the effect of the Enlightenment was the triumph of reason over religion. The question that interested the founding fathers of sociology (Marx, Durkheim and Weber) was that of how modern society would manage without religion (Robertson 1969: 12, Wilson 1966: 14, Wilson 1982: 12). Although it was recognized that the Judeo-Christian tradition had been a crucial element in the historical evolution of Europe as a whole, shaping its laws and social institutions, in modern Britain religion was said to have lost its social significance. As Steve Bruce (1996: 230) has written: 'individualism threatened the communal basis of religious belief and behaviour, while rationality removed many of the purposes of religion and rendered away many of its beliefs implausible.' Religious activity was seen to have retreated to the private sphere and to have become akin to any other leisure activity.

---

1   [2008] ET Case Number: 2201867/07 (29 May 2008).
2   [2010] ET Case Number: 17288862009 (6 April 2010).
3   [2006] ET Case Number: 1801450/06 (6 October 2006); [2007] UKEAT 0009 07 30003 (30 March 2007).
4   [2010] EWCA Civ 80.

This assumption found expression in English law. The dogmatic and often violent religious intolerance and discrimination which followed the break with Rome in the 1530s gradually gave way to limited and piecemeal toleration of religions other than the established Church of England. Important legal milestones include the *Toleration Act 1689*, the *Roman Catholic Relief Act 1791* and the *Unitarians Relief Act 1813* (Sandberg 2011: chapter 2, Rivers 2010: chapter 1, Gunn 2005). The role of the law became minimal; as Hoffmann J commented in 1993: 'the attitude of the English legislator to racing is much more akin to his attitude to religion ... it is something to be encouraged but not the business of government.'[5] Similarly, judges professed themselves to be agnostic in matters of religion,[6] showed deference towards religious beliefs[7] and spoke of a 'well recognized divide between Church and State'.[8] Over the years, although English law extended the accommodation of religious scruples and much was achieved by ad hoc and piecemeal measures (Menski 2008, Hill 2001, Sandberg 2011), the regulation of religion was characterized by a lightness of touch. This is shown, for example, by the fact that (unlike in many European countries) English law lacked detailed and compulsory registration schemes for religious groups (Friedner 2007).

That is not to say, however, that this secularization thesis[9] boasted universal support. Reflections of a Christian heritage can still be found in English law. The legacy of the ecclesiastical courts upon the substantive laws and procedures of modern English law suggests that clerical fingerprints faded rather than disappeared; for example, in relation to marriage law.[10] As Bradney (2000: 89) has noted, although it is often said that there has been a trend towards 'a separation of Church and State, religion and law ... allowing a multi religious country to maintain social stability. Detailed enquiry suggests that this separation is in fact far from complete'. Notably certain incidents of establishment continue in relation to the Church of England, for example, the right to rites of passage in the parish church that continue to belong to parishioners (Sandberg 2011, Hill 2007). The sociological evidence also points to a complex picture: statistics show that

---

5   *R v. Disciplinary Committee of the Jockey Club ex parte Aga Khan* [1993] 1WLR 909 at 932.

6   See *Re Watson* [1973] 1 WLR 1472: 'the court does not prefer one religion to another and it does not prefer one sect to another'.

7   *Gilmour v. Coats* [1949] AC 426: 'No temporal court of law can determine the truth of any religious belief: it is not competent to investigate any such matter and it ought not to attempt to do so'.

8   *R v. Chief Rabbi, ex parte Wachmann* [1992] 1 WLR 1036, 1043.

9   The phrase 'to secularise' originates from the dissolution of the monasteries by Henry VIII in the 1530s (Herbert 2003: 29, Beckford 2003: 33).

10   For example, section 22 of the *Matrimonial Causes Act 1857* provided that the courts of the State should continue to apply the same principles as the ecclesiastical courts had done.

although there has been a steady decline in the membership of most Christian churches,[11] religious belief is not declining as fast as religious practice.[12]

Moreover, in the twenty-first century a vast number of changes have challenged the narrative that religion has disappeared from the public sphere. Sociologists of religion are producing new accounts that seek to move beyond the secularization thesis. These take into account three changes that have occurred in the last decade: (1) a changing moral framework; (2) the rise of consumerism; and (3) immigration. First, as Fevre (2000: 9) has chronicled, Western society is characterized by confusion as to what to do for the best and an inability to rely on morality as a means of dispelling doubts and resolving dilemmas. It now takes 'an extraordinary effort' to hold onto the moral certainties which once were 'as easily grasped as the art of taking breath'; a 'positive act of submission' is now required where previously a 'superhuman exertion' was needed to escape from such constraints. Secondly, the rise of the consumer society (as described, for instance, by Bauman 2002) has led to religion becoming a consumer choice. Some sociologists of religion have said that the prevalent form of religiosity is the 'pick-and-mix' variety (Bruce 1996: 233) and have spoken of the existence of a 'free market in religion' (Beckford and Richardson 2007: 411). Thirdly, as Davie (2006) has noted, new forms of religion are coming from outside Europe largely as a result of immigration. The second wave of immigration in the 1990s ushered in a growth of religious pluralism in general and Islam in particular, challenging 'widely held assumptions about the place of religion in European societies' (2006: 33) – chiefly the notion that religion is a private affair.

These sociological changes have affected the law. Recent years has seen an increase in interest in religion on the part of the State and a widening and deepening of regulation on religion. This trend may be referred to as the 'juridification of religion'.[13] The language of religious rights is becoming common place and a plethora of laws concerning religion have been enacted, interpreted and administered in England and Wales. Collectively, these may be considered to represent a considerable shift towards prescriptive regulation and the active promotion of religious liberty as a right (Hill and Sandberg 2007, Doe and Sandberg 2010, Sandberg 2011). The shift can be seen in the way in which English law deals with religious dress and symbols. Traditionally, the wearing of religious dress and symbols (like much of religious behaviour) was lightly regulated by the law. English law only provided specific statutory exceptions designed to lift particular legal restrictions. This was most notable in relation to the Sikh turban (Poulter 1998). Sikhs alone were exempt from the requirement to wear a safety

---

11   For instance, Davie (1994: 46) says that the Anglicans have lost almost half a million members between 1972 and 1992.

12   Most famously in the 2001 census, over 70 per cent of Britons aligned themselves to Christianity. However, these figures are controversial (see Day: 2006).

13   See Sandberg 2011: chapter 10, which applies the notion of juridificiation (as developed by Teubner 1987, Blicher and Molander 2008) in relation to religion law.

hat on a construction site[14] and were among those exempted from the law relating to the wearing of protective headgear for motor cyclists.[15] Such provisions clearly owed more to the tradition of religious tolerance than to any notion of religious liberty as a widespread positive right (Vickers 2006: 598).[16]

However, from the mid twentieth century onwards the light touch became firmer as a result of developments in human rights and discrimination law. Articles of the European Convention on Human Rights ('ECHR'), including the freedom of religion provisions of Article 9, became important. Although domestic courts lacked the 'jurisdiction directly to enforce the rights and freedoms under the Convention',[17] Convention Articles became regarded as an aid to interpretation by domestic courts and individual petition to the European Court of Human Rights ('ECtHR') in Strasbourg became permitted after 1966. Moreover, important developments occurred in relation to discrimination law. The *Race Relations Act 1976* forbade direct or indirect discrimination on the grounds of colour, race, nationality or ethnic origins and this was interpreted to include members of certain religious groups such as Sikhs[18] and Jews.[19] Although Muslims,[20] Rastafarians[21] and all other religious groups were outside the scope of the protection, the *Race Relations Act 1976* began a trend whereby ethnic (and therefore some religious) practices were not merely tolerated but were legally protected. These developments represented a partial shift from the passive tolerance offered by common law to a more prescriptive regulatory regime.

The laws of the twenty-first century have accelerated this trend, providing explicit positive protection on grounds of religion and belief. Firstly, by virtue of the *Human Rights Act 1998* (in force from October 2000), which made Article 9 of the ECHR directly justiciable in domestic courts, it is now unlawful for public authorities to act in a way which is incompatible with a Convention right[22] and courts are required to interpret United Kingdom legislation so far as is possible in a manner compatible with the rights outlined in the ECHR,[23] and in so doing

---

14 *Employment Act 1989*, s.11.

15 Now found in s.16 of the *Road Traffic Act 1988*.

16 This is illustrated by the fact that Sikhs injured as a result of wearing a turban instead of a safety hat are denied certain forms of legal redress: see *Employment Act 1989*, s.11.

17 *Waddington v. Miah (Otherwise Ullah)* [1974] 2 All ER 377.

18 *Mandla v. Dowell Lee* [1983] 2 AC 548 compare this with the decision in the Court of Appeal which had considered them a religious group and thus outside the scope of the legislation: *Mandla v. Dowell Lee* [1983] QB 1.

19 *Seide v. Gillette Industries Limited* [1980] IRLR 427.

20 Muslims do not constitute an ethnic group because their descent cannot be traced to a common geographical origin; the spread of Islam is the spread of that faith rather than those who share it (Edge 2002, 252).

21 *Crown Suppliers (PSA) Limited v. Dawkins* [1993] ICR 517.

22 s.6(1).

23 s.3(1). In the event of there being an irreconcilable inconsistency, the domestic legislation prevails subject to a 'fast-track' system of executive action to bring English law into

they must 'take into account'[24] – though not necessarily 'follow'[25] – the decisions of the ECtHR. Secondly, pursuant to *EU Directive 2000/78/EC*, regulations were enacted in 2003 to extend discrimination law to explicitly cover religion and belief. The *Employment Equality (Religion or Belief) Regulations 2003* prohibited direct discrimination, indirect discrimination, victimization and harassment on grounds of religion or belief in relation to employment and vocational training (including higher education) whilst Part 2 of the *Equality Act 2006* prohibited direct and indirect discrimination and victimization (but not harassment) in relation to the provision of goods and services and the exercise of public functions (including schools). The *Equality Act 2010* consolidates these pieces of legislation, replacing the substantive law found in earlier legislation without making any general changes.

The HRA and the new law prohibiting discrimination on grounds of religion or belief may be understood as the two pillars of twenty-first century religion law (Sandberg 2011: chapter 6). These are the key legal changes that have led to the juridification of religion in England and Wales. These new provisions protecting religion as a right have led to a significant amount of litigation and many cases have been concerned with the wearing of religious dress and symbols. The remainder of this chapter will explore the current law on religious dress and symbols, focusing upon the position of employees within schools. To what extent does English law now protect the wearing of religious dress and symbols by teachers and other staff? And what does this suggest about the place of religion in the public sphere?

The Legal Framework

Three different areas of English law are relevant to this question.[26] First, there are particular provisions protecting teachers which are found in education law. Second, the HRA provides general human right guarantees which protect people against interferences by public authorities such as schools and Local Education Authorities ('LEAs'). Third, there are legal provisions, now found in the *Equality Act 2010*, which protect employees from discrimination by employers. This section examines these different areas in turn.

---

line with the Convention. See s.4 (declaration of incompatibility) and s.10 (remedial action).

24   s.2(1).

25   Lord Slynn in *R (Alconbury Developments Ltd) v. Secretary of State for the Environment, Transport and the Regions* [2001] UKHL 23, para. 26 has suggested that courts should only feel under an obligation to follow Strasbourg case law where there is a 'clear and constant jurisprudence'.

26   For an argument that these laws are best understood as being part of something called 'religion law', see Sandberg 2011.

Education Law

There are two important distinctions in education law. The first is between maintained schools and independent schools. The second is between schools which have a religious character and those which do not. These distinctions can be summarized as follows (Sandberg and Buchanan this book: Chapter 5, Sandberg 2011). Maintained schools are those which are funded and run by the State: as a general rule, they are maintained by LEAs, follow the National Curriculum and are subject to inspection by the Office for Standards in Education, Children's Services and Skills ('OFSTED') in England and Estyn in Wales. Independent schools, by contrast, are funded by fees paid by parents and investments: they are largely free to run their own affairs, including setting their own curricula and admission policies.[27]

However, not all maintained schools are completely funded by the State. Maintained schools are organized into five statutory categories: (1) community schools; (2) foundation schools; (3) voluntary schools (which include voluntary aided and voluntary controlled schools); (4) community special schools; and (5) foundation special schools.[28] The main differences between these categories are control and financing. Community and voluntary controlled schools are run by the LEA, which employs staff and sets admission criteria. By contrast, foundation and voluntary aided schools are established by voluntary bodies (largely churches and other religious communities) and are run by their own governing body. Where a voluntary body has established a school, it will appoint 'foundation governors' whose duty is to preserve and develop the religious character of the school and to ensure that it is conducted in accordance with its trust deed.

Foundation, voluntary and independent schools can be designated as having a religious character. Such schools are designated by the Secretary of State as schools having a religious character where he is satisfied that the school was established by a religious body or for religious purposes.[29] The protection of the religious freedom of teaching staff differs in schools which have a religious character. Moreover, the protection also varies depending on the type of school which has a religious character. For present purposes, a distinction can be made between teachers at the following types of school:

- Foundation or voluntary schools which do not have a religious character
- Foundation or voluntary controlled schools which do have a religious character
- Voluntary aided schools which do have a religious character

---

27   They do, however, need to be registered with the Department for Children, Schools and Families and are subject to inspection either by Ofsted or by an inspectorate approved by the Secretary of State.

28   *School Standards and Framework Act 1998*, s.20(1).

29   Ibidem, s.69(3), 124B.

- Independent schools which do not have a religious character
- Independent schools which do have a religious character

The general, default, rule is that teachers cannot be required to give religious education or attend religious worship and cannot be refused promotion or paid less because of their 'religious opinions'.[30] This rule applies to all teachers who work in foundation or voluntary schools which do not have a religious character. In schools that do have a religious character, this rule applies to all teachers except 'reserved teachers'. The exception for 'reserved' teachers allows the school to discriminate according to the religious opinions of teachers in order to safeguard the religious character of the school. The number of 'reserved teachers' depends on what type of school the school with a religious character is (Sandberg 2011, Vickers 2009).

In foundation or voluntary controlled schools which have a religious character, only a certain number of staff can be designated as being 'reserved teachers'. These are selected for their fitness and competence to give the required religious education and are specifically appointed to do so. Reserved teachers can be appointed provided that there are more than two teachers in the school and provided that the number of such 'reserved' teachers must not exceed one-fifth of the total number of teachers including the head teacher.[31] Where the head teacher is not to be a reserved teacher, 'regard may be had to that person's ability and fitness to preserve and develop the religious character of the school'.[32]

In the case of 'reserved' teachers, preference may be given in connection with the appointment, remuneration or promotion of teachers at the school to persons whose religious opinions are in accordance with that of the school, who attend religious worship in accordance with those tenets and who give, or are willing to give, religious education at the school in accordance with those tenets.[33] Regard may be had, in connection with the termination of the employment or engagement of any reserved teacher at the school, to any conduct on his part which is incompatible with the precepts or with the upholding of the tenets, of the specified religion or religious denomination.[34] All of the other non-reserved teachers are governed by the general rule that applies to schools which do not have a religious character.[35]

In voluntary aided schools with a religious character, all teachers may be 'reserved' teachers. The general rule does not apply. Instead, the rules which apply to reserved teachers apply across the board.[36] The religious opinions of staff can be taken into account in relation to appointment, remuneration, promotion

---

30   Ibidem, s.59.
31   Ibidem, s.58(2)–(3).
32   Ibidem, s.60(4).
33   Ibidem, ss.60(3), (5)(a).
34   Ibidem, ss.60(3), (5)(b).
35   Ibidem, s.60(2).
36   Ibidem, s.60(5).

or termination of their employment. Therefore, in relation to teachers employed at maintained schools who wish to manifest their religion at work through the wearing of religious dress and symbols it may be said that those who work in a school without a religious character are protected by the provision that the school cannot discriminate against their religious opinions by paying them less, refusing to promote or requiring them to take part in religious education and worship. The same is true of teachers employed in foundation or voluntary controlled schools which have a religious character, provided that they are not 'reserved' teachers. 'Reserved' teachers in foundation or voluntary controlled schools which have a religious character and all teachers in voluntary aided schools with a religious character can be discriminated against if their religious opinions are different to those which are in accordance with that of the school. A teacher in a Catholic voluntary controlled school could be disadvantaged if he or she were to convert to Islam, for example. Such a teacher would not benefit from the general rule. However, it must be remembered that 'reserved' teachers who share the religious opinions of the school are likely to be advantaged.

In relation to independent schools, the general rule protecting the religious opinions of staff does not apply. However, independent schools can be designated as having a religious character.[37] Where this occurs, the independent school can treat all teachers as 'reserved' teachers. Independent schools designated as having a religious character may give preference in connection with the appointment, remuneration or promotion of teachers at the school to persons whose religious opinions are in accordance with that of the school, who attend religious worship in accordance with those tenets, and who give or are willing to give, religious education at the school in accordance with those tenets. Regard may be had, in connection with the termination of the employment or engagement of any teacher at the school, to any conduct on his or her part which is incompatible with the precepts, or with the upholding of the tenets, of the specified religion or religious denomination.[38]

There are a number of other pieces of education law affecting the religious freedom of staff (Sandberg and Buchanan this book: Chapter 5, Sandberg 2011: chapter 8). In particular, it may be noted that there are a number of education-related exceptions to the general law prohibiting discrimination on grounds of religion or belief. Legal prohibitions on religious discrimination do not apply to the school curriculum, to acts of worship and to schools which have a religious character.[39] The general picture appears to be that some of the usual safeguards protecting religious freedom do not apply in schools which have a religious character, allowing for discrimination against some staff who do not share the religious character of the school.

---

37   Ibidem, s.124B.

38   Ibidem, s.124A.

39   *Equality Act 2010*, Part 2 of Schedule 11. Note also the exceptions for LEAs now found in Part 2 of Schedule 3 of the Act.

Overall, however, it may be doubted what effect these general education law provisions would have upon the wearing of religious dress and symbols by school staff. In the cases to date, these legal provisions have not been cited – largely because the protection provided by human rights and discrimination law go beyond the protection provided by the general rule that teachers cannot be disadvantaged by dint of their religious opinions. Having said that, the different provisions applying to 'reserved' teachers shows how the level of protection differs according to the type of school. This perhaps is to be expected. If a teacher chooses to work within a school with a religious character, then surely it is fair for them to expect that manifesting a different religious character might be more difficult.[40]

The remainder of this chapter focuses entirely upon the position of teachers and other staff who work at a school without a religious character who wish to wear religious dress or symbols at work. First, since teachers at maintained schools work for a public authority, it will look at whether they could argue that restrictions on dress or symbols infringe their right to manifest their religion under Article 9 ECHR. Second, the chapter will look at whether teachers could argue that the restriction constitutes discrimination on grounds of religion or belief under the *Equality Act 2010*.

Human Rights Law

Although the HRA incorporated Article 9 into English law, the Act has not led to any great increase in the protection of religious employees who seek to wear religious dress and symbols. The Strasbourg jurisprudence has made it clear that Article 9 has little application in the employment sphere due to the 'specific situation' rule (Sandberg 2011: chapter 5). This states that where a claimant voluntarily submits to a system of rules (typically by signing a contract of employment) they cannot subsequently claim that the terms of those rules breach their right to religious freedom.[41] Although the Court of Appeal in *Copsey v. WBB* Devon Clays Ltd[42] was highly critical of this rule,[43] it was of little doubt that it meant that where

---

40 This is consistent with the 'specific situation' rule applied by Strasbourg. The 'specific situation' rule is discussed further below. However, it is of note that whilst courts have prevented believers from bringing faith into secular situations on the grounds that the believer has voluntarily entered the secular environment, they have never developed this to cover the converse situation where a non-believer voluntarily submits to a religious situation. The religious situation rule would say a non-believer enters a place of worship, a faith school or a religious bookstore, then surely their voluntary submission should be an answer to any claim that the religious setting breaches their Article 9 rights. For further discussion of this see Sandberg 2010, Sandberg 2011: chapter 10.

41 See, *Ahmad v. United Kingdom* (1981) 4 EHRR 126; *Stedman v. United Kingdom* (1997) 23 EHRR CD 168.

42 [2005] EWCA Civ 932.

43 Mummery LJ stated that the rule amounted to 'repeated assertions unsupported by the evidence or reasoning that would normally accompany a judicial ruling' which 'are

an employee agrees to a contract of employment which restricts their religious freedom in some way they cannot subsequently claim that this restriction interferes with their Article 9 right.[44] It is clear, therefore, that if a teacher's contract of employment includes a dress policy then once they sign that contract they cannot subsequently claim that the dress policy infringes their religious freedom.

It may be observed that this is quite unlikely to occur. Although teachers may be required not to dress in an offensive way, there will rarely be detailed regulations concerning their dress. However, this does not mean that the 'specific situation' rule will not apply. Domestic judgments have gone further than the ECtHR and have applied the 'specific situation rule' generally to any situation where the claimant retains the choice to manifest their religion elsewhere. The ECtHR has applied the 'specific situation' rule only where someone has voluntarily submitted to a system of rules, such as in relation to a person who voluntarily submits to military service,[45] a person who voluntarily enters into a contract of employment,[46] those who voluntarily enrol at a university,[47] and prisoners (who have broken the social contract).[48] However, with the exception of one decision which has not been subsequently followed,[49] Strasbourg has not cast this specific situation rule as being of general application. However, the courts of the United Kingdom have done just that. This is shown by the case law that has developed in relation to the wearing of religious dress and symbols by pupils (Hill this book: chapter 15).

The effect of the expansion of the 'specific situation' rule by English courts, notably in *R (on the application of Begum) v. Headteacher and Governors of Denbigh High School*,[50] is that Article 9 claims are unlikely to succeed (Sandberg 2011: chapter 5). Unlike Strasbourg, English courts focus more upon the question of whether there has been interference with the Article 9(1) right rather than the question of whether that interference can be justified by the limitations provided by Article 9(2) (Hill: this book, Chapter 15). This means, as illustrated in R *(on the Application of Playfoot (A Child)) v. Millais School Governing Body*,[51] that decisions can be reached without looking at the merits of the case. In *Playfoot*, the

---

difficult to square with the supposed fundamental character of the rights' and noted that Strasbourg cases alleging breaches of other Articles and recent domestic cases on Article 9 had not followed it: see para. 236.

44   Rix LJ, however, contended that the 'specific situation' rule did not extend to the situation where an *employer* subsequently ought to vary the terms of the employee's contract of employment: para. 65.

45   *Kalaç v. Turkey* (1997) 27 EHRR 552.

46   *Stedman v. United Kingdom* (1997) 5 EHRLR 544; *Ahmad v. United Kingdom* (1981) 4 EHRR 126.

47   *Karaduman v. Turkey* (1993) 74 DR 93.

48   *X v. United Kingdom* (1974) 1 D& R at 41–2.

49   *Jewish Liturgical Association Cha'are Shalom Ve Tsedek v. France* (2000) 9 BHRC 27.

50   [2006] UKHL 15.

51   [2007] EWHC Admin 1698.

High Court also restrictively applied the manifestation/motivation requirement,[52] holding that a practice was not 'intimately linked' to the belief because the claimant was under no obligation, by reason of her faith. This is problematic, in that it requires courts to decide upon questions of religious doctrine and would seem to privilege mainstream religious groups and beliefs. Splinter groups and individuals within religious groups who form different beliefs would lack protection. The decision in *Playfoot* seems to be based on a misunderstanding of Lord Nicholls' speech in *Williamson*;[53] whilst it is true that Lord Nicholls did say that where a belief is obligatory then it is likely to be 'intimately linked',[54] he also said that it is not the case that a belief will not be 'intimately linked' unless it is obligatory.[55]

The decisions in *Begum* and *Playfoot* have therefore introduced misinterpretations of the Article 9 jurisprudence which have severely restricted the chances of litigants bringing successful Article 9 claims. This is underlined by the only successful case brought by a pupil concerning religious dress (*R (on the application of Watkins-Singh) v. The Governing Body of Aberdare Girls' High School*)[56] which succeeded because it was argued under discrimination laws rather than under the HRA (Sandberg 2011: chapter 5). That decision underlines the extent to which Article 9 is now moribund, particularly in claims concerning religious dress and symbols and especially in the employment sphere. This would suggest that school employees are best advised to rely upon discrimination law rather than human rights provisions.

Discrimination Law

There have been a number of religious dress and symbol cases brought by employees under religious discrimination laws. Some of these cases have been successful whilst others have been unsuccessful.[57] All of the successful cases have been cases of indirect discrimination rather than direct discrimination. Indirect discrimination occurs where A applies a provision, criterion or practice

---

52   This rule, as developed by Strasbourg, requires that the claimant's actions manifest their religion or belief as opposed to being merely motivated by it. See for example *Arrwosmith v. United Kingdom* (1981) 3 EHRR 218.

53   *R. Secretary of State for Education and Employment and others ex parte Williamson* [2005] UKHL 15.

54   Ibidem, para. 32: 'If, as here, the belief takes the form of a perceived obligation to act in a specific way, then, in principle, doing that act pursuant to that belief is itself a manifestation of that belief in practice. In such cases the act is "intimately linked" to the belief, in the Strasbourg phraseology.'

55   Ibidem, para. 33: 'This is not to say that a perceived obligation is a prerequisite to manifestation of a belief in practice. It is not: ... I am concerned only to identify what, in principle, is sufficient to constitute manifestation in a case where the belief is one of perceived obligation.'

56   [2008] EWHC (Admin) 1865.

57   For a detailed discussion of the case law see Sandberg 2011: chapter 6, Vickers 2010.

(a PCP) against B which is discriminatory in relation to B's religion or belief. A PCP is discriminatory where it is (1) applied equally to persons who do not share B's religion or belief;[58] (2) puts persons of B's religion or belief at a particular disadvantage compared with others; (3) actually puts B at that disadvantage; and (4) A cannot show it to be a proportionate means of achieving a legitimate aim.[59]

Unlike direct discrimination, indirect discrimination can be justified, for example, by security or health and safety concerns. Its operation is therefore similar to the analysis of the right to manifest under Article 9. The analysis by the court or tribunal is often twofold. First, the court determines whether there is interference with the right. In discrimination law, this is often expressed as asking whether there is a 'disadvantage' but it is effectively the same question. Second, if there has been interference (or 'disadvantage') attention is then given to the question of justification: can the interference be justified?

There have been four significant indirect discrimination cases concerning religious dress and symbols worn by employees:[60] (1) the ET decision in *Noah v. Sarah Desrosiers (t/a Wedge)*[61] in which the religious dress claim succeeded; (2) the EAT decision in *Asmi v. Kirklees Metropolitan Council*[62] in which the religious dress claim lost because although there was a disadvantage, the indirect discrimination was justified; (3) the Court of Appeal decision in *Eweida v. British Airways*[63] in which the religious dress claim lost because there was no disadvantage; and (4) the ET decision in *Chaplin v. Royal Devon & Exeter NHS Foundation Trust*,[64] which followed *Eweida* and dismissed the religious dress claim because there was no disadvantage. Although the decision in *Asmi* was the only case to involve an employee at a school (it involved a teaching assistant), all of these cases would be relevant to such employees. The question is what distinguishes the successful claim in *Noah* from the three other claims which were unsuccessful.

In short, the difference between *Noah* and *Asmi* was the question of whether the discrimination was justified. In *Noah*, the claimant, Mrs Noah, applied for a job as an assistant stylist at the respondent's hairdressing salon. When Noah attended the interview wearing a headscarf, the interview was terminated on the basis that the hair salon was known for 'ultra modern' hair styles which staff were supposed to display to clients. No other person was ultimately appointed to the job. The

---

58 Indirect discrimination also occurs where a PCP would create discrimination if it were applied. Indirect discrimination would therefore protect a claimant who did not apply for a job, knowing that a discriminatory PCP was to be applied.

59 *Equality Act 2010* s.19(2). This mirrors the previous law: *Employment Equality (Religion or Belief) Regulations 2003* reg 3(1)(b); *Equality Act 2006*, s.45(2).

60 See also the decision in *Harris v. NKL Automotive Ltd & Anor* [2007] UKEAT/0134/07/DM; 2007 WL 2817981 (3 October 2007).

61 [2008] ET Case Number: 2201867/07 (29 May 2008).

62 [2006] ET Case Number: 1801450/06 (6 October 2006); [2007] UKEAT 0009 07 30003 (30 March 2007).

63 [2010] EWCA Civ 80.

64 [2010] ET Case Number: 17288862009 (6 April 2010).

Tribunal held Noah had suffered a disadvantage even though no assistant stylist was ever appointed.[65] Moreover, this indirect discrimination was not justified. Although it was reasonable for the respondent to take the view that the issue posed a significant risk to her business, too much weight was accorded to that concern.

By contrast, in *Asmi*, the tribunals concluded that the indirect discrimination had been justified. The claim was brought by a teaching assistant who had been suspended for insisting on wearing a full face veil when male members of staff were present, contrary to a school instruction not to wear the full face veil when teaching children. As in *Noah*, the tribunals accepted that this ban constituted a disadvantage.[66] However, both the ET and the EAT held that the indirect discrimination was justified. It could be justified as a proportionate means of achieving the legitimate aim of children being taught properly. The young children needed to see the facial expressions of their teaching assistant. This distinction between *Noah* and *Asmi* seems fair. Focusing upon the question of justification allows the tribunals to examine carefully the facts of the case in order to arrive at a nuanced decision, reflecting the context in which the claimant operated. Noah could still have done her job properly whilst wearing the headscarf; Asmi could not.

The decision in *Eweida*, however, is more difficult to comprehend. It appears that the difference between *Noah* and *Eweida* is the question of how widely worn the religious symbol is and whether it is seen as being a requirement of a faith. The case concerned a member of check-in staff who wore a silver cross in breach of the airline's then uniform policy which prohibited visible religious symbols unless their wearing was mandatory. The Court of Appeal held that there was no indirect discrimination: the uniform policy did not put Christians at a particular disadvantage. There was no evidence that practising Christians considered the visible display of the cross to be a requirement of the Christian faith and no evidence that the provision created a barrier to Christians employed at the airline. There was no indication that the original Directive intended that solitary disadvantage should be sufficient. It was noted that Eweida herself described it as a personal choice rather than as a religious requirement.

The claim therefore failed on grounds of interference (or disadvantage) rather than justification. Sedley LJ held that if it had been held that there was indirect discrimination then the claim would nevertheless have been defeated on justification. This decision may appear to be unnecessary in that the claim could have been dismissed on grounds of justification instead. Indeed, it may be argued that the claim *should* have been dismissed on grounds of justification instead. There is a long established principle in English law that the courts do not and should not

---

65   The salon had applied provision, criterion or practice (PCP), that an employee would be required to display her hair at work for at least some of the time; this put persons of the same religion as the claimant at a particular disadvantage and disadvantaged the claimant.

66   The 'no face veil when teaching rule' put Muslims at a disadvantage and actually put Asmi at a disadvantage.

readily engage in questions of doctrine (Cranmer this book: Chapter 14). This principle is most fully elucidated in the High Court decision in *HH Sant Baba Jeet Singh Maharaj v. Eastern Media Group Ltd*[67] in which Eady J held that 'that the courts will not attempt to rule upon doctrinal issues or intervene in the regulation or governance of religious groups'.[68] Although exceptionally the courts will need to examine questions of doctrine to resolve disputes about property or money,[69] they are generally very reluctant to become involved in adjudicating internal disputes within religious groups. In the House of Lords decision in *Williamson*, Lord Nicholls of Birkenhead stressed that:

> It is not for the court to embark on an inquiry into the asserted belief and judge its 'validity' by some objective standard such as the source material upon which the claimant founds his belief or the orthodox teaching of the religion in question or the extent to which the claimant's belief conforms to or differs from the views of others professing the same religion. *Freedom of religion protects the subjective belief of an individual.*[70]

Yet, in *Eweida* (as in *Playfoot*) the courts overruled the subjective beliefs of the claimant and sought to judge the validity of the claim by reference to the doctrines of the group. This means that beliefs outside the mainstream are less well protected than those within.

Eweida was followed by the ET decision in *Chaplin v. Royal Devon & Exeter NHS Foundation Trust*,[71] which concerned a nurse who wished to wear a crucifix around her neck. Despite evidence that another nurse had been asked to remove her cross and chain,[72] the ET held that this other nurse had not been put at a particular disadvantage since her religious views were not so strong as to lead her to refuse to comply with the policy.[73] This meant that the uniform policy did not 'place 'persons' at a particular advantage'.[74] *Chaplin* entrenches the Court of Appeal's decision in *Eweida*. On the face of it, Chaplin was disadvantaged and, unlike in *Eweida*, there was clear evidence that she was not alone. Ignoring the other nurse on the basis that her religious objection was not strong enough jars. Even if it is

---

67   [2010] EWHC (QB) 1294.

68   Ibidem, para. 5.

69   *Forbes v. Eden* (1867) LR 1 Sc & Div 568. See also *General Assembly of the Free Church of Scotland v. Lord Overtoun* [1904] AC 515. See Sandberg 2011: chapter 4.

70   *R. v. Secretary of State for Education and Employment and others, ex parte Williamson* [2005] UKHL 15, para. 22 (emphasis added).

71   [2010] ET Case Number: 17288862009 (6 April 2010).

72   Ibidem, para. 15.

73   It was held that in order for there to be a 'particular disadvantage', the disadvantage needed to be 'noteworthy, peculiar or singular': Ibidem, para. 27.

74   Ibidem paras 27–8. This was the decision of the majority. Mr Parkhouse, by contrast, held that both nurses had been placed at a disadvantage but that this was justified. This seems to be a preferable conclusion.

accepted that the courts are entitled to conclude that a ban on wearing a cross would not disadvantage Christians as a whole, these casessuggest that beliefs held by a few individuals (including beliefs held by a minority of believers within a larger religious group) are not protected. This contradicts the general position of religion law – as shown by the text of Article 9 – which protect both religious individuals and religious groups.

This is not to say, however, that these claims should have succeeded. The argument is simply that they should have been decided on grounds of justification. *Eweida* and *Chaplin* could have both easily been decided on grounds of justification. And this would have led to nuanced decisions taking into account the demands of the specific jobs and the cultures of the particular workplaces. The approach of *Noah* and *Asmi*, which focused on justification rather than disadvantage, is to be applauded. Courts and tribunals should distinguish successful and non-successful claims largely by addressing the question of whether the employer's actions were a proportionate means of achieving a legitimate aim. This will allow courts and tribunals to reach nuanced, situation specific conclusions – leading to different results in the differing contexts of the education and retail sectors. Ironically, the unsuccessful claimants in *Eweida* and *Chaplin* arguably suffered more than the successful claimant in *Noah*. It seems ludicrous to say that not being offered a job that never actually existed does constitute a disadvantage but being made to comply with a uniform policy which prohibited visible religious symbols unless their wearing was mandatory or a tidy hair rule does not constitute a disadvantage.

Conclusions

The conclusion seems to be that the success of any litigation by school teachers and other staff who wish to wear religious symbols or dress at work is uncertain. The type of school at which the litigant works may well be a factor, though the general law protecting teachers' rights to have 'religious opinions' is unlikely to be significant. Whilst Article 9 now provides a much fuller right to religious freedom, the cases of *Begum* and *Playfoot* suggest that a claim brought under Article 9 is unlikely to be successful. Litigants are best advised to argue instead that restrictions against them constitute indirect discrimination on grounds of religion. The decisions in *Noah* and *Asmi* indicate that any indirect discrimination claim will hinge upon whether the discrimination was justified. However, problematically, the decisions in *Eweida* and *Chaplin* further suggest that claims will only succeed if the litigant is able to point to a significant number of believers who wear the dress or symbol out of religious obligation. The judges have restricted the scope of the new law failing to protect claims which fall outside a conservative view of religion. Those who can manifest their religion elsewhere have been excluded and so have those whose beliefs are not, in the eyes of the court, required or obligatory to the religion in question or those whose beliefs are not shared by the mainstream of the religion.

The developing case law on religious dress and symbols also reveals much about the general debate concerning the place of religion in the public sphere. The new legal framework concerning religion cannot be understood in isolation from the profound social and political unease concerning the place of religion. The changes in the way in which English law interacts with religion do not point towards a separation of State and religion. Rather, the need to accommodate religious pluralism has led to greater regulation. Although it may be argued that the extension and expansion of protection towards religion is actually evidence of secularization in that the State is forced to protect religion as a minority interest, it is surely a an oversimplification to say that Britain in the twenty-first century is a secular society. The legal changes of recent years reflect a complicated and conflicted move towards a multi-faith society where the State seeks to facilitate (and regulate) a religious free market by increasing the quantity and reach of regulation. As the ECHR has frequently pointed out, the State's role is to facilitate religious freedom. The State is required to be 'the neutral and impartial organizer of the exercise of various religions, faiths and beliefs' striving to 'ensure mutual tolerance between opposing groups'.[75] The case law to date on the wearing of religious dress and symbols suggests that domestic courts are not comfortable with playing this role.

There seem to be two related reasons for this hesitation. The first reason is the novelty not only of the provisions but also of the approach of the new legal framework. The new active promotion of religious freedom as an individual right marks a sharp shift in the attitude towards and the regulation of religion in England and Wales. The judiciary are struggling to find a vocabulary to articulate a consistent and predictable jurisprudence (Hill and Sandberg 2007: 505, Doe and Sandberg 2010, Sandberg 2011: chapter 10). The new laws are expressed in rather abstract ways which make new demands of the judiciary. This is particularly true of the question of justification which requires judges and tribunal chairs to effectively undertake sociological evaluations. Whilst the question of interference is a legal test which can be reduced to a technical analysis of whether the facts fit the language of the provisions, the question of justification is a sociological test which requires reference to social reality. It is not surprising that those schooled in technical legal arguments are keen to avoid determining sociological questions of justification.

The second reason for the unease is the continuing pervasiveness of the notion that the social decline of religion and its retreat from the public sphere was inevitable. The secularization thesis remains deeply ingrained. Judges and tribunal chairs seem to be operating under the presumption that religion does not affect all aspects of a believer's life. However, as discussed above, it seems clear that the secularization thesis no longer holds sway.[76] It has been challenged

---

75   *Refah Partisi v. Turkey* (2003) 37 EHRR 1, para. 91.

76   It is important, however, not to simply swap the secularization thesis with talk of religious resurgence. The fuller picture is more complicated than that. The holding and

and affected by commercialism, changing morals, immigration, international terrorism and numerous other factors. Notions of religion as a private matter and as something that is always good are equally outmoded. The changing social and legal landscape requires a new approach. New legal and sociological tools are needed to understand the immense (and interconnected) legal and sociological changes that have occurred in relation to religion over the last decade in light of one another (Doe 2004, Bradney 1998, Bradney 2001, Sandberg and Catto 2010).

It is clear that the hyperbole in the press which greeted the *Equality Act 2010* was misplaced because the likely impact of the Act has been overplayed. In respect of religious matters, bringing a successful claim is far from easy. The most significant effect of the new laws protecting religion has been an increase in litigation rather than an increase in the protection of religion. Most claims have been unsuccessful. One reason for that increase in (ultimately unsuccessful) litigation is the low level of knowledge concerning the law (Bradney 2010). And that low level of knowledge is perpetuated by the confusion spread by the newspapers. Ironically, if the *Equality Act 2010* is the 'worst law in English history' then the newspapers are partly to blame.

References

Bauman, Z. 2003. *Society under Siege*. Cambridge: Polity Press.

Beckford, J.A. 2003. *Social Theory & Religion*. Cambridge: Cambridge University Press.

Beckford, J.A. and Richardson, J.T. 2007. Religion and regulation, in *The Sage Handbook of the Sociology of Religion*, edited by J.A. Beckford and N.J. Demerath. London: Sage, 396.

Blicher, L.C. and Molander, A. 2008. Mapping juridification. *European Law Journal* 14(1), 36.

Bradney, A. 1998. Law as a parasitic discipline. *Journal of Law and Society* 25(1), 71.

Bradney, A. 2000. Faced by faith in *Faith in Law*, edited by P. Oliver et al. Oxford: Hart, 89.

Bradney, A. 2001. Politics and sociology: new research agenda for the study of law and

religion in *Law and Religion*, edited by R. O'Dair and A. Lewis. Oxford: Oxford University Press, 65.

Bradney, A. 2010. Some sceptical thoughts about the academic analysis of law and religion in the United Kingdom, in *Law and Religion: New Horizons*, edited by N. Doe and R. Sandberg. Leuven: Peeters, 299.

Bruce, S. 1996. *Religion in the Modern World: From Cathedrals to Cults*. Oxford: Oxford University Press.

---

practising of certain religious beliefs and practices are clearly declining.

Davie, G. 1994. *Religion in Britain Since 1945*. Oxford. Blackwell.

Davie, G. 2006. Is Europe an exceptional case? *The Hedgehog Review*, 33.

Day, A. 2006. Belief in Britain. *Anthropology News*, October edition, 58.

Doe, N. 2004. A Sociology of law on religion – Towards a new discipline: legal responses to religious pluralism in Europe. *Law and Justice* 152, 68.

Doe, N. and Sandberg R. 2010. Conclusion: new horizons in *Law and Religion: New Horizons*, edited by N. Doe and R. Sandberg. Leuven: Peeters, 315.

Edge, P.W. 2002. *Legal Responses to Religious Difference*. The Hague: Kluwer Law.

Fevre, R.W. 2000. *The Demoralization of Western Culture*. London: Continuum.

Friedner, L. (ed.) 2007. *Churches and Other Religious Organizations as Legal Persons* (Leuven: Peeters).

Gunn, J. 2005. Religious liberty (modern period), in *Encyclopaedia of Christianity*, edited by E. Fahlbusch et al. Michigan: William B. Eerdmans. vol. 4, 605–17.

Hamilton, M. 2001. *The Sociology of Religion*. 2nd edn. Oxford: Routledge.

Herbert, D. 2003. *Religion and Civil Society*. Aldershot: Ashgate.

Hill, M. 2001. Judicial approaches to religious disputes, in *Law and Religion*, edited by R. O'Dair and A, Lewis. Oxford: Oxford University Press, 409.

Hill, M. 2007. *Ecclesiastical Law*. 3rd edn. Oxford: Oxford University Press.

Hill M. and Sandberg, R. 2007. Is nothing sacred? Clashing symbols in a secular world. *Public Law*, 488.

Knights, S. 2007. *Freedom of Religion, Minorities and the Law*. Oxford: Oxford University Press.

Menski, W. 2008. Law, religion and culture in multicultural Britain, in *Law and Religion in Multicultural Societies*, edited by R. Mehdi et al. Copenhagen: DJØF Publishing, 58.

Poulter, S. 1998. *Ethnicity, Law and Human Rights*. Oxford: Oxford University Press.

Rivers, J. 2010. *The Law of Organized Religions*. Oxford: Oxford University Press.

Robertson, R. 1969. Introduction, in *Sociology of Religion*, edited by R. Robertson. London: Penguin, 12.

Sandberg, R. 2008. Church-State relations in Europe: from legal models to an interdisciplinary approach. *Journal of Religion in Europe* 1(3), 329.

Sandberg, R. 2010. A sign of the times. *e-International Relations* <http://www.e-ir.info/?p=3831>.

Sandberg. R. 2011. *Law and Religion*. Cambridge: Cambridge University Press.

Sandberg, R. and Catto, R. 2010. Law and sociology: toward a greater understanding of religion, in *Law and Religion: New Horizons*, edited by N. Doe and R. Sandberg. Leuven: Peeters, 275.

Sandberg, R. and Doe, N. 2008. The strange death of blasphemy. *Modern Law Review* 71(6), 971.

Teubner, G. 1987. Juridification – concepts, aspects, limits, solutions, in *Juridification of Social Spheres*, edited by G. Teubner. Berlin: Berlin Walter de Gruyter, 3.

Vickers, L. 2006. Is all harassment equal? The case of religious harassment. *Cambridge Law Journal* 65(3), 579.

Vickers, L. 2009. Religion and belief discrimination and the employment of teachers in faith schools. *Religion & Human Rights* 4 (2–3), 137.

Vickers, L. 2010. Religious discrimination in the workplace: an emerging hierarchy? *Ecclesiastical Law Journal* 12 (3), 280.

Wilson, B. 1966. *Religion in Secular Society*. Middlesex: Penguin.

Wilson, B. 1982. *Religion in Sociological Perspective*. Oxford: Oxford University Press.

Chapter 17

Of Crucifixes and Headscarves: Religious Symbols in German Schools

Tobias Lock[1]

The status of religious symbols in German schools has been a hotly debated topic not only in legal circles but also in the wider public domain for almost 20 years. The debate started with the conflict over the crucifix in classrooms, continued with the right of teachers to wear a headscarf at school and currently centres upon a possible ban of the headscarf for students. For instance a newly appointed minister of the *Land* of Lower Saxony suggested that crosses should be banned from classrooms (Schneider 2010). Germany's most prominent feminist Alice Schwarzer argued that girls should not be allowed to wear a headscarf at school (Spiegel Online 2010a). This contribution examines these issues from a legal perspective. It is divided into three sections: the first section is concerned with religious symbols installed by the State, the second section deals with religious symbols worn by teachers and the third section will examine whether students can be prevented from wearing religious symbols. This chapter aims to bring insights into the limits to the freedom of religion, the notion and content of the negative freedom of religion, the demand for neutrality of the German state in religious and philosophical matters and the interpretation of symbols as religious. The contribution is mainly based on the case law of the Federal Constitution Court ('FCC') but also considers the judgments of the lower courts and the relevant legislation, including the transposition of the equality directives of the European Union ('EU') into national law.

The legal framework for the discussion is as follows: Article 4 of the German constitution or *Grundgesetz* ('Basic Law') guarantees freedom of religion, faith and conscience:

(1) Freedom of faith and of conscience, and freedom to profess a religious or philosophical creed, shall be inviolable.

(2) The undisturbed practice of religion shall be guaranteed.

1   I would like to thank Dr Javier García Oliva (University of Manchester) for his valuable comments on an earlier draft, Ms Claudia Müller for her assistance in researching for this chapter and the editor for accepting it and editing it together with Arman Sarvarian to whom I also express my gratitude. All errors remain, of course, my own.

According to German doctrine, freedom of religion has two elements. First, everyone enjoys positive freedom of religion. This means that everyone has the right to adhere to a religion or to hold a belief (so-called *forum internum*). This includes atheism (Kokott 2007). In addition, everyone has the right to behave strictly in accordance with the rules of one's belief and to act according to one's religious convictions (so-called *forum externum*). Secondly, negative freedom of religion gives everyone the right not to share a certain belief (Kokott 2007). The State must not interfere with either of these freedoms. According to the FCC, the State is especially prohibited from prescribing a belief (BVerfGE 32, 98, 106; BVerGE 93, 1, 15; BVerfGE 108, 282, 297). Freedom of religion is a fundamental right enjoyed by everyone, including children and, of course, their parents.

Parents also enjoy a fundamental right to educate their children according to Article 6(2) of the Basic Law: 'The care and upbringing of children is the natural right of parents and a duty primarily incumbent upon them. The state shall watch over them in the performance of this duty.' This right, however, is concurrent with the State's duty to educate, which is derived from Article 7(1) of the Basic Law providing that the entire school system is under the supervision of the State (BVerfGE 34, 165, 183). Thus parents and the State share responsibility to educate children.

It should further be pointed out that according to Article 70 of the Basic Law the organization of schools lies in the competence of the German states (*Länder*) so that that there are 16 different sets of rules which govern the relations amongst schools, students and staff. This means that there can never be a single answer to the questions concerning religious symbols in German schools. Rather, we must compare 16 different systems. What the *Länder*, of course, have in common is that their legislatures are bound by the constitutional limits on legislative regulation set by the Basic Law. It is the aim of this contribution to precisely illustrate these limits and how the *Länder* have positioned themselves within them.

Finally, Germany does not have a state religion. It is a religiously neutral State. According to Article 140 of the Basic Law, Article 137 of the *Weimar* Constitution forms an integral part of the Basic Law and provides that there shall be no state church. This means, on the one hand, that the State is free from the influence of churches but also, on the other hand, that the churches are free from that of the State (Von Campenhausen and de Wall 2006). Moreover, it follows from the constitutional right to freedom of religion that the State must be neutral in matters of religion and philosophy of life (*Weltanschauung*) (BVerfGE 93, 1, 16). At the same time, there is strong cooperation between religious communities and the State. According to Article 137 of the Weimar Constitution, the State grants religious communities, most notably the incorporated churches, certain privileges such as a right to tax their members. The separation of Church and State is thus not strict. The relationship between Church and State is cooperative. This means for instance that state authorities are not prevented from religious avowals (Von Campenhausen and de Wall 2006). A number of early decisions by the FCC show that the State's neutrality must not be confused with the French (Adrian 2006) and

Turkish (Karakas 2007) concepts of *laïcité*, which postulate a strict separation of religion and State. Two decisions of the FCC concerned the legality of legislation passed in two *Länder* which introduced Christian schools. Article 15 of the constitution of the Baden-Württemberg *Land* provided that primary schools (and some secondary schools) are Christian comprehensive schools whereas Article 135 of the Bavarian constitution provided that children in public, primary schools are educated according to Christian principles. In the *Baden-Württemberg* case, the FCC held that the *Länder* enjoy a great degree of independence when it comes to organizing public schools – including their religious orientation (BVerfGE 41, 29, 45). It rejected the argument that the State must keep aloof from introducing religious references into schools (BVerfGE 41, 29, 48).

However, where the legislator chooses to introduce such references, the school must not proselytize or otherwise claim that Christian religious beliefs are binding. Rather, such a school must be open to other philosophical and religious persuasions and its educational mission must not be religious in character. The reference to Christianity is to be understood as the recognition of Christianity as a decisive factor in Western history and culture (BVerfGE 41, 29, 51). The FCC made a similar finding in its decision on the provision of the Bavarian constitution (BVerfGE 41, 65, 78). The Basic Law therefore prescribes 'open' neutrality (Werdmölder 2007).

This openness towards religious elements introduced by the State into schools again arose in the FCC's decision regarding school prayer (BVerfGE 52, 223). The FCC heard two joined cases. In the first case, the parents of a primary school pupil complained that the practice to say a daily prayer before school began had been abandoned following an objection by another pupil. In the second case, the parents of a primary school pupil argued that a school prayer was incompatible with their child's negative freedom of religion. Only the first complaint was successful. The FCC recalled that it is possible for the *Länder* to introduce religious references into schools where the freedom of religion of all concerned is not violated (BVerfGE 52, 223, 238). It acknowledged that it constituted a promotion of Christianity for the State to allow a prayer as part of the school day (BVerfGE 52, 223, 240). The FCC went on to find that the school prayer was not a violation of the negative freedom of religion since the pupil had the possibility to avoid it by either leaving the room or simply not participating in the prayer (BVerfGE 52, 223, 248). Thus, a school prayer is generally compatible with the Basic Law. The decision therefore shows that Germany does not follow the strict French and Turkish models of secularism but a more moderate model of the separation of Church and State.

Symbols Installed by the State: the Crucifix Controversy

Almost 15 years before the *Lautsi* decision[2] by the European Court of Human Rights ('ECtHR') made the headlines, an almost identical case was decided by the FCC (BVerfGE 93, 1). Three siblings and their parents filed a constitutional complaint against the mandatory affixing of crucifixes and crosses in classrooms in Bavaria. The relevant provision in the Bavarian School Regulations for Elementary Schools (*Volksschulordnung*) provided that '[I]n every classroom a cross shall be affixed.' The parents were followers of the anthroposophical philosophy of life as taught by Rudolf Steiner. When one of their children started primary school, they found large crucifixes affixed to the walls of the classrooms in which she was taught. The crucifixes were in direct view of the blackboard. The parents requested that the crucifixes be removed. A compromise was found whereby the school replaced them with plain crosses, which were affixed above the door. Some time later, the parents unsuccessfully requested that the crosses in the classrooms be removed as well. The case ended up in the FCC, which in 1995 delivered one of the most controversial judgments in its history when it held that the affixing of a cross in a classroom violated the complainants' right to religious freedom.[3]

The FCC's Reasoning

The FCC held that the affixing of a cross in a classroom violated pupils' negative religious freedom. The FCC defined 'negative religious freedom' as the freedom to stay away from acts of worship of a faith not shared, which includes the freedom to stay away from the symbols of such a faith (BVerfGE 93, 1, 15). The FCC recognized that, in a pluralist society, an individual has no right to be completely spared from manifestations of other faiths. But the difference in the classroom was that the State itself created a situation wherein the individual was exposed to a religious symbol without any possibility of escape. The FCC's remarks on the cross as a religious symbol, the existence of an interference with freedom of religion and the neutrality of the State were most controversial at the time.

The FCC rejected the argument advanced by the Bavarian government that the cross was merely a symbol of Western culture marked by Christianity. The FCC found that the cross was still the primary symbol of the Christian faith (BVerfGE 93, 1, 19). In interpreting the significance of the cross as a Christian symbol, the FCC based this finding on an objective assessment of the cross and did not take into account the subjective intention of the State affixing it. The FCC distinguished the case from the school decisions referred to above. Whilst it found that the Christian mission of these schools was the recognition of Christianity as

---

2   See notes 4 and 5 *infra*.

3   In that sense, the labelling of the decision as the 'crucifix' decision is a misnomer as the complaint was directed against plain crosses as well.

an important element of Western history and of Western culture, it felt unable to interpret the cross in such a narrow way.

The FCC considered the cross to interfere with negative freedom of religion. The main rationale was that pupils could not escape the cross during lessons. Since education in primary schools was compulsory, pupils were thus forced to study 'under the cross' (BVerfGE 93, 1, 18). This inescapability marked the difference with the school prayer decision discussed above. School prayers only happened at the beginning of a lesson and pupils had the chance to leave the room or simply not participate. Furthermore, the FCC cited its decision on the cross in courtrooms, where the display of the cross had also been held to be unconstitutional since a duty to argue a case 'under the cross' constituted an unreasonable inner burden both for the lawyer and the party represented by him (BVerfGE 35, 366). It was said that this case relating to courtrooms was not a relevant precedent since the FCC had relied on the subjective, inner burden of the particular parties – both the lawyer and his client in this case were former German nationals who had had to flee the country during the Nazi era because they were Jewish (Von Campenhausen 1996). By contrast, the FCC in the crucifix decision no longer took into account the particular circumstances of the individual plaintiff who objected to the cross but found crosses in classrooms to generally interfere with freedom of religion. The FCC expressly disagreed with the decisions of the lower courts which had held that the cross had no effect on pupils. Whilst the FCC admitted that the cross did not compel pupils to identify with it, it ascribed a soliciting character to it (BVerfGE 93, 1, 20). This means that the FCC considered that pupils might interpret the cross as objectively proselytizing and thus interfering with their negative freedom of religion.

The FCC did not regard this interference with freedom of religion to be justified. Negative freedom of religion was not an absolute right and, as was held in the decision on Christian schools and the school prayer, could be restricted because of the State's right to educate children arising from Article 7 of the Basic Law (BVerfGE 93, 1, 20). However, the FCC held that the affixing of a cross violated the neutrality of the State in matters of religion and philosophy of life. It conceded that it had acknowledged in the decisions on Christian schools that the State need not completely abandon all religious or philosophical references when educating children. However, when compulsorily educating children, the State must fulfil its duty in a non-proselytizing fashion. The affixing of a cross was considered to infringe this (BVerfGE 93, 1, 23). Moreover, the FCC made it clear that the positive religious freedom of the majority of pupils (who were Christian) could not override the right of the minority to be protected since fundamental rights were specifically aimed at their protection (BVerfGE 93, 1, 24).

Dissenting Views

The decision of the FCC was not unanimous, however. Three of the eight judges rendered a dissenting opinion arguing that there was no violation of the claimants' freedom of religion. The minority dissented on the basis of the school decisions according to which there is no a violation of the neutrality requirement if the *Länder* base schools on Christian values. This, they argued, also covered the affixing of a cross or crucifix in the classroom (BVerfGE 93, 1, 28). A similar point was made by von Campenhausen (1996) and by Müller-Volbehr (1995) who contended that if Christian schools were constitutional, then the cross as their symbol had to be constitutional as well.

In addition, von Camphausen (1996) and Kokott (2007) criticized the FCC for finding that the exposure of pupils to the cross amounted to an interference with the negative freedom of religion of non-Christian pupils. One of the reasons advanced is that negative freedom of religion does not constitute a superior fundamental right, which always trumps freedom of positive religion (BverfGE 93, 1, 31). However, this contention by the minority is based on the wrong assumption that the case of the crucifix deals with a conflict between the positive freedom of religion of Christian pupils and the negative freedom of religion of non-Christian pupils, that is essentially a question of horizontal application of fundamental rights (so called *Drittwirkung*). But that was not the issue of the case. Rather, the question was whether a binding order by the State to affix crosses in classrooms was compatible with Article 4 of the Basic Law, which is a classical vertical situation wherein an act of the State interferes with fundamental freedoms.

Moreover, the dissenters contended that, for a non-Christian pupil, the cross could not be a *religious* symbol but could only be a symbol representing Christian and Western values. This argument is unconvincing as it essentially negates the existence of negative religious freedom. Were it correct, it would mean that the manifestation of a religion could never interfere with anyone's negative freedom of religion since, as non-members of that particular religious group, they would not be able to understand the religious meaning of that manifestation which, at worst, could only amount for them to a nuisance (Borowski 2006). It was further argued by Müller-Volbehr (1995) that the effects of 'studying under the cross' had been exaggerated and could not be proven. The majority was also criticized for not making any reference to the position of the cross in the classroom. Müller-Volbehr (1995) maintained that it made a difference whether the cross was affixed within sight of the pupils or not.

The decision led to an amendment of the Bavarian legislation. Article 7 of the Bavarian Code on Education (*Bayerisches Erziehungs- und Unterrichtsgesetz*) still provides that a cross shall be affixed in each classroom. However, it was added that where parents object to the affixing of the cross for serious religious or philosophical reasons the head teacher must seek agreement with them. Where such agreement is impossible, the head teacher is bound to find a solution which respects the rights of the minority. The Federal Administrative Court ruled that the provision had to be interpreted in light of Article 4 of the Basic Law. It found that, in the end, the views of objecting pupils and parents had to prevail (Bundesverwaltungsgericht, 6 C 18/98). This, in effect, means that the cross has to be removed where they request it.

Comparison with Lautsi

Given that the facts of the two cases are nearly identical, it seems appropriate to draw a short comparison between the FCC's crucifix decision and the decisions by the ECtHR in *Lautsi*, where the Grand Chamber[4] quashed the earlier Chamber[5] judgment. The Grand Chamber adopted a markedly different approach to the FCC, which warrants a few comments. I shall provide a three-way comparison between the decisions. Both the Chamber and the FCC found that a cross in the classroom was in violation of the negative freedom of religion. However, it appears that the Chamber's definition of what constitutes negative freedom of religion was not the same as that of the FCC. The Chamber defined it as the freedom not to believe. In the FCC's understanding of freedom of religion, not holding a belief would be covered by positive freedom of religion. Negative freedom is defined as the right not to have to follow a certain belief and not to be confronted with religious manifestations. Whilst it stated the above definition of negative freedom, it appears that the Chamber actually applied the FCC's understanding of negative religious freedom when it said that the State must 'refrain from imposing beliefs'. The Grand Chamber did not pronounce on this question. It regarded Article 2 of Protocol 1 ECHR as *lex specialis* to Article 9 ECHR. Article 2 guarantees a right to education and imposes a duty on the part of the State to ensure education in conformity with the religious beliefs of the person educated. The FCC, the Chamber and the Grand Chamber all share the view that the crucifix and the cross are religious symbols and adopt an objective view when interpreting symbols that (also) have a religious meaning.

The most striking differences in the approaches of the FCC and the Chamber on the one side, and the Grand Chamber on the other relate to the issue of the interference that the cross may cause with the religious freedom of pupils and their parents. Both the FCC and the Chamber agreed that a religious symbol can interfere with negative freedom of religion where there is no possibility for pupils to escape. In contrast to the Chamber, the FCC considered that this interference could be justified by the State's right to organize education. The reason for this probably lies in the absence of any such right being mentioned in the European Convention on Human Rights 1950 ('ECHR'). As has been noted by Augsberg and Engelbrecht (2010), the ECHR is not a full constitution but only contains a number of (individual) human rights. However, the Chamber in *Lautsi* went further than the FCC in its unequivocal statement that the State has a duty to (absolute) confessional neutrality in public education, which appears to be the same as *laïcité*. This view is certainly not shared by the FCC, which in the crucifix decision confirmed its older case law on Christian schools. It is regrettable that the Chamber did not at least provide some arguments as to why the State should have a duty to be completely neutral under the Convention. But since this aspect of the

---

4   ECtHR Grand Chamber *Lautsi v. Italy* 18 March 2011, Application no. 30814/06.
5   ECtHR *Lautsi v. Italy* 3 November 2009, Application no. 30814/06.

decision was not upheld by the Grand Chamber, there are no further implications for German schools. In contrast to both FCC and the Chamber, the Grand Chamber did not seem to consider that the cross interfered with the religious freedom of parents and pupils. The Grand Chamber held that Italy had not overstepped the limits of the margin of appreciation granted to it by the Convention when it comes to reconciling its functions in relation to education and teaching with the parents' right to ensure such education in conformity with their own religious convictions (Grand Chamber judgment: para. 69.).

The limit set by the Grand Chamber is whether the provision of education by the Italian State, of which the physical school environment is part, leads to a form of indoctrination. The Grand Chamber did not find that the mere presence of the cross as a religious symbol led to indoctrination. It held that a crucifix on a wall is 'an essentially passive symbol' (Grand Chamber judgment: para. 72). The Grand Chamber thus contradicts the FCC's findings on this question. It is recalled that the FCC highlighted the inescapability of the pupils' situation and the soliciting character of the cross. The Grand Chamber's reasoning deserves some remarks. To begin with, it is regrettable that the reasoning of such an important decision remains short and rather unsatisfactory. It is not entirely clear whether the Grand Chamber regarded the presence of the religious symbol as a potential interference with religious freedom or not. Clarity in this respect is not helped by introducing the category of a 'passive symbol'. Symbols are, one would suggest, always passive. They remind us of a religion, brand or nation and so on and evoke associations we might have with that particular religion, brand or nation. But they never actively speak to us. After the Grand Chamber decision, one must, however, ask whether there is such a thing as an 'active' symbol and if so, what consequences this would have for the decision of a similar case or whether the expression 'passive symbol' is merely a tautology. Furthermore, the Grand Chamber's distinguishing of the *Dahlab* decision[6] (infra), where the ECHR held that the Muslim headscarf constituted a 'powerful external symbol' is hardly convincing (Grand Chamber judgment, para. 73). The Grand Chamber merely distinguished the two cases on the basis of their facts but did not actually address the pertinent question of why the headscarf is a more powerful religious symbol than the crucifix. Both are arguably equally powerful. More importantly, the Grand Chamber fails to appreciate that in *Dahlab* the symbol was worn by a person who was the bearer of fundamental rights whereas in *Lautsi* the symbol was affixed by the State, which does not enjoy fundamental rights (a similar point is made by the dissenting judge Malinverni in the Grand Chamber judgment).

One should briefly ask what consequences the *Lautsi* decision might have for Germany. Judging from a legal perspective there are none. The Grand Chamber decision objects to indoctrination on the part of the State. It does not regard the Italian situation – with a mandatory crucifix on the walls of state classrooms – to amount to such indoctrination. One cannot infer that a ban on the cross as it was

---

6   Note 7 *infra*.

pronounced by the FCC would not be in accordance with the Convention. To the contrary, the decision contains no reason for the FCC to alter its case law. However, could the *Länder*, and especially Bavaria, reintroduce a mandatory affixing of the cross? As long as the decision of the FCC stands, this is not possible. The decision of the Grand Chamber cannot override the FCC's decision in this respect. The protection offered by the Basic Law and voiced by the FCC is thus greater than the protection offered by the Convention. Thus the legal situation in Germany has not been directly affected by the *Lautsi* case.

Cases Involving Teachers

A few years after the FCC's decision, the courts faced the question whether the reasoning would also apply to non-Christian teachers who argued that their negative freedom of religion was affected by having to 'teach under the cross'. In this scenario, the main difference between a teacher and a pupil is that teachers are employed by the State as civil servants so that they owe the State a degree of loyalty. This duty of loyalty is considered to be one of the 'traditional principles of the professional civil service' mentioned in Article 33(5) of the Basic Law. However, notwithstanding this duty, civil servants are also holders of fundamental rights.

Two decisions by the Bavarian administrative courts are worth exploring here. The first case was decided by the Higher Administrative Court of Bavaria (Bayerischer Verwaltungsgerichtshof, 3 B 98.563). The Court drew an analogy between the situation of a teacher and that of a pupil. It pointed out, however, that teachers generally had to comply with their duties which normally trumped their fundamental right to religious freedom. Furthermore, the personalities of teachers were fully developed and they were thus less likely to be indoctrinated by the cross. This means that teachers generally have to accept the cross in the classroom. The Court therefore chose to adopt the FCC's stance in the case concerning the cross in the courtroom mentioned above and tested whether there existed a situation where it was intolerable for the teacher concerned to teach under the cross. In that case, the teacher concerned demonstrated that he was not opposed to Christianity as such but had an aversion to the cross as a symbol. For him, it displayed crucifixion, which in his eyes was the cruellest of all techniques of execution. Furthermore, he considered the cross a symbol of anti-Semitism and the Holocaust. The Court found that, for this reason, it was unacceptable for him to teach classes in front of the cross and upheld his claim to have it removed.

Conversely, in the second case, the Augsburg Administrative Court (Verwaltungsgericht Augsburg, Au 2 K 07.347) found that it was not strong enough a reason for an atheist teacher to politically disagree with the display of the cross. A situation, which did not lead to an inner conflict for the teacher, does not constitute an atypical case. Thus the Augsburg court denied his claim. What is remarkable about both decisions, however, is that they offered a new interpretation of the cross in view of the amended legislation. Both courts argued that with the entry into force of the new legislation, the legislator had changed the symbolism of the cross: it was now to be understood as merely a symbol for Christian and Western values and could no longer be construed as having a soliciting character. This reveals a fundamental misunderstanding of the FCC's reasoning in the crucifix case. The FCC explicitly considered the intentions of the State to be irrelevant. Rather, it based its findings on the impression the cross left on the addressees of the symbol, that is pupils. Similarly, in cases involving teachers, the administrative courts should have considered the addressees as well.

Symbols Worn by Teachers: the Muslim Headscarf

The Ludin Saga

A new facet of the controversy surrounding religious symbols in schools became evident when female Muslim teachers insisted on wearing a headscarf covering their hair and neck while teaching. In these types of cases, the fundamental rights situation differs from the crucifix case law. Courts must not only reconcile the negative religious freedom of pupils with the State's right to educate them and the State's duty to remain neutral in matters of religion and philosophy of life. Courts must also take into account the teacher's positive freedom of religion, which gives her a right to wear the headscarf.

This difficult situation faced the courts in the landmark *Ludin* case. *Ludin* was a German national, who applied to be employed as a primary school teacher by the Baden-Württemberg *Land* having just completed her teacher training there. As aforementioned, teachers in Germany are normally employed as civil servants. Article 33 of the Basic Law regulates access to the civil service:

> (2) Every German shall be equally eligible for any public office according to his aptitude, qualifications and professional achievements.

> (3) Neither ... eligibility for public office, nor rights acquired in the public service shall be dependent upon religious affiliation. No one may be disadvantaged by reason of adherence or non-adherence to a particular religious denomination or philosophical creed.

Article 33(2) is designed to ensure a meritocratic system, which results in the best candidate having a subjective right to be chosen for the office (Battis 2007). In the *Ludin* case the school authorities refused to employ Mrs Ludin, arguing that her insistence on wearing the headscarf in class showed that she lacked the aptitude to perform the job. The school authorities maintained that, as a teacher, she had to represent the values of the State (most notably tolerance) which it deemed impossible for a person wearing a headscarf. Furthermore, the school authorities argued that the wearing of a headscarf by a representative of the State violated the State's duty to be neutral.

Ludin in the administrative courts

The school authorities' decision was upheld by the Stuttgart Administrative Court, (Verwaltungsgericht Stuttgart, 15 K 532/99), the Higher Administrative Court of Baden-Württemberg (Verwaltungsgerichtshof Baden-Württemberg, 4 S 1439/00) and eventually the Federal Administrative Court (Bundesverwaltungsgericht, 2 C 21.01). The main argument of the administrative courts may be summarized as follows. One of the criteria when assessing the aptitude of candidates is an evaluation of whether they will fulfil their duties. Whilst the Federal Administrative Court acknowledged that the wearing of a headscarf is protected by Article 4 of the Basic Law, it stated that the freedom of religion guaranteed therein could be restricted. In the court's opinion, such a restriction follows from the State's duty to be neutral in religious matters. This duty extends to teachers as well since they act on behalf of the State. The teacher's personal religious freedom must be subordinated in such a case because schooling is a very sensitive area with young children who are easily influenced. The argument very much resembles that made by the Swiss Federal Court in the *Dahlab* case, which the ECtHR did not find to be unreasonable.[7] Furthermore, in two decisions from the 1980s concerning teachers wearing Bhagwan dress, the Federal Administrative Court (Bundesverwaltungsgericht, 2 B 92.87) and the Higher Administrative Court of Hamburg (Oberverwaltungsgericht Hamburg, Bs I 171/84) argued along the same lines. The Federal Administrative Court found that the headscarf was a symbol of Islam since it was generally interpreted as an avowal to the Islamic faith. The Court admitted that there was no soft way of resolving the conflict: either the teacher was allowed to wear a headscarf or not. The Court refused, in particular, to allow for a trial period following which the effects of the headscarf on children would be assessed.

What is remarkable about the decision is that it does not once take into account the severe consequences for the teacher. Since the State has a quasi-monopoly on primary schools and since there are virtually no publicly funded Muslim primary schools, the decision had the consequence that the appellant would never be able to work as a teacher. Considering she had spent years studying for her teaching degree and her teacher training, this result was harsh.

Furthermore, it is worthwhile contrasting the reasoning by the administrative courts in the *Ludin* case with the decision of the Lüneburg Administrative Court in Lower Saxony which in 2000 had to decide a case with nearly identical facts (Verwaltungsgericht Lüneburg, 1 A 98/00). The arguments advanced by the school authorities, which refused to employ the plaintiff, were the same as in *Ludin*. The Court, however, quashed the school authorities' decision by finding that the teacher's religious freedom need not be subordinate to the State's neutrality. In

---

7   ECtHR 15 February 2001 *Dahlab v. Switzerland*, Application no. 42393/98.

the eyes of the Lüneburg Court, neutrality means that a teacher must abide by the principle of tolerance when dealing with the different religious and philosophical attitudes present in a school. But the tolerance principle does not require a teacher to abstain from any religious avowal when in school. It pointed out that a pluralism of religious convictions was not only existent in schools but was also the aim of Lower Saxony's school legislation. The Lüneburg Court expressly distinguished cases involving teachers wearing the headscarf from the crucifix decision, in which the situation was created by the State.

Ludin before the FCC – the majority opinion
Having lost her appeal to the Federal Administrative Court, Mrs Ludin filed a constitutional complaint to the Federal Constitutional Court. The FCC by a majority of five to three decided that her complaint was well founded (BVerfGE 108, 282). However, it did not definitively resolve the controversial question of whether a teacher may wear a headscarf at school. Rather, it argued that the denial to employ a teacher on that basis was an interference with her fundamental rights enshrined in Articles 33 and 34 of the Basic Law because it happened without the requisite statutory foundation. Thus the FCC decided the case on the technical point that the *Land* had failed to pass legislation explicitly requiring teachers to refrain from wearing religious symbols in the classroom. According to the FCC's 'doctrine of essentiality' (*Wesentlichkeitstheorie*), interferences with fundamental rights must have a legislative basis. The stronger the interference, the more precise that basis has to be. Notably, decisions concerning the organization of schools cannot be left to the executive branch but must be taken by the democratically elected legislature (BVerfGE 108, 282, 312).

Despite its less definitive result compared with the crucifix case, the *Ludin* decision contains important remarks about the headscarf as a religious symbol and the right of teachers to observe their religion. The FCC emphasized that the question of whether a ban on the headscarf amounted to an interference with religious freedom had to be answered from the point of view of the woman wearing it. If she considers that she must wear it in order to comply with her religion, then the ban on the headscarf constitutes an interference. The discussion within the Muslim community concerning whether women are required to wear the headscarf or not was considered to be irrelevant. (BVerfGE 108, 282, 312). The FCC therefore remained true to earlier case law (BVerfGE 33, 23, 28) by applying a subjective test to the question of whether the wearing of the headscarf falls into the scope of religious freedom. However, when it comes to assessing whether that exercise of religious freedom interferes with the negative freedom of religion granted to others, in this case to pupils, it opted for an objective test. It held that in contrast to a cross, the headscarf was not in itself a religious symbol (BVerfGE 108, 282, 304). Here, the FCC adopted the perspective of the objective observer.

In this context, it is worth discussing a later decision by the Federal Labour Court (Bundesarbeitsgericht, 2 AZR 499/08) concerning a female Muslim social worker employed by a school under a private contract who insisted upon wearing a religiously neutral cap fully covering her hair, hairline and ears while working. The school reprimanded her for violating § 57 of the North Rhine Westphalia School Act (Schulgesetz Nordrhein Westfalen). This provision was added to the Act after the *Ludin* case had been decided by the FCC and provides that teachers must not wear symbols which call the neutrality of the *Land* into question. The social worker, whom the Court assimilated to a teacher because it was her task to mediate conflicts between pupils, argued that she did not wear the cap for religious reasons and thus did not violate her duty to wear religiously neutral clothes. The reason why she chose to wear the cap at school every day was that she had been used to wearing a headscarf for 18 years and felt exposed if she did not cover her head. The Court did not accept her argument but instead adopted an objective approach, preferring an interpretation which seemed likely to correspond to the views of a considerable number of objective observers (namely, parents and pupils). This decision shows that the interpretation of a piece of clothing as amounting to a religious symbol is not only of relevance where a person wishes to rely on provisions protecting freedom of religion but also in cases where a person claims that she wears a piece of clothing without religious motivation.

Having found that the headscarf constituted a religious symbol, the FCC drew a clear distinction between the crucifix case, where the cross was affixed by the State, and the present case, in which the State was only asked to tolerate a situation stemming from teachers' convictions. In the latter, the presence of religious symbols in public schools could not be attributed to the State (BVerfGE 108, 282, 305). The FCC's approach thus shows that teachers wearing the headscarf will fall under the ambit of the fundamental right to freedom of religion. However, it also indicates that since the wearing of a headscarf can lead to a conflict between teachers' rights and the State's duty to remain neutral in matters of religion and philosophy of life as well as with pupils' negative right to religion and their parents' right to educate their children in accordance with their convictions, restrictions on teachers' rights are possible. But such restrictions, the FCC added, could not be left to the executive but had to be decided by the democratically elected legislature.

Ludin before the FCC – the dissenting opinion
The three dissenting judges asserted that the majority had failed to appreciate the specific function of teachers as civil servants. As such, teachers had voluntarily sided with the State and therefore deserved less protection of their fundamental rights than pupils and their parents (BVerfGE 108, 282, 316). They argued that a civil servant only enjoyed fundamental rights insofar as they were compatible with the civil servant's loyalty to the State and other requirements of the job. Thus, a teacher who wore a headscarf in school violated her duty to neutrality BVerfGE 108, 282, 325). The minority maintained that the question of aptitude as contained in Article 33 of the Basic Law should not be confused with an interference with fundamental rights. They therefore did not see a need for a legislative solution as the incompatibility of a teacher's headscarf with her duties could be directly derived

from the Basic Law. It is noteworthy that the minority opinion, in effect, denies the teacher any right to freedom of religion. Unlike the majority, the minority didn't consider it necessary therefore to balance the teacher's right to religious freedom with the neutrality of the State and the freedom of pupils and their parents. Rather, the three judges seemed to fully attribute the teacher's conduct to the State and equate the situation with that in the crucifix decision.

Critical analysis

The majority decision was the subject of much criticism. Most commentators at the time seemed to prefer the line of argument advanced by the dissenting minority, many critics considering the headscarf decision to be inconsistent with the crucifix decision (Käsnter 2003, Bader 2004, Pofalla 2004, von Campenhausen 2004). They argued that the situation was essentially the same since pupils were subjected in both cases to a religious symbol in the classroom which they were unable to escape. These critics disagree with the FCC's distinction between the cross, which was affixed to the wall of the classroom on behalf of the State, and the headscarf which is worn by a teacher and merely tolerated by the State. This criticism is based on two notions. The first is that a teacher, as a civil servant, is a representative of the State and is therefore subjected to the same restrictions as the State itself. The second notion is that the emphasis should be placed on the influence which religious symbols have on pupils, and on the interference it may cause with pupils' (and their parents') fundamental rights.

It is argued here that this view tends to be overly simplistic by neglecting the fact that the teacher is a bearer of fundamental rights too. The situation differs in a fundamental way from the situation in the crucifix decision. As Sacksofsky (2003) pointed out, the State's duty to remain neutral in religious and philosophical matters means that the State must not identify with a certain belief. While the affixing of a religious symbol by the State strongly suggests such identification to an objective observer, a religious symbol worn by a teacher does not. Thus, the critics tend to block out this additional dimension and reduce the issue to a vertical situation where the State, through the teacher wearing the headscarf, interferes with the negative religious freedom of pupils and their parents. Furthermore, it is hardly acknowledged that teachers like the applicant do not feel they have a choice not to wear the headscarf. For them, it is mandatory to do so when they appear in public. Since the State has a quasi-monopoly on primary education, the consequence of the minority opinion would have been to deny the teacher access to the profession for which she trained for many years. Comparing *Ludin* with the crucifix decision, it is remarkable that both the majority and the minority decisions in *Ludin* had no problem in regarding the presence of a religious symbol in the classroom as amounting to an interference with pupils' negative freedom of religion. This, it is recalled, was still very much contested in the crucifix case.

It has been suggested that the FCC deliberately avoided a clearer decision (von Campenhausen 2004) and even refused to decide the case (Kästner 2003). It is submitted that the decision not to fully determine the fate of teachers wearing religious symbols in schools was the correct one. As evidenced by both the public and the academic discussion around the headscarf, the dilemma to be resolved is rather delicate. The FCC thereby gives the legislatures a choice between a pluralistic solution, where religious avowals are relatively unrestricted, and a solution closer to *'laïcisme'*, where every religious avowal outside the context of Religious Education is banned (BVerfGE 108, 282, 310). It is not for a court to decide between these two options. Rather, the principle of democracy demands that such decisions are made by the democratically elected legislature.

The Reaction of the Länder to the FCC's Decision

Eight of the 16 *Länder* reacted and passed legislation designed to outlaw the wearing of headscarves by teachers. The *Länder* concerned opted for different approaches. Berlin chose an unambiguous ban of all religious symbols visibly worn by teachers and other civil servants (§ 2 of the Gesetz zu Artikel 29 der Verfassung von Berlin). Bremen took a less radical stance when legislating that 'the appearance of teachers in school ... must not be capable of disturbing the religious and philosophical sentiments of pupils or their parents' (§ 59b Bremisches Schulgesetz; author's translation). While Berlin opted for a clear-cut approach, the Bremen legislation necessitates that each individual case involving a teacher wearing a headscarf or any other religious symbol to be assessed on its facts.

This contribution focuses on the legislation passed in the remaining six *Länder*. The reason is that the wording of that legislation appears to privilege Christian and Western traditions. In the *Ludin* case, the FCC emphasized that any duty not to wear a headscarf would only be compatible with the non-discrimination provisions of the Basic Law if members of different religions were treated equally (BVerfGE 108, 282, 313). The Baden-Württemberg legislation, for instance, provides that:

> Teachers at public schools ... must not make political, religious, philosophical or similar avowals, which are capable of endangering or disturbing the *Land's* neutrality vis-à-vis pupils and parents or a politically, religiously or philosophically peaceful school environment. ... The realization of the educational mission in accordance with [the] constitution of Baden-Württemberg and the accordant portrayal of Christian and Western cultural and educational values does not contradict the conduct required of teachers [described above] (§ 38 Schulgesetz für Baden-Württemberg; author's translation).

In a similar vein, the Bavarian legislation states:

> External symbols or clothes, which express a religious or philosophical conviction, must not be worn by teachers in class as far as pupils or parents can perceive these symbols or clothes as an expression of an attitude which is incompatible with the core values and the educational aims of the constitution, including Christian and

Western educational and cultural values (Article 59 Bayerisches Gesetz über das Erziehungs- und Unterrichtswesen; author's translation).

The other *Länder* chose similar formulations. At least in some of the *Länder*, the references to Christian and Western culture may be explained by the objective to proscribe the headscarf while at the same time enabling nuns or monks teaching in public schools to wear their habit. This was clearly apparent from the debates in the Baden-Württemberg parliament (Landtag Baden-Württemberg, 4 February 2004, Plenarprotokoll 13/62, 4399; 1 April 2004, Plenarprotokoll13/67, 4700, 4704, 4710, 4717, 4719) and until recently also featured on a website run by the Bavarian school ministry containing information for head teachers on 'Islam in Schools', which expressly stated that the habit of nuns was not affected by the legislation as it was a reflection of Christian and Western values (Dicks 2008). That a nun's habit would normally be covered by the ban is clear since it is an expression of a religious conviction. Therefore, the reference to Christian and Western values has given rise to challenges of that legislation in the courts. On the basis of the newly phrased provision in Baden-Württemberg, Mrs Ludin lost her final appeal before the Federal Administrative Court (Bundesverwaltungsgericht, 2 C 45/03). One of her arguments was that the legislation was unconstitutional because it violated the principle of equal treatment contained in Article 3 of the Basic Law. The Federal Administrative Court interpreted the provision in the same way as the FCC had construed similar references in its school decisions. The reference to Christian and Western cultural and educational values is to be understood not as a reference to Christian doctrine and religious belief as such but to values, which originated in Christianity but which are universally valid, even outside the religious context, such as the protection of human dignity, non-discrimination between the genders or religious freedom. The provisions of most other *Länder* have in the mean time been subjected to challenges of compatibility with the Basic Law. All of them have been upheld on the basis of similar arguments as the ones used by the Federal Administrative Court in the second *Ludin* case (Hessischer Verfassungsgerichtshof, P. St 2016; Bundesarbeitsgericht, 2 AZR 55/09; Verwaltungsgericht Düsseldorf, 2 K 6225/06). The FCC has not yet been called upon to rule.

The only court deviating from this line of argument was the Bavarian Constitutional Court, which upheld the Bavarian provision on different grounds (Bayerischer Verfassungsgerichtshof, Vf. 11-VII-05). Concerning the principle of equal treatment, the court stated that the legislation did not contain an objectionable privilege in favour of the Christian faith since the reference had to be understood as meaning Christian values independent of the actual doctrine. The court nonetheless concluded that some symbols may be in accordance with these values and others may not. Thus, some symbols and some types of clothing may be worn by teachers, and others may not. The latter statement deviates from the statements made in other proceedings. The Bavarian Court does not suggest that, in conformity with constitutional principles, all religious symbols should be illegal.

Rather, the Court appears to accept that unequal treatment is permissible to some extent in view of the Christian and Western heritage of Bavaria. The Court did not have to elaborate further on these statements since the complaint was a popular complaint based on Article 98 of the Bavarian Constitution by which everyone may have Bavarian legislation reviewed by the court as to its compatibility with the fundamental rights contained in the Bavarian constitution independently of litigation and a set of facts. One can easily conclude, however, that the court would generally be willing to accept a ban on the headscarf and yet allow teaches to wear Christian or Jewish religious clothes or symbols. It is submitted that the Bavarian approach would not be shared by the Federal Administrative Court or the FCC.

Challenges under Equality Law Provisions

So far, this contribution has focused on violations of freedom religion guaranteed under Article 4 of the Basic Law. However, in light of the fact that many cases under English law would be argued under anti-discrimination law as well, it seems appropriate to briefly address the courts' reactions to arguments based on equal treatment provisions both in the Basic Law and in the federal legislation implementing the EU's equal treatment directives (*Allgemeines Gleichbehandlungsgesetz – AGG*) which entered into force in August 2006, that is after the second *Ludin* decision. Article 3 of the Basic Law guarantees a right to equal treatment. Furthermore, Article 33(2) of the Basic Law is also an equal treatment provision. The FCC in *Ludin* regarded the refusal of school authorities to employ Mrs Ludin as amounting to an interference with her right to equal access to a public office and emphasized that such an interference could not be justified in the absence of an explicit legislative basis. The FCC then stressed that any such legislation would have to guarantee equal treatment of all religions (BVerfGE 108, 282, 313).

After the entry into force of the legislation implementing the EU's directives on equal treatment, applicants were able to rely on these provisions alongside those of the Basic Law. Article 31 of the Basic Law provides for the precedence of federal law over *Länder* law. Since the AGG is federal law, the *Länder* legislation banning religious symbols has to be compliant with it. Furthermore, any dismissal of an employee or refusal to employ a prospective employee must not infringe the AGG. This is also true where civil servants are concerned since §24 AGG provides that the Act also applies to the public sector. The AGG has unsuccessfully been invoked in a number of cases concerning the headscarf. The discriminations on grounds of religion were deemed justified in each instance (Verwaltungsgerichtshof Baden Württemberg, 4 S 516/07; Verwaltungsgericht Düsseldorf, 2 K 6225/06 (5 June 2007).

In the case of the social worker, mentioned above, the Federal Labour Court admitted a direct discrimination on the basis of religion but considered that discrimination to be justified under § 8 AGG, which provides that a 'difference of treatment ... shall not constitute discrimination where, by reason of the nature of the particular occupational activities or of the context in which they are carried out, such grounds constitute a genuine and determining occupational requirement, provided that the objective is legitimate and the requirement is proportionate'. The Federal Labour Court considered the restriction to serve a legitimate purpose, namely the preservation of a peaceful school environment. It was also deemed proportionate since the ban would only affect her during the school day and since it served the purpose of protecting the negative freedom of religion of others (Bundesarbeitsgericht 2 AZR 499/08). In another case, a female Muslim Turkish language teacher was dismissed for insisting on wearing the headscarf in class even though she only taught pupils of Turkish origin all of whom were Muslims. The Federal Labour Court upheld the dismissal with the same reasoning as in the case just discussed and regarded the discrimination to be justified (Bundesarbeitsgericht 2 AZR 55/09).

What is remarkable about these two cases is that the Federal Labour Court, without any discussion, adopted the reasoning of the administrative courts, ignoring the fundamental difference between a teacher or social worker who is employed under private law and a civil servant. While there is some room for the argument that civil servants represent the State and therefore have to accept more far reaching restrictions of their fundamental rights, this is not the case for private law employees. Furthermore, upholding the dismissal of the Turkish language teacher who only taught Muslims goes rather far. As is evident from paragraph 23 of the preamble to *Directive 2000/78/EC*, on which the AGG is based, discrimination can only be justified in 'very limited circumstances'. It is submitted that the Federal Labour Court failed to appreciate the very exceptional nature of the justification provision in this case.

It is further noteworthy that none of the decisions mentions § 4 AGG, which deals with multiple discriminations and requires justification under all those grounds. In the case of the ban on the headscarf, the courts are not only confronted with a potential discrimination on the basis of religion but also an indirect discrimination on the basis of gender (Vickers 2008). This failure to appreciate the existence of multiple discriminations in these cases is evidence of a slightly underdeveloped anti-discrimination jurisprudence by the German courts.

Overall Comments

The *Ludin* decision, albeit much-criticized, has provided a certain degree of legal certainty with regard to religious symbols and religiously inspired clothing worn by teachers. Where a *Land* wishes to ban such symbols, it must do so by way of legislation and must not discriminate between religions. With the exception of the Bavarian Constitutional Court, all courts held that a reference to the *Land*'s Christian and Western heritage could not lead to a privileging of Christian and Western religious convictions. Rather, this reference must be understood to mean that the Western values marked by Christianity are to inspire teaching and cannot allow for indoctrination of Christian religious content.

The legislation of the eight *Länder* has created a situation for schools and teachers, which comes quite close to '*laïcisme*'. They are effectively banned from avowing to any religious belief when in school. To some observers this may seem ironic since the legislation, which contains explicit references to the Christian and Western heritage, was passed by *Länder* parliaments with a strong conservative majority consisting mainly of Germany's Christian parties. Examples are the Christian Social Union in Bavaria and the Christian Democratic Union in Hesse, Baden-Württemberg, Lower Saxony, North Rhine Westphalia and Saarland.

Symbols Worn by Pupils: Any Room for Regulation In View of Religious Freedom?

The final point which this contribution briefly aims to address is the situation of pupils. At present there is no legislation or executive practice banning pupils from wearing religious symbols in schools. Yet the political discussion revolving around immigration and integration has recently seen some politicians and commentators call for a ban of the headscarf even for pupils (Akgün 2009, Sarrazin 2009). According to media reports, a few head teachers have tried to ban the headscarf in their schools (Dicks 2008, Spiegel Online 2010b). Yet, in each case the school authorities were quick to lift the ban.

Viewed from the perspective of the law, it would be very difficult to achieve such a ban in a constitutional manner. The *Ludin* case showed that a ban of the headscarf for teachers would require a legislative basis and could not merely be imposed by the executive. Since the interference with pupils' freedom of religion would be at least as strong, there is much reason to believe that any such ban for pupils would have to be passed by the legislature. Of course, a ban on the headscarf only would not be possible either. In view of Article 3 of the Basic Law, which prohibits discrimination, the legislation would have to treat all religions equally and ban all religious symbols.

But even if that were to happen, such a ban would probably be considered an unconstitutional interference with the pupils' freedom of religion by the FCC. That there would be an interference with that freedom is clear from the *Ludin* case and needs no further discussion. When it comes to justifying that interference, the fundamental difference between a teacher and a pupil in school would become pertinent. Pupils, at least until they have completed nine years of schooling,[8] are subjected to compulsory education. This means that they have to attend school. If they were not allowed to wear the headscarf in school, this would in effect result in the State forcing them to violate their religious duty, which would constitute a grave interference with their freedom of religion. This interference could only be justified to protect other conflicting constitutional principles, such as the fundamental rights of others. In contrast to a teacher, where the neutrality of the State in religious and philosophical matters constitutes such a colliding principle, it would be hard to find a pressing interest to justify a similar ban for pupils. As

---

8   The length of compulsory education differs between the *Länder*.

has been pointed out, the neutrality of the German State in religious matters is not to be confused with *laïcité*. Thus, the reasoning of the Turkish State justifying the ban of the headscarf in Turkish universities in the *Şahin* case before the ECtHR would not work for Germany.

One argument for a ban would be to consider it necessary to protect young girls from being forced to wear the headscarf. Apart from the difficulties of distilling the State's duty to protect pupils from the Basic Law, this would have to be squared with parents' right to bring up their children according to their religious convictions, which is guaranteed by the Basic Law. This right inevitably involves a degree of religious indoctrination. Thus a ban on the headscarf for pupils would interfere with their parents' rights as well.

This line of argument finds some support in the Federal Administrative Court's decision on the right of a Muslim pupil not to be forced to take part in classes of physical education where boys and girls are taught in mixed classes (Bundesverwaltungsgericht, 6 C 8/91). The Court acknowledged that the state has a right to educate pupils arising from Article 7 of the Basic Law and that this right was of equal weight as the pupil's religious freedom, which demanded that she had to wear wide dresses and a headscarf so that male pupils would not be able to see her body shape. However, the court held that the state would have had the choice of teaching physical education in single sex classes. Thus the pupil's right to freedom of religion prevailed.

It would therefore be very difficult for a school or even the legislator to ban pupils from wearing a headscarf in school. Even though they are run by a religiously neutral State, schools are places which are open to religious avowals of the pupils attending them. This shows the difference between the German cooperative model of State/Church relations and the French and Turkish models of *laïcité*.

Conclusion

The controversies surrounding religious symbols in schools are testimonies of Germany's pluralistic society. Since politicians tend to shun making decisions which affect people's religion, these controversies are often decided in the courts. As a result, there is now a relatively settled case law on religious symbols. The courts interpret these symbols from the point of view of an objective observer. However, when deciding whether a religious symbol is compulsory for the person wearing it, the courts adopt a subjective test. Furthermore, the courts now seem to accept that a religious symbol can interfere with other people's negative freedom of religion. The situation for teachers wearing a headscarf has been clarified to a large extent. In the *Länder* which introduced a ban on the headscarf, teachers who wear a headscarf may be refused employment and those who are employed can be dismissed if they insist on wearing it in class. In the *Länder* which did not legislate for a ban, it is clear from the *Ludin* case that teachers are allowed to wear it. This fragmentation of the legal situation in the different *Länder* is regrettable but inherent in a federal system. The only way in which teacher wishing to wear a headscarf in schools might still be successful is under EU's anti-discrimination law. As this contribution has shown, the case law of the German courts in this respect is not developed in a very sophisticated manner. It is only a matter of time until the Court of Justice of the European Union will be asked to address these questions as well.

References

Adrian, M. 2006. Laïcité unveiled: a case study in human rights, religion and culture in France. *Human Rights Review* 8(2), 102–14.

Akgün, L. 2009. Nicht vor dem 14. Jahr! *Emma*, 5/2009. [Online]. Available at: http://www.emma.de/hefte/ausgaben-2009/inhalt-emma-2009–5/lale-akguen-2009–5 [Accessed: 22 January 2011].

Augsberg, I. and Engelbrecht, K. 2010. Staatlicher Gebrauch religiöser Symbole im Licht der EMRK. *Juristenzeitung* 65(9), 450–8.

Bader, J. 2004. Cuius regio, eius religio – Wessen Land, dessen Religion. *Neue Juristische Wochenschrift*, 3092–4.

Battis, U. 2007. Artikel 33 Grundgesetz, in *Grundgesetz*, edited by M. Sachs. 4th edn. Munich: C.H. Beck, 1078–1101.

Borowski, M. 2006. *Die Glaubens- und Gewissensfreiheit des Grundgesetzes*, Tübingen: Verlag Mohr Siebeck.

Dicks, B. 2008. Wie Rektoren das Kopftuchverbot ausweiten wollen. *Spiegel Online*, 16 October 2008. [Online]. Available at: http://www.spiegel.de/schulspiegel/wissen/0,1518,584023,00.html [Accessed: 22 January 2011].

Karakas, C. 2007. Turkey: Islam and laicism: between the interests of State, politics, and society. *PRIF Reports* no. 78 [Online]. Available at: http://www.hsfk.de/fileadmin/downloads/prif78.pdf [Accessed: 22 January 2011].

Kästner, K.-H. 2003. Anmerkung. *Juristenzeitung* 58, 1178–80.

Kokott, J. 2007. Artikel 4 Grundgesetz, in *Grundgesetz*, edited by M. Sachs. 4th edn. Munich: C.H. Beck, 235–70.

Müller-Volbehr, J. 1995. Positive und negative Religionsfreiheit. *Juristenzeitung* 50, 996–1000.

Pofalla, R. 2004. Kopftuch ja – Kruzifix nein? Zu den Widersprüchen in der Rechtsprechung des BverfG. *Neue Juristische Wochenschrif*, 1218–20.

Sacksofsky, U. 2003. Die Kopftuch-Entscheidung – von der religiösen zur föderalen Vielfalt. *Neue Juristische Wochenschrift*, 3297–301.

Sarrazin, T. 2009. Sarrazin fordert Kopftuchverbot für Schülerinnen. *Die Welt Online*, 12 December 2009. [Online]. Available at: http://www.welt.de/politik/deutschland/article5507124/Sarrazin-fordert-Kopftuchverbot-fuer-Schuelerinnen.html [Accessed: 22 January 2011].

Schneider, J. 2010. Das Kreuz, ein Vorbild zu sein. *Süddeutsche Zeitung*, 27 April 2010, 2.

Spiegel Online. 2010a. Alice Schwarzer fordert Kopftuch-Verbot für Schülerinnen. *Spiegel Online*, 21 September 2010. [Online]. Available at: http://www.spiegel. de/politik/deutschland/0,1518,718785,00.html [Accessed: 22 January 2011].

Spiegel Online. 2010b. Kultusministerium prüft Kopftuchverbot. *Spiegel Online*, 23 November 2010. [Online]. Available at: http://www.spiegel.de/schulspiegel/ wissen/0,1518,730730,00.html [Accessed: 22 January 2011].

Vickers, L. 2008. *Religious Freedom, Religious Discrimination and the Workplace*. Oxford: Hart Publishing.

Von Campenhausen, A. 1996. Zur Kruzifix-Entscheidung des Bundesverfassungsgerichts. *Archiv des Öffentlichen Rechts* 121, 448–64.

Von Campenhausen, A. 2004. The German headscarf debate. *Brigham Young University Law Review*, 665–700.

Von Campenhausen, A. and de Wall, H. 2006. *Staatskirchenrecht*. 4th edn. Munich: C.H. Beck.

Werdmölder, H. 2007. Headscarves in public schools, in *Religious Pluralism and Human Rights in Europe: Where to Draw the Line?*, edited by M.L.P. Loenen and J. Goldsmith. Antwerp: Intersentia, 155–65.

Case law

Federal Constitution Court

BVerfGE 32, 98.
BVerfGE 93, 1.
BVerfGE 108, 282.
BVerfGE 34, 165.
BVerfGE 41, 65.
BVerfGE 41, 29.
BVerfGE 52, 223.
BVerfGE 35, 366.
BVerfGE 108, 282.

Administrative Courts

Bundesverwaltungsgericht, 2 B 92.87 (8 March 1988).
Bundesverwaltungsgericht, 6 C 8/91 (25 August 1993).
Bundesverwaltungsgericht, 6 C 18/98 (21 April 1999).
Bundesverwaltungsgericht, 2 C 21.01 (4 July 2002).
Bundesverwaltungsgericht 2 C 45/03 (24 June 2003).
Oberverwaltungsgericht Hamburg, OVG Bs I 171/84 (26 November 1984).
Verwaltungsgerichtshof Baden-Württemberg, 4 S 1439/00 (26 June 2001).
Bayerischer Verwaltungsgerichtshof, 3 B 98.563 (21 December 2001).
Verwaltungsgerichtshof Baden Württemberg, 4 S 516/07 (14 March 2008).

Verwaltungsgericht Lüneburg, 1 A 98/00 (16 October 2000).
Verwaltungsgericht Stuttgart, 15 K 532/99 (24 March 2003).
Verwaltungsgericht Düsseldorf, 2 K 6225/06 (5 June 2007).
Verwaltungsgericht Augsburg, Au 2 K 07.347 (14 August 2008).

Federal Labour Court

Bundesarbeitsgericht, 2 AZR 499/08 (20. August 2009).
Bundesarbeitsgericht, 2 AZR 55/09 (10 December 2009).
Bavarian Constitutional Court
Bayerischer Verfassungsgerichtshof, Vf. 11-VII-05 (15 January 2007).
Hessian Constitutional Court
Staatsgerichtshof des Landes Hessen, P. St 2016 (10 December 2007).

European Court of Human Rights

App. no. 42393/98 *Dahlab v Switzerland* (15 February 2001).
App. no. 44774/98 *Şahin v Turkey* (10 November 2005).
App. no.30814/06 *Lautsi v Italy* (3 November 2009).
App no. 30814/06 *Lautsi v Italy* (Grand Chamber) (18 March 2011).

Legislation

Allgemeines Gleichbehandlungsgesetz (Act Implementing European Directives Putting Into Effect the Principle of Equal Treatment) of 14 August 2006 (BGBl. I S. 1897) or in English [Online]. Available at: http://www.antidiskriminierungsstelle.de/RedaktionBMFSFJ/RedaktionADSen/PDF-Anlagen/2009–08–28-agg-englisch-neues-design,property=pdf,bereich=adsen,sprache=en,rwb=true.pdf [Accessed: 22 January 2011].
Bayerisches Gesetz über das Erziehungs- und Unterrichtswesen (Gesetz- und Verordnungsblatt 2004, 443).
Bremisches Schulgesetz (28 June 2005, Bremisches Gesetzblatt S. 245).
Gesetz zu Artikel 29 der Verfassung von Berlin (Gesetz- und Verordnungsblatt für Berlin S. 92, Nr. 4).
Grundgesetz für die Bundesrepublik Deutschland. [Online]. Available in English at: http://www.gesetze-im-internet.de/englisch_gg/index.html [Accessed: 22 January 2011].
Schulgesetz für Baden-Württemberg (Gesetzblatt 2003, 359)
Schulgesetz Nordrhein Westfalen (Gesetz- und Verordnungsblatt für das Land Nordrhein-Westfalen, 2005, S. 102).
Verfassung des Freistaates Bayern (Gesetz- und Verordnungsblatt 1946).
Verfassung des Landes Baden-Württemberg (Gesetzesblatt 1953, 173).

Index

Page numbers including an "n" refer to notes.